COMMENTARY ON LUTHER'S CATECHISMS

TEN
COMMANDMENTS

COMMENTARY ON LUTHER'S CATECHISMS

TEN
COMMANDMENTS

ALBRECHT PETERS

CHARLES P. SCHAUM,
GENERAL EDITOR, ENGLISH EDITION

TRANSLATED BY HOLGER K. SONNTAG

FOREWORD BY GOTTFRIED SEEBASS

CONCORDIA PUBLISHING HOUSE · SAINT LOUIS

English translation © 2009 Concordia Publishing House
3558 S. Jefferson Ave., St. Louis, MO 63118-3968
1-800-325-3040 • www.cph.org

Ten Commandments translated from *Die Zehn Gebote*, © Vandenhoeck & Ruprecht, Albrecht Peters: *Kommentar zu Luthers Katechismen*, 5 volumes, edited by Gottfried Seebaß, Göttingen, 1990–94.

Unless otherwise noted, all quotations from Scripture, the Confessions, and other authors in this work are translated from *Die Zehn Gebote*, volume 1 of Albrecht Peters *Kommentar zu Luthers Katechismen*, edited by Gottfried Seebaß (Göttingen: Vandenhoeck & Ruprecht, 1990).

Manufactured in the United States of America

Library of Congress Cataloging-in-Publication Data

Peters, Albrecht, 1924–87
    [Kommentar zu Luthers Katechismen. English]
    Commentary on Luther's catechisms / Albrecht Peters ; Charles P. Schaum, general editor, English edition ; translated by Holger K. Sonntag ; foreword by Gottfried Seebass.
        p. cm.
    Includes bibliographical references.
    ISBN 978-0-7586-1197-0
    1. Luther, Martin, 1483–1546. Kleine Katechismus. 2. Luther, Martin, 1483–1546. Grosse Katechismus. 3. Lutheran Church—Catechisms—History and criticism. I. Schaum, Charles P. II. Title.
    BX8070.L8P3713   2009
    238'.41—dc22   2008050520

2   3   4   5   6   7   8   9   10   11   22   21   20   19   18   17   16   15   14   13

CONTENTS

Abbreviations

AC	Augsburg Confession
AE	*Luther's Works*. American Edition. 55 vols. General editors Jaroslav Pelikan and Helmut Lehmann. St. Louis: Concordia; Philadelphia: Muhlenberg/Fortress, 1955–.
Ap	Apology of the Augsburg Confession
BDAG	Bauer, W., F. W. Danker, W. F. Arndt, and F. W. Gingrich. *A Greek-English Lexicon of the New Testament and Other Early Christian Literature.*
Bill.	Billerbeck, Paul, and Hermann Leberecht Strack. *Kommentar zum Neuen Testament aus Talmud und Midrasch.* 2d ed. Munich: Beck, 1956.
BSLK	*Die Bekenntnisschriften der evangelisch-lutherischen Kirche.* Edited by Deutscher Evangelischer Kirchenausschuß. 9th ed. Göttingen: Vandenhoeck & Ruprecht, 1982.
CCSL	Corpus Christianorum: Series latina. Turnhout, 1953–.
CR	Corpus reformatorum
Ep	Epitome of the Formula of Concord
ESL	*Evangelisches Soziallexikon.* Edited by Friedrich Karrenberg. Stuttgart: Kreuz, 1954.
EKL	*Evangelisches Kirchenlexikon.* 4 vols. Göttingen, 1956–61.
FC	Formula of Concord
GCS	Die griechische christliche Schriftsteller der ersten [drei] Jahrhunderte
LC	Large Catechism
LCMS	The Lutheran Church—Missouri Synod

Liddell and Scott	Liddell, H. G., R. Scott, and H. S. Jones. *A Greek-English Lexicon*. 9th ed. with revised supplement. Oxford: Clarendon, 1958.
LTK	*Lexicon für Theologie und Kirche*
LXX	Septuagint
MCG	Monumenta conciliorum generalium saeculi decimi quinti
MGP	*Monumenta Germaniae Paedagogica*. Vols. 20–22. Edited by K. Kehrbach.
PL	Patrologia latina. Edited by J.-P. Migne. 217 vols. Paris, 1844–64.
RGG	*Religion in Geschichte und Gegenwart*. Edited by Kurt Galling. 7 vols. 3d ed. Tübingen, 1957–65.
SA	Smalcald Articles
SC	Small Catechism
SD	Solid Declaration of the Formula of Concord
TWNT	*Theologische Wörterbuch zum Neuen Testament*. Edited by G. Kittel and G. Friedrich. Stuttgart, 1932–79. Translated by G. W. Bromiley. 10 vols. Grand Rapids: Eerdmans, 1964–76.
TU	Texte und Untersuchungen
WA	*D. Martin Luthers Werke: Kritische Gesamtausgabe*. Weimar: Herman Böhlau, 1883–.
WABr	*D. Martin Luthers Werke: Kritische Gesamtausgabe. Briefwechsel*. Weimar: Herman Böhlau, 1930ff.
WADB	*D. Martin Luthers Werke: Kritische Gesamtausgabe. Deutsche Bibel*. Weimar: Herman Böhlau, 1906–61.
WATR	*D. Martin Luthers Werke: Kritische Gesamtausgabe. Tischreden*. Weimar: Herman Böhlau, 1912ff.

Publisher's Preface
to the English Edition

Concordia Publishing House is pleased to present this important scholarly work that interprets Martin Luther's Small and Large Catechisms, together with the sermons and other documents by Luther that make up their context. This series originally was undertaken by the late Professor Dr. Albrecht Peters, longtime member of the theological faculty of the Ruprecht-Karls-Universität in Heidelberg, Germany. His material was gathered and edited by Gottfried Seebaß, his junior colleague, and published by Vandenhoeck & Ruprecht as the five-volume *Kommentar zu Luthers Katechismen*. Most recent scholarship regarding Luther's catechisms refers to this work in some fashion. Concordia extends its thanks to the Reverend Paul Strawn for his efforts in organizing the initial work on this series, especially regarding this volume. We thank the Commission on Doctrinal Review of The Lutheran Church—Missouri Synod for their approval to publish these volumes as resources for study purposes.

Format of the Translation

The body text of this volume retains titles in the original language for all works except those of Luther. The first occurrence of titles of Luther's works in the body text generally includes both the title in the original language and a translation; generally the translated form is used in subsequent references. This convention is observed because in many cases these works do not exist in the American Edition of Luther's Works, thus translating all titles into English might create the false impression that the represented works themselves had been translated into English. In the footnotes, titles are given in their original language. The reader is encouraged to consult Heinrich J. Vogel's *Cross-Reference and Index to the Contents of Luther's Works* and Kurt Aland's *Hilfsbuch zum Lutherstudium*. To aid the reader in this effort, cross-references to extant works in the American Edition have been included in this volume, but only to the selected works as respective page ranges, not to exact corresponding page numbers. References to the *Bekenntnisschriften* are not mapped to an English version of the Lutheran Confessions in this volume. Subsequent volumes will demonstrate improvement in this matter.

Quotations in the body text have been translated into English unless doing so would adversely affect the places where Peters refers specifically to the features and content of the material in its original language. The bulk of the notes, though translated, refers generally to non-English research. The translation intends to remain faithful to the original text. We have also given attention to the consistent use and translation of technical terms. Titles in the notes and of the suggested reading material at the end of each chapter are not translated because many of these resources do not exist in English. This also helps the student or theologian who wishes to look deeper into the Weimar Edition.

HISTORICAL-CRITICAL METHODS

The reader will notice that historical-critical exegetical methods are used throughout the series, but the use remains less extreme than that of some formerly within the LCMS.[1] Peters does look for a Lutheran middle way when he speaks of a Lutheran orthodox "confessionalist hardening" on the right and a humanist tradition on the left, with Luther in the center. He does not embrace the same view of confessional theology long held by the LCMS. Peters does not support the Mosaic authorship of Scripture. The clear position of the Missouri Synod remains that Moses wrote the Pentateuch, the ultimate basis for that being the words of Jesus Christ Himself, who knew the canon of Scripture and who identified Moses as the author of the Pentateuch. There will be points in this volume where the reader who confesses Mosaic authorship of the Pentateuch, and rejects the documentary hypothesis, will come into sharp disagreement with the author on issues such as the JEDP documentary hypothesis, the assertions regarding source and form criticism, the assertions of a supposed religious evolution of the primitive Israelite religion into the cult of Yahweh, and related topics. The Lutheran Church—Missouri Synod rejects the errors of the higher-critical study of Scripture, as explained most pointedly in *A Statement of Scriptural and Confessional Principles*.[2]

Although Peters criticizes the radical rejection of the third use of the Law based on the philosophy and influence of Albrecht Ritschl, nevertheless he has some points of conflict with the third use of the Law. The Lutheran

---

1   See Paul A. Zimmermann, *A Seminary in Crisis: The Inside Story of the Preus Fact Finding Committee* (St. Louis: Concordia, 2007).

2   Zimmermann, 430–36. See also *A Statement of Scriptural and Confessional Principles* (St. Louis: LCMS, 1973).

Church—Missouri Synod affirms the Lutheran Confessions' teaching that there is a third use of the Law.[3]

RENEWED INTEREST IN THE CATECHISMS

In recent years, scholarly interest in Luther's catechisms has been rekindled in the LCMS by the original German edition of this work. For example, consider the recent work of Charles Arand, such as his book on the setting, content, and purpose of Luther's catechisms, *That I May Be His Own* (St. Louis: Concordia, 2000). One sees an opportunity to examine again the catechisms of Luther that has only started to realize a scholarly awakening after a hiatus in the LCMS for the better part of a century.

This work by Albrecht Peters sheds needed light on Luther's catechisms. At the same time it brings a different set of presuppositions to the table. It allows individuals within the LCMS to examine how people outside the LCMS may view, study, and use Luther's catechisms. It will doubtlessly create points of friction with readers who reject higher-critical approaches. Nevertheless it remains a translation that seeks to uphold the responsibility to be faithful to the author's texts and viewpoints yet also provide material usable by a faithful Church. We pray that it succeeds to that end.

---

3   A helpful resource in this area is Scott R. Murray, *Law, Life, and the Living God: The Third Use of the Law in Modern American Lutheranism* (St. Louis: Concordia, 2002).

PREFACE AND INTRODUCTION

GENESIS AND CHARACTERIZATION
OF THIS WORK

When Albrecht Peters was torn out of the circle of students, colleagues, and friends too early and unexpectedly on October 26, 1987, he had been permitted some years in which he could reap at least part of the benefits of a rich and fruitful career in research and teaching. The volumes of the *Handbuch systematischer Theologie* that were published by him in rapid succession—all of them the center of the author's life, treating the theme of man before God—show in an exemplary manner how Peters wanted to make Reformation theology meaningful and alive for our times.[1] On his sixtieth birthday, a selection of his essays was published to express gratitude to the friend, colleague, and teacher. The preface of the volume reads, in part: "Of his many essays, we here present a representative selection. The numerous works on Luther's catechisms were left out in view of the planned historical commentary on the catechetical writings of the reformer that are part of the Confession of Evangelical Lutheran Christendom."[2]

Already then, the plans to publish this commentary had been ongoing for some time because the manuscript had been finished in the mid-1970s. Peters had taken on the writing of such a commentary in the context of a larger project that was intended to be a historical-theological commentary on the Confessions of the Evangelical Lutheran Church. Only two parts of this project were completed: Despite his dwindling strength, my teacher, Wilhelm Maurer, was able to present the two-volume historical commentary on the *Confessio Augustana*.[3] And beginning in the mid-1960s, Peters had been working on his commentary on Luther's catechisms. Especially in

---

1   Albrecht Peters, *Der Mensch*, Handbuch systematischer Theologie 8 (Gütersloh: Gütersloher, 1979); *Gesetz und Evangelium*, Handbuch systematischer Theologie 2 (Gütersloh: Gütersloher, 1981); *Rechtfertigung*, Handbuch systematischer Theologie 12 (Gütersloh: Gütersloher, 1984).

2   From p. 5f. of the preface by Reinhard Slenczka and Rudolf Keller for Albrecht Peters, *Rechenschaft des Glaubens: Aufsätze zum 60. Gerburtstag des Autors*, ed. Reinhard Slenczka and Rudolf Keller (Göttingen: Vandenhoeck & Ruprecht, 1984).

3   Cf. Wilhem Maurer, *Historischer Kommentar zur Confessio Augustana*, 2 vols. (Gütersloh: Gütersloher, 1976–78).

the time of major social upheaval between 1968 and 1972, when the theological faculty, the university, and the city of Heidelberg were rocked by severe and long-lasting unrest, this work had a special meaning for Peters. Returning from the turbulent, tumultuous vicinity of the university to his work on the commentary meant that he could breathe easier, concentrate on what is essential, and experience the possibility of calm and calming distance. The dramatic events did not stir in him "apocalyptic" fears for the existence of the German university, but he did believe that he was witnessing a profound turning point in its history. He often confided to a small, trusted circle that in his work on the commentary he felt somewhat like a Boethius at the threshold to the Middle Ages, marked by the decay of the Western Roman Empire. And in his commentary, Peters wanted to preserve and pass on what he had experienced as a source of spiritual strength in those years. Yet he did not consider the material that was growing larger and larger under his hand in his study rooms at Pfaffengrund and Peterstal to be a result of "lonesome scholarly work." He knew himself to be supported and borne by his "brothers and sisters"—by the fraternities of Ansverus and St. Michael, as well as by St. Peter's Church (the Protestant university chapel in Heidelberg), whose services were shaped by him not just in those years but permanently. All his writings, including his commentary, were shaped by the insight that all theology has a spiritual goal, that it time and again in exhortation and comfort has to return to its center: "We come out of God's hand and go toward Him."

Because Peters was convinced that the catechism concentrates on "what is necessary for life and death"[4] and because he, therefore, believed he could pass on spiritual treasures in the interpretation of the catechisms, beginning in the mid-1970s, he repeatedly presented on various aspects of his work on the catechism. He thus published a relatively large number of essays, indirectly anticipating his great work. These essays by themselves would be well worth publishing as a collection.[5] However, they can by no means replace the commentary itself. Peters always wanted to publish it, though he

---

4   Albrecht Peters, "Vermittler des Christusglaubens: Luthers Katechismen nach 450 Jahren," *Luther* 51 (1980): 34.

5   Cf. Albrecht Peters, "Die Theologie der Katechismen Luthers anhand der Zuordnung ihrer Hauptstücke," *Luther Jahrbuch* 43 (1979): 7–35; "Die Vaterunser-Auslegung in Luthers Katechismen," *Lutherische Theologie und Kirche* 3 (1979): 69–87; 4 (1979): 101–15; 3 (1980): 66–82; "Die Bedeutung der Katechismen Luthers innerhalb der Bekenntnisschriften: Eine Thesenreihe," *Luther* 50 (1979): 19–22; "Vermittler des Christusglaubens: Luthers Katechismen nach 450 Jahren," *Luther* 51 (1980): 26–44; "Die Bedeutung der Katechismen Luthers innerhalb der Bekenntnisschriften," pages 46–89 in *Luther und die Bekenntnisschriften,* Veröffentlichungen der Lutherakademie Ratzeburg 2 (Erlangen: Martin-Luther Verlag, 1981); "Die theologische Konzeption des Kleine Katechismus," *Katechismus und Öffentlichkeit, Themenheft der Pastoraltheologie* 73 (1984); "Taufe und Glaube beim Luther der Katechismen," *Homiletisch-liturgisches Korrespondenzblatt,* NS 2 (1984/85): 379–400.

doubted he would ever find a publisher for the large manuscript, which is why he planned a revised and abridged version. Yet he never got back to this project, certainly not only because the collaboration on the *Handbuch systematischer Theologie* constrained his efforts but also because he knew that the condensed abridgment would have taken away from the work the very approach that characterized it. This approach yields a catechism interpretation that not only fearlessly understands Luther's work against the backdrop of the teachings of the early and medieval churches but also one that examines exegetically, in the true spirit of the Reformation, the extent that Luther's conviction of the catechism being "a brief digest and summary of the entire Holy Scriptures"[6] was indeed validated by him. The result was a commentary that was not only historical but also theological, integrating the various theological disciplines. What it was lacking, though—and Peters was conscious of this and would have liked to undertake the necessary studies at the Herzog August Bibliothek at Wolfenbüttel—was the history of the reception and interpretation of the catechism from the sixteenth century to our own time. Yet what would the dimensions of the work then have become?

ABOUT THE EDITION

There was no question for Mrs. Gisela Peters, the friends, and the colleagues of Albrecht Peters that what he sometimes jokingly expected—namely, that "the commentary had to be published posthumously"—now had to be undertaken indeed. The purpose was not to carry out the revision of the manuscript that Peters had not even begun; rather, the commentary was to be published as the author himself left it. Readers and users will appreciate that we decided to publish the work in five volumes according to the catechism itself: Prefaces and Decalogue; Creed; Lord's Prayer; Baptism and Lord's Supper; Confession with Prayers[7] and Table of Duties, Marriage Booklet, and Baptismal Booklet. For the sake of its readers, a more transparent outline was put in place in only a few instances.

To be sure, Peters always considered important the conversation with those who, like him, worked to understand and pass on the Reformation heritage, especially where he thought he needed to contradict respectfully, but he did not want to consult exhaustively the literature on the topics given by the catechism. There are in particular no references to publications that

---

6   Cf. *BSLK*, 552.30–32.

7   The comments on Luther's prayers are not by Peters but were prepared by D. Frieder Schulz, whom Peters early on had identified as the greatest expert in the field. Cf. Albrecht Peters, "Gebetserwachen in neuer Gestalt: Überlieferung—Erfahrung—Gestaltung," in *Freude am Gottesdienst: Festschrift für Frieder Schulz*, ed. Heinrich Riehm (Heidelberg, 1988), 428–56, esp. 429. The contribution by Frieder Schulz, "Die Hausgebete Luthers," *Pastoraltheologie* 72 (1983): 478–90.

came out after the manuscript was concluded in the mid-1970s. Therefore, there were no corrections or additions made in this area. All information was thus taken over the way it was found in the manuscript. It was wanting in only two areas: the notes to the section on the prefaces could not be found, despite all attempts to do so. They were supplied, as well as possible, based on older publications by Peters and our own efforts. Furthermore, the combined bibliography to the Fourth Commandment was missing. Here, too, a replacement was attempted.

TIPS FOR THE USER

In order not to disrupt the reading of the text, all references to the catechisms and other writings by Luther and to the Confessions were put into the footnotes. Page and line numbers, unless otherwise noted, always refer to the fourth and subsequent editions of the *Bekenntnisschriften der evangelisch-lutherischen Kirche* (Göttingen: Vandenhoeck & Ruprecht, 1959f.). References to writings of Luther are always given with a short title to which page information is related. References to the Church fathers were partly retained, partly replaced by newer editions. Sources and secondary works are listed in the bibliography. Other references, such as those for documents in the Book of Concord and Migne's Greek and Latin series, are included in a table of abbreviations. Any remaining references that are not found in the bibliography or on the abbreviations table correspond to those of Siegfried Schwertner, *Theologische Realenzyklopädie: Abkürzungsverzeichnis* (Berlin: de Gruyter, 1976).

To me it remains to give much thanks. I begin where Albrecht Peters would have begun had he been able to finish the commentary himself: I thank Gisela Peters, who, as with Luther's translation of Genesis, also in the work on this commentary was her husband's "helper" and "around him." She also supported this edition wherever she could. I further have to thank Mr. Jürgen Kaiser, who, with great energy and above and beyond what could be expected, brought the footnotes into one format and who hopefully will take over this work also for the following volumes. The Vereinigte Evangelisch-Lutherische Kirche thankfully made the publication of the work possible by a significant publication subsidy. I conclude by remembering the author himself, the colleague to whom I owe stimulating conversation, many an instruction, and much advice and help. *Requiem aeternam dona ei, Domine, et lux perpetua luceat ei.*

Heidelberg, September 1990

G. Seebaß

The Prefaces[1]

Origin, Meaning, and Usage of the Word "Catechism"[2]

The term "catechism" probably did not originate as a Latinization of the Late Greek κατηχισμός; rather, it seems to have been derived from the Latin verb *catechizare*, which later Greek usage borrowed. As a product of ecclesiastical Latin in North Africa, both Tertullian and Augustine[3] use it for oral instruction, for the doctrinal presentation in prebaptismal instruction. Therefore, even Leidradus (eighth century) still says: *catechizare est instruere* ("to catechize means to instruct").[4]

When infant baptism became the general practice, the word "catechism" meant "the liturgical acts preparing for the rite of Baptism"[5] in which the sponsors acted as the child's proxies, that is, for the handing over of the Creed and the Lord's Prayer, as well as the renunciation of Satan and the child's dedication to the triune God. Alongside this "catechism" appeared the exorcism, which became more and more elaborate. As the child grew, the sponsors, as *catechistae*,[6] were supposed to introduce to the growing child that faith and prayer which they had spoken over that child in Baptism. Thus *catechismus* can take on the meaning of sponsorship or of being godparents.[7] Different than the exorcism, the catechetical parts of the baptismal liturgy receive their structure from the alternate speaking of question and answer. Toward the end of the Middle Ages, this style is taken up

---

1   The original footnotes by Albrecht Peters for the subsections 1–6 of this chapter are lost. As far as possible, they have been reconstructed by the editor.

2   See Hans-Werner Surkau, "Katechismus II," *RGG* 3:1179–86; Albrecht, "Vorbemerkungen zu beiden Katechismen," 448–65; *Luthers Katechismen*, 24–41. See also κατηχέω in BDAG and the unabridged Liddell and Scott.

3   Tertullian, *Adv. Marc.* 4.29; Augustine, *De fide et op.* 6.13.

4   Leidradus, *De sacr. baptismi*, c.1 (PL 99.856B).

5   Surkau, "Katechismus II," *RGG* 3:1180.

6   "Brief an Nikolaus v. Amsdorf vom 5.5.1529," WABr 5:61.11 (see also AE 49:218–19); cf. "Brief an Konrad Cordatus vom 3.1.1530," WABr 5:216.5.

7   Cf. von Zezschwitz, *Katechetik*, 2.1:36ff., referencing sources.

in the instruction for penance and finds its way into the instruction of the young. The penitential books prefer the form of a dialogical conversation. Using primarily the example set by the Bohemian Brethren, the reformers renew the early Church's catechumenate and enlarge it into post-baptismal instruction.

Out of this development grows the usage of the word "catechism" that Luther, above all, made normative. (1) "Catechism" means, principally and basically, the instruction in the foundational elements of the Christian faith. Luther highlights this in his first public use of the word, which is in the preface to the 1526 *Deutsche Messe* ("German Mass"): "Catechism . . . means the instruction in which the heathen who want to be Christians are taught and guided in what they should believe, do, refrain from, and know according to the Christian faith. This is why the candidates who had been admitted for such instruction and learned the Creed before their Baptism used to be called *catechumenos*."[8] The reformer takes up this definition in his prefaces to the catechisms: " 'Catechism,' that is, instruction for children. It contains what every Christian should know."[9] (2) This instruction, as a back-and-forth of question and answer, takes place as an addendum to the practice of penance, as well as in the development of the school. Enabled by a kind of popular etymology, one embedded this specific form of interrogation into the meaning of the word itself.[10] From this late medieval approach, the reformers developed special catechism services. Accordingly, "catechism" also can denote those services as they are actually carried out.[11] (3) The focus of the reformer here is obviously on the content that is to be learned and witnessed. This is why the word already in Luther's preface to the German Mass has the meaning "subject matter for elementary instruction."[12] It circumscribes the "sum of certain fixated and clearly delineated doctrinal articles."[13] "This instruction or teaching I cannot put better or more plainly than has been done from the beginning of Christendom and retained till now, namely, these three parts: the Ten Commandments, the Creed, and the Lord's Prayer. These three parts plainly and briefly contain almost everything a Christian needs to know."[14] However, Luther adds to these three central parts Baptism and the Lord's Supper for the weekly lessons for Monday

---

8   WA 19:76.2 (see also AE 53:51–90).

9   *BSLK*, 553.36.

10   Cf. "Sendschreiben an die zu Frankfurt a.M., 1533," WA 30.3:567.19–21. Cf. Melanchthon, *Cat. puerilis* (Reu, *Quellen*, 1.2.2:17.30–46); *CR* 25:690; Andreas Althamer, *Kat. Vorrede* (MGP 22.20) .

11   Cf. "Vorreden zu den 3. Predigtreihen über den Dekalog, 1528," WA 30.1:2.2, 27.26–28, 57.6f. (see also AE 51:137–41), as well as *BSLK*, 554.9.

12   This quotation could not be located.

13   Von Zezschwitz, *Katechetik*, 2.1:31.

14   "Vorrede zur Dt. Messe, 1526," WA 19:76.7 (see also AE 53:51–90).

and Tuesday,[15] as the catechisms of that period make normative. This third usage—"catechism" as another word for the central doctrinal content of the Christian faith—is intended in Luther above all others. (4) With the codification of what necessarily needs to be known in a book, we arrive finally at the meaning most common today: "catechism" as referring to the contents of a book or as an abbreviation for the book itself. Already in the 1525 letters to Hausmann,[16] in which the project of a catechism is touched upon for the first time, Luther uses the term as another word for such a book. Almost by necessity this meaning then arises from the titles of the two works by Luther: from the April 1529 *Deutsch Catechismus* ("German" or Large Catechism) and from the May 1529 summary of the catechism charts in the *Enchiridion* that has the title *Der kleine Katechismus fur die gemeine Pfarrherr und Prediger* ("The Small Catechism for Common Pastors and Preachers"). Luther himself introduces this term in his preface to the *Enchiridion*: "After you [the pastor is addressed here] have taught the people a short catechism like this one, then take up the Large Catechism and impart to them additionally a richer and fuller understanding."[17]

This fourfold meaning is always to be kept in mind for the term "catechism," with the last three—catechism service, catechism parts, catechism book—resting on the first and basic one, the elementary instruction in the Christian faith. "'Catechism' is thus instruction in the Christian religion, elementary instruction in Christianity; first conceived of as an activity, then a delimited subject matter, then to denote a book's content, and finally a book itself."[18]

The Intentions of Luther's Catechisms

In his September 14, 1528, sermon, Luther calls the catechism "a children's sermon or layman's bible."[19] The preface to the Large Catechism speaks of an "instruction for children" that covers "what every Christian should know."[20] The Formula of Concord picks this up. It considers both the Small and Large Catechism "a Bible of the laity, in which everything is summarized that is treated in detail in Holy Scripture and that is necessary for a Christian to know for salvation."[21]

---

15 See "Vorrede zur Dt. Messe, 1526," WA 19:79.17ff. (see also AE 53:51–90). Cf. Albrecht, "Vorbemerkungen zu beiden Katechismen," 440.

16 WABr 3:582.

17 *BSLK*, 504.35.

18 Albrecht, "Vorbemerkungen zu beiden Katechismen," 454.

19 "Vorrede zur 2. Predigtreihe," WA 30.1:27.16.

20 *BSLK*, 553.37.

21 Ep Preface (*BSLK*, 769.7–10). Cf. WATR 5:581.30.

The catechism sets as a goal for itself to summarize what is essential and vital, what is elementary and fundamental of the Christian faith in simple language. For this purpose, Luther looked into a fourfold direction. (1) The catechism, as "a brief summary and digest" of the Bible,[22] strives to comprehend its central content. It desires to summarize and lay out in simple terms the statements of the biblical witness of the revelation of God the Father through Jesus Christ, the Son, in the Holy Spirit that are decisive for salvation. (2) The catechism enunciates the spiritual core of Scripture not as an insight gained by a spiritually gifted individual, but by means of those texts that have prevailed in Christendom and, at the same time, within the context of the history of interpretation of these decisive texts. In this way, the catechism summarizes in a highly conscious manner the artisan and town privileges of Christendom.[23] This is how the reformer circumspectly makes his confession a part of the witness of the Western Church. Together with the fathers and brethren he listens to the biblical message. This is why a theologically relevant interpretation of the catechism will necessarily keep an eye on the history of the tradition up to Luther. "Nowhere are we dealing with a catechism statement by itself; always there is also its history."[24] (3) The catechism looks at the concrete daily life of the simple members of the Church. It takes our calling and estate into consideration and understands both as the place in life God gave us in the coordinate system of natural/creaturely, societal/social, as well as historical/cultural, relations. In our daily life, we Christians should exercise and prove faith in love. The catechism desires to instruct for this purpose, not only as a doctrinal, confessional book but also as a book of prayer and comfort.[25] (4) The catechism moves Scripture, the confession of the Church, and our daily life into the light of the Last Day. Unlike the humanist educational tradition that found its way into the Lutheran Church from Erasmus via Melanchthon, but also unlike the confessionalist hardening, Luther does not offer a miniature dogmatics textbook nor even a "popular abstract of the entire doctrine of faith and morals."[26] Rather, he consciously focused on what was necessary for life and death, on the iron ration, as it were. This is why we do well always to keep the beginning of Luther's 1522 Invocavit Sermons in mind: "The summons of death comes to us all, and no one can die for another. Every one must fight his own battle with death by himself, alone. . . . Therefore, every one for himself must know and be armed with the chief things that concern a Christian."[27]

---

22 *BSLK*, 552.32.
23 *BSLK*, 554.6, 504.9.
24 Origin of quotation unknown.
25 *BSLK*, 546.15–31.
26 Origin of quotation unknown.
27 WA 10.3:1.7 (see also AE 51:70–75).

In this fourfold direction the catechism is basic: As a true "lay bible," it desires to offer what is foundational in the Christian faith. It desires to make the center of Scripture, expressed in the core parts of the churchly tradition, fruitful for daily life. By doing so, it desires to hammer into us what is decisive in life and death for our salvation. In this, the catechetical struggle of Christianity, as it reaches an apex in Luther's Small Catechism, remains able to offer directive aid to us today. What is basic is presented in an equally simple yet profound way. It can be recognized and uttered as what is exemplary only in the spiritual discipline of the praying mind. In the twentieth century it is no less important than in the sixteenth to find what is decisive for our salvation. Today, as well as then, this does not happen by "security and boredom"[28] but only by humble kneeling and through the disciplined thinking of faith. Time and again it remains impressive how little is truly decisive for salvation and, at the same time, how infinitely much this "little" is.

ORIGIN AND STRUCTURE OF THE PREFACES

The prefaces to the catechism articulate what is decisive for salvation in a precise way and concretize what is true for all people and all times for the situation of the Saxon peasant-citizens of the sixteenth century. The three "holy orders and true religious institutions"[29]—the pastoral office, marriage and house, and secular authority—within the one *corpus Christianum* serve the catechism, as God Himself does not disdain teaching it constantly.[30] The reformer prefaces the Small Catechism with a letter to "all faithful and upright pastors and preachers."[31] Luther added this preface in May 1529 when he had the catechism charts assembled into a handy enchiridion. The preface can be structured as follows:

A. After the greeting,[32] which is patterned after the beginning of the New Testament Letters, especially the greetings at the beginning of the Pastoral Letters, the reformer outlines the precarious situation that was uncovered by the first major church visitation.[33] About a quarter of the pastors had to be removed from office. This need forced Luther finally to put his long-entertained plan for a catechism into practice and, alongside the Large Catechism (which might serve as a sermon outline), to place into the clergy's

---

28   *BSLK*, 547.11
29   "Vom Abendmahl Christi, 1528," WA 26:504.30 (see also AE 37:151–372).
30   *BSLK*, 552.3–10.
31   *BSLK*, 501.4; entire preface *BSLK*, 501–7.
32   *BSLK*, 501.4–7.
33   *BSLK*, 501.8–502.27.

hands the Small Catechism. For this purpose, the enchiridion brought together the "tables and forms,"[34] that is, the catechism tables[35] that had been printed clearly as memorization aids.

B.   The body of this preface[36] outlines the methodical steps of that pedagogical task, namely, to "bring the catechism to the people, especially to the young."[37] To this end, Luther lays out these three steps: (1) tireless teaching of a precisely fixed wording that will remain unchanged;[38] (2) careful and step-by-step introduction to the meaning of what has been memorized;[39] (3) expansive deepening and concrete application of what has been learned.[40] In this, preachers are to look out for trouble spots, to accentuate the existential connection to the daily life of the congregation, to adduce examples from Scripture, and in all of it to make visible God's zealously holy vigilance over the catechism. Into these three steps, which are not merely formal methodology, Luther weaves the harsh instruction to exclude from the Christian and political community those who do not want to learn.[41] Whoever does not want to learn the "town laws" of Christendom is to be mercilessly excluded from Christian society.

C.   The demand to drill especially those things "where your people suffer the greatest need"[42] leads the reformer to underline two particularly critical points on which he has spoken again and again, namely, the decay of the schools and the despising of the Sacrament.[43]

1.   In view of the school, Luther directs an eschatologically motivated appeal to the authorities, as well as to the parents: they are not to allow God's two kingdoms to be laid waste. What Luther hints at here is unfolded in the Fourth

34   *BSLK*, 502.36.
35   On these charts, cf. Albrecht, "Besondere Einleitung in den Kleinen Katechismus," 561–68; *Luthers Katechismen*, 112–24; Meyer, *Historischer Kommentar*, 131.
36   *BSLK*, 502.28–505.18.
37   *BSLK*, 502.33.
38   *BSLK*, 502.41–503.32.
39   *BSLK*, 504.13–14.
40   *BSLK*, 504.35–505.18.
41   *BSLK*, 503.33–504.12.
42   *BSLK*, 504.44.
43   *BSLK*, 505.19–507.17.

Commandment[44] and is tirelessly supported in the writings and sermons on schools.[45]

2. The increasing fear or also indifference when it came to the Lord's Supper in the "evangelical" congregations occasions Luther to instruct pastors on how to preach the Sacrament according to the Gospel.[46] Here Luther again outlines what he has just pointed out in the admonition to the Sacrament and to confession.[47]

D. The reformer concludes his letter by describing the reformation form of a true preaching and pastoral ministry.[48] As a ministry serving the eschatological salvation of human souls, it is drawn into the battle between God and Satan.

We will deal later with the specific school-related issues,[49] as well as with the independent exhortation to the Lord's Supper[50] given in this preface.[51] We have already discussed the term "catechism"; the interesting oscillation within the triad Decalogue, Creed, and Lord's Prayer we will pick up when analyzing the organization of the chief parts for sponsors.[52] First, we want to focus on those carrying out the instruction in the catechism, on the three steps that structure the method, and on the horizon of the eschatological battle in which praying the catechism stands.

The short preface to the Large Catechism[53] grew out of the introduction to the first sermon series given on May 18, 1528.[54] As with its earlier form, the preface is directed not so much to pastors as to the members of the congregations, especially to the fathers of the household.

A. In a first step, Luther focuses the catechism on the traditional triad: Decalogue, Creed, and Lord's Prayer.[55] (1) He paraphrases the catechism as "instruction for children" or "instruction of

---

44 Cf. *BSLK*, 603.17–605.34, as well the commentary on pp. 197–208.

45 "Daß man Kinder zur Schule halten solle, 1530," WA 30.2:517–88 (see also AE 46:207–58); "An die Ratherren . . . daß sie christl. Schulen aufrichten und halten sollen, 1524," WA 15:27–53 (see also AE 45:339–78).

46 *BSLK*, 505.48–507.16.

47 *BSLK*, 707.47–725.29 ("Von dem Sakrament des Altars"); *BSLK*, 725.30–733.29 ("Eine kurze Vermahnung zu der Beichte").

48 *BSLK*, 507.16–34.

49 *BSLK*, 505.19–47.

50 *BSLK*, 505.48–507.16.

51 Cf. pp. 26–31 and the commentary on the Lord's Supper.

52 Cf. pp. 40–51.

53 *BSLK*, 553.31–560.3.

54 WA 30.1:2.2–30.

55 *BSLK*, 553.33–557.33; cf. WA 30.1:2.15f.

children and the uneducated,"[56] which is meant to introduce chiefly the next generation to the "artisan rules" of Christianity.[57] (2) He places the father of the house into the office of teacher and examiner.[58] (3) He briefly touches on the unworthy situation that even the elderly go to the Lord's Supper without knowing what Christianity is all about.[59] (4) For the "common masses" he will leave it at the Decalogue, the Creed, and the Lord's Prayer.[60] (5) Luther next quotes these three chief parts in a version that has been reviewed neither mnemonically nor theologically.[61] (6) Finally, he summarizes the basic theses of the preface.[62] Here he underlines that those three texts summarize the content of Scripture "in short, plain, and simple terms."[63]

B. The second step in Luther's thought similarly adds Baptism and the Lord's Supper as the two sacraments instituted by the Lord Himself[64] and makes pedagogical remarks.[65] (1) Here, too, the biblical texts quoted by him (Matt. 28:19; Mark 16:16; 1 Cor. 11:23–25) have not been examined according to the catechetical guidelines established by Luther himself. (2) Finally,[66] he mentions the pedagogical steps that he offers in the preface to the Small Catechism[67] in a reflective manner. At the same time, the cooperation between house (school) and church, between fathers of the household and pastors, becomes visible. To the cosmos of the five chief parts (confession is still missing) psalms and hymns are added.[68] Strangely, the Scripture verses are missing, the *loci communes*, in which, according to Luther's preface to the German

---

56 *BSLK*, 553.34f., 553.37.

57 *BSLK*, 553.33–554.16.

58 *BSLK*, 554.16–24.

59 *BSLK*, 554.24–555.2.

60 *BSLK*, 555.2–11.

61 *BSLK*, 555.12–557.4.

62 *BSLK*, 557.5–33.

63 *BSLK*, 557.25–33; cf. "Einl. zur 1. Reihe d. Kat.-Pred.," WA 30.1:2.20–23.

64 Cf. *BSLK*, 691.22–692.39, 707.47–709.21.

65 *BSLK*, 557.34–560.3.

66 *BSLK*, 558.34–560.3

67 *BSLK*, 502.41–505.18.

68 *BSLK*, 559.8f.; cf. especially the catechism hymns "Dies sind die heiligen zehn Gebot" (WA 35:426–28 [see also *Lutheran Service Book* 581; AE 53:277–79]); "Vater unser im Himmelreich" (WA 35:463–67 [see also *Lutheran Service Book* 766; AE 53:295–98]); "Christ unser Herr zum Jordan kam" (WA 35:468–70 [see also *Lutheran Service Book* 406; AE 53:299–301]); "Der du bist drei in Einigkeit" (WA 35:473 [see also AE 53:308–9]).

Mass, "all Scripture" is comprehended into a "complete sum of Christian thought."[69]

The more elaborate preface[70] is first found in Rhau's quarto edition of 1530; already there it introduces the catechism. The Jena Edition puts it in second place and adds a lengthy title.[71] The first edition of the *Book of Concord* follows the Jena Edition.[72] It seems that Luther wrote this new preface during the summer of 1530 at Coburg castle. This is suggested by the almost verbatim allusions to a letter written on June 29 (?), 1530, to Justus Jonas, as well as to the interpretation of Psalm 117 that was written there as well.[73] While the first preface (with the sermon on May 18, 1528) was addressed primarily to the fathers of the household and had an instruction for children and the uneducated, Luther now addresses the pastors and preachers and makes suggestions for an evangelical catechism breviary.[74]

A. In a first set of thoughts,[75] the reformer calls on the evangelical preachers to deal with these central texts by way of daily meditation. (1) To this end, he first describes the horrifying ignorance concerning basic truths.[76] (2) Then he juxtaposes to that false "carnal liberty" a simple form of biblical meditation and daily prayer that was to replace, in evangelical freedom, the seven canonical hours (*horae*).[77] (3) He again addresses carnal security as the counterimage that is to be overcome and sees this dangerous aberration also in the people's despising of the Gospel and in some of the nobility's disrespect for the pastoral office.[78] (4) As a positive example, he outlines his daily remembrance and meditation of the text of the catechism. He sets this intensive praying of the catechism against the despising of God's Word.[79]

B. In a second set of thoughts, Luther highlights the godly meaning and the spiritual benefit of truly praying the catechism.[80] The structure of these elaborations, as well as many a detail, is

---

69   "Vorrede zur Dt. Messe, 1526," WA 19:78.18, 77.13 (see also AE 53:51–90).

70   *BSLK*, 545.1–553.30

71   It is reprinted in Albrecht, "Bibliographie zum Großen Katechismus," 519f.

72   Cf. Albrecht, "Bibliographie zum Großen Katechismus," 518f.

73   WABr 5:408; WA 31.1:223–57 (see also AE 14:1–39).

74   Especially *BSLK*, 546.15–31.

75   *BSLK*, 545.2–548.30.

76   *BSLK*, 545.2–546.14.

77   *BSLK*, 546.15–31.

78   *BSLK*, 547.1–10.

79   *BSLK*, 547.31–548.30.

80   *BSLK*, 548.31–553.30.

reminiscent of the admonition to prayer.[81] (1) God's Spirit is present in such a meditation and leads us into the depths of divine mysteries.[82] (2) The meditation of God's Word protects us from the attacks of Satan and his minions. It especially drives away evil thoughts.[83] (3) God's Word is a "master of a hundred thousand arts" against the daily cunning and attacking of the devil, the "master of a thousand arts."[84] (4) It is God's gracious command that we should meditate on His Word without ceasing, for it is our weapon against satanic attacks.[85] (5) From the beginning to the end of the world, God teaches the catechism, and His saints delight in remaining His pupils in this. How can we think that we have already fully mastered the catechism?[86] (6) In the catechism, especially in the First Commandment, the entire Holy Scripture is concentrated, as well as all true human wisdom.[87] (7) Growing into the catechism remains an infinite task. The more intensively we wrestle with it, the more acutely will we recognize our ignorance and the more will we also hunger for being instructed by God.[88]

These two prefaces to the Large Catechism again afford us further insight into Luther's understanding of the term "catechism." They offer a deep look into the theocentric horizon, as well as the spiritual dimension of truly praying the catechism. At the same time, those responsible for catechism instruction are named more concretely and a pedagogical method is developed.

THOSE RESPONSIBLE FOR PROVIDING CATECHISM INSTRUCTION

The catechism addresses a confusing plethora of persons. The prefaces, as well as the catechisms themselves, are addressed to pastors and fathers. The fathers were "simply to hold before" the members of their household the printed catechism tables. Also, texts, especially of the Small Catechism, are placed into the mouth of the father. This is confirmed by the explanations to the Sixth Commandment, to the First Article, as well as to the Fourth

---

81 *BSLK*, 662.41–670.28.

82 *BSLK*, 548.31–549.20.

83 *BSLK*, 549.21–550.8.

84 *BSLK*, 550.9–36.

85 *BSLK*, 550.37–551.26.

86 *BSLK*, 551.27–552.15.

87 *BSLK*, 552.16–37.

88 *BSLK*, 552.38–552.30.

Petition. The *Enchiridion* is dedicated to the unlearned holders of a parish pastorate, as well as to the preachers assigned to the greater parishes. The Latin translation is entitled: *Parvus catechismus pro pueris in schola* ("Small Catechism for Students in School").[89] In the individual chief parts, pedagogues replace the fathers, and the students take the place of the members of the household. The catechism also serves at the same time the visitation ordered by the prince, which he, as "emergency bishop,"[90] carries out "for God's sake for the good of the Gospel and for the benefit and salvation . . . of the miserable Christians."[91] The Christian home, the church, and the school submit to the discipline of the catechism; the Christians holding offices of civil authority direct and supervise this instruction. Thus the three "holy orders and true religious institutions"[92] within the *corpus Christianum* serve the catechism.

All these fathers—"of blood, in the house, and in the country,"[93] and above all the spiritual fathers—have the very same duty: the *cura* or *custodia utriusque tabulae* ("care or guardianship of both Tables"). And according to Luther's customary way of speaking, this means they are "not only to feed and care for their children, workers, subjects, etc., physically, but also chiefly to raise them to the praise and glory of God."[94] This task grows not only out of the demands of human society, but it is also more a stern command of the triune God who is the Lord of both kingdoms.

According to the Fourth Commandment, God commands first the *patres et matres familias* to carry out this task. Fathers and mothers, as house bishops ordered by God,[95] place the catechism before their children and servants. They have them pray daily the old chief parts for sponsors—the Creed and the Lord's Prayer—and guide them in the prayers of the house-congregation. They have the growing youth recite Scripture and psalm verses and check at least once weekly the catechism knowledge commended to them.[96] Although the questions of the Small Catechism are directed at the youth and the servants, the answers are formulated in view of the father. Those growing up confess in the same manner as potential fathers. Luther's catechism does not want its situation in life to be limited to isolated events in school,

---

89   *BSLK*, 507.34.

90   "Exempel, einen rechten christlichen Bischof zu weihen, 1542," WA 53:255.5, 256.3.

91   "Unterricht der Visitatoren, 1528," WA 26:197.26 (see also AE 40:263–320).

92   "Vom Abendmahl Christi, 1528," WA 26:504.30 (see also AE 37:151–372).

93   *BSLK*, 601.25.

94   *BSLK*, 603.35.

95   "Vorrede zur 3. Predigtreihe über den Kat. vom 30.11.1528," WA 30.1:58.8–10, 58.23f. (see also AE 51:137–41); "Von den guten Werken, 1520," WA 6:254.9 (see also AE 44:15–114); "Pred. über Ex. 20 vom 5.11.1525," WA 16:504.11; "Gen.-Vorl., 1535–45," WA 42:159.34 (see also AE 1:1–359).

96   *BSLK*, 554.11–16; cf. "Vorrede zur 1. Predigtreihe vom 18.5.1528," WA 30.1:2.8–12.

much less in catechism class, but to be in daily lives together at home.[97] The primary confessor is the Christian father, since the house (*familia, oeconomia*) is the point where the secular and spiritual kingdoms coincide.[98]

The schoolmasters support the house bishops. According to "Unterricht der Visitatoren" ("Instruction for Visitors"), one day (either Wednesday or Saturday) is to be dedicated to "Christian instruction."[99] In the Wittenberg church order, Bugenhagen reserves Friday for catechism instruction, while Saturday serves to prepare for Sunday's Gospel.[100] Instruction is framed by daily Matins and Vespers, which the students, as successors to the monks, take upon themselves.[101] Here they daily sing three psalms each service (in German or Latin); the antiphons; the hymns, as well as the responsories; the canticles (Magnificat, Te Deum, Benedictus, Quicumque) or the prayers, as well as German hymns. They also take care of the Scripture and catechism lessons[102] and listen to the interpretations on Wednesday and on Friday. All this is done so that "the youth may remain in Scripture."[103] By means of this "daily exercise in the church,"[104] the children are schooled also to take upon themselves the prayer life at home.

The pastor is given the model sermons of the Large Catechism to help him to conduct meaningfully the catechism services that had been instituted by the reformers for this purpose.[105] Early on Sunday morning or in the afternoon,[106] as well as during the week, but especially on ember days,[107] pastors were called to impress upon their congregations the five chief parts.[108] At Wittenberg, the fourth deacon was "ordered to hold catechism instruction in particular for the peasants and their children."[109] Every Sunday he rode out to the villages belonging to Wittenberg, gathered young and old, and instructed them in the catechism.[110] However, the theologians did not want to introduce only the laymen to the catechism, but the pastor

97   E.g., "Vorrede zur 3. Predigtreihe," WA 30.1:57.10–14 (see also AE 51:137–41).
98   Cf. pp. 197–200 and pp. 205–8.
99   "Unterricht der Visitatoren, 1528," WA 26:238.32 (see also AE 40:263–320).
100 Sehling, *Kirchenordnungen*, 1.1:707A.
101 Sehling, *Kirchenordnungen*, 1.1:706B, 707A.
102 Sehling, *Kirchenordnungen*, 1.1:701B.
103 "Unterricht der Visitatoren, 1528," WA 26:230.23 (see also AE 40:263–320).
104 "Unterricht der Visitatoren, 1528," WA 26:230.1 (see also AE 40:263–320).
105 Cf. "Wittenberger Ordnung," in Sehling, *Kirchenordnungen*, 1.1:701B; *BSLK*, 559.20, 559 n. 5; Meyer, *Historischer Kommentar*, 48.
106 "Unterricht der Visitatoren, 1528," WA 26:230.35–39 (see also AE 40:263–320); "Wittenberger Ordnung," in Sehling, *Kirchenordnungen*, 1.1:700B.
107 Sehling, *Kirchenordnungen*, 1.1:701B.
108 Sehling, *Kirchenordnungen*, 1.1:700B, 701A.
109 Sehling, *Kirchenordnungen*, 1.1:701A.
110 Sehling, *Kirchenordnungen*, 1.1:701A.

himself also was at least "to read about one page or two in the morning, at noon, and in the evening from the catechism, prayer book, New Testament, or something else from the Bible and to pray a Lord's Prayer for himself" and his parishioners.[111] The reformer himself also was not ashamed, "like a child that is being taught the catechism," to memorize the chief parts word for word and to meditate on them prayerfully.[112]

Finally, the castle or town hall is set behind the house of the peasant or burgher, as well as behind church and school, in order to enforce the catechism's ordinances for the household, artisan guild, and town. For this, even the Christians holding civil authority bow under the catechism. Obviously, they do not submit to the catechism understood as a doctrinal booklet authored by the reformer for the simple, but they submit to the Christian faith in its central parts. According to Luther, in this way God Himself steps behind the catechism.[113] God is not ashamed to drill the catechism daily to His Christendom, and His true believers are not ashamed to study the catechism tirelessly.[114] The triune God as the one Lord in all three hierarchies— in *familia, politia*, and *ecclesia*[115]—drives the catechism home by means of His servants. In the catechism, God Himself in His zealous holiness watches over our lives. This shows itself in His blessing as well as in His curse.

In this eschatological horizon of judgment we have to understand Luther's sharp words against those members of the congregation who do not want to learn the catechism and against those pastors who do not eagerly teach it. The reformer does not establish these seemingly grim "pedagogical guidelines" in order to chase after "the ideal of a community church" or to defend the "unified ecclesiastical culture"[116] of the late Middle Ages. Instead, the reformer, in the way of the Old Testament, looks strictly to God's zealous holiness. Whoever does not want to learn the catechism commits a public act of renunciation against God. In this way, the person excommunicates himself in a highly concrete and active way from God's community that stands under promise and commandment.[117]

Luther's comparison with the customs within a trade guild[118] or a town community[119] means, first, whoever refuses to learn the catechism separates himself from Christendom, since he does not want to know about the basic

---

111 *BSLK*, 546.18.
112 *BSLK*, 547.33–548.6.
113 *BSLK*, 549.8–16.
114 *BSLK*, 551.33–40.
115 Cf. Maurer, *Lehre von den drei Hierarchien*.
116 The quotes could not be located.
117 *BSLK*, 503.33–504.2, 554.2–4.
118 *BSLK*, 554.4–7.
119 *BSLK*, 504.8–12.

order given to it. This is why the Church cannot offer him a place in its midst. If he does not want to assume the duties of a Christian, he also cannot enjoy the rights of a Christian. He is excluded from the Lord's Supper, from the office of sponsor, and from Christian burial. He loses all the rights of the Christian estate, falls under the church ban, and in this way is abandoned to the dominion of Satan.[120] Luther only threatens this excommunication in the prefaces. To be sure, his conclusions are rigorous but consistent. Whoever does not want to have anything to do with the God who turned His face to us in Jesus Christ thereby excommunicates himself from Christendom. The Church has the duty to proclaim this to him, lest he entertain the delusion of a God of "cheap grace."

However, Luther does not only threaten the ecclesiastical punishment of the lesser ban, but he also adds the threat of civil punishments: "*Additionally,* the parents and masters of the houses should refuse to give them (that is, those who refuse to learn the catechism in its chief parts) food and drink. They should also tell them that the prince wants to drive such rude people out of the country, etc."[121] Does this not again mingle secular and spiritual punishments? The analogy of the town privileges and guild rules apparently embraces not only the order within the Christian congregation but also affects the *corpus Christianum* in the house and in the political realm. Certainly, the reference to driving out of the country is important.

The distinction between the secular and spiritual realm goes beyond the separation of state and church. Parents, pastors, teachers, and the civil magistrates answer immediately to God, who is the one Lord of both realms. Because God has established His holy law of grace over all of humanity and watches over His Commandments, this is why every father, every pastor and teacher, every councilman and prince, on penalty of God's eternal wrath and temporal punishment, has the duty to protect and provide not only physically for the people entrusted to him but also and especially to rear them to God's praise and honor. The non-Christian will be able to do this more or less well only in view of the Second Table of the Decalogue. The Christian holding political office, on the other hand, will attempt not only to suppress public disobedience but also to quell public denial of God. For he protects the community entrusted to him not only in the horizon of the Second Table but also in the horizon of the First Table, and that means primarily against the "horrible wrath of God."[122] Unquestionably strange though it may be for us today, this is the context in which Luther's admonitions to show the door to the despisers of the catechism are to be interpreted.

---

120   *BSLK*, 503.33–40, 554.1–4; cf. "Vorreden zu den 3. Predigtreihen über den Kat., 1528," WA 30.1:2.5–7, 27.33, 57.8–10, 58.16f., 58.30f.

121   *BSLK*, 503.41.

122   "Vom Mißbrauch der Messe, 1521," WA 8:491.10 (see also AE 36:127–230).

Studying and praying the catechism takes place on the battlefield between God and anti-god; there is no neutrality here. Nobody stands for himself here. The decision of each individual negatively affects the entire community in which God has called us to live. Whatever happens in a person's heart is known to God alone and will be judged by Him alone. Yet whatever is said and done necessarily touches the community, which is why those responsible before God have to act in these cases. Luther makes a noteworthy distinction here. The magistrates are to respect the free independence of the house community. Whatever takes place in the house is none of their business so long as it does not become public.

In this way the hierarchies and estates ordered by God exercise their office of service and guardianship in an artful interplay of mutual aid and supervision. This mutual visitation is to be carried out as a fraternal service of love, since here man's eternal salvation and earthly welfare are at stake. Yet this mutual visitation must not shrink from harsh action, since God, guarding His supremacy over mankind in His zealous holiness, stands above it.

Yet in all this the point is not merely some external, legalistic obedience to the catechism but the willing self-sacrifice of the free children of God. Especially in his Coburg preface, the reformer therefore urges the joyous service of the pastor,[123] the grateful and cheerful praying of the catechism in the home of the burgher and pastor,[124] the unforced and longing race to the Lord's Supper. God does not want the fear of servants that hides smoldering hatred behind memorized obedience. He seeks the reverence of children that is connected to spontaneous love. Whoever bows under the catechism merely for external servile fear will certainly remain a part of the worldly realm of God, but he will have no part in the eternal realm of loving and fearing God that springs from true faith. This is why every true exercise in the catechism remains under the standard of the First Commandment: "We should fear, love, and trust in God above all things."[125]

THE METHODS OF TRUE CATECHISM INSTRUCTION IN THEIR PEDAGOGICAL AND THEOLOGICAL HORIZON

After discussing those responsible for instruction, we now have to reflect on the method of catechetical instruction. In loose analogy to the "three groupings" of the school in Melanchthon's "Visitationsunterricht" ("Saxon

---

123   *BSLK*, 548.31–549.20.
124   *BSLK*, 546.15–31.
125   *BSLK*, 507.42.

Visitation Articles"),[126] Luther outlines three steps in his preface to the Small Catechism.[127]

1. First, a concisely fixed and unchanging text is tirelessly taught.[128] The reason for Luther's careful conservatism in view of the versions of the Decalogue, Creed, and Lord's Prayer, which had already been more firmly established, as well as his greater freedom in view of the words of institution of Baptism and the Lord's Supper, is found in this pedagogical insight: "Choose for yourself whichever form you wish and stick to it forever."[129] This first step is marked by the interplay of speaking before a group and common repetition, solitary learning, and individual review. However, the decisive thing for Luther is saying the text out loud constantly, not as a catechetical recitation but as a living praying before God. He has crafted the texts extremely carefully so that they may be prayed aloud.

2. Once the text is memorized, a first introduction to its meaning is to take place.[130] In this way, the words of prayer and confession received out of the hand of the Church are brought near to the youth, who are thereby introduced to the town laws and guild rules common to all Christendom. According to the Luther of the catechisms, this first understanding again presses on toward a fixed formulation in which it is to find a preliminary support.[131] Those fixed answers to the repeated questions—What does this mean? How does this take place also among us?—invite all to pray aloud together. Especially Luther's explanations to the Decalogue and the Creed are carefully, thoroughly composed. They can be graphically displayed for the eye, as well as rhythmically taught for the ear. The following is true of them in an eminent way: "Memorizing means: experiencing content by practicing a form of speech and by being tied to this form of speech. Such impression and imprinting of forms of words, based on the nature of language, reaches into the depth of human existence. In this way, memorization rightly understood becomes learning by heart."[132] The lively rhythm of the phrases encourages the immature in the

---

126 "Visitationsunterricht," WA 26:237–40 (see also AE 40:263–320).
127 *BSLK*, 502.41–505.18.
128 *BSLK*, 502.41–503.32.
129 *BSLK*, 503.11.
130 *BSLK*, 504.13–34.
131 *BSLK*, 504.16–20.
132 This quotation could not be located.

faith to participate in speaking. By agreement or "tuning up," it takes them helpfully by the hand into the confession, the public faith, and draws them into its inner movement. The teacher is to unlock this exemplary form of speech for the growing youth and is to instruct them to entrust themselves to the rhythm of speech. In this active participation, the dimension of giving a true witness to the faith emerges. We do not recite a poem; we do not repeat a difficult formula. Rather, we join in a confession that is first spoken to us in order that God's will for it to be shared creates, in turn, our will to share it. Such an introduction wishes to unlock for us carefully and step by step the realm of the Christian faith. This is why Luther warned against unmethodical haste[133] and against selfish autonomy.[134]

3.   The third step expands, deepens, and applies what has been learned.[135] Here Luther has two things in mind: On the one hand, the whole of Scripture becomes unlocked for us by means of its "short summary."[136] On the other hand, our daily life is to be placed under the judgment and forgiveness of the catechism. Especially the Large Catechism serves this purpose.[137] Holy Scripture, the historical experience of humanity, and the specific knowledge of the nearby community are marshaled to witness tirelessly and to impress based on concrete examples that, in His zealous holiness, God watches over each and every one of us in judgment and grace and daily visits us with His curse and with His blessing.

The "New Preface" to the Large Catechism puts Luther's rather pedagogical hints once again in a more theological light. Praying the catechism is not merely for children and the simple; it is no less the duty and the joy of the mature Christian. Because the triune God Himself is the true teacher of the basic mysteries of the faith, all Christians are His pupils. Prayerful meditation on those central texts of our Christian faith draws our inner man into the dynamic of the Spirit of God.[138] These texts and the light of faith breaking forth from them pull us out of evil thoughts, still the diffuse unrest of our hearts, and form a sturdy protective barrier against demonic temptations.

---

133   *BSLK*, 504.20–26.
134   *BSLK*, 503.13–17.
135   *BSLK*, 504.35–505.18.
136   *BSLK*, 552.32.
137   *BSLK*, 504.37.
138   *BSLK*, 549.6–11.

At the same time, constantly new insights emerge, and contexts we could not have imagined become visible. Just as, according to Luther's preface to the German Mass,[139] the children are trained playfully to place the individual verses of Scripture either into the golden pouch of faith or into the silver pouch of love, so the mature Christians will penetrate all of Scripture by taking the Small Catechism as their point of departure. The reformer merely hints at this in that preface, though in his Table Talk he came back to this repeatedly. The Psalter will become for them an unfolding of and exercise in the First Commandment, even as it simultaneously and continually encompasses the Lord's Prayer.[140] The Decalogue, applied as a mirror for confession, instructs us to bring all of Scripture into a fruitful and healing conversation with our daily life here on earth. It offers a coordinate system that helps us to locate all areas of our political and spiritual communities.[141] Indeed, the entire catechism, especially in its three core parts—Decalogue, Creed, and Lord's Prayer—turns out to be "a short abstract and copy of the entire Holy Scripture."[142]

As "the laymen's bible,"[143] the catechism contains "everything that is in the Scripture and may be preached always":[144]

> As Solomon's Song of Songs becomes a *canticum canticorum*, a song above all songs, thus may the *Decalogus* become a *doctrina doctrinarum*, a doctrine above all doctrines, from which we may learn God's will, what God demands of us, and what we lack.
>
> *Symbolum* (the confession of our holy Christian faith) *est historia historiarum*, a true story above all stories, the highest *historia* of all, in which are set before us the inexhaustible miracles of divine majesty from the beginning until eternity: how we and all creatures were created; how we were redeemed by the Son of God by means of His incarnation, suffering, death, and resurrection; how we are renewed, sanctified, and made a new creature and altogether gathered into one people of God, have forgiveness of sins, and become eternally saved.
>
> *Oratio dominica* (the Lord's Prayer) *est oratio orationum*, a prayer above all prayers, the very highest prayer, which the very highest Master has taught and in which all spiritual and physical need is included and which is the best comfort in all temptations, afflictions, and in the last hour.[145]

---

139   WA 19:76.1–78.24 (see also AE 53:51–90).
140   *BSLK*, 552.24–26.
141   *BSLK*, 552.16–24.
142   *BSLK*, 552.31.
143   "Vorrede zur 2. Predigtreihe vom 14.9.1528," WA 30.1:27.26.
144   "Eine kurze Form d. 10 Gebote, 1520," WA 7:204.9.
145   WATR 5:581.32–582.4 (no. 6288).

These decisive three chief parts the triune God Himself teaches to His creatures that are given the gift of reason. God the Father carved the Decalogue on Moses' tablets of stone, as well as on mankind's hearts of flesh. The Lord's Prayer was taught by the Son. The Creed was composed by the Holy Spirit. The Sacraments, as *ceremoniae ceremoniarum*, join these three chief parts, since they are instituted and established directly by the Lord.[146]

Those simple words and actions contain the true bread of life for all men. This is why they are to be taught and practiced perseveringly. By means of the catechism God wants to preserve His Christendom against all satanic attacks.[147] After all, "every day a new church grows up, which needs the first principles. This is why we should just drive the catechism diligently and hand out the milk."[148] The Reformation has placed the catechism again on the lamp stand, "which had not been the case for a thousand years."[149] After all, all the writings of the Church fathers do not afford such clarity as could be concentrated in the Small Catechism. This is why the reformer, together with those charges learning their ABCs, patiently and continually wants to suckle these central words of God and remain daily "the catechism's student."[150]

Thus, for the reformer, the catechism, this instruction for children, this "layman's bible," "does not only stand at the beginning of the way into Scripture but also at its end. It does not only function as an opening key but also as a gathering repository."[151] Day by day Luther has placed all his theological insights and spiritual experiences into the earthen vessels of these simple formulae. These simple words "in which the Word of God became nourishing food and protecting shelter for generations"[152] are not too difficult for the young pupil, yet they contain abyssal mysteries into which the mature Christian sinks. The catechism is accessible to the beginner learning the ABCs and goes infinitely beyond the insight of the wisest. This property it shares with God's revelation.[153]

---

146   WATR 5:582.5–11 (no. 6288).

147   *BSLK*, 549.21–550.8, 551.6–22.

148   WATR 3:310.6 (no. 3421).

149   This quote could not be located.

150   "Ausl. von Ps. 117, 1530," WA 31.1:227.22 (see also AE 14:1–39); cf. *BSLK*, 547.33–548.6.

151   This quote could not be located.

152   This quote could not be located.

153   Cf. *BSLK*, 551.33–38.

AN ALTERNATIVE WAY OF ARRANGING
THE CATECHISM NOT USED BY LUTHER

Before we turn to the three foundational texts of the catechism—Decalogue, Creed, Lord's Prayer—and analyze their systematic coordination, I would like to point out a second model of a catechism that Luther outlined but never developed further. In his preface to the German Mass, in which Luther for the first time brings up the issue of a "plain, simple, basic, good catechism,"[154] he begins with the three traditional chief parts and shows how they can be memorized and appropriated.[155] Yet without marking the transition, he then outlines a different instruction. The children are to remember Scripture passages from the sermons and recite them for their parents at home during the meal and order them according to the basic outline: faith—love.[156] The reformer illustrates this powerfully. The individual verses are like coins that are to be put into one of two pouches. Each of the two pouches has for its part two pockets. This is how the dual pattern of faith—love unfolds into a fourfold outline: "Faith's pouch ought to have two pockets. In the one place, we find the part that we believe how we are—every one of us—corrupted, sinners, and damned by Adam's sin. . . . In the other place, we find the part that we all are redeemed by Jesus Christ from such a corrupt, sinful, and damned nature."[157] Foundational faith emerges out of judgment and grace, Law and Gospel. "Love's pouch also ought to have two pockets. In the one place, there is the part that we ought to serve and do good to everyone, as Christ has done to us. . . . In the other place, there is the part that we should gladly suffer and endure all kinds of evil."[158] Love issuing forth from faith proves itself in dedication to fellow men and in patient endurance of the suffering imposed. In joyful play, children are to place all passages they can lay hold of into those two pouches with their double pockets until they thereby comprehend "the sum total of the Christian understanding"[159] and through this, on their part, would become "souls rich in Scripture and knowledge of God."[160] Every bit of child's play is holy seriousness for the reformer. Here he reminds the reader of God's becoming man in the Son: "And let no one consider himself to be too sophisticated and despise such child's play. Christ,

---

154   WA 19:76.2 (see also AE 53:51–90).
155   WA 19:76.7–11.
156   WA 19:76.11–77.22 (see also AE 53:51–90).
157   WA 19:77.15 (see also AE 53:51–90).
158   WA 19:77.19 (see also AE 53:51–90).
159   WA 19:77.13 (see also AE 53:51–90).
160   WA 19:78.16 (see also AE 53:51–90).

because He wanted to instruct men, had to become man. If we are to instruct children, we also have to become children with them."[161]

Already in the first of his famous 1522 Invocavit Sermons, Luther hammered this fourfold pattern—faith from Law and Gospel, love in serving the neighbor, and suffering obedience—into his restless Wittenberg congregation: "We are all, every one of us, summoned to death, and no one will die for the other!"[162] This is why "everyone must know well and be armed with the chief parts that concern a Christian. . . . First, how we are children of wrath and how all our work, mind, and thoughts are each nothing. . . . Second, that God has sent us His only-begotten Son so that we would believe in Him and that he who believes in Him shall be free from sin and a child of God."[163] Thus already here in total clarity: faith out of God's judgment and acquittal, out of the Law and out of the Gospel. "Third, we must also have love and do to each other in love as God has done to us by means of faith; without this love faith is not. . . . Fourth, patience is also necessary for us,"[164] for whoever trusts God in faith and serves his neighbor in love will be exposed to the attacks of Satan and will thereby be driven into a patient waiting for God's gracious aid. Thus faith is exercised and grows strong in the service of love and in the obedience of suffering. In this sermon, too, Luther supports his four theses tirelessly with quotes from Scripture. After all, we all ought to "be well-versed in the Bible and equipped with many verses to fend off the devil."[165]

We can trace this outline back one step further, into "Von der Freiheit eines Christenmenschen" ("On Christian Liberty"), Luther's missive to Pope Leo X. After all, in this writing the reformer summarizes the anthropological scope of the doctrine of justification in the famous dual thesis: "A Christian is (in faith according to his inner spiritual existence) a free lord over all things and subject to no one.—A Christian is (in love according to his outward bodily existence) a meek servant of all things and subject to everyone."[166] Thus in the same year (1520), both crucial catechetical outlines begin to be developed: on the one hand in the "short form" of the Decalogue, Creed, and the Lord's Prayer,[167] and on the other hand in the freedom tract.[168]

The double or fourfold outline—faith out of Law and Gospel, love in service to neighbor and following Christ in suffering—contains in itself the

161 WA 19:78.12.
162 WA 10.3:1.7 (see also AE 51:70–75).
163 WA 10.3:2.1, 2.4, 2.10 (see also AE 51:70–75).
164 WA 10.3:3.5, 4.13 (see also AE 51:70–75).
165 WA 10.3:2.14 (see also AE 51:70–75).
166 WA 7:21.1 (see also AE 31:327–77).
167 WA 7:204–29.
168 WA 7:20–28, 42–73 (see also AE 31:327–77).

core of the crystalization of the Reformation approach. Thus it is not surprising that one attempts to develop a catechism out of it. Encouraged by Luther, Melanchthon did this in his 1527 *Spruchbüchlein*.[169] In the preface to the German Mass, Luther already indicated that, going beyond those four core theses, one ought to encourage the children to "make more of these pouches as *loci communes* and therein comprehend all of Scripture."[170] Accordingly, Melanchthon unfolds the dimension of our existence in the world more broadly and adds as a new locus the "married life." The *Articuli, de quibus egerunt per visitatores*[171] and the "Saxon Visitation Articles," expand this outline. In these documents, Melanchthon deals with repentance, faith, good works (unfolded according to the Ten Commandments and the Lord's Prayer), as well as grief, but then adds the Sacraments, as well as churchly and secular orders.

It is curious and gives pause that Luther does not attempt to construct a stand-alone catechism of the Reformation out of this anthropological core outline of justification, as Johannes Brenz and Martin Bucer did, at least with respect to the basic approach.[172] Indeed, it is more puzzling and more peculiar yet that Luther, unlike John Calvin in the Geneva Catechism and Ursinus in the Heidelberg Catechism,[173] did not at least attempt to develop this guiding model within the catechism in a precise way and to impress it thus on the next generation. On the contrary, in Luther's catechism the trinitarian salvation-historical outline of the "short form" prevails fully over the rather anthropological-psychological outline of the document on freedom.

Melanchthon's drafts confirm how easily this one-sided anthropological approach to justification by faith alone can be separated from God's gracious turning to the world in Jesus Christ. In his practical guidebooks from 1527–28, the emphasis quickly moves to the second pole of tension, to our loving dedication to society among humans. In the "Saxon Visitation Articles" there is an elaborate part on the danger posed by the Turks, but Christology is barely touched upon.[174] Thus it remains quite unclear how our justification is founded in God's world-transforming acts of salvation and how it relates back to the Christ event.

---

169   In *Supplementa Melanchthoniana* 5.1:61–73.

170   WA 19:78.17 (see also AE 53:51–90).

171   In CR 26:7–28.

172   Brenz, *Fragstücke*, in MGP 22:146–85; Bucer, *Katechismus*, in Reu, *Quellen*, 1.1:23–66.

173   Calvin, "Geneva Catechism (1545)," in Müller, *Bekenntnisschriften der reformierten Kirche*, 117–53: On faith—On law—On prayer—On sacraments. Cf. Heidelberg Catechism: On man's misery—On man's redemption—On gratitude.

174   On Christology in the "Visitationsunterricht," see the topic "Von der echten christlichen Genugthuung fur die sunde," WA 26:220.20–222.7 (see also AE 40:263–320). On the danger posed by the Turks, see WA 26:228.32–229.46 (see also AE 40:263–320).

Thus if one starts with the outline of the document on freedom, *fides qua* is more easily separated from *fides quae*, the carrying out of faith is better detached from the basis of faith. It is not by fortuitous accident that nearly all neo-Protestant interpreters, along with Albrecht Ritschl, would like to construe such a formalized understanding of faith in the catechisms. To this end, they play off personal trust against a fact-oriented assertion of truth.[175] The reformers certainly did not intend such an isolation of the anthropological dimension of trust. In the Augsburg Confession, Melanchthon again places the pattern of justification[176] into the comprehensive movement of trinitarian salvation and churchly history[177] and, at the same time, anchors it Christologically.[178] In the 1528 Confession, Luther orients himself on the outline of the Creed and has the Apostles' Creed with its Second Article form the core in his catechisms as well.

Yet it still remains quite curious that Luther does not at least add the distinction to his catechisms as a meaningful aid to understand Scripture. The preface to the German Mass would have suggested such an approach. In this way, the Reformation's doctrine of justification would have gained without question a fixed place in the catechism. Maybe Luther considered this task accomplished in Melanchthon's writings. At the same time, he thought that the children were introduced to the *sola fide absque operibus* ["by faith alone without works"][179] by means of the traditional texts of the catechism. In his 1530 notes for *De loco iustificationis* ("Concerning the Topic of Justification"),[180] Luther lists three relevant points: (1) In the Creed we confess the forgiveness of sins by grace alone, without any hint to our works. (2) God's self-introduction at the beginning of the Decalogue bears witness to the fact that, prior to all our works, He wants to be our God and adopt us as His children. (3) In the address of the Lord's Prayer, we, prior to all deeds, place ourselves prayerfully into the heavenly Father's protective hand of grace. At these key points Luther hints at the anthropological pattern of faith and love also in the catechisms. According to this distinction, the First Commandment proves to be effectual in all the other commandments.[181] This pattern shows in the sanctifying work of God's Spirit that grows out of the constant forgiveness of sins; it permeates the interpretation of the Lord's Prayer and structures especially the petition for forgiveness; and in the coordination of promise and faith, the Sacraments find their right

---

175   Ritschl, *Rechtfertigung*, 3:6, 21, 201ff., 369f., etc.
176   AC II–VI, with the additional articles XVIII–XX.
177   AC I–XVII.
178   AC III.
179   "Entwurf zu *De loco iustificationis*, 1530," WA 30.2:663.25.
180   WA 30.2:663.25–664.12.
181   Cf. pp. 134–41.

place.[182] In this way, the double and fourfold outline subliminally structures time and again Luther's interpretations, yet it is not made solemnly explicit anywhere.

Subtly different from Melanchthon's elaborations, Luther, especially on the Third Article and on the Lord's Prayer, directs the pole of that outline that faces the world—love in service of the neighbor and following Christ in suffering—more strongly toward the kingdom of God. "The dear holy cross"[183] does not primarily grow out of our creaturely existence, but it arises all the more as genuine suffering of Christians results from the rebellious struggle of a world alienated from God and resisting the Gospel. Thus the legitimate place of the cross is not properly in the First but in the Third Article. Luther describes the dual scope's pole facing the world by means of the "true order of a Christian." This *verus ordo Christianae vitae*[184] is something that Luther works out especially in 1525 against Carlstadt. In the catechisms, it forms a hidden red thread in the interpretation of the Lord's Prayer. In this sense, Luther constantly took the decisive insights, which he formulated as a precise dual thesis first in the document on liberty, as points of reference for his interpretation of the catechism.

Yet the impasse remains: Luther does not use in his catechisms the central anthropological patterns of the doctrine of justification that he had extolled very pointedly between 1520 and 1526. Although the reformer himself outlined in the German Mass how a catechesis based on this could look, and though (or because?) Melanchthon elaborated on those hints in catechetical books, Luther drops this approach. He orients himself on the traditional texts as reference points for his catechisms. By doing so, he at the same time accepts their trinitarian salvation-historical breadth. In this way the catechisms become a work of the ecumenical Luther. Our interpretation will tirelessly point to this ecumenical horizon. At the same time, it wishes to underline the specific contribution of Luther.

THE ORDERING
OF THE THREE CENTRAL CHIEF PARTS

The ordering of the catechism parts, especially of the three parts considered indispensable by the reformer (Creed, Lord's Prayer, Decalogue), has generated controversies in scholarship. The controversies have concentrated on the Small Catechism.[185] The alternative is this: Did Luther want to develop

---

182 Cf. the commentary to the respective places.
183 *BSLK*, 677.21.
184 "Dtn.-Vorl., 1523/24," WA 14:682.2 (see also AE 9:1–311).
185 An overview of the discussion is offered by Fraas, *Katechismustradition*, 25–31, 248–63, 288–92, 298, 305–11. Cf. furthermore Albrecht, "Vorbemerkungen zu beiden Katechismen," 446–48;

an "inner progression of thought" by placing the Decalogue first, placing the Creed in the center, and having the Lord's Prayer follow, or is this outline merely random and therefore to be disregarded by the interpreter?

The thesis of an "inner progression of thought" was developed by the great catechists and Luther scholars of the nineteenth century, primarily by Gerhard von Zezschwitz and Theodosius Harnack:[186]

> The Decalogue leads up to faith in a preparatory way as teacher of the knowledge of sin. Once on this way, the possession of salvation is found in the Creed, then out of it flows, ideally descending, the fruit of the engagement of the new spirit. Faith alone determines in a fundamental way what the other two parts are in the whole of Christian doctrine. Faith takes the Decalogue and prayer to be its companions: the Decalogue as an expression for going through repentance; prayer as sum and outgrowth of the engagement of its own life.[187] Moses, Christ, the Spirit is then the shorthand for the great catechetical trilogy that, based on history, enunciates the law of the entire revelation, the sum of the way of salvation and of all of dogmatics and ethics.[188]

The antithesis, according to which the three parts are merely loosely connected blocks, begins to emerge in Johannes Gottschick[189] and dominates the current interpretation. Kurt Frör formulated it most clearly:

> The chief parts of the Small Catechism form, according to Luther, no coherent system of doctrine. Rather, they form a blocklike, insular compilation of the traditional texts most important for elementary and exemplary instruction. Each individual chief part always presupposes simultaneously the whole of tradition. To be sure, it does not contain the whole but addresses it based on a specific question. No chief part can be understood apart from the context of the others. The sequence found in the Small

---

Luthers Katechismen, 39–41; Bachmann, "Die Reihenfolge der drei ersten Haupstücke"; Meyer, *Historischer Kommentar*, 82–85; Heintze, *Luthers Predigt von Gesetz und Evangelium*, 104–10; Hoffmann, "Der Kleiner Katechismus als Abriß der Theologie Luthers"; Frör, "Theologische Grundfragen zur Interpretation des Kleinen Katechismus"; Krusche, "Zur Struktur des Kleinen Katechismus."

186   Von Zezschwitz, *Katechetik*, 2.1:272–84; Harnack, *Katechetik*, 2:15–18; Girgensohn, *Katechismus-Auslegung*, 1:10–13.

187   Publisher's note: This understanding of faith relates historically to the position on election to which C. F. W. Walther and the Missouri Synod were opposed. Related also thereto are Francis Pieper's arguments against psychological religion and interpretation according to the totality of Scripture.

188   Von Zezschwitz, *Katechetik*, 2.1:278; cf. Fraas, *Katechismustraditionen*, 26f., 257f., 261.

189   Gottschick, *Luther als Katechet*, 39: "The progress from one chief part to the next is thus—as each step makes an impression on the whole of Christianity—each time an enrichment and deepening of the Christian knowledge in which, to be sure, the correlations become more clear and distinct, but in which no new and hitherto unknown part is added." Cf. Gottschick, "Die Seligkeit und der Dekalog," vol. 1 of "Katechetische Lutherstudien"; Achelis, *Der Dekalog als katechetisches Lehrstück*, 63f.; Hardeland, *Katechismusgedanken*, 186; Heintze, *Luthers Predigt von Gesetz und Evangelium*, 110; Fraas, *Katechismustradition*, 26ff., 259ff., 290.

Catechism is not determined by the subject matter and necessity. Therefore the interpretation in instruction is not bound by this sequence.[190]

The concise thesis thus reads: the sequence Decalogue—Creed—Lord's Prayer wants to mark out the God-given way of salvation from the Law to Jesus Christ, from Jesus Christ to the Spirit. The antithesis that possesses equal clarity reads: The sequence does not want to establish a theological principle; it is merely supposed to construe a "methodical aid." Each chief part of the triad directs the eyes "anew . . . toward the center . . . God's grace revealed in Jesus Christ."[191]

We have to examine thesis as well as antithesis, constantly keeping in mind the tradition inherited by Luther as well as his own catechetical works. Johannes Meyer compiled the arrangements that are found in late medieval writings.[192] Until the middle of the fifteenth century, the sequence Creed, Lord's Prayer, Decalogue dominates. This reflects the historical growth. Beginning in the thirteenth century, the Decalogue gains significance as an aid for confession.[193] It is mostly interpreted as an unfolding of the dual commandment (love of God and love of neighbor). Around the end of the fourteenth century and in the course of the fifteenth century, the Decalogue replaces the manifold alternative confessional outlines or absorbs them. At the same time, the Lord's Prayer increasingly gains importance as lay prayer within the rosary. Beginning about 1450, the Lord's Prayer moves to the top in synodical decisions and in catechetical handbooks. Johann Surgant gives the reason for the emerging sequence in his *Manuale Curatorum*: "Prayer is powerless without faith; faith is powerless without keeping the Commandments."[194]

In Luther we observe a peculiar tension. On the one hand, all sorts of combinations are found where he mentions these three chief parts only in passing.[195] On the other hand, where he interprets the chief parts combined,

---

190 Frör, "Theologische Grundfragen zur Interpretation des Kleinen Katechismus," 482. The theses have been adopted by Krusche, "Zur Struktur des Kleinen Katechismus," 321; and especially by Fraas, *Katechismustradition*, 298, 305–11.

191 Fraas, *Katechismustradition*, 28; cf. Albrecht, *Luthers Katechismen*, 40: "Each chief part contains from its peculiar angle all of Luther's understanding of Christianity."

192 Meyer, *Historischer Kommentar*, 82. However, this overview is problematic insofar as those three texts are often taken out of the variety of other arrangements.

193 Cf. on this p. 72f.

194 Meyer, *Historischer Kommentar*, 82. Surgant: "When prayer does not have power, it takes place without true faith (for without faith it is impossible to please God); then do speak the Creed" (that is, after the Lord's Prayer). For after the Creed, this is urged: "Since faith is entirely powerless and dead without the works and does not become alive without the keeping of the Ten Commandments, therefore also keep and learn the Ten Commandments" (quoted according to Albrecht, "Vorbemerkungen zu beiden Katechismen," 448 n. 1).

195 In these manifold arrangements, "Sach-Ausl., 1527" (WA 23:486.29 [see also AE 20:153–347]) and the Large Catechism (*BSLK*, 547.37) have Lord's Prayer—Decalogue—Creed. "Vorrede

he inexorably clings to the sequence Decalogue—Creed—Lord's Prayer.[196] Prior to Luther, this sequence is found only rarely and without any inner reason being given for it.[197] Luther not only maintains it consistently, but he also time and again gives reasons for it.

In the 1520 "Kurzen Form" ("Short Form"), Luther programmatically sets out with this thesis: Decalogue, Creed, and Lord's Prayer "contain thoroughly and abundantly . . . everything written in Scripture and what always may be preached, also everything a Christian needs to know."[198] The Decalogue tells everyone "what he should do and leave undone" and thereby teaches him "to recognize his disease, so that he might see and feel what he can do and cannot do, leave undone and cannot leave undone, and thus recognize that he is a sinner and an evil person."[199] The Creed shows to him who has recognized his own powerlessness and inability to undivided obedience "where he should take it and seek and find it . . . where he should find the medicine, the grace."[200] The Lord's Prayer teaches him "how it is to be sought and taken," how he should "desire, take, and bring to himself" grace.[201]

As an all-inclusive mirror of sin, the Decalogue does not merely remain at the beginning of this introduction to the faith. Rather, as God's unchanging command, it remains normative for the entire way of the Christian. Creed and Lord's Prayer are added to the Decalogue.[202] The Creed offers

---

zur Dt. Messe, 1526" (WA 19:75.16 [see also AE 53:51–90]) has Creed—Decalogue—Lord's Prayer. The Small Catechism (BSLK, 502.43) has Decalogue—Lord's Prayer—Creed. All these seem to be governed only by the principle "variety delights," and only some broader patterns emerge. Where Luther has the early Church in view, the order prior to 1450 appears occasionally, for example, "Ein Brief an die zu Frankfurt a. M., 1532" (WA 30.3:567.17) and "15 ps. grad. comm., 1532/33" (WA 40.3:90.4). However, when he speaks about tradition and urges praying the catechism, he primarily follows the customary, well-known post-1450 order; see "Vorrede zur Dt. Messe, 1526" (WA 19:76.26–77.11 [see also AE 53:51–90]); "Sach.-Ausl., 1527" (WA 23:485.28, 485.33 [see also AE 20:153–347]); the Small Catechism (BSLK, 502.4, 509.5); "Brief an die zu Frankfurt a. M., 1532" (WA 30.3:566.37); and "Pred. zum Credo vom 11.2.1537" (WA 45:12.7). When he invites others to take up and study the catechism, frequently his own order appears; see "Eine kurze Form d. 10 Gebote, 1520" (WA 7:204.7); the Small Catechism (BSLK, 503.20); and "Vorrede zur 1. Reihe d. Kat.-Predigten, 1528" (WA 30.1:2.15).

196 "Eine kurze Form d. 10 Gebote, des Glaubens, des Vaterunsers, 1520," WA 7:205–29; "Katechismuspredigten, 1523," WA 11:36–59; and "Katechismuspredigten, 1528," WA 30.1:2–122.

197 Meyer, Historischer Kommentar, 82, mentions the Spierer Beichttafel (1495) and Honnef (1500). Frör points to John Wycliffe, The poor Caitiff, but he begins with the Creed (cf. Geffcken, Bildercatechismus, app., col. 214ff.).

198 WA 7:204.9.

199 WA 7:204.14, 204.23; cf. WA 7:214.18–22.

200 WA 7:204.16, 204.26.

201 WA 7:204.18, 205.1.

202 Heintze, Luthers Predigt von Gesetz und Evangelium, 105f.: "Contrariwise, God's will revealed in the Decalogue is, in this arrangement, the actual dominating force. Symbol and Lord's Prayer serve it, in order to bring it to fulfillment."

the medicine of grace to man, "which helps him to become pious so that he might keep the Commandments."[203] And the Lord's Prayer instructs him actually to receive that grace, "namely, with orderly, humble, comforting prayer. This is how it is given to him, and thus he will be saved by keeping the Commandments of God."[204]

This phrase sounds like late medieval works-righteousness.[205] It shows how strongly Luther's first catechism attempt from 1520 was still shaped by beginning with the Ten Commandments as the most important confessional manual. After all, between 1516 and 1520 Luther had interpreted the Decalogue several times to prepare for confession.[206] Beginning with the Ten Commandments in this way doubtlessly belongs to the conditions in which the catechisms of Luther originated.

In the 1523 and 1528 catechism sermons,[207] the reformer retains the systematizing ordering of the three central chief parts, which is outlined in the "Short Form." This order also structures the Large Catechism. Especially in the second sermon series of September 1528, Luther places the entire interpretation of the Creed[208] and the beginning of the Lord's Prayer[209] under this scope: The triune God gives Himself in creation, redemption, and sanctification so that we would fulfill His will expressed in the Commandments. "It is necessary for the Father, Son, Holy Spirit to come with His power and works so that we might observe the Ten Commandments."[210]

---

203   WA 7:204.26.

204   WA 7:205.1.

205   Cf. "Eine kurze Form, 1520," WA 7:214.21f.; "Vorrede zum Betbüchlein, 1522," WA 10.2:377.12 (see also AE 43:3–45); "Pred. zur 1. Vaterunserbitte, 9.3.1523," WA 11:55.2–5; "Kat.-Pred., Vorrede zum Vaterunser, 22.9.1528," WA 30.1:46.17f. According to the medieval instructions for confession, the purpose of keeping the Commandments is entering eternal life. One refers to Mark 10:17–31 and parallels, the pericope of the rich young man. See, for example, the saying quoted in Geffcken, *Bildercatechismus*, 42: "Now may merciful God help us / that we may keep His Commandments / so that by it we would be given / grace here in time and eternal life there." Or Geffcken, *Bildercatechismus*, app., col. 1: "If you want to enter eternal life, you should stand firmly in the Commandments of God."

206   "Eine kurze Erklärung d. 10 Gebote, 1518," WA 1:250–56; "Instructio pro confessione peccatorum, 1518," WA 1:258–65 (see also AE 51:35–43); "Eine kurze Unterweisung, wie man beichten soll, 1519," WA 2:59–65.

207   "Kat.-Pred., 24.2.1523," WA 11:31.3–5: "First, the Ten Commandments teach what to do and what not to do. The Symbol [Creed] teaches where to get it; the Lord's Prayer, that it may increase." Cf. "Kat.-Pred. 4.3.1523/9.3.1523," WA 11:48.16–24, 55.2–5. See also "Kat.-Pred., Vorrede zum Vaterunser, 24.2.1523," WA 30.1:46.9: "For also the Ten Commandments teach the best life. Then the Symbol shows where strength is to be gotten and fetched so that we would lead a holy life. The Lord's Prayer follows . . . so that God might give the fulfillment of the Commandments by faith and might not impute where not enough is done."

208   "Vorrede zum Credo, 21.9.1528," WA 30.1:43.27–46.6.

209   "Vorrede zum Vaterunser, 22.9.1528," WA 30.1:46.8–17.

210   "Kat.-Pred. zum Credo, 21.9.1528," WA 30.1:46.5; cf. WA 30.1:45.36ff.

In the Large Catechism, as already in the first and third sermon series of 1528, the reformer preserves more distinctly the individual character of the individual chief parts. As in the Small Catechism, they stand side by side like blocks. However, at the beginning of the Creed[211] and the Lord's Prayer,[212] Luther does resort to the foundational formulae from the 1520 "Short Form," but reformulates them independently: The Decalogue teaches us "what God wants us to do and to leave undone."[213] The Creed offers to us "everything we must expect and receive from God."[214] The Lord's Prayer tells us "how one should pray."[215] As already the different lengths of the individual interpretations show,[216] the accent is still unequivocally on the Decalogue. The dark experience Luther had to have as a visitor probably had an exacerbating effect. The Creed and the Lord's Prayer are ordered according to the Ten Commandments also concerning content; both help us to fulfill the Decalogue.[217] Similar to the "Short Form," the Large Catechism still ties the Creed more tightly to the Decalogue than to the Lord's Prayer. In doing so, Luther even takes up entire statements made in the second sermon series, namely, that "God gives Himself fully with all He is and has and can do to help and direct us to keep the Ten Commandments: the Father, all His creatures; the Son, all His work; the Holy Spirit, all His gifts."[218]

However, the reformer submits this one-sided ordering of the creedal Symbol and Lord's Prayer according to the Decalogue to the harsh tension between Creed and Decalogue. In this clear opposition, the relation between Law and Gospel is reflected. Already the phrase at the beginning of the interpretation of the Creed—the Commandments show "what God wants us to do and to leave undone," while the Creed teaches what God wants to give us[219]—makes this opposition obvious. At the end of the interpretation of the Symbol, Luther underlines it again: The Decalogue "is written in the hearts of all men." It cannot make us into believers in Christ since it leaves us under God's judgment concerning our disobedience. However, "no human wisdom

---

211 *BSLK*, 646.3–12.

212 *BSLK*, 662.17–31.

213 *BSLK*, 646.5.

214 *BSLK*, 646.7.

215 *BSLK*, 662.19.

216 About eighty-six pages for the Decalogue, fifteen pages for the Creed, and twenty-nine pages for the Lord's Prayer. The Creed is discussed rather briefly because especially the Second Article is unfolded in the sermons in the course of the church year; cf. *BSLK*, 653.4–10.

217 *BSLK*, 640.39–45, 646.10–12, 662.20–31.

218 *BSLK*, 661.38–42.

219 *BSLK*, 646.3–8. It is modeled after "Kat.-Pred. zum Credo, 10.12.1528" (WA 30.1:94.19ff. [see also AE 51:169–76]); "Kat.-Pred., Vorrede zum Vaterunser, 14.12.1528" (WA 30.1:95.2ff. [see also AE 51:169–76]). Cf. already "Pred. zum Credo, 4.3.1523," WA 11:48.23: "The entire Gospel is in the Symbol, which certainly can encompass the entire Gospel."

can comprehend" the Creed. It has to be given to us out of the proclamation of Christ by the Holy Spirit Himself in order to change our hearts and to strengthen us for new obedience.[220] Because Luther strongly distinguishes between the Decalogue as the Law and the Creed as the Gospel, the Second Article must necessarily take center stage in the Creed. After all, God the Father has opened His loving heart only in Jesus Christ.[221] Scholarship has always underlined: "The actual core of the Small (and the Large) Catechism is the Second Chief Part with the three articles of the faith. Here, in turn, the Second Article is the core and heart with its statements on Christ's person and work."[222] In our search for the arrangement of the three foundational chief parts, we have thus hit upon two centers. On the one hand, Luther lifts up the Decalogue already from the time of the "Short Form" and coordinates Creed and Lord's Prayer with it in a serving function. On the other hand, he accentuates the tension between commandment and Gospel, which moves the Symbol with its Second Article into the center. Two movements go out from these two centers, which have led to the two traditions of interpretation in scholarship. Somewhat schematically, that antagonism can be made understandable and clear in three steps.

1.   First, one needs to maintain that the center of the catechism is the interpretation of the Creed as it moves from creation to redemption all the way to sanctification.[223] Justification's "by grace alone" is hinted at already in the First Article: the heavenly Father gives to the confessor His blessing as Creator "out of fatherly, divine goodness and mercy without any merit or worthiness in me."[224] This "by grace alone" is anchored in the "Jesus Christ alone" of the Second Article: "Jesus Christ [is] my Lord who has redeemed me, a lost and condemned creature."[225] Both reach their completion in the "by faith alone" of the Third Article: I cannot, "by my own reason or strength,"[226] believe in Jesus Christ as my Lord and Redeemer. This takes places only by virtue of the office and work of the Holy Spirit.[227]

---

220   *BSLK*, 661.21–35.

221   *BSLK*, 660.38–46.

222   Hoffmann, "Der Kleine Katechismus als Abriß der Theologie Luthers," 57. Similarly, Krusche, "Zur Struktur des Kleinen Katechismus," 322; and Fraas, *Katechismustradition*, 255f., 259, 306.

223   Girgensohn, *Katechismus-Auslegung*, 1:106: "In Luther's catechism, the second chief part is a great hymn that grows out of faith and glorifies God."

224   *BSLK*, 511.3.

225   *BSLK*, 551.23.

226   *BSLK*, 511.46.

227   Hoffmann, "Der Kleine Katechismus als Abriß der Theologie Luthers," 60: "Thus the *gratis* of justification is already foreshadowed in the First Article, is continued by means of the *propter*

The Decalogue points forward to the Christ-center of the Symbol by demanding fear and love toward the source of all temporal and eternal blessings. The Lord's Prayer comes from this center, both in its interpretation of the address (though it was first added later)[228] and in the interpretation of the central Second Petition.[229] The Sacraments refer to the Second Article.[230] In this sense the assertion of the Smalcald Articles is also true for the catechisms: core and center is and remains the "office and work of Jesus Christ," the basic article of our redemption,[231] as it is unfolded and defined by the threefold "alone"—Christ alone, grace alone, faith alone. Also for the catechism holds true: "This article cannot be given up or compromised, even if heaven and earth or whatever else does not want to remain are destroyed."[232] This is the first and foundational insight.

2. In a second step, however, we now need to realize that the reformer in the catechisms—unlike, for example, in the Smalcald Articles—has distanced the realm of the First Article and the dimensions of the Third Article quite significantly from the Second Article and has treated them quite independently.

As Luther focuses strictly on the goodness of God the Creator, he clearly differentiates the First Article from the Christ-center and simultaneously assigns the Decalogue clearly to the work of the Creator. In keeping with the First Commandment as the "head and source"[233] of all the other commandments, Luther addresses God as the "eternal Source" of all good things, "from which one receives all good things and is delivered from all misfortune."[234] The name Jesus Christ is not mentioned. The focus is on the earthly/bodily blessing of God. Eternal salvation is hinted at in merely formulary phrases and in a concluding outlook.[235] Those scholars who, according to the New Testament exhortations (paraneses), wish to interpret the Decalogue in light of the Second

---

Christum in the Second Article as a foundational statement, and by means of the *per fidem* of the Third Article it is finally completed and concluded."
228 Cf. *BSLK*, 512 n. 1.
229 Cf. the comments on the Second Petition.
230 Cf. the comments on the Sacraments.
231 *BSLK*, 415.4f.
232 *BSLK*, 415.21.
233 *BSLK*, 644.18.
234 *BSLK*, 565.41, 565.35.
235 *BSLK*, 571.40–572.8.

Article as Christ-formed *usus practicus evangelii*[236] have major problems with their interpretation, because the reformer, likely under the impression of the visitations, emphatically moves the threat and promise attached to the prohibition of images (Exod. 20:5f.; Deut. 5:9f.) to the end in the Small Catechism. In the Large Catechism, he interprets these words in conjunction with the First Commandment and takes them up again at the end of the Decalogue.[237] In this way, all the commandments are permeated by God's zealous holiness.

In the First Article, Luther also describes the goodness of the heavenly Father in creating and sustaining without making any explicit mention of Jesus Christ as His only-begotten Son. Our eschatological salvation is again only hinted at in the transition to the Second Article: "Here we see how the Father has given Himself with all creatures and provides for us more than richly in *this* life, *apart from additionally* showering on us also ineffable, *eternal* goods through His *Son* and *Holy Spirit, as we shall hear*."[238]

In the Decalogue, the reformer thus accentuates slightly differently than, for example, in the "Sermon von den guten Werken" ("Sermon on Good Works").[239] The First Commandment is not interpreted here in relation to God's will to save in the Son and to full faith in Christ given thereby. Rather, Luther focuses on our creaturely relationship to God. Analogously, the interpretation of the First Article is different than the 1528 Confession[240] and the Smalcald Articles.[241] Although in these other texts the statements about us are made strictly from Christ and thus our enslavement to original sin is featured prominently, the catechisms seem to allow for an at least conditionally independent realm of creatureliness that lies before the Second Article with the fall into sin and redemption by Christ.

Something analogous can be seen regarding the Third Article. Unlike Melanchthon in the Augsburg Confession, Luther has further removed this article from the Christ-center and has unfolded it independently under the head of our sanctification by God the

---

236   Joest, *Gesetz und Freiheit*, 132.
237   *BSLK*, 567–71, 641–45.
238   *BSLK*, 650.27.
239   WA 6:204–16 (see also AE 44:15–114).
240   WA 26:500.27–505.28 (see also AE 40:321–77).
241   *BSLK*, 414ff.

Spirit.[242] However, here the connection with the central Second Article is closer than in the case of the First Article. After all, "sanctifying is nothing other than bringing to the Lord Christ."[243] Already in the Second Article, Luther had not described Christ primarily as the one who blots out our guilt before God, but at least equally important as the conqueror of the powers of doom, urging that our sanctification directly ties into this. The Lord's Prayer underlines this aspect impressively.

These observations can be compressed into the following insight: in the catechisms, Luther removes especially the First Article with the Decalogue, and to a lesser degree also the Third Article, surprisingly far from the Second Article of the Creed, which remains the center.

3. In a third step, we now have to consider those strange back references that Luther constantly carries out. In the case of the Symbol, he formulates this most emphatically at the end of the Third Article, similar to what he had done already in the 1528 Confession:[244] In Christ alone, as the mirror of the heart of God the Father, we regain the favor and goodness of the Father and Creator that we lost in the original fall. In the Spirit alone, Christ reveals Himself to us as the Redeemer.[245] Thus redemption is offered to us in sanctification, and it is first through these two that creation becomes anew the gift of the heavenly Father.

Luther situates an outer ring around this inner ring of back references within the Symbol. The outer ring has to do with this insight: first, by faith and prayer the Decalogue is changed from the condemning Law of the holy Judge into the gracious direction of the merciful Father. In this insight, the coordination Law— Gospel—exhortation (paranesis) is articulated.

Yet, at the beginning of the Lord's Prayer, Luther locates this triad in the ongoing battle against devil, world, and one's own flesh.[246] He had already hinted at this battle in connection with

---

242 This does have a certain parallel in the 1528 Confession; see WA 26:505.29–509.18 (see also AE 37:151–372).

243 *BSLK*, 654.39.

244 WA 26:505.38–506.12 (see also AE 37:151–372).

245 *BSLK*, 660.32–47. Cf. "Kat.-Pred. zum Credo, 10.12.1528," WA 30.1:94.14–19 (see also AE 51:169–76).

246 *BSLK*, 662.23ff.

the Second and Third Articles.[247] Thus the Lord's Prayer becomes an in-depth repetition of the Decalogue. What Luther presented in outline only in the Decalogue, he now fills in using bright colors. In the Decalogue, he had in view the obedience of the believers vis-à-vis the Creator and Giver of blessings. In the Lord's Prayer, Luther drastically describes our wrestling with the powers of chaos, in which our sanctification appears as justification claimed time and again. The central petition for the breaking-in of the kingdom of God summarizes what has been pointed out regarding the Second and Third Articles.[248] The First Petition ties in with the command to sanctify God's name,[249] and the Third Petition puts the foe, against whom the ground is to be held, right in the sights.[250] All three "Your petitions" thus unfold the breaking-in of the spiritual kingdom of God in this perishing world of death.

The bread petition restates what has been said regarding the First Article and the Fourth Commandment under the scope of God's government of this world in its battle against the dominion of Satan.[251] The additional "Our petitions" stretch out toward God's eschatological future. Out of the daily forgiveness of our sins we cry out to be saved in soul and body through the battles of this life. The reformer outlines a similar movement also regarding Baptism and the Lord's Supper: out of the ongoing Christ-forgiveness we, in the daily death of the old Adam and emergence of the new man, press on toward coming before God's gracious presence.

Thus we come to see the third characteristic of the catechisms: a tireless back referencing, a continuous taking up and deepening continuation of earlier thoughts.

Based on this threefold observation, we formulate our thesis on the ordering of Decalogue, Creed, and Lord's Prayer in Luther's catechisms: Luther neither offers a systematic *ordo salutis* (Moses—Christ—Spirit) nor did he place the individual chief parts side by side in an isolated manner. Rather, the reformer by means of that triad opens for us the eschatological path of Christendom and the individual believer, from our being creatures to the final completion. In all this, the Christ-center is constantly in focus. Based

---

247 *BSLK*, 651.34–652.30, 652.47–653.3, 655.22–29, 661.5–18.

248 Especially *BSLK*, 673.27–39.

249 Especially *BSLK*, 672.6–26.

250 Especially *BSLK*, 677.14–40; cf. the comments on the Third Petition of the Lord's Prayer.

251 *BSLK*, 679.44: ". . . in summary, everything that is both related to house and neighbor or civil business and government." Cf. *BSLK*, 681.35–51.

on the Second Article of the Creed, Luther unveils the deep dimensions of our Christian existence.

To be sure, the order of the basic catechism parts grew out of intensively working on the Decalogue as a confessional manual, but it is reflected in a responsible manner and filled with substance. This is why a change in the order of the chief parts would affect Luther's interpretation. One should hold fast to this against modern catechesis. The reformer, on the other hand, did not mean to construct a fixed order of salvation. This is the error of the great catechists of the nineteenth century. Rather, Luther meant carefully to introduce the people entrusted to him to the eschatological path of faith of the mature Christian. For this purpose, he needed a delicate coordination of the individual chief parts to the whole of church doctrine, which can only be unfolded in three steps:[252] (1) The interpretation of the Creed, which is centered in the Second Article concerning our redemption by means of Christ's becoming our Lord, represents the ever-present hidden center of the catechisms. (2) However, the First Article and the Decalogue are removed remarkably far from the Christ-center. Under the guiding idea of the sustaining goodness of the Creator and the grateful obedience of the believers, this complex forms something like a vestibule to the Second Article. At the same time, the Third Article and the Lord's Prayer are correlated to the Second Article as a third center. The guiding idea here is our constant sanctification in the struggle against the forces of chaos. (3) In a deliberate back reference, on the one hand, the Creed and the Lord's Prayer are placed under the scope of the fulfillment of the Commandments. On the other hand, the First Article is shown to be already in the light of the Second and Third Articles. At the same time, a constantly deepening continuation opens a vista on the eschatological goal of our wrestling with the forces of death, namely, on the eschatological rule of God through Christ in the Holy Spirit.

These living three steps not only shape the Large Catechism, they also and especially structure the Small Catechism, though Luther was unable to explain this expressly. A historical-systematic interpretation that desires to be guided by the intention of the author should not overlook this living movement; instead, it should carefully follow it.

---

252   Pointing in the same direction as the solution for the conflict within Luther research outlined here is Bachmann, "Die Reihenfolge der drei ersten Hauptstücke," 379: "In the pious life of the Christian, the Law, the Creed, and the Prayer lie and work next to each other. They are constant contents, and each in its way is an exhaustive expression of the Christian being. . . . But these entities do not merely lie next to each other; they influence each other and arrange themselves into an inner sequence." Cf. also Fraas, *Katechismustradition*, 308f.

THE DECALOGUE

Luther's Understanding
of the Decalogue[1]
in the Context of Churchly
Interpretation

Unlike the Creed and the Lord's Prayer, the Decalogue could gain no proper function in the catechumenate of the early Church. While the Decalogue is rarely mentioned prior to Augustine,[2] that Church father employed it to unfold the double commandment concerning love of God and neighbor; yet he, too, does not know of a solemn *traditio* and *redditio decalogi*.[3] Only in the thirteenth century is the Decalogue officially commended by the Church as an aid for confession. In the fifteenth century, it begins to absorb or to replace the other outlines for confession. The reformers step into this development and bring it to a conclusion. The practice to develop the Christian ethos solely based on the Decalogue was first adopted by the reformers. Recently, Hugo Röthlisberger attacked this sharply: Not the Law of Sinai but Jesus Christ Himself must be "the starting point and center of our ethical instruction."[4] Like Augustine, Röthlisberger wants to base the Christian ethos on the double commandment of love of God and neighbor. Unlike Augustine and Thomas, Röthlisberger does not want to unfold it by means of the Decalogue but in constant reference to Jesus Christ, "whose deeds and words are the only legitimate interpretation of what God gives and demands with the commandment of love."[5]

Those historical observations and this material criticism of the catechism force us to ask a threefold question: What is the meaning and function of the Decalogue in the Old Testament? Under which aspects is the Decalogue received in the New Testament and by Christendom? How did

---

1   The texts in which Luther expounds the Decalogue are given on p. 86.

2   Cf. Rentschka, *Dekalogkatechese*, 8–55; Röthlisberger, *Kirche am Sinai*, 43–55.

3   Thus Eggersdorfer, *Augustinus als Pädagoge*, 164ff.; and Röthlisberger, *Kirche am Sinai*, 59ff.; against Rentschka, *Dekalogkatechese*, 117–26.

4   Röthlisberger, *Kirche am Sinai*, 151; cf. Röthlisberger, *Kirche am Sinai*, 143–51.

5   Röthlisberger, *Kirche am Sinai*, 149.

Luther evaluate the Decalogue in general terms? We can answer these questions only in a brief manner. A fourth section on the structure of the Decalogue according to Luther concludes this first chapter.

THE DECALOGUE IN THE OLD TESTAMENT[6]

The "ten words" (Exod. 34:28; Deut. 4:13; 10:4) are inserted in Exodus 20 and Deuteronomy 5 in two slightly different versions[7] into, respectively, the inauguration and the renewal of the covenant between Yahweh and Israel through Moses.[8] Alongside these well-known series of commandments we find other lists that are also formulated in the style of apodictic participles.[9] Outstanding examples of these are, on the one hand, the "cultic Decalogue"[10] in Exod. 34:10–28, which was probably handed down by the Yahwist, and, on the other hand, the series of twelve curses in Deut. 26:15–26, the so-called "Shechemite dodecalogue" of the divine curses that the Levite priests "in the great amphitheater between Mount Ebal and Mount Gerizim at the Pass of Shechem"[11] were called to lay upon the tribes returning home from the sanctuary.

These four series are closely connected to the establishment of the covenant that according to Joshua 24 and Deuteronomy 27 might have been renewed and represented as the Festival of Booths/Festival of Covenant of the Yahweh-Amphictyony at Shechem. By pointing to Joshua 24, Gerhard von Rad, in his study on the form-historical problem of the Hexateuch,[12] has outlined the consummation of the covenant and its cultic representation as follows:

---

6   Cf. on this: Alt, "Die Ursprünge des israelitischen Rechts"; Fohrer, "Das sog. apodiktisch formulierte Recht und der Dekalog"; Gerstenberger, *Wesen und Herkunft*; Gese, "Der Dekalog als Ganzheit betrachtet"; Mowinckel, *Le Décalogue*; "Zur Geschichte der Dekaloge"; von Reventlow, *Gebot und Predigt im Dekalog*; Stamm, "Dreißig Jahre Dekalogforschung"; *Der Dekalog im Lichte der neueren Forschung.*

7   A third late combination of both texts can be found in Papyrus Nash; cf. Würthwein, *Der Text des Alten Testaments*, 98. Both versions are compared in Stamm, *Der Dekalog im Lichte der neueren Forschung*, 7–11.

8   For the LCMS position, see the publisher's introduction, pp. 10–11.

9   Cf. on this the essays by Mowinckel, Fohrer, and Gese mentioned in n. 6 above.

10   In its traditional form, it is a "secondary amalgamation" (Alt, "Die Ursprünge des israelitischen Rechts," 317 n. 1), out of which the original ten words can only be reconstructed hypothetically; cf. Fohrer, "Das sog. apodiktisch formulierte Recht und der Dekalog," 68ff.; and Gese, "Der Dekalog als Ganzheit betrachtet," 130f.

11   Alt, "Die Ursprünge des israelitischen Rechts," 324; Friedrich Horst, "Dekalog," *RGG* 2:69; and Gese, "Der Dekalog als Ganzheit betrachtet," 129f., think that here, too, a commandment aimed at God was placed at the top of an original decalogue (Deut. 26:15) and a concluding Deuteronomist formula was added at the end (Deut. 26:26).

12   Von Rad, "Das formgeschichtliche Problem des Hexateuchs," 33–41; cf. Stamm, *Der Dekalog im Lichte der neueren Forschung*, 30.

1. Promise or parenesis of Joshua with the exhortation to worship
    Yahweh in an undivided manner (Josh. 24:14f.) and with the ac-
    clamation of the people (Josh. 24:16f., 24: "We will serve Yahweh,
    our God, and obey His voice"). This corresponds to the historical
    account with the parenesis in Exod. 19:4–6, 19f., and Deuterono-
    my 1–11.

2. Proclamation of the Law (Josh. 24:25: "Thus Joshua made a cove-
    nant with the people on that day and gave them law and statute at
    Shechem"). This corresponds to the bodies of laws—in Exodus,
    the Decalogue and the covenant code; in Deuteronomy, the body
    from Deuteronomy 12:1–26:15.

3. The making of the covenant (the renewal of the covenant) (Josh.
    24:27), connected with the erection of the stone of witness. Exo-
    dus 24:1–11 mentions the witness stones, the joint sacrifice, and
    the covenant meal.[13] Deuteronomy 26:16–27:10 reads similarly.

4. Promise of blessing for the keeping of the statutes and proclama-
    tion of curse for breaking them (Josh. 8:34; Deut. 27:12f.). This
    corresponds to the promise of blessing in Exod. 23:20ff. and to
    the annunciation of blessing and curse in Deuteronomy 27ff.[14]

In Exodus 20 as well as in Deuteronomy 5, the Decalogue is placed cen-
trally in the account of Yahweh's covenant-making with His people. "The
self-introduction of Yahweh, which implies the idea of the covenant—'I am
Yahweh, your God'—along with the promulgation of the covenant represent
the real content of the revelation of Yahweh at Sinai; in fact, it represents *the*
revelation of Yahweh."[15] The Decalogue attempts to "summarize and outline
the being of an Israel *coram Deo* as a partner of God in a most fundamental
way." It constitutes "that state of *šalōm*, in which Israel finds itself as recipi-
ent of the revelation. The Law is not the condition of the covenant but its
salutary content. . . . God gives a new being by separating it from absence of
salvation. The boundaries of this being are marked for protective purposes.
In this way, a realm of salvation comes about in which Israel can live."[16]

---

13   Cf. Noth, *Das zweite Buch Mose*, 157–61.

14   At first glance, the parallels to Hittite public treaties dating from the fourteenth and thirteenth
      centuries seem astounding, yet they cannot be explained as exact historical copies. In those
      treaties we are dealing with legally codified conditions with detailed sanctions. They represent
      a secondary form that actualizes the primordial order of the sacred covenant into new socio-
      political circumstances. It is from here that parallels arise. Cf. Mendenhall, *Law and Covenant*;
      Baltzer, *Das Bundesformular*; Beyerlin, *Sinaitraditionen*; McCarthy, *Treaty and Covenant*.

15   Gese, "Der Dekalog als Ganzheit betrachtet," 123.

16   Gese, "Der Dekalog als Ganzheit betrachtet," 124.

The form in which the Decalogue has come upon us no longer shows the stylistic tightness, coupled rhythms, and striking brevity of the old sets of commandments. As the Law in general, the Decalogue, too, "at one point in its history entered fully into the parenetic instruction of the congregation; a host of preachers adopted it." It is no longer simply pronounced over the assembly; now it is offered to them for the purpose of warning and exhorting, comforting and encouraging, it is explained, reasons for it are given. In this way, the Decalogue is divine Law that is preached continually. "This broad layer of preaching . . . has enveloped it with its forms like a coat."[17]

The Decalogue's place in the life of the covenant festival probably was not, as Sigmund Mowinckel assumed by pointing to Psalm 15 and 24, the entrance *torôt*, but the central act in the sanctuary itself.[18] Thus the Decalogue is not held before the pilgrim desiring to enter the sanctuary as a catechism-like confessional mirror;[19] rather, the *šalōm*-order of the Lord is again established over the festal assembly, which desires to lead everyone into their daily life in the Diaspora. This is why of all the feasts and ceremonial orders, merely the Sabbath is enjoined.[20] This is also why the daily life together with one's neighbor is front and center; God establishes His order of blessing over this life.

In Deuteronomy 5, as well as in Exodus 20, the Decalogue is placed before the body of laws. It is elevated as a direct and immediate revelation of God to Israel, while the later legal bodies are mediated by Moses.[21] The priesthood that is primarily interested in the cult similarly has the tablets written by God Himself stored in the ark.[22] Nonetheless, the Decalogue seems to have been added only later to the theophany of God. This makes any assessment of its origin and age difficult.

Reconstructions of a "primal Decalogue"[23] are based on an ideal of perfection that hardly could have been achieved at the beginning of such a rich

---

17   Von Reventlow, *Gebot und Predigt im Dekalog*, 15; cf. Breit, *Die Predigt des Deuteronomisten*; von Rad, *Deuteronomium-Studien*.

18   Mowinckel, *Le Décalogue*, 141ff.; cf. Stamm, *Der Dekalog im Lichte der neueren Forschung*, 21f.

19   Galling, "Der Beichtspiegel," 125–30; von Reventlow, *Gebot und Predigt im Dekalog*, 16ff.

20   Von Rad, *Theologie des Alten Testaments*, 1:195: "The laity is addressed by the Decalogue specifically in view of their daily lives, in view of their secular living together in their orders out in the country. That means they are addressed in view of the life that they were to lead after the establishment of the covenant and after their return to their native districts. The priests were to take care of the cult."

21   This was accomplished by postponing Exod. 20:18–21, which originally stood before Exod. 20:1ff., and by tying in the Covenant Code as supplementary revelation.

22   Cf. von Rad, "Zelt und Lade."

23   E.g., in Kittel, *Geschichte des Volkes Israel*, 1:383f.; Rabast, *Apodiktische Recht*, 35ff.; Fohrer, "Das sog. apodiktisch formulierte Recht," 60f.; Gese, "Der Dekalog als Ganzheit betrachtet," 125f.

historical development. Rather, several smaller sets were combined into one unit.[24] In its comprehensive form, the Decalogue seems to be rather late. More meaningful is the quest for the original place in life of the individual commandments.[25] In doing this, a dual focus emerges, as especially Erhard Gerstenberger[26] has demonstrated: on the one hand, the revelation of Yahweh's zeal for salvation; on the other hand, the hallowed order of the clan's bond. Both are older than the settlement of the tribes in the fertile land, yet both have probably first gradually grown together. According to Rolf Knierim,[27] the prohibition of idolatry at the Shechem sanctuary became the basic law of the amphictyony and pushed the prohibition of images into second place. However this might have been in detail, both places held by the sets of commandments in the life of the communities can still be clearly discerned.

The prohibitions of the "Second Table" have their place in life in the ethos of the clans, which is older than Israel.[28] "In the ancient Near East there existed a genre of rules, formulated predominantly negatively in the second person singular, which has been preserved in many a literary form and whose primal form perfectly agrees with the prohibitions known from the Old Testament."[29] Out of these prohibitions grow wisdom's warnings, admonitions, and explanations. The prohibitions are mainly directed at the male members of the clan and exhort them not to do violence to its basic order. Transgressing this order was punished by the ban. The prohibitions cover the whole range of the order of the clan's bond and their life together in it. First, honoring the clan elders is demanded. The commandment is directed not so much at the children but at the grown members of the clan. Next, a protective wall is erected around the clan member close by: his life (Do not murder!), his marriage (Do not break into the marriage!), his freedom (Do not steal and do not enslave a free clan member!),[30] his honor and legal standing (Do not give false witness in the gate against your neighbor!), his house (You shall not strive for the house of your neighbor!).[31] The commands are meant for the male clan member. The one speaking them—thereby the guarantor of the order of taboo protected by them—is originally the head of the extended family, the elders of the clan. Instruction is entrusted

---

24   This is how Fohrer sees it in "Das sog. apodiktisch formulierte Recht," 63ff.

25   Cf. Knierim, "Das erste Gebot," 20ff.

26   Gerstenberger, *Wesen und Herkunft*, 89–117.

27   Knierim, "Das erste Gebot," 38f.

28   Cf. Gerstenberger, *Wesen und Herkunft*, 130–44.

29   Gerstenberger, *Wesen und Herkunft*, 137.

30   Cf. Gerstenberger, *Wesen und Herkunft*, 166f.

31   Gese offers a slightly different order that is probably too complex; see "Der Dekalog als Ganzheit betrachtet," 125–28.

to them; they watch over the commandments. Gerstenberger here points to what is said in Isaiah 35 concerning the faithfulness of the Rechabites.[32] They refuse the wine by claiming a *mişwah*, an entire set of commandments, of their clan's father Jonadab: "You shall not drink wine . . . you shall not build houses; you shall not sow seeds; and vineyards you shall not plant" (Isa. 35:6f.). In the case of the Rechabites, we are dealing with the adherence to the seminomadic way of life even in the Promised Land. The Decalogue codifies in its Second Table the "foundations of human life together in general."[33] The ethos of the clans is what binds Israel and the surrounding nations together.[34] These primal orders are not created by the Commandments but are recognized and protected as something given and found. They lie at the basis of all genuine life together and are received as a good.

These primal orders are not secular orders but are surrounded by a sacred taboo. All peoples of the ancient Near East relate them to a supreme divine power. "The idea that the godhead itself is guardian of the order of life is universal and is evident from the fact that the confessions of sin and innocence hearken back directly to the old orders."[35] According to Exod. 22:28, the *elohim*—the guarantors standing behind and above the heads of the clan—have their place in the specific directions: "You shall not revile god (the *elohim*), and a prince of your people you shall not curse!"[36] Here we see how the ethos of the clan opens up to the worship of God. Thereby the one focus of the ellipse (the preservation of the interhuman order of the clan) begins to transition to the other one: the commandments regarding the worship of God. Two commandments of the "First Table," especially the prohibition of misusing the name but probably also the command to honor the Sabbath, go beyond the community of the Yahweh-worshipers. Even if the origin of the Sabbath is lost in the mist of history, it is certainly older than Israel.[37]

The tribal orders with their prohibitions know that they are founded in a divine numen; Yahweh's Sinai-revelation steps into this knowledge. The self-introduction "I am Yahweh, your God," hearkens back to the basic salvific act on which Israel's covenantal relationship is based[38] and permeates the Commandments all the way to the one concerning honoring parents. The prohibition of images, as well as that of foreign gods, is originally connected

---

32   Gerstenberger, *Wesen und Herkunft*, 110ff.

33   Von Reventlow, *Gebot und Predigt im Dekalog*, 65.

34   Gerstenberger, *Wesen und Herkunft*, 148: "By and large, Israel shares its ethical norms and its ideas of a well-ordered society with the surrounding peoples."

35   Gerstenberger, *Wesen und Herkunft*, 141f.

36   Cf. 1 Kings 21:10.

37   Cf. p. 170.

38   See Smend, *Die Bundesformel*.

to Yahweh's zeal in wrath and salvation, as this is confirmed by the word of curse and blessing in Exod. 20:5f.[39] These two commandments form, as it were, the inner circle of the prohibition that relates to Yahweh's theophany.

Yahweh also reaches into the other commandments in blessing and curse. The curse fends off the abuse of the name of God, and God's blessing over the promised land of inheritance rests especially on that person who observes the basic commandment of the clan's order: honoring the heads of the family.[40] The numinous point, and the divine guarantor, of the clan-ethos now bears the name of that God who led Israel out of the land of bondage into the land of promise. Between that threat and this promise is given the peculiar dual reason for the Sabbath. Exodus 20:11 points to the rest of the Creator; Deut. 5:15 remembers the leading out of Egypt.[41]

From the preamble through the sermonlike expansions of the commandments, Yahweh's zealous holiness permeates all areas of life. The ancient commandments of the clan are focused on Yahweh's revelation and given a new motivation. "The proclamation of the divine legal will is like a net cast over Israel; it is the execution of its being handed over to Yahweh."[42] The priests and preachers at the covenantal sanctuary have replaced the father of the clan.[43] They proclaim God in His zealous holiness as the guarantor of the ancient ethos of the clan. Thus the obedience in the daily human relationships is consciously grounded in the reverent fear and the thankful love to the God who has chosen the congregation of salvation for Himself.

Yahweh's theophany must have permeated the traditional clan-ethos on all levels. (1) The Decalogue is inserted into the establishment of the covenant as a *verbum abbreviatum* of the *šalōm*-order of Yahweh. (2) Within the Decalogue, all commandments are placed under Yahweh's self-introduction. (3) In the preaching of priestly Levites, Yahweh's zeal in wrath and salvation permeates the individual commandments and reaches all the way to the commandment to honor the parents as the foundational commandment of the interhuman ethos. This process took place over centuries; its individual stages are now no longer accessible to us.[44] What is very clear, though, is that faith in Yahweh, not the clan-ethos, represents the active element in this process of amalgamation. To be sure, the Decalogue is formulated as an ellipse with two foci, but the actual center lies in the preamble concerning Yahweh's zealous holiness.

---

39   Cf. p. 113.

40   Cf. pp. 188–92.

41   Cf. pp. 169–72.

42   Von Rad, *Theologie des Alten Testaments*, 1:193.

43   On the office of "covenantal mediator," cf. Kraus, *Gottesdienst in Israel*, 128ff; Zimmerli, *Ezechiel*, 1:397ff.; von Reventlow, *Wächter über Israel*, 116, 124f.

44   See the summary in von Reventlow, *Gebot und Predigt im Dekalog*, 93ff.

Taking the focus of the preamble as a starting point, the Decalogue attempts to place all of life under obedience to God. The traditional dual form of the Decalogue thus shows a dual purpose: on the one hand, the Decalogue seeks to express the will of God as comprehensively and as precisely as possible; on the other hand, it seeks to outline an inner connection of motivation.

When it comes to the codification of God's will, we observe two manners of proceeding: on the one hand, the commandments are formulated as broadly and as vaguely as possible; on the other hand, the added instructions for execution delimit the realm of the commandment. Critical research assumes the former for the prohibition of theft, which originally applied to the enslavement of full Israelite citizens;[45] for the commandment to honor the parents, which originally read, "You shall not curse your father and mother";[46] as well as for the Sabbath commandment, which had been handed down also as a prohibition against carrying out work.[47] While the process of expanding on the actual text of the Decalogue cannot be shown anymore and, therefore, has to remain hypothetical, we can clearly discern the corresponding process—delimiting the area—because it is first carried out in the sermonlike additions of the Levites. Thus "many generations of proclaimers and preachers" have worked on the prohibition of images,[48] have added the instructions for execution to the Sabbath commandment,[49] and have carefully circumscribed the neighbor's area of life in the concluding double commandment.[50] These three examples unequivocally show the will to determine the cases and possibilities envisioned by the commandments as comprehensively and as precisely as possible.

We have now given three key examples for the two ways in which the original prohibitions were broadened, by opening them from within as well as by limiting the recognizable area. These examples show that in the formation of the Decalogue generations have struggled to unlock the area of life open to man in a basic yet detailed fashion and to comprehend this in ten words that are both transparent and memorable. This has not remained in such a complete state in the remaining apodictic sets of the Old Testament. Therefore it is not surprising that already Hellenistic Judaism and, following its lead, the early Christian apologists and finally all of Christendom thought to recognize in the Decalogue something like a basic law for

---

45   Cf. pp. 267f.

46   Cf. p. 190.

47   Cf. p. 169.

48   Von Reventlow, *Gebot und Predigt im Dekalog,* 40.

49   Cf. p. 172.

50   Cf. pp. 307f.

all worship of God and interhuman order, the *lex naturae* written on man's heart as *lex Dei*.

In the Decalogue in its traditional form another direction is hinted at: all obedience and all ethos in the expansive realm of our earthly existence are founded in the fear and love of the God who predicates Himself as the Lord and Savior of Israel. The reasons given for the prohibition of alien gods and images, for the prohibition of abusing the name, for the honoring of the Sabbath, as well as for the blessing promised to that person who honors his parents—all this points toward an informed and free obedience, not for the sake of the Commandments as such, not even for the sake of the interhuman order that is to be protected by them, but for the sake of the zealous God Himself.[51] Where this is tirelessly aimed at, there the entire complex of commandments begins to move inwardly. The *šm'a yiśra'ēl* emerges from the other individual commandments as the one commandment corresponding to the preamble and its foundational promise: "Hear, O Israel: The Lord, our God, is one Lord. And you shall love the Lord, your God, with all your heart, with all your soul, and with all your strength" (Deut. 6:4f.). Here, in the unequivocal *yes* of the covenant people to its covenant God, lies the center of its existence: "We shall fear, love, and trust in God above all things."[52]

However, every turn of the core of the believer's heart to God does not remain isolated alongside or above the specific obedience in all other commandments but wishes to become its inner drive. The force emanating from the one focus of the preamble changes the inner structure of the Decalogue. The sermonlike reasons ultimately aim at founding all the following commandments of the Decalogue on the basic commandment to fear and love God and at developing them out of it.[53] This intention is first made conscious and carried out all the way through the last commandment in Luther's explanatory formula in the Small Catechism for the Second through Tenth Commandments: "We should fear and love God, so that we do not . . . but rather . . . ."

This formula implies once again a twofold further development of the prohibitions of the Decalogue, a development that can be demonstrated in the Old Testament form of the prohibitions only by artificial means. In a first step, the negative prohibitions are driven into the heart of those addressed. The Christian tradition here makes use of the antitheses of the Sermon on the Mount with its scope: not primarily—but already. The manifest act is not

---

51   Von Rad, *Theologie des Alten Testaments*, 1:199: "In non-Israelite bodies of law, no such explanations and reasons are given. This is why we have to regard them as something specific to the Israelite legal tradition."

52   *BSLK*, 507.42f.

53   Perhaps originally the set of prohibitions in Lev. 19:13–18 had each individual commandment issue into a liturgical exclamation giving the reason: "For I am Yahweh!"

primarily a violation of the prohibition, but already the secret longings of the heart qualify us before God as transgressors. In a second step and following the tradition, Luther unfolds the positive commandment that stands behind the negative prohibition. God not only wants us to respect His prohibitions, but He also wants us to walk in His Commandments. There might be some slight references in the Decalogue to driving the commandments from the outside to the inside in this manner and to changing the negative into the positive[54] in this way;[55] however, both operations go beyond the traditional wording. This explains why it took Christendom centuries to come to appreciate the Decalogue as a basic formula for the New Testament ethos. This was only possible by broadening it again and deepening it at the same time. This new interpretation we now need to outline.

THE DECALOGUE IN THE NEW TESTAMENT AND IN THE CHURCH UNDER THE CANON OF THE DOUBLE COMMANDMENT[56]

The Decalogue, along with the *šm'a yiśra'ēl*, was part of the daily readings of the synagogue. In the New Testament it is remarkably less prominent. The baptismal pareneses take up very heterogeneous traditions. Hellenistic popular philosophy is combined with Jewish proverbial wisdom, and dominical words are unfolded alongside apostolic mandates. The household tables[57] and rules regarding behavior toward the authorities[58] are received from the tradition of the Hellenistic synagogue. The lists of virtues and vices[59] paraphrase the "ways in Christ" (1 Cor. 4:17) in the apocalyptic perspective of opposing light and darkness; following Jewish examples, the way leading to life is contrasted with the way leading to death.[60] Many New Testament Letters insert these heterogeneous formulae into a fourfold unfolding of the Christian ethos:

---

54   Cf. on this the section "Structure and Arrangement of the Decalogue," pp. 97f.

55   The drive from the outside to the inside changes the second *lō tamōd* in Deut. 5:21 into the stronger *lō tit'awweh*; cf. p. 309. The transformation of the prohibition into a command might have taken place in the Third and Fourth Commandments; cf. pp. 169, 190.

56   Cf. on this Rentschka, *Dekalogkatechese*; Röthlisberger, *Kirche am Sinai*; von Zezschwitz, *Katechetik*, 2.1:161–272.

57   Eph. 5:22ff.; Col. 3:18ff.; 1 Tim. 2:8ff.; 6:1f.; Titus 2:1ff. Cf. on this Weidinger, *Die Haustafeln*; Wendland, "Zur sozial-ethischen Bedeutung."

58   Rom. 13:1ff.; 1 Pet. 3:13ff.; Titus 3:1.

59   Rom. 1:29ff.; 13:13; 1 Cor. 5:10f.; 6:9f.; 2 Cor. 12:10f.; Gal. 5:19ff.; Eph. 4:31; 5:3ff.; Col. 3:5ff.; 1 Tim. 1:9f.; 2 Tim. 3:2ff. Cf. on this Vögtle, *Tugend- und Lasterkataloge*; Wibbing, *Tugend- und Lasterkataloge*; Schrage, *Die Einzelgebote*.

60   Cf. *Didache* 1–6; 16:3–8; *Barnabas* 18–20.

1. Therefore put off (the former evil).   (*Deponentes*)
2. Be subject.   (*Subjecti*)
3. Watch and pray.   (*Vigilate*)
4. Resist the devil.   (*Resistite*)[61]

This fullness of moral exhortation is based on the indicative of salvation of the Christ-event and is shaped by the double commandment of love of God and neighbor, into which Jesus of Nazareth stepped as the free man for God and neighbor and which He has filled with the concrete form of His loving devotion.

The inner coordination of turning to God and to fellow man, which began to emerge already in the Decalogue, gains clear contours in the time of Jesus. The *šm'a yiśra'ēl*, prayed daily, articulates the foundational command of full, undivided devotion to God. Leviticus 19:17f. enjoins it as a summary of every turning toward fellow man: "You shall love your neighbor as yourself." The "I am the Lord" of the God who vies for undivided obedience stands also behind this "second" commandment. This double turn, first to God and then to fellow man, is pointedly summarized in the double commandment of love of God and neighbor.[62]

This double commandment, which became concrete in the life and sacrificial death of Jesus, turns out to be the inner core and the critical norm of all commandments. The conflict breaks open when it comes to the Sabbath and the purity laws. Here the relationship of the free children to God and the spontaneous love of the neighbor break through the casuistic fences of tradition. The love of the invisible God becomes manifest in the love of the visible human brother, which also includes the enemy.[63] This is why, for John, the love of the brother is the old/new commandment of Jesus and the sign of the love of God, established and fulfilled in the ministry of Jesus Himself.[64]

This new approach regarding the double commandment, which has gained concrete form in Jesus' life and death for the many and also in being a disciple of Jesus, pushes back the Decalogue.[65] In Paul and the other New Testament Letters, the Decalogue is alluded to here and there,[66] yet nowhere does it structure the parenesis. The Christ-event seems to have pushed back the Decalogue into the past as the old Mosaic commandment.

61 Cf. Carrington, *Primitive Christian Catechism*, 30f., 40ff., 48, based on Col. 3:8–4:12; Eph. 4:22–6:19; 1 Pet. 1:1–4:11; 4:12–5:14 (originally two letters, according to Carrington); and James 1:1–4:10. See also Seeberg, *Katechismus* and *Didache*; Dodd, *Gospel and Law*.

62 Mark 12:28–31; Matt. 22:36–40; Luke 10:25–28; cf. Rom. 13:9f. and James 2:8, as well as the parallels in *Bill.*, 1:353–64, 907.

63 Matt. 5:43f.; 25:1–46; Luke 10:25–37.

64 John 13:12ff., 34f.; 1 John 2:3, 11; 3:10ff.; 4:7–13, 19–21; and elsewhere.

65 Cf. Röthlisberger, *Kirche am Sinai*, 13–42.

66 Rom. 7:7; 13:8ff.; Eph. 6:2; Col. 3:5f. Cf. 1 Tim. 1:8ff. Röthlisberger, *Kirche am Sinai*, 32f. n. 88, thinks that it prevails more in James.

Yet also the New Testament instruction, especially in the household tables, reaches back not only to insights of the Hellenistic synagogue but also to the moral teachings of pagan Stoicism that had already been received by the Hellenistic synagogue. "Everything the household tables have to say about love and obedience, about freely serving Christ, is related to the fact of a given traditional, societal morality that interprets social realities as duties and moral obligations; as δίκαιον; as equity (Col. 4:1); as virtue (Phil. 4:8); as what is fitting and proper and what, therefore, also among men provides to man, the social being, a good reputation (Col. 3:18; Phil. 4:8). The social teachings on duty and virtue really have not first come into the world with the Gospel of Christ."[67]

Thus just as in the Old Testament Decalogue, we observe in New Testament ethics this ellipse with its two foci. The Decalogue's pole of the preamble, as well as that of Yahweh's zeal in salvation and wrath spilling over from the preamble into all relations of life, corresponds in the New Testament to the foundational commandment of love of God and, emerging from it, the turn to the neighbor under the Lordship and discipleship of Christ. The pole of the ancient-oriental clan order seen in the Decalogue corresponds in the New Testament to the recourse to pagan Stoic and Jewish Hellenistic moral teachings.[68] The former determines the inner impulse out of which the community of faith exists; the latter delimits the field in which it has to prove itself. The double commandment of love of God and neighbor keeps the field of tension between the two poles together and guarantees the unity of the ellipse. It is thus not far-fetched that the Decalogue gains new weight in Christendom, especially in Augustine and Thomas Aquinas, as an unfolding of the *verbum abbreviatum* of the double commandment.

The early Church, just as the New Testament itself, lacked a clear center and fixed outline of moral instruction.[69] The Decalogue is mentioned here and there only in passing. From the early apologists to the Middle Ages, the Church's basic position regarding the Decalogue remained strangely ambivalent.[70] The general judgment begins to emerge in Irenaeus, is formulated

---

67   Wendland, "Zur sozial-ethischen Bedeutung," 42. The pagan Stoic and Jewish Hellenistic forerunners of the New Testament household tables are gathered in Weidinger, *Die Haustafeln*, 23–39.

68   For the LCMS position, see the publisher's introduction, pp. 10–11.

69   Origen mentions the Books of Esther, Judith, Tobit, and the wisdom books (Origen, *Hom. in Num.* 27:1). Athanasius adds the *Didache* and the *Shepherd of Hermas* (Athanasius, *Festbriefe* 39). At the time of Ambrose of Milan, the Books of Job and Tobit were read during the first five weeks (Ambrose, *De mysteriis* 1:4.25, 7.59, 9.89). The "catechetical-ethical instruction of the first four centuries" followed "mainly the books of the Old Testament and the Apocrypha, sometimes the *Didache* and the *Shepherd of Hermas*" (Röthlisberger, *Kirche am Sinai*, 49).

70   Cf. von Zezschwitz, *Katechetik*, 2:164–97; Rentschka, *Dekalogkatechese*, 8–55; Röthlisberger, *Kirche am Sinai*, 43–49.

by Augustine, and is unfolded by Thomas. It can be summarized in four theses:

1. The Decalogue, as the center of Mosaic Law, renews the law of nature written on the hearts of all men. Already in creation, God implanted in man the "natural commandments." Already the patriarchs possessed the *virtus Decalogi*, as well as the *iustitia legis* inscribed in their souls.[71] When man forgot this original commandment because of the overwhelming force of sin, God revealed it anew in the Decalogue.

    The apologists followed Philo of Alexandria, who, based on the νόμοι ἄγραφοι, saw in the patriarchs embodiments of the Greek cardinal virtues.[72] This is how they connected the Decalogue with the Stoic idea of the *lex naturae*, the ἔννοιαι φυσικαί or ἔμφυσαι, which Cicero summarized in the saying: "The law is the highest reason implanted in nature that commands what is to be done and prohibits the opposite."[73] Following Cicero's teaching on order, Augustine and Thomas also let the law of nature still be surrounded by and grounded in the *lex aeterna* itself. Thomas paraphrases it as "*ratio divinae sapientiae, secundum quod est directive omnium actuum et motionum*,"[74] as "divine wisdom's structure of meaning insofar as it directs the actions and movements of all things."[75] Since by means of God's radiating (*irradiatio*) into our souls man participates in that original divine order, the *lex naturalis* is nothing less than that "participation of the eternal law in the rational creature."[76] Irenaeus underlined more strongly the truly historical movement from creation and fall to the recapitulation (*recapitulatio*) of all of creation.[77]

2. The Decalogue, however, contains the Law of God engraved on man's heart as a statute that the Lord through Moses imposed on His rebellious people from the outside.

    In this thesis, the early Christian fathers sought to comprehend the difference between the Law of the old covenant and the *nova*

---

71 Irenaeus, *Adversus haereses* 4:16.3.

72 Philo, *De Abrahamo*, in Mangey, ed., *Opera*, 2:1–40; *De Josepho*, in Mangey, ed., *Opera*, 2:41–79; *De decalogo*, in Mangey, ed., *Opera*, 2:180–290.

73 Cicero, *De legibus* 1:18.

74 Thomas Aquinas, *Summa theologiae* I/II, q. 93, a. 1. Cf. Cicero, *De legibus* 2:10: "*Lex vera atque princeps apta ad iubendem et vetandum ratio est recta summi Jovis.*"

75 Kühn, *Via caritatis*, 142; cf. Schubert, *Lex-aeterna Lehre*; Meyer, *Thomas von Aquin*, 591ff.

76 Cf. Thomas Aquinas, *Summa theologiae* I/II, q. 91, a. 2.

77 Irenaeus, *Adversus haereses* 4:11–16.

lex Christi. At the same time, however, they did notice that the Decalogue holds a special place also among the Old Testament commandments. This is why it ends up in between: on the one hand, the original law of nature, written on man's heart and renewed by Christ, and, on the other hand, the commandments imposed on Israel alone. This special place is hinted at here and there but is not precisely defined. The Decalogue is the original commandment given in Paradise, but it is that only in a disfigured and hardened form. Irenaeus, for example, writes thus: "The natural precepts are common to us and them (the Jews). Among them, however, they have their beginning and source, but among us they received their augmentation and fulfillment."[78] And Ambrose harshly points out the distance: "The Jews do not have the true Law . . . . The Law given by Moses is a figure of the Law."[79] One takes recourse to the Pauline juxtaposition of the tablets of stone and of human hearts (2 Cor. 3:3), remembers the promise of the new covenant with its law written on hearts (Jer. 31:31ff.; Ezek. 11:19; 36:26f.), and is thereby inspired to interpret Exodus 32–34 allegorically: The first set of tablets destroyed by Moses in view of the golden calf represents the destruction of the original law written on the heart; the tablets renewed by God's command symbolize the Law renewed by the Holy Spirit.[80]

3. The Decalogue is to be differentiated from the remainder of the old covenant law, especially from the ceremonial law and the judicial law. God added them first by Moses after Israel's apostasy. As "commandments of servitude," they were meant to serve as a yoke for the fallen and rebellious people to guide them to Christ.

The Gnostic Ptolemaeus, in his *Letter to Flora*, distinguishes between the pure Law of the Decalogue, which was not abrogated by Jesus; the second law that is mixed with injustice and evil, which is why it was abrogated by Jesus; and the ceremonial law, which, while abrogated in its literal sense, also has a typological-allegorical meaning that now has become visible.[81] Irenaeus takes up this distinction but says that the "laws and statutes that were not good" (Ezek. 20:24f.) were imposed on an apostate people as

---

78   Irenaeus, *Adversus haereses* 4:13.4.

79   Ambrosius, Psalm 118, Opp. 1.2:1206; quoted in von Zezschwitz, *Katechetik*, 2.1:174, further proofs in von Zezschwitz, *Katechetik*, 2.1:166ff. Thomas offers a more reflective perspective; cf. Pesch, *Rechtfertigung bei Luther und Thomas*, 418–24.

80   Texts offered by von Zezschwitz, *Katechetik*, 2.1:172f.

81   According to Röthlisberger, *Kirche am Sinai*, 51.

a yoke of slavery that had to correspond to its wild lusts.[82] The Syriac *Didascalia Apostolorum* and the *Apostolic Constitutions*[83] both take up, though with different accents,[84] this difference between a first and second giving of the Law. Christ has redeemed us from the ceremonies of the second giving of the Law. He has newly interpreted and deepened the first giving of the Decalogue. It is incumbent on the bishop to distinguish between the two.

The Law's division into three parts—the moral, ceremonial, and judicial commandments—is not yet known to the early Church. It emerges in the Middle Ages and is fully developed in Thomas's treatise on the Law, and he focuses it on Christ.[85] The moral commandments unfold the natural law, which culminates in the double commandment;[86] the ceremonial law prepares hearts for the Christ-mystery, whose typological foreshadowing they represent;[87] the judicial law orders the status of the Jewish people *secundum iustitiam et aequitatem*[88] and thereby helps it to abide in the expectation of what is promised.

4.   The Decalogue, and the original commandment of God present in it, is not abrogated by Christ; rather, the Decalogue as *paedagogus ad gratiam*[89] is perfected and opened toward the Gospel in the double commandment of selfless love of God and neighbor. As *verbum consummans et brevians* (Isa. 10:23; Rom. 9:28), the double commandment pushes back the Decalogue.[90] As a gift of the Pentecost Spirit, the love of God and neighbor exhibited by the children of God is free from external force, free from the fear of punishment, as well as free from the longing for earthly rewards. The Decalogue of Mount Sinai, on the other hand, remains under God's discipline toward servants and minors. This

---

82   Irenaeus, *Adversus haereses* 4:15.1.

83   *Didascalia Apostolorum* I; *Apostolic Constitutions*, esp. 1:6; 4:19ff.

84   Cf. Rentschka, *Dekalogkatechese*, 44–49; Röthlisberger, *Kirche am Sinai*, 52ff.

85   Cf. Kühn, *Via caritatis*, 173–91.

86   Thomas Aquinas, *Summa theologiae* I/II, q. 100, a. 3 ad 1: "These two commandments (of love of God and neighbor) are the first and common commandments of the law of nature, which by themselves are known to human reason, either by nature or by faith. And this is why all commandments of the Decalogue refer back to these two as conclusions refer back to common principles."

87   Thomas shows this in the longest *quaestio* of the *Summa theologiae* (I/II, q. 102), in which he is inspired by Moses Maimonides.

88   Thomas Aquinas, *Summa theologiae* I/II, q. 104, a. 2.

89   Concerning the function of the Law as *paedagogus*, cf. von Zezschwitz, *Katechetik*, 2.1:169f.

90   Proof texts offered by von Zezschwitz, *Katechetik*, 2.1:184–97; and Röthlisberger, *Kirche am Sinai*, 43–71.

is confirmed by the externally imposed prohibitions and by the threats of worldly punishments and the luring with earthly promises. At the same time, the Decalogue is more and more positively correlated to the double commandment, as the former is used to unfold the latter into all areas of daily life.

This negative as well as positive coordination of Decalogue and double commandment begins to emerge in Irenaeus, is firmly established by Augustine, and is handed down in the medieval interpretations of the Decalogue. According to Irenaeus, Christ, by taking up the Decalogue in the Sermon on the Mount, leads the original natural commandments of Paradise out of their Mosaic servant-form and into freedom.[91] By means of external prohibitions, Moses sought to train slavish souls in the obedience of God without being able to disclose to them the true will of God. The God-Logos, on the other hand, liberated the souls from within by revealing to them the gracious will of salvation of the heavenly Father, thus enabling them to render a free and spontaneous obedience of the heart. These two items—the inner knowledge as well as the free obedience—set the New Testament friends of God apart from the Old Testament's forced servants of God.

Augustine develops his doctrine of the Decalogue in his struggle against the Manichaean Faustus, who considered it spiritual adultery to be subject to the Law and to Christ at the same time.[92] Against the demotion of the Old Testament Law, Augustine points to Rom. 13:9f. and concludes from this word of Paul that the double commandment summarizes the Law and, by way of consequence, also its core, the Decalogue. The first three commandments, the First Table, unfold the basic command of love of God; the following seven, the Second Table, unfold the basic command of love of neighbor.[93] The Church father has proved the perfection of the Decalogue in his catechetical writings with many an exercise in numerology.[94] However, at the same time, in his anti-Pelagian writings, Augustine sought to determine the difference between the Old Testament and the New Testament obedience to the Law. For this purpose, he uses the Pauline juxtaposition old covenant—new covenant, Law—grace, letter—spirit. What has changed is not the Law as the good and just will of God, but man's relationship to the Law. The Jews stand as servants under the Law, as dead or even deadly let-

---

91   Irenaeus, *Adversus haereses* 4:13.2f.

92   Cf. Rentschka, *Dekalogkatechese*, 63–81; and Röthlisberger, *Kirche am Sinai*, 55–59.

93   Cf. Augustine, *Sermo* 9.14 (CCSL 41:135): "For the Ten Commandments refer to these two, as we have heard, that we love God and the neighbor—and these two to this one. This one, however, is: What you do not want to be done to you, this also do not do to others. There the ten are contained; here, the two." Cf. also *Sermo* 8.18, 9.6f., 33.2f.; *Quaestiones in Heptateuchum* 2:71 and passim.

94   On the numerology, cf. von Zezschwitz, *Katechetik*, 2.1:184; Rentschka, *Dekalogkatechese*, 63f., 83ff.; Röthlisberger, *Kirche am Sinai*, 56f.

ters under the Law without the grace of the Spirit. The Christians have died to that Law which applies force from without, that is, to the grace-less Law. Instead, they live under the law of Christ's grace. For them, the letter of the Law is permeated by God's Spirit; the commandment given by Moses has become grace and truth through Christ.

Especially in his theological summation, Thomas adopts these juxtapositions of Augustine from the latter's writing *De spiritu et littera*.[95] He sharply contrasts the new law as the law of grace and love, of the Holy Spirit and of Christ,[96] and the old Law. While the old Law is imposed from without and, therefore, has a forced character, the law of the Spirit, as *lex indita*, lets us spontaneously recognize what is demanded by God and simultaneously leads us to fulfill it joyfully.[97] While no longer subject to the Law as an external mandate, the Christian still willingly bows under it in Christlike humility.[98]

At the end of his life, during Lent 1273, Thomas preached to students and citizens in Naples on the Creed, the Lord's Prayer, and the Commandments. In the sermon series *In duo praecepta caritatis et in decem legis praecepta*,[99] he initially distinguishes sharply between the Mosaic Law and the law of Christ.[100] Because the natural law, originally implanted by God into human reason, was corrupted by the law of concupiscence (Rom. 7:23: *lex concupiscentiae*) sown over it by Satan, God had to call man back from vices to works of virtue by the law of Scripture (*lex scripturae*). To reach this goal, God used two means: first, the Law of Moses, which was to restrain from evil by fear, then the law of Christ, which leads to the obedience of love. The first remains insufficient because, as the *lex timoris*, it enslaved those who observe it, used only temporal goods as lures, weighed heavy upon its followers, and overcame only the bodies and not the hearts of its followers.

95 Kühn, *Via caritatis*, 192–218.
96 Thomas Aquinas, *Summa theologiae* I/II, q. 106, a. 1: "The one thing, however, that is chief in the law of the New Testament and in which its entire power consists is the grace of the Holy Spirit, which is given by faith in Christ. And this is why the new law is principally the grace of the Holy Spirit itself that is given the believers in Christ."
97 Thomas Aquinas, *In Rom.* VIII, lect. 1 (*Expositio*, 75a): "The Holy Spirit inhabiting the mind not only teaches what ought to be done, thereby illuminating the intellect concerning the things to be done, but He also inclines the affect to act rightly."
98 Thomas Aquinas, *Summa theologiae* I/II, q. 93, a. 6 ad 1, on Gal. 5:18: "For in yet another way it can be understood in what sense the works of man done in the Holy Spirit are called works of the Holy Spirit rather than works of man himself. Because the Holy Spirit is not under the Law, neither is the Son . . . . It follows that such works, insofar as they are the Holy Spirit's, are not under the Law." Q. 96, a. 5 ad 2: ". . . spiritual men, insofar as they are led by the law of the Holy Spirit, are not placed under the (human) law insofar as it disagrees with being led by the Holy Spirit. However, it nonetheless pertains to the leading of the Holy Spirit that spiritual men are placed under human laws."
99 Cf. on this Grabmann, *Die Werke des hl. Thomas*, 316f.
100 Thomas Aquinas, *Duo praecepta* §§ 1129–37.

First, the *lex evangelica* and the *lex Christi* as *lex amoris* led to perfection; as easy commandment and soft yoke, the new law changes the heart from within and leads the liberated toward what is eternal.[101]

After this basic introduction, Thomas interprets the commandment of love of God and neighbor[102] and unfolds it by means of the Decalogue in both directions. By doing so, he simultaneously moves the Decalogue into the light of the *lex caritatis* and opens it thus for the old-new commandment of Christ.[103]

When the institution of auricular confession was made mandatory for all in 1215 by the Fourth Lateran Council, this practice is expanded into a remedial instruction for catechumens. To prepare for confession, a colorful assortment of categories is cobbled together from Scripture and churchly tradition.[104] These outlines often stand under the double commandment. The Decalogue appears in the synodical decisions of the thirteenth century. The *Speculum Ecclesiae* of Archbishop Edmund of Canterbury is the first confessional booklet that contains it.[105] Bonaventure and Thomas interpret it for future father confessors.[106] Following Augustine, the Decalogue is first understood as a tool to unfold the double commandment. Toward the end of the fourteenth century and in the fifteenth century, the Decalogue becomes more and more independent and starts to push back or absorb the other outlines that lead to a knowledge of sin. Perhaps Master Johannes Wolff goes the farthest in his posthumously printed confessional booklet.[107] He inserts all the other aids for confession into the coordinate system of the Ten Commandments and thereby earns the honorific title *Doctor decem praeceptorum Dei*.[108] The Reformation continues this development as the Decalogue grows independent of the double commandment and is understood as a fully valid expression of the Christian ethos. At the same time, Luther takes

---

101   Thomas Aquinas, *Duo praecepta* § 1133.

102   Thomas Aquinas, *Duo praecepta* §§ 1160–92.

103   Cf. Thomas Aquinas, *Duo praecepta*, esp. §§ 1193, 1332.

104   Cf. von Zezschwitz, *Katechetik*, 2.1:197–239; Geffcken, *Bildercatechismus*, 20–22; Weidenhiller, *Untersuchungen*, 20–24.

105   Synods of Trier (1227), Clermont (1268), Lambeth (1281), Utrecht (1294 and 1310), the *Confessional Sum* of Raymond of Peñafort, as well as Edmund of Canterbury (d. 1242), *Speculum ecclesiae*, ch. 11: *De decem praeceptis dei*.

106   Thomas in the sermons mentioned above (*Duo praecepta*) and Bonaventure in his *Collationes de decem praeceptis*. Furthermore, Hugh of St. Victor's *Institutiones in decalogum legis dominicae* have been handed down (PL 176:9–18). In the writings of Bernard of Clairvaux there is an exposition of the Decalogue in his fourth sermon on the *Salve Regina* (PL 184:1075f.), which seems to originate from the transition to high scholasticism.

107   See the bibliography.

108   Cf. Wolff, *Beichtbüchlein*, 112–17. On the Decalogue from antiquity to the Middle Ages, see Rentschka, *Dekalogkatechese*, 158–72. On the late Middle Ages, see Geffcken, *Bildercatechismus*.

up the insights gained especially by Irenaeus, Augustine, and Thomas and reflects on them anew.

THE DECALOGUE IN LUTHER'S THEOLOGY

Luther rethinks the Decalogue's intermediate position between the original commandment of God written on the hearts of all men and the double commandment of selfless love of God and neighbor as Christ showed it in His life and death. Luther does so not so much from the vantage point of an observer arranging the matter under headings, but as someone pulled into the midst of the battle between God and anti-god. With that, the Law again grows together to an inner unity. In the 1510 *Galaterbriefkommentar* (*Commentary on Galatians*), on Gal. 5:14, the reformer opines that the traditional scholastic distinctions between the natural, written, and evangelical laws have to be used with circumspection and restraint. For him, they merely are the different forms, dimensions of depth, and directions of impact concerning the one and only Law of God that permeates all times, impresses itself on all men, and leaves no one with an excuse.[109] Behind those various expressions of the Law, the zealous, holy Creator God Himself becomes visible, the God who wrestles with the powers of destruction on behalf of His rational creatures.

Augustine and Thomas establish a position more strongly related to the pagan traditions of antiquity, with the *lex aeterna* as the impulse toward perfection implanted in all living beings. They aim this impulse in the direction of the transcendent God. In doing so, they push forward to a point of departure from the maxim of a eudemonistic movement of life to perfection ("We all want to become happy!")[110] to Jesus' giving Himself in suffering to God and men.[111] In a contrary manner, Luther establishes his position with the biblical tradition from the attack of the commandment of God on man as he is curved in upon himself (*incurvatus in se*). By means of the double commandment, which God constantly impresses on our hearts and consciences,

---

109 WA 2:580.7 (see also AE 27:151–410): "No less cautiously is to be understood that most common distinction of natural law, scriptural law, evangelical law." WA 2:580.18 (see also AE 27:151–410): "Thus the Law is one that goes through all times, is known to all men, is written in all hearts, and does not leave anyone from beginning to end with an excuse." Cf. "Röm.-Vorl., 1515/16," WA 56:355.14 (see also AE 25:1–524); and "Gal.-Komm., 1519," WA 57:101.3.

110 Cf. Aristotle, *Eth. Nic.* 1:1 (1094a): "Good is what all desire," which is taken up by Thomas Aquinas, *Summa theologiae* I, q. 5, a. 1. Cf. Augustine, *De civ. Dei* 11:26.1: "There is no one who does not want to be happy."

111 Thomas Aquinas, *Summa theologiae* I/II, q. 109, a. 3 ad 1: "Charity loves God above all things, more than nature does. For nature loves God above all things as He is the principle and goal of the good of nature; charity, however, loves God insofar as He is the object of blessedness and insofar as man has a certain spiritual fellowship with God."

God tirelessly drives us out of diabolical selfishness and liberates us to give of ourselves selflessly.[112] This is also how Luther looks at the *lex naturae*; however, he does not find it enunciated in the ancient tradition of natural law, but concretely lived out and died out in Jesus of Nazareth. Only with the persistent view of the one man who exhibited perfect love for God and man do we see clearly the original writing of the *lex naturae* in our own conscience, which had been made nearly illegible by the original fall. According to Luther, the law written into the hearts of all men therefore means nothing less than Jesus Christ's selfless love of God and neighbor.[113]

In keeping with ecclesiastical tradition, Luther relates the Decalogue, on the one hand, to the divine commandment written onto man's heart and, on the other hand, to the spiritual interpretation by Jesus Christ, especially in the Sermon on the Mount. Seen positively, the Decalogue appears to be a kind of "help for reception"[114] in view of the *lex naturae*, given by God Himself in the Sinai revelation, since "the natural laws are nowhere as nicely and orderly . . . arranged as in Moses."[115] Seen negatively, even the Decalogue appears as a divine Law imposed solely on the people of Israel led out of Egypt, a Law that does not bind the Gentiles. Thus it appears as "the Jews' *Sachsenspiegel*."[116]

In his struggle against Carlstadt, Luther harshly argues that the Christians are, in principle, free from the Decalogue. Carlstadt opined that the Decalogue in its entirety is part of the moral law, and therefore it must be clearly distinguished from the ceremonies and laws added specifically for the Jews in the old covenant. Luther comments on this: "I know very well that this is given as an old distinction, but out of ignorance. For all the other commandments and everything given by Moses flow from, and hang on, the Ten Commandments."[117] The Decalogue is not limited to a perennial moral order. What is also historical and contingent upon Israel's cultic and legal

---

112   There is perhaps a hint at the vision of the *lex aeterna* in "Operationes in Psalmos" (WA 5:38.14ff. [see also AE 14:279–349]). However, here Luther clearly proceeds from the principle of self-commitment, not from self-perfection.

113   Cf. Heckel, "Naturrecht."

114   Schloemann, *Natürliches und gepredigtes Gesetz bei Luther*, 103 n. 319: "Rather, one could say almost the opposite (against E. Wolf and J. Heckel) that for Luther the Decalogue is a 'help for reception' for the *lex naturae*, if it were not always 'already there.' "

115   "Wider die himml. Proph., 1525," WA 18:81.19 (see also AE 40:73–223).

116   WA 18:81.16 (see also AE 40:73–223): "Therefore let Moses be the Jews' *Sachsenspiegel*, and let us Gentiles be unconfused thereby, just as France does not observe the *Sachsenspiegel* yet agrees with it perfectly in view of natural law." Cf. "Einl. zur Pred. über Ex. 19–20," WA 16:378.1, 378.11, 378.23 (see also AE 35:155–74); "Epistel aus Jeremia, von Christus' Reich und christl. Freiheit, 1527," WA 20:576.34; "Eine Unterrichtung, wie sich die Christen in Mose sollen schicken," WA 24:9.5; "Pred. über Dtn. 1:4," WA 28:543.7; "Wider die Sabbather, 1538," WA 50:332.14ff. (see also AE 47:57–98).

117   "Wider die himml. Proph., 1525," WA 18:76.23 (see also AE 40:73–223).

order has found its place in it. The cultic order is concentrated in the prohibition of images and in the Sabbath commandment. The legal and clan order is hinted at in that, for example, merely breaking into another marriage is prohibited; that the Eighth Commandment has the court in the gate in view; and that in the concluding double commandment the women and the slaves of the neighbor belong to the Lord's goods and chattel.

For Luther, however, not only this or that detail of the Decalogue respective to cultic and social history has become outdated; rather, the entire Decalogue does not apply to us anymore. It has lost its binding character because we are no longer the Old Testament covenant people to whom the preamble was addressed: "I am the Lord, your God, who led you out of the land of Egypt, out of the house of slaves" (Exod. 20:2; Deut. 5:6). We have been granted a different sign of the gracious revelation of God, in which we as Gentiles are to know and worship God. Our creed reads:

> O God, Creator of heaven and earth: You have sent Your Son, Jesus Christ, into the world for me, so that He would be crucified for me, would die and rise again on the third day, would ascend into heaven; that He would sit there at Your right hand and have everything in His hand and send His Spirit; that we should wait for His coming to judge both the living and the dead, and thus reach with Him the eternal kingdom, our inheritance, which You wish to give to us through Him—for this, O Lord God, You have given us and instituted Baptism and the Sacrament of the body and blood of Your Son, etc. For He has bound us Christians to these Sacraments of His and has revealed Himself therein.... This title we should thus use, just as the Jews used their title, since they are led out of Egypt out of the house of servitude.[118]

Luther replaces the Old Testament creed in the self-introduction of Yahweh with the New Testament confession according to the Apostles' Creed. Not a changed cultural and sociopolitical situation has delivered us from being bound by the Decalogue, but God's new salvific action in Jesus Christ. To such extent we as Christians are absolutely free in relation to the Decalogue. As the order of the people of God at Sinai, the Decalogue is in principle not binding on the Church of Jesus Christ.[119]

Yet why is the Church's instruction carried out so exclusively based on the Decalogue? In what does the Decalogue's remaining authority consist? The reformer answers: "We therefore read Moses not because he concerns us so that we must keep him, but because he agrees with natural law and is

---

118   "Pred. über Ex. 19:14ff., 20, 1525," WA 16:425.22. Cf. "Dtn.-Vorl., 1534/24," WA 14:604; WA 16:426.27–33, 429.10–18; "Wider die Sabbather, 1538," WA 50:331.30–36; and Melanchthon, *Loci,* in *Studienausgabe,* 2.1:286.8–287.27; Calvin, *Inst.,* 2:8.13ff.

119   "Pred. über Ex. 20, 1525," WA 16:431.1–3; "Eine Unterrichtung, wie sich die Christen in Mose sollen schicken, 1525," WA 24:12.8–28, 14.19ff. Thus far the thesis by Röthlisberger, *Kirche am Sinai,* 1 (cf. p. 55), agrees quite well with the view of the reformers.

written better than the Gentiles could have possibly done it. The Ten Commandments are thus a mirror of our life in which we see what we lack."[120] "Therefore wherever Moses' Law and nature's law are one and the same, there the Law remains and is not abrogated externally, except spiritually by faith."[121] The Decalogue also retains its validity for Christians, not as the šalōm-order of the people of God at Sinai, but as a paradigmatic version of the divine commandment written into the hearts of all men.[122] Primarily following Augustine,[123] Luther does not look merely at the wording of the Decalogue but at Jesus' spiritual interpretation of the same, especially in the antitheses of the Sermon on the Mount. Primarily the spiritual concentration of the Decalogue on the radical double commandment of selfless love of God and neighbor made the Old Testament Decalogue, as well as the original will of God engraved upon each person's heart, shine brightly in such a way that both became able to convict the hearts and consciences in an authoritative way and to make the total demand clearly heard, "by which every man is placed before God and fellow man in an immediate and responsible way."[124]

In equal view of Luther's no and yes to the Decalogue, a set of reciprocal elucidations results. "We want to regard Moses as a teacher, but not as a lawgiver unless he agrees with the New Testament and the natural law."[125] The Decalogue is not interpreted within itself but in constant confrontation with, on the one hand, our human knowledge of good and evil and, on the other hand, the bodily fulfillment of the double commandment by Jesus. In this way, the Decalogue helps us to know the will of God in our hearts more clearly. At the same time, this original sentence, recognized more clearly in light of Christ's obedience, enables us to eliminate those aspects of the Decalogue that are part of Israel's temporary and particular order of cult and law.

In this reciprocal elucidation, an anthropological-existential and a salvation-historical element interlock. Seen from an anthropological-existential viewpoint, Luther, on the one hand, highlights the continued ethical

---

120 "Eine Unterrichtung, wie sich die Christen in Mose sollen schicken, 1525," WA 24:14.25. Cf. "Einl. zur Pred. über Ex. 19–20," WA 16:390.26ff., 380.23ff. (see also AE 35:155–74); "Wider die Sabbather," WA 50:330.28–37 (see also AE 47:57–98).

121 "Wider die himml. Proph.," WA 18:81.4 (see also AE 40:73–223).

122 "1. Disp. gg. die Antinomer, 1537," WA 39.1:374.2: "The Decalogue still is present in the conscience. For even if God had never given the Law by Moses, the human mind nonetheless has this knowledge by nature: God is to be worshiped; the neighbor is to be loved." Cf. "1. Disp. gg. die Antinomer, 1537," WA 39.1:402.14–403.3.

123 On Augustine, see Rentschka, Dekalogkatechese, 64–68, 140–48, 152–57.

124 Schloemann, Natürliches und gepredigtes Gesetz bei Luther, 92.

125 "Eine Unterrichtung," WA 24:7.13. Cf. "Eine Unterrichtung," WA 24:9.20–10.5, 14.25–29; "2. Disp. gg. die Antinomer, 1538," WA 39.1:454.4–16, 460.17–461.18.

dimension of conscience; on the other hand, he underlines the abysmal self-blinding of man. Both aspects he moves into the all-inclusive battle between God and anti-god.[126] God as our Creator and Judge tirelessly bears witness to Himself through the call to conscience. In this, the power of the *lex indita* is seen. "The Law is in the heart by nature. If the natural law had not been written and given by God into the heart, one would have to preach a long time until consciences are struck. One would have to preach to donkey, horse, ox, or cattle for a hundred thousand years before they accept the Law, though they have ears, eyes, and heart just like a man. They can hear it, but it does not fall into the heart. Why? What is the matter? The soul is not built and created in such a way that such matters ought to fall into it. Yet a man, as soon as the Law is presented to him, says: Yes, this is how it is; I cannot deny it. One would have a hard time convincing him of this, unless it had been written into his heart previously."[127] This is one side of the anthropological phenomenon, the ethical qualification of human existence.

The other side, however, runs counter to it. Man's knowledge of good and evil, let alone of God and of His commandments, is by no means a bright sentence of God engraved in hearts once and for all that automatically lights up when transgressed. This knowledge is neither a permanent possession of reason nor an enduring faculty of conscience. Rather, man tirelessly seeks to silence that call to conscience and to blur this original sentence. In this, he is supported by the satanic force of opposition that "blinds and possesses hearts so much that they do not always feel such Law."[128] That man hears God's call in his conscience as a convicting force is something that he is unable to produce at will from his own reason or power; rather, he suffers this event from the outside.[129] It is not man who calls out to himself in conscience, but he is reached and confronted by God's call in the Law.[130]

In this, the salvation-historical dimension of the Law is added to its anthropological-existential one. God awakens the *lex indita* by means of the *lex praedicata*. Conscience, constantly suppressed and distorted by the satanic foe and one's own reason, has to be awakened and sharpened tirelessly by

126 Cf. Barth, *Der Teufel und Jesus Christus in der Theologie Luthers*, 98ff., 179ff.
127 "Pred. über Ex. 20, 1525," WA 16:447.26. Cf. "Pred. über Ex. 20, 1525," WA 16:447.6–12; "Wider die himml. Proph.," WA 18:80.35–38 (see also AE 40:73–223); "Eine Unterrichtung," WA 24:9.14–10.11); "3. Disp. gg. die Antinomer, 1538," WA 39.1:540.3–13.
128 "Wider die himml. Proph.," WA 18:80.38 (see also AE 40:73–223).
129 "Pred. über Ex. 20," WA 16:448.7: "Although the devil is strongly opposed to man's feeling, knowledge, and doing. Yes, man equally is unable to do any of these without the word and light of the Holy Spirit."
130 Martin Heidegger, *Sein und Zeit*, 275, excellently described the phenomenon of being called in conscience: "The call is not and never planned, prepared, or willingly carried out. 'It' calls, against expectation and even against the will. On the other hand, the call certainly does not come from another one who is with me in the world. The call comes from inside of me and yet comes over me."

the preaching of the Law. The reformers seek to show that chain of tradition of the preached Law from the proclamation of Adam before the trees of life and knowledge to the fall, to the new order of Noah, to the Sinai revelation through Moses, and to Jesus' Sermon on the Mount.[131] The handing down of interpretation and the renewing proclamation of God's will go hand in hand here. Also the peoples and nations of the Gentiles participate in mysterious ways in that historical witness of God concerning Himself in the Law.[132] Thus the knowing, enunciating, and handing down of the Law of God is an eminently historical process.

Analogously to the Gospel, the Law also has its historical extension. At the same time, both entities have a different point of contact. The Gospel is centered on the cross and raising of Jesus; the Law, in the original knowledge of God's commandments shared by all men.[133] However, just as the Gospel casts its light from the Christ-center forth into the Old Testament and reaches all the way to the promise of the *Christus venturus* in Gen. 3:15, the *Protevangelium*,[134] thus the original knowledge of all men concerning the commandment of God reaches beyond the Law of Sinai all the way to the Sermon on the Mount. If Moses, authorized by God Himself through a special revelation, served as the interpreter and illustrator of the *lex naturae*, then Jesus Christ for His part takes the Law of Moses into His divine hands and interprets it spiritually in the Sermon on the Mount.[135]

Where the reformer thus interprets the Decalogue as expression of the Law written into the hearts of all men, he as a Christian does not cease to stand before the cross and resurrection of Christ. For Luther, our general knowledge of good and evil is filled to the brim with the obedient life and sacrificial death of this One for the many. Put differently: Into the anonymous demand for an obscure, quasidivine superiority, as well as into the ethical directions that arise from common social interaction, the concrete man Jesus and the picture of true obedience erected by Him have entered in a real history, therefore one that cannot be undone. To be sure, Luther did see that historically contingent process[136] but did not consciously analyze

---

131 Cf. "Gen.-Vorl., 1535–45," WA 42:79ff., 408f. (see also AE 1:1–359; 2:1–399); and "1. und 2. Disp. gg. die Antinomer, 1537/38," WA 39.1:402.14–403.3, 454.4–16.

132 On the understanding of tradition, cf. Mauer, "Die geschichtliche Wurzel von Melanchthons Traditionsverständnis."

133 "2. Disp. gg. die Antinomer, 1538," WA 39.1:454.14: "Thus Moses was merely something like an interpreter and illustrator of the laws written in the minds of humans wherever they might be on earth under the sun."

134 Cf. Bornkamm, *Luther und das Alte Testament*, 126–39.

135 Cf. "40. Antinomerthese," WA 39.1:352; "2. Disp. gg. die Antinomer, 1538," WA 39.1:454.4–16, 461.3ff.

136 Cf. "Prop. disp. Witt. pro doctoratu Weller et Medler, These 52–61, 1535," WA 39.1:47f. (see also AE 34:105–32).

it. With the entire ecclesiastical tradition, he rather projects, or better casts backward, the antitype of the Second Adam into the type of the first Adam.[137] Yet Luther does so in all clarity. This is why, for him, the *lex naturae* as *lex caritatis* is first and last the Christ exemplar, the archetype of the fulfilled double commandment of selfless love of God and neighbor. In the form of this one man, who lived and died for His human brothers before the invisible God in an undivided form, the original commandment, written into the hearts and consciences of all from the beginning, again stepped bodily out of all sinful deformations and demonic distortions. The *lex naturae*, as a law fulfilled in Jesus Christ, is identical with the *lex caritatis*. In this it is no longer knowledge of God's demand that is corrupted by sin but *lex naturae sanae et incorruptae*.[138]

Already in the 1518 "Kurzen Erklärung der Zehn Gebote" ("Short Explanation of the Ten Commandments"), the reformer summarizes the transgression and fulfillment of the Decalogue by taking recourse to the double commandment of love of God and neighbor, which he sharply contrasts with self-love. The mnemonic verse concerning the violation of the Decalogue reads:

> Self-love and the despising of God and neighbor
> Takes away from God what is His and withholds from Him
>   what belongs to Him;
> Takes away from the neighbor what is his and does not offer to him
>   what belongs to him—
> This is what nature, left to itself, does because of Adam's first sin.[139]

The mnemonic verse on the fulfillment of the Decalogue reads:

> Love of God and neighbor and the despising of self
> Abstains from the goods and names of God and offers Him its
>   mere nothing,
> Abstains from the goods of the neighbor and offers him what belongs
>   to it and itself—
> This is what God's grace does through Christ, our Lord.[140]

---

137 Cf. on this the comments on the Creed regarding the *imago dei*.
138 Cf. "Decem praecepta Wittenbergensi praedicata populo, 1518, zu Mt. 7:12," WA 1:502.22: "For this is the Law and the Prophets, namely, that the Law and the Prophets are fulfilled by love alone. Therefore if it is the law of nature, it is that of sound and uncorrupted nature, which is the same as love." Cf. "Gen.-Vorl., 1535–45" (WA 42:124.4–21 [see also AE 1:1–359]), the description of Adam's righteousness before the fall.
139 WA 1:254.10. The same in "Instructio pro confessione peccatorum, 1518," WA 1:262.31: "Self-love to the point of despising God and neighbor. Theft of things and names of God and withholding one's own. Usurping the things of the neighbor and withholding one's own."
140 WA 1:255.19. The same in the "Instructio," WA 1:264.5: "The life-giving Spirit. Love of God and neighbor to the point of despising oneself. Abstaining from the things and names of God and offering one's nothing. Abstaining from the things of the neighbor and offering one's own."

The reformer seeks to prove, in ongoing confrontation with being enslaved to one's own self, that both Tables—the commandments of the First Table that are summarized in the commandment of selfless love of God and those of the Second Table that are concentrated in the commandment of selfless love of neighbor—are originally engraved in our humanity, and in the case of both, Luther looks first and last to Jesus Christ.

It is true for the First Table: as *Deus semper actuosus*,[141] the eternal Creator and Sustainer holds and surrounds us from all sides. Behind the *larvae* and masks of His creatures, all men sense His potent omnipresence. The mystery of our existence constantly points us to His invisible hand. We do not live out of ourselves but out of, before, and toward His overpowering divinity, which both graciously gives itself and sublimely withholds itself. Pointing to Rom. 1:19, Luther takes up the faith of all peoples. According to him, the natural light of reason is quite capable of grasping the basic concepts, the *notiones communes*, of natural religion:[142] There is a numinous power above all life. It is good, gracious, merciful. It wants us to call upon it and serve it. To this end, it gave us the ability to distinguish between good and evil. It destroys the blasphemer and exalts the righteous,[143] "for to have a God does not only pertain to the Law of Moses but also to the natural law."[144]

Yet man always tries to hold this original revelation down. However, he is able to do so only against better knowledge and conscience. This is why atheism bears militant and violent traits.[145] At the same time, however, this creaturely relation to the Creator remains under the uncertainty of faithless doubt and under the contortion of sinful false belief. We certainly have a feeling that there is a merciful Lord above all things. However, the natural knowledge of God—how He relates to us, whether He looks out for us at all, whether He is merciful and wants to call us to Himself—remains hidden. It is "a tremendous difference between knowing that there is a God and knowing

---

141 Cf. on this the commentary on the Creed.

142 On the *notiones communes* of E. H. of Cherbury, see Hirsch, *Geschichte der neuern evangelischen Theologie*, 1:248.

143 Cf. "Röm.-Vorl., 1515/16," WA 56:174.11–179.25 (see also AE 25:1–524); "Pred. über Ex. 20, 1525," WA 16:431.3ff.; "De servo arbitrio, 1525," WA 18:718.15–20 (see also AE 33:3–295); "Jona-Auslegung, 1526," WA 19:205.27–208.35, 238.20–239.5 (see also AE 19:33–104); "Eine Unterrichtung," WA 24:9.20–31; "Pred. über Dtn. 5:6, 1529," WA 28:611.26ff.; "Gal.-Komm., 1535," WA 40.1:607.28ff. (see also AE 26:1–461); "Gen.-Vorl., 1535–45," WA 42:408.19–409.29, 631.25–632.36 (see also AE 2:1–399; 3:1–365); "Wider die Sabbather, 1538," WA 50:331.1ff. (see also AE 47:57–98).

144 "Wider die himml. Proph., 1525," WA 18:80.18 (see also AE 40:73–223).

145 "Jona-Auslegung, 1526," WA 19:206.1 (see also AE 19:33–104): "There were certainly those who, like the Epicureans, Pliny, and so forth, denied it with their mouths. Yet those who do it with violence and seek to extinguish the light in their hearts are like those who violently stop their ears and close their eyes in order not to see and hear."

what or who God is. Nature knows the first, which is written in all hearts. Only the Holy Spirit teaches the other."[146] Out of this uncertainty, our reason constantly contorts the image of the invisible Creator God, which tirelessly urges Himself upon it, into the image of its sinful presumptuousness. As when playing blindman's bluff, reason always misses the Creator and either worships itself or idolizes other creaturely powers. Yet by doing so, it falls to the prince of this world, "so that now its presumptuousness is its idol and image of the devil in its heart."[147]

The Creator nonetheless watches over the First Commandment, as well as over the entire First Table of the Decalogue, by always bearing witness to Himself in conscience as well as in nature and history—even in idols He does not permit His name to be blasphemed.[148] In this, the Creator God waits for the man who does not misplace what is majestically apparent in the images of the idols, who has not become immovably mired in every available worldly thing, who does not additionally debase the eternal Lord into being the pedestal of that person's own self-glory. The invisible God waits for the man who stretches out to him as his Father the hand of genuine childlike trust through all his life and death. Only one man did this, Jesus of Nazareth. God confirmed and testified to it by raising Him from the dead. This is how this one also became for everybody else God's hand stretched out to them. At the same time, God here uncovered the ultimate depth of the original guilt of all men. It consists only in this: that we reject this hand of the invisible Creator and Redeemer as it is stretched out to us, either because we haughtily trust ourselves or because we timidly doubt it. The original sin of free will against the commandment of selfless love of God is thus ultimately the continuous *no* to our salvation in Jesus Christ alone. "Of all men, no one could think what the sin of the world is: not to believe in Christ Jesus, the crucified."[149]

---

146 "Jona-Auslegung, 1526," WA 19:207.11 (see also AE 19:33–104). Cf. "Gal.-Komm., 1535," WA 40.1:607.30 (see also AE 26:1–461): ". . . but what God thinks about us, what He wants to give and do, how we would be liberated from sins and death and be saved (which is the proper and true knowledge of God)—this men did not know." See also "Sermon von Stärke und Zunehmen des Glaubens und der Liebe, Eph. 3:14–21, 1525," WA 17.1:431.2f.; "Pred. über Dtn. 5:6, 1529," WA 28:609–12; "Gen.-Vorl., 1535–45," WA 42:486.14–488.3 (see also AE 2:1–399).

147 "Jona-Auslegung, 1526," WA 19:207.25 (see also AE 19:33–104).

148 Cf. "Habakuk-Auslegung, 1526," WA 19:404.16 (see also AE 19:149–237): "God so stiffly holds to His name that He will not have it blasphemed even in idols. Since all idols use God's name and have people call them God, those still have been punished who ridiculed the idols or blasphemed them, as the pagan books show." Cf. Bornkamm, *Luther und das Alte Testament*, 38ff.

149 "Disp. de iustificatione, 7. These, 1536," WA 39.1:84 (see also AE 34:145–96). Cf. "Sermon von dem neugeborenen Kindlein Jesu, 1523," WA 9:533.3: "Therefore, whoever is not ready in his heart to help his neighbor with all he has . . . also does not know what it means: God's Son became man." Cf. "Chrl. Sermon von Gewalt S. Peters, 1522," WA 10.3:209.4–210.16; "De servo

In view of the commandment of love of God, for Luther thus these two elements interlock: on the one hand, the active power of the living God that ceaselessly imposes itself on all men in their daily lives, as well as God's demand to trust Him wholeheartedly, which He makes heard in all consciences; on the other hand, the historically singular and unique life and death of Jesus of Nazareth under this original commandment of the Father. Both interpret and elucidate each other; both are constantly driven against crude idolatry as well as against the subtle self-idolization of man.

Luther analogously views the Second Table of the Decalogue, which is summarized in the commandment of selfless love of the neighbor. The tradition of the Church, the theologians of the early as well as the medieval Church, coupled the *lex naturae* with the *regula aurea* (Matt. 7:12f.).[150] Luther takes up this insight in his 1518 "Instructio pro confessione" ("Instruction for Confession");[151] however, he also pointedly drives the commandment of love of neighbor to a harsh either/or: either love of self or love of neighbor.[152] Also in the realm of the Second Table the jealous God enforces His sovereign Law among us men. In the holiness code, Leviticus 19, the highly exalted ego of Yahweh stands behind the commandment: "You shall love your neighbor as yourself" (Lev. 19:18).

God enforces His Law among us men, according to Luther, by laying hold of us in a double way. From within, He lays hold of us in consciences by means of the Golden Rule; from without, He places us in the coordinate system of estates and vocations.

Let us first outline God's hold on us from without. Here Luther, summing up the exposition of the Decalogue in the Large Catechism,[153] uses the Ten Commandments and the divine estates almost synonymously.[154] Both are intertwined. God lays hold of us from the outside, as we still have to show in greater detail,[155] by casting us into His creative institutions, and He protects the latter by means of the Commandments. Thus the estates and the Commandments are the grip by which God sustains His creatures against

arbitrio, 1525," WA 18:778.17–779.14 (see also AE 33:3–295); "1. Disp. gg. die Antinomer, 1537," WA 39.1:404.5ff..

150   Cf. Schilling, *Die Staats- und Sozialiehre des Heiligen Thomas von Aquin*, 20f.

151   "Instructio pro confessione peccatorum, 1518," WA 1:259.13–19; "Kurze Erklärung der 10 Gebote, 1518," WA 1:251.26–32.

152   Cf. "Gal.-Komm., 1519," WA 2:581.4 (see also AE 27:151–410): "This is why, as I said, the commandment seems to be talking about perverted love because of my temerity, a love by which everybody, forgetful of the neighbor, only seeks what is his. Love becomes the right kind when it, being forgetful about oneself, serves the neighbor alone." Cf. also "Röm.-Vorl., 1515/16," WA 56:518.4–21 (see also AE 25:1–524); "Gal.-Vorl., 1516/17," WA 57:100.18–101.3; "Wider die Sabbather, 1525," WA 50:331.2–6 (see also AE 47:57–98).

153   *BSLK*, 640.31–641.5, 645.30ff.

154   On this, see pp. 124–25.

155   See pp. 197–208.

the cunning attacks of the forces of destruction and preserves them into the eschaton.

The inner call to loving sacrifice corresponds to that more defensive outward grip of God. God lays hold of us in the heart by means of the Golden Rule. "There is no one who does not feel or does not have to confess that it is right and true when the natural law speaks: What you want done and left undone to yourself, that do and leave undone also to another; this light lives and shines in all men's reason."[156] God does not reach out to us simply by means of external commandments—neither, strictly speaking, by means of rational cogitation. Rather, He takes hold of us by the deeply rooted will of our ego. Our own ego spontaneously and without any reflection tirelessly establishes the standard by which we judge how our neighbor deals with us. By just that standard, which we apply with great care and precision to our neighbor, God nails us in our conscience by directing it back at us in boomerang-like fashion. Rudolf Bultmann and Günther Bornkamm here quote a saying by Søren Kierkegaard:

> If the neighbor is to be loved as oneself, then the commandment opens the lock of self-love as with a lock pick and rips it away from man. . . . This "as yourself" cannot be turned or twisted. Judging with the sharpness of eternity, it penetrates into the innermost hiding place where man loves himself. It does not leave the slightest excuse for self-love, not the tiniest escape. How wonderful! One could certainly give lengthy and incisive speeches as to how man should love his neighbor, and time and again self-love would find excuses and escapes. . . . Yet this "as yourself"—indeed, no wrestler can cling to his opponent in such an inescapable way as this commandment clings to self-love.[157]

Luther shows in his interpretation of the Sermon on the Mount (on Matt. 7:12f.) how God's outer grip by means of the estates and His inner call in conscience interlock: "If you are a craftsman, you find the Bible [Law and Prophets] placed in your workshop, in your hand, in your heart, which teaches and preaches to you how you are to do to the neighbor: Just look at your tools, your needle, thimble, your beer barrel, your comb, your scales, ell, and measure, you would have this verse engraved on it. . . . All this cries out over you: My dear man, use me in such a way in relation to your neighbor as you want him to deal with you with his property."[158]

---

156 "Fastenpostille, 1525, zu Röm. 13:8ff.," WA 17.2:102.8.

157 Kierkegaard, *Leben und Walten der Liebe*, 19f.; cf. Bultmann, *Jesus*, 99f.; and Bornkamm, *Jesus von Nazareth*, 104.

158 "Das 5., 6. und 7. Kap. Matthaei gepredigt u. ausgelegt, 1532," WA 32:495.29 (see also AE 21:1–294). Cf. WA 32:494.20–495.4 (see also AE 21:1–294); "Decem praecepta Wittenbergensi praedicata populo, 1518," WA 1:480.1–481.27; "Gal.-Komm, 1519," WA 2:577.28–578.10 (see also AE 27:151–410); "Fastenpostille, 1525, zu Röm. 13:8ff.," WA 17.2:102.4–39.

Luther diametrically juxtaposes the commandment of love of neighbor as summarizing the Second Table of the Decalogue to self-love because also here he looks first and last on the One who alone was the selfless man who was open to His fellow men. In his "Sermo du duplici iustitia" ("Sermon on the Twofold Righteousness"), Luther for the first time paints the archetype of Christ's sacrifice within the commandment of love of neighbor. To this end, he offers a detailed interpretation of Phil. 2:5–11.[159] As Christ set aside His being God to take the form of a servant in order to serve us all the way to the death of a martyr, so He incorporates us into His self-giving. We, too, may and should be Christ to our neighbor.[160] In his writing on civil authority, Luther combines this with the estate when he has the Christian prince say: "Behold, Christ, the supreme prince, has come and has served me. He did not seek how to gain power, goods, and honor from me, but He only saw my need and did everything so that I would have power, goods, and honor from Him and by Him. Thus I will do likewise, not to seek what is mine from the subjects but what is theirs. This is how I also wish to serve them with my office . . . that they, not I, might reap goods and use from it."[161]

Also in view of the Second Table of the Decalogue and, respectively, the commandment of love of neighbor, we thus observe the same inner movement as in the case of the First Commandment. Luther takes the Law written in each person's heart, which he sees concentrated in the Golden Rule, as a point of departure. Yet he lets the *lex naturalis* penetrate from the outside to the inside. At the same time, Luther seeks to read the full commandment of selfless love out of the defensive prohibition. In this, he takes Jesus Christ as the archetype of the *lex caritatis* as his constant reference point.[162]

However, between the *lex naturalis* and the *lex caritatis* remains a hiatus that even Luther was not fully able to bridge. As the ancient tradition of natural law shows, natural thought and law are able to understand the Golden Rule only in a reciprocal way.[163] Everything we want our fellow men to grant us we also want to do for them—however, only to the extent and so far as something is not expected of us that the other also would not take

---

159 See "Sermo du duplici iustitia, 1519," WA 2:147.19–150.31 (see also AE 31:293–306). Cf. also "Sermon von dem neugeborenen Kindlein Jesu, 1523," WA 9:531–35.

160 According to the famous phrase from "De libertate Christiana, 1520," WA 7:34.23–36.10, 64.38–66.38 (see also AE 31:327–77).

161 "Von weltlicher Oberkeit, 1523," WA 11:273.7 (see also AE 45:75–129). Cf. also "Pred. von weltlicher Oberkeit, 1522," WA 10.3:382.4ff..

162 This was correctly seen by Karl Holl and defended against Max Weber and Ernst Troeltsch; cf. Holl, "Der Neubau der Sittlichkeit," 244 (note) and 249 (note).

163 On this hiatus, cf., e.g., "Von Kaufshandlung und Wucher, 1524," WA 15:294.31f. (see also AE 45:231–310); "Ermahnung zum Frieden auf die 12 Artikel der Bauerschaft in Schwaben, 1525," WA 18:308.34–314.36 (see also AE 46:3–43); Melanchthon, *Loci*, in *Studienausgabe*, 2.1:317.14–321.7.

upon himself in our place. This mutual limitation has to be preserved necessarily where the Second Table is founded in human socialization willed by God.[164] It comes to the fore in manifold individual rules that cause trouble also for Luther in his interpretation of the Decalogue, for example, that there is a right of self-defense,[165] that a merchant may adjust the price according to the law of supply and demand,[166] that Christians are not in principle forbidden to take and give interest.[167]

The reformer continually runs into conflict with these and similar principles that are derived from a reciprocal understanding of the Golden Rule because for him the "as yourself" in the commandment of love does not include a legitimate self-love but rather is meant to exclude it. According to Luther, it demands in a one-sided and radical way "the free love of everyone, regardless of who he is, whether he is enemy or friend. For it does not seek what is useful or good but gives and does what is useful and good."[168] This demand of selfless love of neighbor is no longer reciprocal, but it ruthlessly attacks us. It goes beyond the natural consciousness. It can no longer be explained by means of rational argumentation. In his writings to the peasants, where he addresses this cross-mystery of unreserved commitment, Luther therefore speaks of the "Christian and evangelical law,"[169] which is participation in the sacrifice of Christ: "suffering, suffering, cross, cross, is the Christians' law, this and no other."[170] For Luther, this loving devotion is the *lex Christi*,[171] which, as the *lex naturae incorruptae*, constantly has to be uncovered from selfish distortions of the *lex naturae corruptae*. This "*lex Christi* is . . . in reality no Law but the divine sermon concerning the divine meaning of the divine Law, be it the natural law, be it the Decalogue. It proclaims the commandment of perfect love of God and neighbor."[172]

Luther, with tradition, uses the Decalogue to explain the original commandment of the *lex Christi* as *lex caritatis*. Yet unlike in the "Sermon on Good Works," Luther lets the relation to Christ recede in the catechisms. In the section on the correlation between Decalogue, Creed, and Lord's

---

164 Cf. on this, e.g., Thomas Aquinas, *Summa Theologiae* I/II, q. 94, a. 2; Melanchthon, *Loci*, in *Studienausgabe*, 2.1, 313.17, 317.9.

165 On self-defense see Heinz Zipf, "Notwehr," *ESL*, col. 1381f.

166 See p. 277.

167 See pp. 277–78.

168 "Fastenpostille, 1525, zu Röm. 13:8ff.," WA 17.2:101.11.

169 "Ermahnung zum Frieden," WA 18:308.34 (see also AE 46:3–43).

170 "Ermahnung zum Frieden," WA 18:310.28 (see also AE 46:3–43).

171 Cf. "Gal.-Komm., 1519," WA 2:604.10 (see also AE 27:151–410): "Thus love everywhere finds what to endure, what to do. But love is the law of Christ." "Gal.-Komm., 1535," WA 40.2:145.7 (see also AE 27:1–144): "The law of Christ . . . the law of love."

172 Heckel, "Naturrecht," 254f. Cf. Althaus, *Ethik Luthers*, 41f.

Prayer,[173] we already anticipated two things: on the one hand, Luther lets God's holy will be fulfilled first through Creed and Lord's Prayer; on the other hand, he disconnects the Decalogue, in relation to the First Article of the Creed, from the witness to Christ in the Second Article and ties it primarily to the Creator God. This is how Luther's interpretation gains an Old Testament color. We best demonstrate what this implies for the Decalogue's connection to Christ based on the First Commandment.

TEXTS IN WHICH LUTHER INTERPRETS THE DECALOGUE

WA 1:250–56: Eine kurze Erklärung der zehn Gebote, 1518

WA 2:59–65: Eine kurze Unterweisung, wie man beichten soll., 1519

WA 7:204–14: Eine kurze Form der zehn Gebote, 1520

WA 1:258–65: Instructio pro confessione peccatorum, 1518

WA 1:398–521: Decem praecepta Wittenbergensi praedicata populo, 1518

WA 6:202–76: Sermon von den guten Werken, 1520 (see also AE 44:15–114)

WA 11:30–33, 36–41, 45–48: Fastenpredigten über den Dekalog vom 24.2, 26.2, 27.2, 28.2, 2.3, und 3.3.1523

WA 16:363–393, 422–528: Predigen über Exodus, 1524–27, zu Ex. 19 und 20

WA 30.1:2–9, 27–43, 57–85: Katechismuspredigten über den Dekalog vom 18.–22.5, 14.–19.9, und 30.11–7.12.1528 (for WA 30.1:57–85, see also AE 51:137–61)

WA 30.2:358f.: Glossen zum Dekalog, 1530

WA 35:426–28: Hymn: "Dies sind die heiligen zehn Gebot" (*Lutheran Service Book*, 581; see also AE 53:277–79)

WA 38:364–73: from Eine einfältige Weise zu beten für einen guten Freund, 1535 (see also AE 43:187–211)

ADDITIONAL IMPORTANT TEXTS FOR UNDERSTANDING THE DECALOGUE (SEE ALSO THE TEXTS GIVEN FOR THE FIRST COMMANDMENT)

WA 56:482–85: from Römerbriefvorlesung, 1515/16, zu Röm. 13:10 (see also AE 25:1–524)

WA 2:43–47: Sermo de triplici iustitia, 1518

WA 2:145–52: Sermo de duplici iustitia, 1519 (see also AE 31:293–306)

WA 2:575–82: from Galaterbriefkommentar, 1519, zu Gal. 5:14 (see also AE 27:151–410)

WA 24:2–24: Eine Unterrichtung, wie sich die Christen in Mosen sollen schicken, 1525

WA 17.2:88–104: Fastenpostille 1525, zu Röm. 13:8ff.

WA 18:67–84: from Wider die himmlischen Propheten, 1525 (see also AE 40:73–223)

WA 19:205–9, 234–39: from Der Prophet Jona ausgelegt, 1526 (see also AE 19:33–104)

---

173 See pp. 40–51.

WA 32:494–99: from Wochenpredigten über Mt. 5–7, 1532, zu Mt. 7:12f. (see also AE 21:1–294)

WA 39.1:44–53: Thesen de fide et de lege, 1535 (see also AE 34:105–32)

WA 39.1:83–86: Thesen de iustificatione, 1536 (see also AE 34:145–96)

WA 39.1:342–58: Thesen gegen die Antinomer, 1536–40

WA 50:330–37: from Ein Brief D. M. Luthers Wider die Sabbather, 1538 (see also AE 47:57–98)

WA 50:468–77: Wider die Antinomer, 1539 (see also AE 47:99–119)

STRUCTURE AND ARRANGEMENT
OF THE DECALOGUE

Among the denominations and faith communities, the numbering of the individual commandments of the Decalogue is contested.[1] Only in the late medieval confessional manuals and in the catechisms at the time of the Reformation did the numbering become firmly established. The Talmud places the presentation of Yahweh at the top, and then counts nine words. "The tradition that came from Philo and Josephus to the early Church and from there to the Greek Orthodox and the Reformed, and which modern scholarship usually follows,"[2] counts the prohibition of images as the Second Commandment. During the Middle Ages, the apodictic commandments were taken out of the deuteronomic context of sermons so that one need not learn the extensive text of Exodus 20 and Deuteronomy 5. This created a text for memorization that was certainly quite variable but also short and that, during the fifteenth century, was "commonly read from the pulpit on Sundays."[3] These texts were influenced by a Latin mnemonic verse;[4] following this verse, the self-introduction of God, the instructions of how to carry out the Commandments, and the threats of curse and the promises of blessing were left out.[5] Following Augustine,[6] there was a split of the prohibition to covet rather than a separation of the prohibition of images from the prohibition of

---

1   Cf. Vaccari, "De distinctione et ordine," 317–20, 329–34; Meyer, *Historischer Kommentar*, 85–91.

2   Zimmerli, "Das zweite Gebot," 234.

3   Bader, *Gesprächbüchlein* (MGP 20:278).

4   Believe in one God (1), do not swear by Him falsely (2). / Sanctify the Sabbath (3), hold your parents in honor (4). / Do not be a slayer (5), robber (7), adulterer (6), unjust witness (8), / Neither your neighbor's bed (9), nor his property should you covet (10). See Geffcken, *Bildercatechismus*, app., col. 37: "Unum credo deum (1), nec jures vane per ipsum (2). / Sabbata sanctifices (3), habeas in honore parentes (4). / Non sis occisor (5), fur (7), moechus (6), testis iniquus (8), / Vicinique thorum (9) resque caveto suas (10)." "In einen got solt du glouben. Bey seinem namen nit üppiklichen schweren. Die feiertag heiligen. Und deinen aelteren eren. Bisz nit ein todschleger. Dieb. Unkeüscher. Noch falsch gezüg. Froemdes gut nitt beger." A slightly different version can be found in Weidenhiller, *Untersuchungen*, 112, 200.

5   Meyer, *Historischer Kommentar*, 86f., offers the proofs for the individual commandments.

6   Augustine, *Sermo* 8:18; 9:6f.; *Quaestiones in Heptateuchum* 2:71, et pass. Cf. also Peter Lombard, *Sent.* III, dist. 37.

idolatry. Luther follows the conventional numbering as he consciously draws the prohibition of images into the prohibition of idolatry and thus subordinates the former to the latter. The artificial splitting of the commandment to covet the neighbor's wife and house he accepts only to arrive at the number ten. In his interpretation, he always treats both commandments as one.[7]

The Greek Orthodox and Reformed numbering seems to correspond to the "original Decalogue."[8] The Roman Catholic and Lutheran numbering follows the intention of the Deuteronomist editors who move the prohibition of images into the shadow of the prohibition of idols.[9] The talmudic order that places the self-predication of God before the Commandments would correspond to Luther's intention to hear the Gospel out of the First Commandment; however, the reformer reads the entire revelation of Christ into the preamble.[10]

The sequence of the prohibition to kill, commit adultery, and steal was always uncertain in ecclesiastical tradition. Against the Masoretic text of Exodus 20 and Deuteronomy 5 stood the LXX text of Deuteronomy 5 given in Luke (codex B), offering "committing adultery, killing, stealing," which influenced the New Testament.[11] To make the confusion complete, the medieval mnemonic verse, probably because of metric considerations, ordered "killing, stealing, committing adultery," and many confessional manuals followed this sequence.[12] With Augustine, Luther goes back to the Masoretic text and typically follows Exodus 20 closely. Following the tradition that was popularized by Augustine, handed down by Peter Lombard, and put

---

7   Cf. "Pred. über Ex. 20, 8.–10. Gebot, 1525," WA 16:525.32: "Many divide the two commandments; this division is not very important. St. Paul combines it into one." Cf. Calvin, *Inst.* 2:8.12.

8   Cf. the attempts to reconstruct it in Stamm, *Der Dekalog im Lichte der neueren Forschung,* 11–14; Fohrer, "Das sog. apodiktisch formulierte Recht und der Dekalog," 49–74; Gese, "Der Dekalog," 121–38; Auerbach, "Das Zehngebot," 255. For a critique, see Perlitt, *Bundestheologie,* 87–92.

9   Cf. Zimmerli, "Das zweite Gebot," 242; von Reventlow, *Gebot und Predigt im Dekalog,* 41; Knierim, "Das erste Gebot," 20–40; Perlitt, *Bundestheologie,* 85f. On literary-critical issues, cf. also Lohfink, *Das Hauptgebot.*

10   Cf. "Pred. über Dtn. 5, 1529," WA 28:604.21, where Luther combines Deuteronomy 5 with the promise in Deut. 18:15: "There He (God) has established the Ten Commandments until Christ, whom they are to accept and believe, because Christ is comprehended in the First Commandment. He is the God who led them out of Egypt, who gave them the bread from heaven. He also was the rock from which they drank in the desert, the pillars of cloud and fire that went before them by day and by night." Perlitt, *Bundestheologie,* 86f.: "The bipartition of the Decalogue in a speech of God and in a collection of prohibitions does not only mark a formal distinction but also a historical one concerning the tradition and a theological one, namely, the subordination of the manifold commandments under this one basic commandment, and this subordination took place during the Deuteronomist collation and concentration of traditional topics and materials." See also Botterweck, "Form- und überlieferungs geschichtliche Studie zum Dekalog," 394f.

11   Mark 10:19; Luke 18:20; Rom. 13:9.

12   Cf. Meyer, *Historischer Kommentar,* 88.

into outline by Bonaventure,[13] Luther also subdivides the Decalogue into the Two Tables according to the double commandment of love of God and neighbor. The "first and right-hand Table of Moses contains the first three commandments in which man is taught what he is to do and is obligated to do respective to God, that is, how he is to behave in relation to God."[14] The "other and left-hand Table of Moses" comprehends the remaining seven commandments "in which man is taught what he is obligated to do and to leave undone respective to other people and his neighbor."[15]

For Luther, the commandments of the First Table thereby have a separate and direct meaning even independent of the remaining seven of the Second Table. In them, God acts with us and we with Him in a deeply direct way, "without the mediation of any creature."[16] The First Table, as it is centered in the First Commandment, watches over our direct relation to God in which our relation to the world is to be grounded. The love of God thus does have "a realm of activity outside the love for the brethren,"[17] albeit not disconnected from the dedication to the neighbor, as Luther shows in the interpretation of the prohibition to kill.

Following Augustine,[18] Luther unfolds the first three commandments not in a trinitarian[19] but in an anthropological threesome. The First Commandment directs our heart with its thoughts to God above; the Second governs our mouth with its words; the Third makes our body with its works subject to itself.[20] This group of three is found already in "Decem praecepta Wittenbergensi praedicata populo" ("Preaching of the Ten Commandments"),[21] though still veiled in mystical images. The more Luther focuses the Third Commandment on listening to the Word of God, the

---

13   Augustine, *Quaestiones in Heptateuchum* 2:71; *Sermo* 8:13; 9:6f., 14; 33:2f., et pass.; Peter Lombard, *Sent.* III, dist. 37; Bonaventure, *Collationes de decem praeceptis* 1:21–24; 3:2; 4:2; 5:2f.; 8:2, 7.

14   "Eine kurze Form d. 10 Gebote, 1520," WA 7:205.8. Cf. "Von den guten Werken, 1520," WA 6:229.23 (see also AE 44:15–114); "Pred. über Ex. 20, 4. Gebot, 1525," WA 16:485.28.

15   WA 7:206.1. Cf. WA 6:250.20 (see also AE 44:15–114); 16:485.34ff.

16   WA 6:229.26 (see also AE 44:15–114).

17   Ritschl, *Unterricht,* § 6: "The love of God does not have a realm of activity outside the love of the brethren (1 John 4:19–21; 5:1–3)."

18   Augustine, *Enchiridion* 17:64.

19   The trinitarian triad was handed down by Peter Lombard (*Sent.* III, dist. 37, a. 3; cf. Hugh of St. Victor, *De sacramentis* 1:12.6ff.). Bonaventure elaborated on it in a playful way; cf. *Collationes de decem praeceptis* 2:9; 3:2; 1:22: "majesty—truth—goodness; power—sonship—procession; efficient cause—exemplary cause—final cause; power—wisdom—benevolence."

20   "Von den guten Werken, 1520," WA 6:229.21 (see also AE 44:15–114): "The First commands how our heart ought to behave toward God in thoughts; the Second, how the mouth in words; the Third commands how we ought to behave toward God in works."

21   WA 1:436.17: "Therefore these three commandments provide man to God as pure matter so that he would rest with heart, mouth, work—that is, in the inner and outer and middle man who are sensual, rational, spiritual—and be pure rest."

more the threesome recedes. In the 1528 catechism sermons,[22] as well as in the Large Catechism,[23] only traces are left, while the wording of the Commandments determines the summaries in a clearer way.

However, the foundational preeminence and superiority of the First Commandment vis-à-vis all other commandments are characteristic of Luther. This, too, begins to emerge in some formulations in the late medieval confessional booklets where, however, the accent lies on the opposite proposition: Only one who keeps all other commandments fulfills the First Commandment.[24] Already in the 1518 "Preaching of the Ten Commandments," Luther pointedly formulates: "For, behold, we declare this, that the First Commandment contains all the other ones in itself. For whoever observes it, observes them all, and whoever does not observe one of them, does not observe it either, because his heart regards something else than God alone."[25] Then Luther connects this central insight for the first three commandments with the anthropological distribution of heart, mouth, and work.[26]

In the Large Catechism, the reformer lets the First Commandment continually run through all the others, since it is "the head and source"[27] that permeates all the others or is like the light that radiates through everything.[28] In this context, Luther again points to the anthropological relation of heart to body: "Where the heart is on good terms with God and this (First) Commandment is kept, there the others all follow."[29] In the Small Catechism, Luther builds the obedience in all the other commandments on the First Commandment by the classical expression "we should fear and love God." The threat of punishment and the promise of blessing (Exod. 20:5f.) support this; they comprehend all commandments like an iron clasp and penetrate

---

22   WA 30.1:6.2: "In the first three commandments we are taught to trust in God with heart, mouth, and whole body." Cf. WA 30.1:33.8–16, 66.9–11.

23   *BSLK*, 586.35–40.

24   Gerson/Geiler, quoted in Geffcken, *Bildercatechismus*, app., col. 37: "This commandment is kept by man only if he fulfills the Law of God and other commandments by his works."

25   WA 1:438.7.

26   Cf. "Decem praecepta, 1518," WA 1:430.22:

"Therefore { Just as whoever does not sin in the heart does not sin with mouth and work,
So whoever sins in the heart cannot do right with mouth and work.
Whoever does not observe the First Commandment, does not observe the Second and the Third,
Whoever truly observes the First, also observes the Second and Third."
Cf. "Von den Guten Werken, 1520," WA 6:249.7–37 (see also AE 44:15–114); "Pred. über Ex. 20, 4. Gebot, 1525," WA 16:484.48–485.24.

27   *BSLK*, 644.18.

28   See the comments on the First Commandment.

29   *BSLK*, 572.12. "Katechismuspredigten, 1528," WA 30.1:65.16 (see also AE 51:141–45): "The First calls for a fearing and trusting heart. This must go through all the Commandments, since it is *summa* and light of all, because all commandments forbid because of fear and command because of trust."

them at the same time. The words of threat and blessing take the place held by the double commandment in the Augustinian tradition.[30] In his 1518 confessional manuals, Luther still concentrated on the Golden Rule in the interpretation of the Decalogue[31] and summarized the transgressions as well as the fulfillment of the Commandments according to the double commandment.[32] Even if here Luther, unlike Thomas, no longer proceeded from the double commandment, he still preserved the connection to it. The Old Testament words of threat and promise take the place of the double commandment in the 1528 catechism sermons and in the catechisms. We will have to ponder the dogmatic weight of this change.

The commandments of the Second Table turn the attention to one's neighbor; they unfold the other half of the double commandment: "You shall love your neighbor as yourself." Luther takes the term "your (our) neighbor" from the Eighth through Tenth Commandments, where it appeared in the mnemonic text, into the explanation of the Fifth and Seventh. The Sixth, alongside the Fourth Commandment to honor parents, represents an exception. It is formulated entirely positively in the Small Catechism and demands, in general, disciplined chastity and, in marriage, the respectful, loving life. In the Large Catechism, Luther explicitly undoes the Jewish narrowing of the commandment on adultery and expands it to a *no* to "all unchastity,"[33] and he places us right next to the neighbor: each should live "chastely for himself" and "also help the neighbor to do likewise."[34]

These last words merge again into the tenor of the interpretation of the Fifth through Tenth Commandment in the catechisms. The reformer interprets them as protective commandments that God Himself has established for the preservation of the human community in what is good against the breaking in of what is chaotic/evil: "And in summary, He desires to have protected, delivered, and pacified everybody against everybody else's assault and violence; and to have erected this commandment as wall, citadel, and privilege surrounding the neighbor so that he would not be harmed or hurt in his body,"[35] as Luther writes concerning the prohibition to kill.

From this flows the structure of the series of prohibitions from the Fifth through the Tenth Commandment. Each prohibition protects a specific

---

30   Especially Röthlisberger, *Kirche am Sinai*, 66–88, has examined the relationship between Decalogue and the double commandment.

31   Cf. "Eine kurze Erklärung der 10 Gebote, 1518," WA 1:251.24–32; "Instructio pro confessione peccatorum, 1518," WA 1:259.13–18.

32   Cf. "Eine kurze Erklärung der 10 Gebote," WA 1:254.10ff., 255.19ff.; "Instructio pro confessione peccatorum," WA 1:262.31ff., 264.5ff.

33   *BSLK*, 611.28.

34   *BSLK*, 611.43.

35   *BSLK*, 607.3.

gift or possession of the neighbor: body and life, wife (and child), money and goods, honor and good reputation.[36] The final double commandment summarizes the world of the neighbor once more under the symbol of the house and simultaneously unfolds it into specific details. Attention is thereby turned to the ways and manners in which we can take away from the neighbor "what is his." Even deception, what merely appears to be right, is prohibited.[37] The neighbor as *pater familias* with his house is under God's protection.

This understanding especially of commandments Five through Eight as God's protective wall around our neighbor begins to emerge in "Preaching of the Ten Commandments." Already here Luther turns our attention to God's wonderful and highly harmonious order. The prohibition stretches from the greater to the lesser, from killing one's neighbor himself (*occisio hominis*), violating his wife (*violatio coniugis*), and stealing his goods (*ablatio facultatis*), all the way to damaging his good reputation (*laesio famae*), and it finally penetrates to the hatred of our heart itself.[38]

In his instructions for confession, Luther only alludes to the protective nature of the Commandments.[39] In his 1525 sermons on Exodus,[40] he emphasizes it more: the Commandments are God's iron bars and strong walls against the beast in man.[41] The Lord "thinks thus: I have wild, unreasonable, mad, raging animals in the world, wolf, bears, lions, etc. This is why I need to lock them up behind iron bars and strong walls, lest they strangle each other and work great damage. For if God did not care, what caused Him to give the Commandments?"[42] In the third sermon in the 1528 series on the Fifth

---

36 *BSLK*, 644.9: ". . . may it affect body, spouse, goods, honor and rights, as it is commanded in series." Cf. Stamm, *Der Dekalog im Lichte der neueren Forschung*, 58f. Gese, "Der Dekalog," 137, of course, takes a different approach.

37 Cf. Herrmann, "Das zehnte Gebot," 69–82; Stamm, *Der Dekalog im Lichte der neueren Forschung*, 56ff.

38 "Decem praecepta Wittenbergensi praedicata populo, 1518," WA 1:461.4–10: "And look at the wonderful and apt order. For the prohibition begins with the greatest all the way to the least. For most damnable is to kill a man; then doing violence to the spouse; third, stealing his goods. Since those who cannot do harm in these matters at least do damage by the tongue, therefore the damage of reputation comes in fourth place. Since if they cannot accomplish anything in all these matters, nonetheless they damage the neighbor in the heart by desiring what belongs to him, in which properly consists envy." Cf. WA 1:499.9–23, 506.9–13.

39 Especially "Eine kurze Form der 10 Gebote, 1520," WA 7:206.9–26.

40 Especially in the sermons on Nov. 5 and 12, 1525, "Pred. über das 4.–7. bzw. 8.–10. Gebot," WA 16:506–28.

41 "Pred. über das 4.–7. bzw. 8.–10. Gebot," WA 16:507.4: "Ita cogitat deus: habeo wutete thier, oportet repagulum, gitter et frenum iniiciam."

42 "Pred. über das 4.–7. bzw. 8.–10. Gebot," WA 16:507.25.

Commandment, Luther again points to the function of that divine fence of protection: It is to protect my neighbor's body and life from my anger.[43]

The reformer does not inquire only about the specific goods of the neighbor that are to be protected by the individual commandments. He simultaneously analyzes our attempts to scale this protective wall by all means imaginable. This aspect should yield a different structuring of the Commandments: negatively, so to speak, according to the individual vices with which we attack the Commandments; positively according to the virtues by which we help to build the protective wall around the particular goods of our neighbor. Already in "Preaching of the Ten Commandments," Luther establishes the analogy mirroring the First Table: as the Third Commandment, the Fifth and the Seventh address first our hand; the Eighth applies, like the Second, to the tongue; while the Ninth and Tenth, like the First, mean the heart.[44] Yet this order is too playful and too schematic. Exegetically, it cannot be sustained. This is why Luther formulates it more precisely, especially in "Sermon von den guten Werken" ("Sermon on Good Works"),[45] for which he might have taken recourse to the examples of Augustine[46] and Bonaventure.[47] God demands in the prohibition against killing that we by "meekness" overcome our "angry and vindictive covetousness." The prohibition of adultery commands the battle of "purity or chastity" against "unchastity" and "evil lust." The prohibition of theft seeks ultimately the "mildness" springing from faith, which overcomes greed begotten by unbelief. The prohibition of false testimony seeks the person who, as a witness to truth, rejects the seduction to lying. The double prohibition of coveting attacks the basic evil of original sin itself; this struggle ends first in death. "Eine kurze Erklärung des Dekalogs" ("Short Explanation of the Decalogue") offers a richer catalog that is not so focused, however, on one virtue each. Both compilations have in common that the reformer "seeks the individual transgressions and fulfillments in the attitudes indicated by the mortal sins and their

---

43 WA 30.1:75.8 (see also AE 51:150–55): "Et 5. praeceptum inspiciendum est tamquam murus quem deus aedificat contra meam iram." Cf. WA 30.1:74.11–15 (see also AE 51:150–55).

44 WA 1:461.3–16.

45 WA 6:265–76 (see also AE 44:15–114).

46 Augustine, *Sermo* 9:13: The First Commandment is set against *superstitio*; the Second, against *error nefandarum haeresum*; the Third, against *amor saeculi huius*; the Fourth, against *impietas*; the Fifth, against *libido*; the Sixth, against *crudelitas*; the Seventh, against *rapacitas*; the Eighth, against *falsitas*; the Ninth, against *cogitatio adulterina*; the Tenth, against *cupiditas*.

47 Bonaventure, *Collationes de decem praeceptis* 7:8: He posits for each commandment the *affirmatio* as well as the *negatio*: to the First, *humilis adoratio—idolatria*; to the Second, *fidelis assertio divinae veritatis—periurium*; to the Third, *devota dilectio divinae bonitatis—indevotio*; to the Fourth, *pietas ad parentes—inhonoratio*; to the Fifth, *mansuetudo—iracundia*; to the Sixth, *pudicia—moechia*; to the Seventh, *largitas—furtum*; to the Eighth, *veritas—mendacium*; to the Ninth, *liberalitas cordis—concupiscentia rei temporalis*; to the Tenth, *castitas mentis—concupiscentia carnis*.

corresponding virtues."[48] This focus of the interpretation of the commandment on the vice to be combated and on the virtue commanded that helps
to overcome it remains in the catechisms. On the one hand, in the Small
Catechism, unlike in the "Sermon on Good Works," this is not concentrated
in one virtue, in one vice; rather, as in the earlier instructions for confession,
it is circumscribed as comprehensively and as concisely as possible. To this
end, several verbs are lined up, and adverbial sentences are formed. On the
other hand, in the Large Catechism Luther strives to summarize in a few
memorable words what has been unfolded broadly. Yet here, too, unlike in
earlier interpretations, he retains sentences.[49]

These observations show that the tension between two types of interpretation accentuated by Johannes Meyer[50] does not do full justice to Luther.
The reformer, from the beginning, combined both: To him, the commandments of the Second Table are God's protective wall around our neighbor
and a call to conversion of the heart. An "evangelical ethics of conviction"
that, out of fear of "medieval confessional casuistry," loses sight of the concrete neighbor is certainly not what Luther wanted. For him, an ethics of
conviction without constant reference to the neighbor given us by God mili-
tates against the Decalogue. In "Preaching of the Ten Commandments," the
steady references to crass sins and the urging of conversion of the heart stand
side by side, yet relatively disjointedly. In the "Sermon on Good Works," Luther puts the stress on the internal dimension of conviction. On the other
hand, in the catechisms he puts the protection of the neighbor at the center.

This definite shift of accent can be observed clearly in the final double
commandment. Luther was thoroughly familiar with the original meaning of the verb *hamad*. As modern scholarship has rediscovered,[51] it does
not mean the inner desire of the heart but "manifest activities to obtain the
possessions of somebody else," legal tricks and dark practices.[52] Nonetheless, the reformer, with Peter Lombard and Bonaventure,[53] interprets this
double commandment in his early exegetical works to address the *concupiscentia carnis*. This he does not because it corresponds to the Old Testament
wording; that rather seems to be open to the "understanding of the Jews or,

48   Meyer, *Historischer Kommentar*, 224. Cf. "Decem praecepta, 1518," WA 1:516–21; "Eine kurze Erklärung, 1518," WA 1:254.3–9; "Instructio, 1518," WA 1:262.14–31; "Eine kurze Form, 1520," WA 7:211.28–212.3.

49   Summary of the Fifth Commandment, *BSLK*, 607.41–44; of the Sixth Commandment, *BSLK*, 611.41–612.2, 615.25–35.

50   Meyer, *Historischer Kommentar*, 223–29.

51   See the works cited in p. 94 n. 37.

52   "Decem praecepta, 1518," WA 1:516.13: ". . . attempt among jurists"; "Kat.-Pred. zum 8.–10. Gebot, 19.9.1528," WA 30.1:42.36: "They used tricks to take each other's house."

53   Cf. Peter Lombard, *Sent.* III, dist. 40.1; Hugh of St. Victor, *De sacramentis* 1:12.7; Bonaventure, *In sent.* 3, dist. 37, dub. 5; *Collationes de decem praeceptis* 7:6.

preferably, pigs."[54] He does so because the New Testament interpretation by the apostle Paul in Rom. 7:7; 13:9 demands this. Paul unambiguously aims at the dark coveting of the heart that is at the bottom of all active desiring and that indicates the original depravity of our humanity. This is why these two commandments do not belong to the confession before men. Rather, they point to the goal of our eschatological perfection, toward which we rush through our death as well as through the fire of the Last Judgment.[55]

In the Small Catechism, Luther returns to the Old Testament understanding of the last commandments. We should not try to take away from our neighbor what is his with lust and the appearance of right. In the Large Catechism, Luther likewise starts with the coarse interpretation and thinks that these commandments were "almost given especially to the Jews."[56] Following Paul, and perhaps already the Deuteronomist preacher,[57] he then adds that God wants to eliminate the "cause and root" of that deceptive attack on the neighbor and what is his. God also wants to uncover "the envy and miserable greed" of a "rogue's heart" and "chiefly wants to have the heart pure, though we, as long as we live here, cannot attain this."[58]

The tension between the Old Testament wording of the Decalogue and its New Testament reception has become paradigmatic in Jesus' reception of the prohibition to kill in the Sermon on the Mount (Matt. 5:21–26). Already Peter Lombard, Thomas, and Bonaventure[59] draw on this section to explain the commandment.[60] Luther follows them and gains from this the key to interpreting the commandments of the Second Table:[61] in the prohibitions of the Decalogue one finds the beginning of a double movement that the spiritual interpreter, Christ, made conscious, namely, from the outside to the inside and from the negative to the positive.

---

54   "Decem praecepta, 1518," WA 1:516.10.

55   "Eine kurze Erklärung, 1518," WA 1:253.35–254.2; "Instructio, 1518," WA 1:264.2ff.; "Decem praecepta, 1518," WA 1:515.1–516.24; "Von den guten Werken, 1520," WA 6:276.10–20 (see also AE 44:15–114); "Eine kurze Form, 1520," WA 7:210.23–271.

56   *BSLK*, 633.38.

57   Cf. Stamm, *Der Dekalog im Lichte der neueren Forschung*, 59; von Reventlow, *Gebot und Predigt im Dekalog*, 86f.

58   *BSLK*, 638.20, 638.39, 638.44.

59   Peter Lombard, *Sent.* III, dist. 37.3; Thomas Aquinas, *Duo praecepta* §§ 1275ff.; Bonaventure, *Collationes de decem praeceptis* 6:4.

60   Matthew 5:20–26 was the historic pericope for the Sixth Sunday after Trinity. Sixteen sermons by Luther on this text have come down to us (cf. WA 22:xlvif.). A selection is offered by Mühlhaupt, *Evangelien-Auslegung*, 2:84–97.

61   He manages to do this already in "Preaching of the Ten Commandments," where he formulates: "Yet what I said about this commandment is to be understood about all of them, in a similar fashion" (WA 1:467.12).

1.　The Lord, by means of the motif of His antitheses "Not only—
but already"[62] drives the prohibition from what is external into
what is internal, from man and his body and deeds to the core
of the heart. This is how a series of steps emerges for the reflect-
ing interpreter: "For the first is not to kill by deeds, yet one must
also make this neither by word nor by sign and, therefore, nor
in the heart."[63] In the Large Catechism, Luther again rehearses
these steps: "Do not kill. This means we should do no harm to
anyone, neither by hand or deed, nor by words or advice, nor by
any means or ways, until the prohibition finally penetrates to the
thoughts of our heart."[64]

2.　In a second step, Luther unfolds the positive commandment that
lies dormant in the negative prohibition.[65] God wants more from
us than that we endure all hatred and that we stoically bear all in-
sults. God seeks an active and imaginative love of neighbor. Spiritually interpreted, the prohibition means the active love of neighbor in all circumstances of life. We should not only "not hurt or
harm our neighbor in his body, but help and be of service to him
in all physical needs."[66] As Thomas before him, Luther points to
a word by Ambrose: "If you did not feed, you killed,"[67] and draws
attention to the six works of mercy mentioned by Christ in Matt.
25:42f.[68] Both help him to deliver the commandment out of the
prohibition.

62　Cf. Bornkamm, *Jesus von Nazareth*, 95: "All these antitheses are permeated by one constant
motif that can be summarized in these few words: 'Not only—but already.'"

63　"Decem praecepta, 1518," WA 1:467.22. Parallels can be found in Thomas Aquinas, *Duo praecepta* § 1262: "First by hand, then by mouth, third by aid, fourth by consent." Cf. Thomas
Aquinas, *Duo praecepta* §§ 1273ff.; Peter Lombard, *Sent.* I, dist. 42.6; Hugh of St. Victor, *De
sacramentis* 1:12.7; Bonaventure, *In sent.* 3, dist. 37, dub. 5.

64　Cf. "Kat.-Pred. über das 2. u. 3. Gebot, 15.9.1528," WA 30.1:30–32; *BSLK*, 608.6–12.

65　"Decem praecepta, 1518," WA 1:470.16: "Therefore this commandment is, to be sure, negative
according to the letter but highly positive according to the Spirit, because the Lord requires
them to be meek and peaceful." Cf. WA 1:470.13–471.29, where this turn from the negative to
the positive is carried out for all commandments.

66　*BSLK*, 508.32.

67　Luther quotes this word several times, e.g., "Von den guten Werken, 1520" (WA 6:273.6 [see
also AE 44:15–114]); "Kat.-Pred., 1528" (WA 30.1:37.1, 75.13 [for WA 30.1:75.13, see also
AE 51:150–55]). It is already found in Thomas Aquinas, *Duo praecepta* § 1262: "Feed the one
starving of hunger; if you did not feed, you killed." Ambrose, *Expos. in Ps. 118*, sermo 12:44
(PL 15:1449), is adduced.

68　On the works of mercy, see "Eine kurze Erklärung, 1518," WA 1:253.11, 254.4; "Instructio,
1518," WA 1:261.15, 261.37; "Eine kurze Unterweisung, 1519," WA 2:62.33f.; "Eine kurze Form,
1520," WA 7:210.13. See already perhaps the earliest sermon, "Pred. über Mt. 7:12, 1514(?),"
WA 4:590–95 (see also AE 51:5–13), as well as the proofs collected by Peters, *Glaube und Werk*,
115f.

Both of these movements—from without to within and from negative to positive—Luther carries out paradigmatically for the Fifth Commandment and then for each of the following commandments.[69] Constantly it is shown that God primarily "has not only externally prohibited deeds"[70] but also that in His act of prohibition He wishes to pull out from the slavery of sin the entire person according to both the external body and the internal heart. God wants our heart all for Himself; this is why the reformer in a first step drives the prohibition into the core of our existence. In the second step, he then shows positively how God wants to create in us the desire and love of the new obedience. Probably that he not overload the mnemonic formulae, Luther has only unfolded the transition from prohibition to commandment, from harming to helping and fostering, in the Small Catechism. After all, the movement from negative to positive includes the one from outside to inside, since only a heart renewed in faith is able to serve the neighbor in selfless dedication.

At the same time, the reformer assigned something specific to each commandment of the Second Table. Only the Fifth Commandment serves almost exclusively the purpose of unlocking the inner structure of the interpretation of the Decalogue in light of the antitheses of Jesus. While Luther developed his understanding of the two kingdoms based on the Fourth Commandment, the Sixth Commandment is dedicated to the estate of marriage as the "most common and most noble estate that pervades all of Christendom, even the entire world."[71] Here Luther gives a rough sketch of his view on marriage. For the Seventh Commandment, he establishes God's zealous holiness over the human economic community. For the Eighth Commandment, he develops the difference between the public punitive office of the authorities and private calumny. For the concluding double commandment, he describes the specific sin of the "pious" who, in their attacks on the neighbor, seek to preserve the appearance of right and decency. This is how he works out one characteristic point in each commandment, on which we will have to concentrate primarily in our interpretation.

Between the commandments of the First and of the Second Table, the Fourth Commandment holds a special place, since parents and clan heads are seen in the brightness of God's majesty.[72] "The Lord has established parents

---

69   Cf. *BSLK*, 608.3–609.26, 611.25–612.2, 619.13–22, 623.37–47, 632.7–22, 638.29–639.4.

70   *BSLK*, 611.29.

71   *BSLK*, 613.23.

72   The special position of the Fourth Commandment has been shown exegetically by Kremers, "Die Stellung des Elterngebotes im Dekalog"; cf. also Gerstenberger, *Wesen und Herkunft*, 130–44. Bonaventure notes its special place in *Collationes de decem praeceptis* 7:7: "In the first three commandments is commanded the right ordering toward God; in the fourth, the right ordering and honorable treatment toward the parents. In the other six is commanded the right ordering and innocence toward the neighbor." Cf. *Collationes de decem praeceptis* 5:3; *In sent.*

and elders in His place and has mandated them as His representatives."[73] To the love of the neighbor, which we owe all people, therefore here honor is added, which is a shadow of the fear of God.[74] We deal with our parents and lords not only in love but also in "fear, reverence, discipline,"[75] because in them we honor God's creative majesty and His sovereign design.[76] This is why it is understandable that Luther in a few summary overviews combines the first four commandments under this common aspect: here obedience to everything that is above us is in view—first, to God; second, to all who stand in His stead.[77] This is why he takes the Fourth Commandment as an occasion to assert his understanding of the secular and spiritual kingdom in the Decalogue,[78] just as he outlines the true understanding of the estate of marriage in the context of the prohibition of adultery.

Luther takes this intermediate position of the Fourth Commandment between the two tables as an occasion to show that parents as well as spiritual and secular authorities correspond to the following commandments of neighborly love in a specific way. Because they stand on God's side in the divinely established hierarchical order among men, God gave them a share in His holy zeal watching over the Commandments. Holding thus an office of service in relation to the Commandments, they often have to act in a way that appears contrary to them. In the Large Catechism, Luther develops this especially on the Fifth and Eighth Commandments. With the sword, God has made the authorities stewards of His office of wrath and punishment. Because they are "in God's stead,"[79] they have power over life and death. According to Deut. 21:18–20, heads of family themselves are called to bring their disobedient sons before the court of judgment and sentence them to

---

3, dist. 37, a. 2, q. 2f., as well as Peter Lombard, *Sent.* III, dist. 37.5. Hugh of St. Victor, *De sacramentis* 1:12.5 (PL 176:352B/C): "The first commandment of the First Table pertains to God the Father; thus the first commandment of the Second Table pertains to the human father, so that in both cases paternity be honored in the authority of the beginning."

73 "Instructio, 1518," WA 1:258.21.

74 "Decem praecepta, 1518," WA 1:448.32: "Since God therefore wants parents to be honored and the cause is most just, namely, because the representative is also the workshop of God, this commandment differs from the preceding ones (1–3) only in this, that God is honored in them as in Himself, in this one as in somebody else, namely, in the rulers who are His seats, workshop, altar, mercy seat. Therefore this is true honor."

75 "Kat.-Pred., 1528," WA 30.1:6.6ff. Cf. "Instructio, 1518," WA 1:258.19: "Honor includes beyond love also honor and reverence."

76 *BSLK*, 587.18: ". . . a discipline, humility, and fear as toward a majesty hidden there."

77 See the summaries in "Decem praecepta, 1518," WA 1:461.10–16; "Pred. über Ex. 20, 1525," WA 16:506.28–507.14; "Eine kurze Form, 1520," WA 7:206.3–6; "Kat.-Pred., 1528," WA 30.1:74.9 (see also AE 51:150–55).

78 Cf. Kinder, "Geistlichen und weltlichen 'Oberkeit.'" In this, Luther followed the tradition; cf. Maurer, *Lehre von den drei Hierarchien.*

79 *BSLK*, 606.23.

death.[80] "For God and whatever is in divine estate ought to be wrathful, rebuke, and punish precisely because of those who transgress this and other commandments."[81] Analogously, the authorities have to watch over the honor and good reputation of their subjects; at the same time, they have to uncover and judge secret sin since they are not to let the evil go unpunished. The authorities placed at the top of the Second Table by the Fourth Commandment have been instituted by God precisely in order to watch with Him and under Him that the protective wall erected in the Commandments to surround the neighbor is not torn down. Thus the authorities share in God's holy zeal for His Commandments.

---

80   Luther references Deut. 21:18–20 in *BSLK*, 606.7ff. Cf. the interpretation in "Dtn.-Vorl., 1523/24," WA 14:696.25–36 (see also AE 9:1–311).

81   *BSLK*, 606.24.

THE FIRST COMMANDMENT[1]

WORDING OF THE COMMANDMENT
AND STRUCTURING OF THE INTERPRETATION

In the medieval mnemonic texts, the wording of the prohibition of idolatry is handed down with great variety and instability. To better explain the "having" of other gods, one took recourse not to Exod. 20:3 but to texts such as Matt. 4:20: "You shall worship the Lord your God and serve Him only"; to Deut. 6:5, the *šm'a yiśra'ēl*; to Exod. 34:14: "You shall not worship any other god"; as well as to the mnemonic verse: "*Unum crede deum*, 'You shall believe in one God.'"[2] Or one quite freely tied together the verbs used in the prohibitions of idolatry and images with faith and love (worship and serve, believe and love).[3] Luther foregoes changing the wording itself. He sticks to Exod. 20:3: "You shall have no other gods," but he replaces the customary translation "alien gods" with "other gods."[4]

The Small Catechism's explanation: "We should fear, love, and trust in God above all things," loosely follows the 1518 "Eine kurze Erklärung" ("Short Explanation")[5] and, respectively, the 1520 "Eine kurze Form" ("Short Form"),[6] where "fear and love of God in true faith and firm trust" was used to paraphrase the fulfillment of the First Commandment. Already these early Decalogue interpretations offer a more precise paraphrase of the abstract "having" of a god: "To have a god means to have someone to whom one looks to be fostered in all good things, to be helped in all bad things. This

---

1   For some central texts on the First Commandment, see pp. 146–47.

2   "Eine kurze Unterweisung, wie man beichten soll, 1519," WA 2:60.35: "Du sollt in einen einigen Gott glauben."

3   See the compilation in Meyer, *Historischer Kommentar*, 88. Already Augustine paraphrases the commandment freely; cf. Rentschka, *Dekalogkatechese*, 127.

4   "Eine kurze Erklärung, 1518," WA 1:250.3; "Eine kurze Form, 1520," WA 7:205.19; *BSLK*, 507.40, 560.5. The addition "besides Me" is found only in the introduction to the Large Catechism, *BSLK*, 555.14. The Latin version reads: "Non haberis deos alienos" ("Decem praecepta, 1518," WA 1:398.5; "Instructio, 1518," WA 1:258.3).

5   WA 1:254.17ff.

6   WA 7:212.14ff.

is what the one true God Himself wants to be, and this is also what He is."[7] The 1528 sermons[8] and the Large Catechism take up this interpretation: "A god is that to which one should look for all good things and to which one should take refuge in all needs."[9] Thus fear, love, and trust are the right ways to have a god. The only true God, our Creator and Redeemer, wants to turn the heart of man away from all other places of comfort and refuge to Himself alone as the only giver of life. The phrase "above all things" hints at this constant movement away from all creaturely places of refuge and means of comfort to the Creator Himself and thus puts the prohibition of idolatry in positive terms.

Luther's classical explanation in the Small Catechism summarizes a late medieval tradition of interpretation that gained a fixed form in Jean Gerson's *Opusculum tripartitum* and that from there enters into the confessional manuals as a stereotypical phrase. Jean Gerson/Johann Geiler concludes the explanation of the Commandments with these words: "Only God is the true and faithful friend who is able to help us in extreme need, and this is why He is to be faithfully honored, worshiped, and loved above all things in purity of heart."[10] In subsequent confessional manuals these phrases are varied constantly, for example, in the Lübeck *Spiegel der Tugenden*: "We should love above all things God our Creator who is above us."[11] Following the Augustinian tradition, faith in God is understood as love striving toward God in reverence, humility, and worship.[12] The triad fear—love—faith is not found; it is Luther's very own.[13]

In the Large Catechism, Luther describes this inner movement away from idolizing of the creature to trusting in the Creator in several lines of thought. In this, he follows the sequence of the second sermon series and inserts particular insights from the first sermon series. Insights from the third sermon series get their due at the very end of the Decalogue explanation

---

7   "Eine kurze Erklärung, 1518," WA 1:250.4. "Eine kurze Form, 1520," WA 7:205.12: "The First Commandment teaches how man should behave inwardly in the heart toward God, that is, what he always is to think of Him, hold, and observe; namely, that he is to look for all good things to Him as to a father and good friend, in all faithfulness, faith, and love, with fear at all times, lest he offend Him like a child his father."

8   WA 30.1:2.32ff., 3.14ff., 28.2ff., 59.4f. (see also AE 51:137–41), et pass.

9   *BSLK*, 560.10.

10   Geffcken, *Bildercatechismus*, app., col. 38.

11   Geffcken, *Bildercatechismus*, app., col. 142; cf. col. 53, 86, 93, 100, 108, 148, 150, 164, 167. See also Weidenhiller, *Untersuchungen*, 46, 67, 192, 229ff.

12   See, e.g., *Spiegel des Sünders*, in Geffcken, *Bildercatechismus*, app., col. 51: "You shall briefly understand the commandment in this way: that you may not love any good nor creature more than God, by which love you would lose the love of God."

13   Especially close to Luther is the confessional manual preserved in a manuscript at the Hamburg State Library in Geffcken, *Bildercatechismus*, app., col. 86.

when Luther again takes up the threats and promises.[14] Luther follows the pedagogical rules established in the prefaces.[15] The threefold pattern of brief explanation—deepening exposition—application to the reader is followed, with negative examples contrasting and thereby clarifying the positive propositions.

As in the Small Catechism, the reformer primarily puts the negative formulation of the prohibition of idolatry in the positive sense: "You should have Me alone as your God."[16] The actual scope of the interpretation is unfolded in a threefold movement of thought. Existential analysis and existential preaching are interwoven in a peculiar way; insights into the structure of our being as humans, as well as observations regarding human history, are surrounded by faith's hinting at the all-encompassing wrestling between God and anti-god. After all, it is only the bright light of faith's witness to God's holy zeal for His sovereign right among men that unlocks our external fate as well as our internal essence.

The first as well as the second explanation unfold the positive meaning of the commandment by employing negative counterimages, "everyday examples of opposition,"[17] which are to demonstrate: "Upon what you now ... hang your heart and rely, this is actually your god."[18] In a first circle of ideas, this is demonstrated regarding dependence on money and goods; on Mammon as the most common idol on earth;[19] on one's own and somebody else's personal power;[20] on taking refuge with the saints,[21] as well as with dark antidivine powers.[22] Luther tirelessly emphasizes everywhere the characteristic of the personal relationship of trust: "To have a god means to have something on which the heart totally relies."[23] From these counterexamples, the First Commandment again turns our attention to the Creator God in

---

14   Section 1 (*BSLK*, 560.10–563.27) follows "Kat.-Pred., 1528," WA 30.1:27.35–28.15, and inserts WA 30.1:3.4–10. Section 2 (*BSLK*, 563.28–565.24) follows WA 30.1:28.15–22 with recourse to WA 30.1:3.20ff. Section 3 (*BSLK*, 565.25–567.13) is dependent on WA 30.1:3.34–4.9. Section 4 (*BSLK*, 567.14–572.22) follows almost verbatim WA 30.1:28.22–29.34. The end of the Decalogue interpretation (*BSLK*, 639.11–645.52) offers thoughts that are first hinted at in WA 30.1:43.12–26. They are elaborated on in detail in WA 30.1:58.18–61.22 (see also AE 51:137–41) under the scope: "*Timor* is on the left side, *fiducia* on the right" (WA 30.1:60.14 [see also AE 51:137–41]). Their echo can be heard in WA 30.1:85.5–16 (see also AE 51:155–61).

15   See the interpretation of the prefaces, pp. 31–35.

16   *BSLK*, 560.7.

17   *BSLK*, 561.9.

18   *BSLK*, 560.23.

19   *BSLK*, 561.7–38.

20   *BSLK*, 561.39–562.9.

21   *BSLK*, 562.10–26.

22   *BSLK*, 562.27–38.

23   *BSLK*, 562.3.

His zealous holiness: whatever we have previously looked for among those creaturely idols, we are to seek from Him who alone is living.[24]

The second set of ideas corroborates the insight by means of two more counterexamples, that is, the crass pagan recourse to vain idols[25] and the subtle self-reliance on works of the erring church.[26] The latter goes beyond what the growing youth can understand and comprehend.

While the reader hereby was twice brought back, as it were, from looking to and building on what is vain to the one true and life-giving God, in a third set of thoughts, Luther positively unfolds the essence of this God.[27] He is the "eternal fountain" of all natural and supernatural goods. In all the things we receive from creatures, therefore, we should look to His creative commanding and His commanding giving. The concluding application implants in the heart of each person the question for confession: whether he in his concrete daily life fears, loves, and trusts in God alone.[28]

For the three explications, this results in the following structure:

Scope: "You should have Me alone as your God."[29]

I.   Explication: "What does it mean to have a God" under the basic commandment of the zealous Creator God?[30]

     A.   The positive exposition: Hang your heart on Me alone.[31]

          1. Existential analysis: Faith and God belong together.[32]

          2. Existential proclamation: Your true faith belongs to the one true God alone.[33]

     B.   The negative explication based on "opposing examples."[34]

          1. Trust in dead material values: money and goods.[35]

          2. Trust in personal gifts and interpersonal values.[36]

---

24   *BSLK*, 562.39–563.27.

25   *BSLK*, 564.1–39.

26   *BSLK*, 564.40–565.24.

27   *BSLK*, 565.25–567.13.

28   *BSLK*, 566.44–567.13.

29   *BSLK*, 560.7.

30   *BSLK*, 560.11–563.27. Cf. "Kat.-Pred. zum 1. Gebot vom 14.9.1528," WA 30.1:27.35–28.15.

31   *BSLK*, 560.11–561.6.

32   *BSLK*, 560.11–29.

33   *BSLK*, 560.30–561.6.

34   *BSLK*, 561.7–562.38.

35   *BSLK*, 561.7–38.

36   *BSLK*, 561.39–562.9.

3. Trust in dead saints.[37]

4. Trust in satanic powers.[38]

C. Turning attention away from the creaturely powers to the living Creator God.[39]

II. Explication: The false worship of the pagans and the subtle idolatry in Christendom as counterimage of the true worship demanded in the First Commandment.[40]

A. Summary of the First Commandment.[41]

B. Idolatry relating to God negatively.[42]

1. The simple idolatry of the pagans who, in their conceit, set their minds on the creature.[43]

2. The dual idolatry of the false Christians who build on their own works before the munificent God.[44]

III. Explication: Who is the living God?[45]

A. God as the fountain of temporal as well as eternal goods.[46]

B. True receiving of God's gifts through the cooperation of the creatures according to God's command and ordinance.[47]

C. The First Commandment applied as question for confession.[48]

The appendix to the First Commandment and, respectively, to the Decalogue as a whole unfolds twice the word of threat and promise (Exod. 20:5f.), which Luther applies to the whole Decalogue.[49] The first exposition follows consciously the order of pedagogical steps. First, the word of Scripture is

---

37   *BSLK*, 562.10–26. Cf. "Kat.-Pred. zum 1. Gebot vom 18.5.1528," WA 30.1:3.4–10.

38   *BSLK*, 562.27–38.

39   *BSLK*, 562.39–563.27.

40   *BSLK*, 563.28–565.24. Cf. "Kat.-Pred. zum 1. Gebot vom 14.9.1528," WA 30.1:28.15–22.

41   *BSLK*, 563.28–39.

42   *BSLK*, 563.39–565.24.

43   *BSLK*, 564.1–39. Cf. "Kat.-Pred. zum 1. Gebot vom 18.5.1528," WA 30.1:3.20ff.

44   *BSLK*, 564.40–565.24.

45   *BSLK*, 565.25–567.13.

46   *BSLK*, 565.25–566.11. Cf. "Kat.-Pred. zum 1. Gebot vom 18.5.1528," WA 30.1:3.31–34.

47   *BSLK*, 566.12–43. Cf. "Kat.-Pred. zum 1. Gebot vom 18.5.1528," WA 30.1:3.34–4.9.

48   *BSLK*, 566.44–567.13.

49   See the interpretation on p. 130.

offered,[50] albeit not yet in the version worked through for memorization.[51] Then the understanding of the same is explicated both in relation to the threat of curse and in relation to the promise of blessing, where the reformer points to God's zeal for man's obedience, which is powerfully at work in Scripture, human history, and daily experience.[52] Then the "This applies to you!"[53] follows. In it, what has been recognized by faith is now practiced existentially against superficial appearances. By this, Luther disengages the view of the Christian from this world and turns it upward to God's future kingdom.[54]

The conclusion of the interpretation of the Decalogue[55] returns again to the First Commandment. In itself, it is not structured as clearly. First, Luther harshly contrasts the Ten Commandments as "summary of divine doctrine" with all self-chosen piety of man[56] and reminds the reader that the Decalogue is fulfilled by faith alone, that is to say, by the triune God working in faith. Those words of threat and promise merely underline the First Commandment; they do not want anything but our heart for God alone. Where this happens to us, there our entire outward life is right before God. There the walking in the First Commandment permeates the obedience to all the remaining commandments. Both strands of thought drive toward the perpetual remembrance and the daily practice for which Luther reminds the readers of the commandment in Deut. 6:8f. and 11:20 to have God's Law always before their eyes.[57] Thus at the end of the Decalogue interpretation, we find included the text prepared for memorization in a twofold unfolding that, for its part, moves toward application and practice.

The two appendices are thus arranged as follows:

IV.   First exposition of the word of threat and grace.[58]

A.   Presentation of God's Word.[59]

B.   Unfolding of the understanding.[60]

---

50   *BSLK*, 567.14–33.
51   The different versions of the word are analyzed by Meyer, *Historischer Kommentar*, 184.
52   *BSLK*, 567.34–570.7.
53   *BSLK*, 570.10.
54   *BSLK*, 570.8–572.22.
55   *BSLK*, 639.11–645.32.
56   *BSLK*, 639.11–641.29.
57   *BSLK*, 645.11, 645.13. Cf. the interpretation of the prefaces, pp. 31–35.
58   *BSLK*, 567.14–572.22, following "Kat.-Pred. zum 1. Gebot vom 14.9.1528," WA 30.1:28.28, 22–29.34.
59   *BSLK*, 567.14–33.
60   *BSLK*, 567.34–570.7.

1. The word added to the First Commandment
   as the head of all commandments.[61]

2. God's zeal for His majesty against all idolatry.[62]

3. God's promise of earthly and heavenly blessing.[63]

C. Application of God's Word.[64]

1. God's Word.[65]

2. God's prevailing against the appearances
   and the resistance of the world.[66]

3. The Christians' rushing toward God through
   this world in their calling and estate.[67]

4. The heart's obedience to God in the First
   Commandment as source of the obedience
   in all the other commandments.[68]

V. The conclusion of the interpretation of the Decalogue: The Decalogue centered on the First Commandment as "summary of divine doctrine."[69]

A. The Decalogue as *ordo* commanded by God and fulfilled in God alone against all self-chosen orders and works of man.[70]

1. The lowly work of the Decalogue; the
   exalted works of self-chosen holiness.[71]

---

61   *BSLK*, 567.34–42.
62   *BSLK*, 567.42–569.31.
63   *BSLK*, 569.32–570.7. Cf. "Kat.-Pred. zum 1. Gebot vom 14.9.1528," WA 30.1:29.1–4.
64   *BSLK*, 570.8–572.22, following "Kat.-Pred. zum 1. Gebot vom 14.9.1528," WA 30.1:29.4–34.
65   *BSLK*, 570.8–23.
66   *BSLK*, 570.23–571.39, following "Kat.-Pred. zum 1. Gebot vom 14.9.1528," WA 30.1:29.15–22.
67   *BSLK*, 571.40–572.14.
68   *BSLK*, 572.14–22.
69   *BSLK*, 639.11–645.52, summarizing "Kat.-Pred. zum 1. Gebot vom 30.11.1528," WA 30.1:58.18–61.22 (see also AE 51:137–41). Cf. "Kat.-Pred. vom 19.9. und 7.12.1528," WA 30.1:43.12–26, 85.5–16 (see also AE 51:155–61).
70   *BSLK*, 639.11–641.29.
71   *BSLK*, 639.11–640.30.

2. Fulfillment of the commandment
by faith and prayer alone.[72]

3. Call to obedience in the Decalogue.[73]

B.   The word of threat and promise as the inculcation of the
First Commandment in all commandments.[74]

1. The dual direction of the word of threat
and blessing in all commandments.[75]

2. The First Commandment as a call to fear and
trust in God as the center of Scripture.[76]

3. The First Commandment as head and source
of all other commandments in both tables.[77]

4. Perpetual remembrance and daily
practice of the Decalogue.[78]

5. God's holy zeal and kindness of
blessing in the Decalogue.[79]

THE PROHIBITION OF IDOLATRY
IN THE OLD TESTAMENT DECALOGUE[80]

The prohibition to worship alien gods is found in the Old Testament in various formulations. In addition to Exod. 20:3; Deut. 5:7: "You shall not have other gods before My face," there is, for example, Exod. 34:14: "You shall not prostrate yourself before another god," or the combination in Ps. 81:10: "No alien god shall be found with you, and you shall not prostrate yourself before an alien god." The oldest version seems to be preserved in Exod. 22:19. The instruction on how it is to be carried out is found in Deut. 13:2–19: "Whoever sacrifices to other gods is to be banned," that is, is to be brought from life to death. "The sentence in the Decalogue to have no other gods in defiance

---

72   *BSLK*, 640.31–641.5.
73   *BSLK*, 641.6–29.
74   *BSLK*, 641.29–645.52.
75   *BSLK*, 641.29–642.44.
76   *BSLK*, 642.45–643.23.
77   *BSLK*, 643.24–644.35.
78   *BSLK*, 644.36–645.29.
79   *BSLK*, 645.30–52.
80   Cf. Knierim, "Das erste Gebot"; von Rad, *Theologie des Alten Testaments*, 1:201–11; Rost, "Die Schuld der Väter"; Smend, *Die Bundesformel; Die Mitte des Alten Testaments*; Perlitt, *Bundestheologie*, 77–102, 156–238; Zimmerli, "Ich bin Jahwe."

of Yahweh is . . . of all the versions the most general and least specific. Yet it is precisely on account of its inner broadness and its tendency toward what is foundational that this commandment was well-suited to make binding this aspect of Yahweh's will on His people across all times and their particular conditions."[81]

The term 'al-panay, rendered by Luther as "besides Me," means—taken literally—something that the person in question can see; to put oneself or something before somebody's face; or, respectively, to let pass by either in an adversarial or in an amicable sense so that another person can or must see it.[82] Originally, the images of the idols facing the ark of Yahweh might have been in mind. As this "existing in the presence of . . ." takes place, the coram-dimension of our human existence in its relation to God is revealed to reflective theology.[83] We lead our lives "facing" the zealous holy God whose eyes penetrate the abysses of our heart that are hidden to us.[84]

Following the mnemonic texts of the Middle Ages, Luther skips the prohibition of images. To be sure, this hardly corresponds to the original wording of the Ten Commandments, but it has some support in the text that has come down to us. After all, in the latter "the prohibition of images has come to be overshadowed by the prohibition of alien gods and has lost the dignity of a separate commandment."[85] By means of a plural suffix, the words "Do not prostrate before them and do not serve them" are added to the prohibition of images, which goes beyond the singular graven image to the alien gods of the First Commandment. Likewise, the priestly instruction "neither of what is up in heaven nor below on earth nor in the waters beneath the earth" marks out the provenance of the possible idols. Walther Zimmerli has investigated the phrase "to prostrate oneself and serve." Neither an image nor Yahweh appears as its object. It is always referring to "alien gods" who are specified here and there as, for example, the gods of the Canaanites, Baal, the heavenly host, as well as the sun, moon, and stars. The exhortation "You shall not prostrate before them and serve them" thus takes us back to the prohibition of idolatry.[86]

This is confirmed by the word of curse and blessing for which the prohibition of images seemingly offers the reason (Exod. 20:5f.). Like the preamble to the entire Decalogue, this curse and blessing also is a self-predication of Yahweh, admittedly in the form of a sermonlike parenesis. It refers to Yahweh's zeal for His covenant people to preserve them from falling away to

81   Von Rad, Theologie des Alten Testaments, 1:203.
82   According to Knierim, "Das erste Gebot," 203.
83   See Ebeling, Luther, 219–38. On Deuteronomy, see Lohfink, Das Hauptgebot, 271–85.
84   Cf. Rom. 2:16; 1 Cor. 4:5; 2 Cor. 5:10; and Calvin, Inst. 2:8.16.
85   Zimmerli, "Das zweite Gebot," 242.
86   Zimmerli, "Das zweite Gebot," 236–38.

alien gods. Rolf Knierim supports Zimmerli's observations by asserting that the prohibition of foreign gods grew out of the core vow of the amphictyony at Shechem. It pushed the older prohibition of images back to second place. The vow to serve Yahweh only corresponded to the renunciation of all alien gods.[87] Thus the prohibition of images was included in the prohibition of alien gods; both were comprehended by Yahweh's zeal for His people. "The entire history of Israel's worship" thereby becomes "a single battle for the First Commandment."[88]

Yahweh's zealous holiness has been evident since the time in the desert.[89] It grows out of the physical taboo-zone of the holy that takes the offensive, penetrates, and seeks to integrate what is profane.[90] Yahweh's zealous holiness is understood in a more personal way than in the other religions of the Near East.[91] Yahweh finds His glory in historical acts; He hallows Himself in His history with His people.[92] The land is to be filled with His blessing power.[93]

The prohibition of alien gods is no cultic axiom, much less is it an intellectual one. Because Yahweh time and again proves Himself to be Israel's God and Lord, this is why Israel shall and may turn to Him time and again. In this, the First Commandment opens up increasingly broad horizons. In the ongoing process of updating it by the prophets, it reaches from the cultic realm into social and political life. The expectant trust in Yahweh's miraculous action fends off the idolization of earthly means of power and resists a trust in military armament and political alliances.[94]

The First Commandment continually updates the carrying out of rejection and promise, of renunciation and confession, all the way into the baptismal act of Christendom. Behind both stands the loving zeal of God, who wants His covenant people for Himself only[95] and who woos the apostate and resistant people with the intensity of holy love.[96] This is why His zeal

---

87   Josh. 24:17f.; 22:22; 1 Kings 18:39; Gen. 35:1ff.

88   Von Rad, *Theologie des Alten Testaments*, 1:209; see also the discussion in Smend, *Die Mitte des Alten Testaments*, 44ff.

89   For an alternate reading, see John W. Kleinig, *Leviticus*, Concordia Commentary (St. Louis: Concordia, 2001). For the LCMS position, see the publisher's introduction, pp. 10–11.

90   Cf. Otto, *Das Heilige*; Friedrich Horst, "Heilig und profan im AT und Judentum," *RGG* 3:148–51.

91   Cf. von Rad, *Theologie des Alten Testaments*, 1:205.

92   On Yahweh's self-glorification and self-sanctification, cf., e.g., Exod. 14:4f., 7; Num. 20:13; Lev. 10:3; Ezek. 20:41; 28:22, 25; 38:16, 23.

93   Isa. 6:3–5.

94   Cf., e.g., Isa. 7:9; 30:1–3; 31:1–9; Ps. 20:8.

95   Deut. 18:13.

96   Hosea 11:9.

is at the same time both zeal of wrath[97] and zeal of salvation.[98] Here wrath breaks out for the sake of blessing and salvation.[99]

The word of curse and blessing unfolds the two sides of this holy zeal of love. First, Yahweh predicates Himself as the "strong zealot."[100] In the parallel texts,[101] the Lord struggles in this wrathful zeal of love to turn His covenant people away from the alien gods: "You shall not prostrate yourself before any other god, for Yahweh is called 'zealous.' He is a zealous God" (Exod. 34:14). "As if He was to say: This is the greatest summary. Let go of your idolatry; you have to change and get better; you cannot and may not pass by; you have to desist fully from idolatry and all godless plans, for God does not desist from His zeal. I do not know any harsher word or text in the Bible than this one, that God is a consuming fire."[102]

This foundational confession of God as the "strong zealot" is first specified on the side of His wrath. For this, as Leonhard Rost[103] has made probable, an old formula might have been used at the court of law in the gate. It exhorted the judicial community to execute the ban in the case of a guilty member. That ban affected the three or four generations that lived together as an extended family. The Lord Himself demanded and executed that holy ban: "Yahweh punishes the sons and grandsons for the guilt of the fathers to the third and fourth generation" (Exod. 34:17; Num. 14:18). This formula is here taken out of its original place in life, the court in the gate, and it is integrated into the doxology. At the same time, it is supported and exalted by the confession of Yahweh's loving care and faithful mercy. In hymnic praise, the "exuberant measure of Yahweh's grace is to be emphasized over against the relatively short-lived wrath."[104] The almost pedantic definitions—"namely, on those who hate Me," I will pour out My wrath, but "to those who love Me and keep My commandments" I will show My grace—probably were not meant to weaken the traditional understanding of a collective responsibility

97 Zeph. 1:18; Nah. 1:2; Ps. 79:5.
98 Isa. 9:6; Ezek. 39:25; Joel 2:18; Zech. 1:14; 2 Kings 19:31. God's saving zeal is often considered to be the center of the Old Testament; cf. the texts assembled by Smend, *Die Mitte des Alten Testaments*, 34–38.
99 "Dtn.-Vorl., 1523/24," WA 14:596.4 (see also AE 9:1–311): "Zeal relates to love. Zeal is the envy of love."
100 *BSLK*, 567.4. Cf. on Exod. 34:14, "Pred. über Ex. 20," WA 16:466.4, 448.21ff.
101 Exod. 34:14; Deut. 4:24; 6:14f.; Josh. 24:19.
102 "Pred. über Dtn. 4 vom 20.6.1529," WA 28:562.12. Cf. "Pred. über Dtn. 4 vom 20.6, 27.6, 1.8.1529," WA 28:557–68, 581–88; "Dtn.-Vorl., 1523/24," WA 14:596.2 (see also AE 9:1–311): "God is a zealot, zeal is envy, zealous is envious; it is hatred, envy. We have translated it as zeal, but it is new word. Zeal is envy when I love something in such a way that I cannot endure its being damaged."
103 Rost, "Die Schuld der Väter," 229–33.
104 Von Reventlow, *Gebot und Predigt im Dekalog*, 37f.

but only wished to relate once more wrath and grace to Israel's *no* and *yes* to Yahweh.[105]

The word of threat and blessing unfolds in the form of a doxological parenesis of Yahweh's zeal for His sovereignty over His covenant people. Thereby it again integrates the prohibition of images into the prohibition to worship alien gods and lets both commandments grow out of the self-predication of the preamble that bears the character of an epiphany.

CHARACTERISTICS OF LUTHER'S INTERPRETATION

Like no interpreter before him, Luther placed the First Commandment above all other commandments. In fact, in the First Commandment he saw God's entire acting on humanity focused like light in a concave mirror. Thus our interpretation could and should make the First Commandment become recognizable as the center of Luther's theology.[106] However, this would go beyond this commentary. We have to focus on the catechisms and can only offer some outlook on Luther's total understanding of the commandment.

In the catechisms, the reformer consciously enters into the holy zeal of the covenant God for His covenant people and broadens it to include the zeal of the Creator for the obedience of His rational creatures. "For He extirpated all idolatry from the beginning and overthrows for its sake both heathen and Jews, as well as today all false worship, so that finally all who remain in it must perish."[107] This zeal of God for man lasts from the beginning of the human race to the end of the world. It is the core signature of the history of the nations and of the world. In this sense it is true that not only the history of Israel's religious and social institutions but also world history itself is to be seen as the wrestling of faith with unbelief for the validity of the First Commandment. "Out of this commandment flows all the doctrine of the prophets and psalms as out of a spring and fountain, likewise all curses, threats, and all promises."[108] In Luther's interpretation of the commandment in the Large Catechism, this insight is only sketched in outline and explained primarily from its anthropological-existential side.

---

105   Cf. von Reventlow, *Gebot und Predigt im Dekalog*, 37f.
106   This has been stated repeatedly in the literature on the First Commandment mentioned at the beginning.
107   *BSLK*, 568.24.
108   "Pred. über Dtn. 5 vom 15.8.1529," WA 28:601.21.

1. TURNING AWAY FROM THE CREATED FORCES— TURNING TO THE CREATOR

The scope of the First Commandment—"You shall keep Me alone for your God"[109]—is expounded by Luther by combining existential analysis and preaching. The existential analysis takes as a point of departure the question "What does it mean to have a god?"[110] The famous answer to this question reads: "On that which you now . . . set your heart to rely, that is really your god."[111] "The trust and faith of the heart makes both God and idol. . . . For these two belong together: faith and god."[112] The existential formulae have been received in modern theology especially by Ludwig Feuerbach, who explicitly refers to Luther.[113] According to Feuerbach,[114] the reformer opened the path from theology to anthropology by turning his eyes from the God by Himself to the God for us. This is how Luther made possible the apotheosis of man and started what cultural Protestantism perfected, namely, to turn "men from theologians into anthropologists, from theophiles into philanthropists, from candidates of the next world into students of this world."[115]

However, with these controversial phrases of the Large Catechism, Luther does not want to deduce the existence of God from the trusting faith of man; rather, he wants to guide the simple hearers of his sermons and readers of his catechism to the concrete "situation of understanding God's speaking."[116] To achieve this, Luther makes reflective the faith relationship of our humanity. The entire inner and outer existence of man is combined in the act of that trust: "To have a god means to have something on which

---

109 *BSLK*, 560.7.

110 *BSLK*, 560.9.

111 *BSLK*, 560.22.

112 *BSLK*, 560.16, 560.21. "Instructio pro confessione peccatorum, 1518," WA 1:258.4: "To have a god is to have someone from whom you trust to receive help in all bad things and being fostered in all good things. Since no one but the one true God can do this, it is also to be expected from no one else." "Dtn.-Vorl., 1523/24," WA 14:648.16 (see also AE 9:1–311): "For as is your conscience, such is God." "Kat.-Pred. zum 1. Gebot vom 14.9.1528," WA 30.1:28.2: "Trusting and believing makes God. If faith, trust in God, is right then God, too, is right." "Jes.-Vorl., 1527/30," WA 31.2:346.10: "We see God through our nature as through some tinted glass; however our thinking goes, as such we see God." "Ausl. v. Mt. 5–7, 1530/32," WA 32:456.12 (see also AE 21:1–294): "This is why also St. Augustine says: *Deus meus amor meus*; what I love, that is my god." "Ausl. v. Joh. 14f., 1537/38," WA 45:478.4 (see also AE 24:1–422): "Whatever now concerns such and similar idolatry, one sees here that these two, trust and god, belong together. Where there is a heart that comforts itself by something and relies on it, that is certainly its god, even if it is a false god."

113 Feuerbach's recourse to Luther is described by Barth, *Die protestantische Theologie im 19. Jahrhundert*, § 18, 486ff.; cf. Ebeling, *Luther*, 288–300; Hans-Martin Barth, "Glaube als Projektion."

114 Feuerbach, *Werke*, 7:311ff.

115 Feuerbach, "Vorl. über das Wesen d. Religion," in *Werke*, 8:28f.

116 Ebeling, *Luther*, 293; cf. Ebeling, *Gott und Wort*, 57, 61ff.

the heart fully relies."[117] "What man loves, that is his god, for his heart carries him to it, deals with it by day and night, sleeps and wakes with it—be it money or goods, lust or honor, etc."[118] The little word "god" does not simply want to be labeled as something envisioned by humans; rather, it wants to signify the central teleological goal of our concrete existence.[119]

Luther does not shrink back from saying that each genuinely human situation circles around the mystery of that "basic situation" and always practices it with whatever distortions and contortions there may be. For, indeed, "really to have a god, also according to every heathen opinion," means to "trust and believe."[120] Within these suggestive clues of the Large Catechism resonates the insight that moves even closer to Feuerbach, namely, that faith is "creator of the godhead in us": *Fides est creatrix divinitatis, non in persona, sed in nobis.*[121] In true faith the eternal Creator God receives the divinity that is due Him. In false belief a created entity, be it something tangible in the world or something supernatural and demonic, is loaded up with *doxa*. Part of being human is looking for help and salvation; part of being human is praising and exalting because our being human cannot stand by itself.[122] Luther merely hints fleetingly at this deep structure of human nature in the Large Catechism.

All anthropological-existential analyses are comprehended by tirelessly pointing to the zeal of the Creator for His creatures. Here the reformer does bear witness to the absolute "irreversibility of the relation to God."[123] We cannot create or beget God by means of our trusting and believing, our praising and glorifying, because God's entire acting as Creator, Redeemer, and Consummator precedes all our presence in acknowledging trust and praising glorification. For Luther, it is not we who project the powerful mirror image

---

117   *BSLK*, 562.2.

118   "Auls. v. Mt. 5–7, 1530/32," WA 32:444.29 (see also AE 21:1–294).

119   Schott, "Luthers Verständnis des ersten Gebots," 201: "In Luther, God is the whereto of trust (560.22ff.); in Schleiermacher, God is the wherefrom of the utter dependence (*Glaubensl.* 4.4)."

120   *BSLK*, 564.19.

121   "Gal.-Komm., 1535," WA 40.1:360.5 (see also AE 26:1–461); *BSLK*, 560.16: "The trusting and believing of the heart *makes* both God and idol."

122   Westermann, *Das Loben Gottes in den Psalmen*, 122: "Part of existence is exalting. It is part of it so much so that, when one has ceased to exalt God, something else must be exalted. . . . This is exactly what world history shows: men must exalt something; without exalting, existence is apparently impossible."

123   Against Barth, *Die protestantische Theologie im 19. Jahrhundert*, 488; see also "Vermahnung zum Sakrament des Leibes und Blutes unseres Herrn, 1530," WA 30.2:602.39 (see also AE 38:91–137): "If you now want to be a God-maker, come here, listen; He will teach you this art that you may not fail and make not an idol, but the true God to be the true God; not that you should make His divine nature, for it remains unmade forever. But that you can make Him God for you so that He may become a true God for you, you, you, as He is a true God for Himself." Furthermore, "Pred. über Dtn. 7 vom 31.10, 7.11, 21.11.1429," WA 28:679–713.

of our broken human existence onto the infinite nothingness of eternity, but the zealous, holy watch of the Creator over His fallen creature proves effective even in the most abominable perversions of idolatry.

The chain or stepladder of idolatry, which Luther unfolds in a dual line of attack, summarizes briefly what the late medieval confessional booklets and Luther's 1518 "Decem praecepta Wittenbergensi praedicata populo" ("Preaching of the Ten Commandments") offer in greater detail.[124] This stepladder does not have any weight in itself; using "common examples of opposition,"[125] it merely makes manifest the meaning of "Trusting and believing alone make both God and idol."[126] Characteristic of those deformations is the self-centered will of man. Tirelessly, we turn away from the true Creator God and gawk[127] here and there, wherever the shifting hubris of the heart leads us.[128]

The first explanation[129] sets out from material valuables, money and goods, from the god Mammon, the "most common idol" and almighty lord of this "filthy, deadly realm of the belly."[130] It transitions to the personal gifts of artistic skill, intelligence, and power that set a human being apart from others, as well as to the interpersonal honors that are bestowed on an individual by others.[131] It concludes with the veneration of saints as well as satanic covenants,[132] both of which already go beyond what is inner-worldly and interpersonal.[133] By this hanging on to what is material and tangible, interpersonal and personal, as well as holy or demonic, the reformer tirelessly

---

124 "Decem praecepta, 1518," WA 1:401–30. See also the brief summaries in "Eine kurze Erklärung"; "Instructio, 1518," WA 1:252, 259f.; and "Eine kurze Form, 1520," WA 7:207f. Here, Luther summarizes the catalogs of transgressions from the medieval confessional mirrors. Cf. Thomas Aquinas, *Duo praecepta* §§ 1194–97; Gerson/Geiler, *Opusc. tripartitum*, in Geffcken, *Bildercatechismus*, app., col. 37f.; *Spiegel d. Sünders*, in Geffcken, *Bildercatechismus*, app., col. 51–53; *Spiegel d. Christen-Glaubens*, Geffcken, *Bildercatechismus*, app., col. 91–93; and the overview in Geffcken, *Bildercatechismus*, 54–56, as well as Weidenhiller, *Untersuchungen*, 46, 68f., 112f., 150, 182f., 229ff.

125 *BSLK*, 561.8.

126 *BSLK*, 560.16.

127 *BSLK*, 564.23.

128 *BSLK*, 564.9.

129 *BSLK*, 561.7–562.38.

130 "Ausl. v. Mt. 5–7, 1530/32," WA 32:467.24 (see also AE 21:1–294). Cf. WA 32:436–72 (see also AE 21:1–294) for Luther's interpretation of Matt. 6:18–34; Mülhaupt, *Evangelien-Auslegung*, 2:162–92.

131 *BSLK*, 561.39–562.9. "Instructio, 1518," WA 1:260.11: ". . . who flatter themselves and take pride in their justice, wisdom, or any other virtue or goodness of theirs."

132 *BSLK*, 562.10–38.

133 On the veneration of the saints, cf. *BSLK*, 83b–83d (AC XXI), 316.45–328.36 (Ap XXI), 424.10–425.25 (SA II II), as well as Lackmann, "Thesaurus sanctorum"; Pinomaa, "Die Heiligen in Luthers Frühtheologie"; "Luthers Weg zur Verwerfung des Heiligendienstes."

turns the eye toward the attitude of the heart: on what man bases the heart and core of his existence, that is his god.

God's First Commandment, however, confiscates this center of our entire human nature for itself. God, as our Creator, calls our heart out of clinging to what is created and demands it for itself in an exclusive and undivided way. Here the First Commandment and the Creed interlock.[134] The rejection of creatures transitions into commitment to the Creator: "I ponder and put my trust alone in the bare, invisible, incomprehensible, only God who created heaven and earth and alone is above all creatures."[135]

In the second explanation of "having God,"[136] Luther remembers the heathen who "made their self-concocted thinking and dreaming of God into an idol and trust in absolutely nothing."[137] They still belong to the first step in that they do not direct their trust toward the one true Creator God.[138] The false worship of man, however, only turns into the highest idolatry[139] where it turns to the true God Himself, thus in the midst of the Christian Church. Here men approach the one true God, but they do so in a wrong way. By approaching Him in a superficial, corporeal form of worship and dedication, they do not offer to Him the trusting heart but hold it back, tightly bound to the act of building on their self-chosen righteousness.[140] They do not seek help and refuge with Him; they achieve the certainty of their being right before Him from their own actions.[141] In this way and in view of the living God, they turn on its head the basic order that Luther tirelessly emphasized. They separate God from their trust. For themselves they claim the giving righteousness of the feudal lord and make God into their vassal.[142] "The beggar comes here to the mighty king and begs thusly, that he does not want to take the alms for free but wants to give him some four pennies or lice in return."[143] This is nothing other than "worshiping God outwardly, but

---

134 Cf. the commentary on the Creed.

135 "Eine kurze Form, 1520," WA 7:216.1.

136 *BSLK*, 563.28–565.24.

137 *BSLK*, 564.16. Cf. Vossberg, *Luthers Kritik aller Religion*; Holsten, *Christentum und nichtchristliche Religionen nach der Auffassung Luthers*.

138 *BSLK*, 564.1–39.

139 *BSLK*, 564.40–565.24.

140 "Pred. über Dtn. 5 vom 15.8.1529," WA 28:599.11: "Thus every made-up worship has the addition, muck, and mire hanging on it that man trusts in it. This is why they are all against the First Commandment, which teaches to fear, love, and trust in God alone."

141 "Kat.-Pred. zum 1. Gebot vom 18.5.1528," WA 30.1:3.29: "Therefore all religions sin against the First Commandment since where they ought to give thanks to God, there they themselves wish to receive praise. Thus they totally turn the commandment of God upside down."

142 *BSLK*, 565.9f.

143 "Pred. über Dtn. 4 vom 27.6.1529," WA 28:568.23.

inwardly setting oneself up as an idol."¹⁴⁴ The idolaters at least still looked among the created nobodies for what is to be entreated from the living God, namely, refuge, help, and comfort. Here the pious person, in view of the God who alone gives life, locks himself up in self-reliance. This is how in the very midst of Christendom the original sin of the old man erupts. He wants to sit in the stead of his Creator and Lord because he cannot leave God's Godhead in peace. "By nature, man cannot will God to be God; in fact, he wants himself to be God and God not to be God."¹⁴⁵

These brief hints summarize Luther's rejection of the scholastic doctrine of merit. They go beyond the horizon of the catechisms, since the danger in view here can first emerge where people day by day and night by night labor for obedience to God, but not where young people begin to grow into the love of the Commandments by means of a first instruction. The need in view here is the problem of the monks and thinking Christians, not that of peasants and young students. Luther says about this, "This is a little too sharp."¹⁴⁶ Does he indicate thereby that he has interpreted the statements of the late medieval theologians in a one-sided manner? The theses of the "schoolmen" are compiled in the Smalcald Articles.¹⁴⁷ In the interpretation of those sayings, Luther removes from view all that had been said about the prevenient, concurrent, and subsequent "grace of Christ the Head." At the same time, those texts gain for him a totally new importance as he transfers them out of the sapient-descriptive horizon of scholastic distinctions into the existential-confessional context of sermonlike instruction in the faith. Thus, by necessity, the question emerges of how one should interpret especially the words about the works and merits of the believers.¹⁴⁸ Now, they really cannot or will not guide believers, as they serve God in the free dedication of love, to withdraw themselves from God in their hearts and to approach Him by insistently trusting in their own works, will they?¹⁴⁹ The reformer, by seeing the core commandment of undivided fear and love of

---

144 "Von den guten Werken, 1520," WA 6:211.28 (see also AE 44:15–114). The phrase in *BSLK*, 565.9ff., appears in Luther often in similar form: "Decem praecepta, 1518," WA 1:399.18: "This means to worship God in the body and in the flesh, but within to worship the creature in spirit." "Kat.-Pred. zum 1. Gebot vom 18.5.1528," WA 30.1:3.26: ". . . because here I want to be my own god, that is, I do not want to have a God, but an idol and fool."

145 "Disp. contra scholast. theol., 1517," thesis 17, WA 1:225 (see also AE 31:3–16). Cf. "Disp. pro doctoratu Weller et Medler, 1535," thesis 71, WA 39.1:48 (see also AE 34:105–32): "Therefore as it is blasphemy to say one is one's own God, Creator, and Father, so it is blasphemy to be justified by one's own works."

146 *BSLK*, 565.15.

147 See *BSLK*, 434.13–435.8.

148 Cf. Pesch, "Die Lehre vom 'Verdienst' als Problem für Theologie und Verkündigung"; "Pöhlmann, *Rechtfertigung*, 193–214; Fagerberg, *Theologie der lutherischen Bekenntnisschriften*, 130–68.

149 This is how Luther sees it; cf. *BSLK*, 565.3–11.

God applied also to the obedience of the Christians, uncovers particularly in "pious" works the old man marked by self-righteous self-will and work-enamored self-confidence. The First Commandment penetrates all the way to the deeply covered sin of the pious, to that withdrawal of the trusting, believing center of the heart out of the undivided dedication to God.

The reformer merely hints at these deep relations vis-à-vis the "simple."[150] He guides them primarily on the path away from the idolization of creatures to the trust in the Creator. Hereby the realm of what is to be sought from God is indirectly implied rather than thematically elaborated. First, Luther simply says, What we previously sought from Mammon, from ourselves or other people, from the saints or demonic forces, namely, to be rid of misfortune and to obtain what is good—this we are now to seek from the One who is "the one eternal Good."[151] Our seeking here seemingly does not gain any new content. At stake are the simple things of daily life, the concrete life, as the First Article and the Fourth Petition will circumscribe it more carefully.[152]

The reformer summarizes this in the popular etymology: God = good.[153] God is the inexhaustible primal wellspring of all goods.[154] "We Germans have given God a fitting name, as have the Danes, 'Good,' because from Him comes nothing but that which is good. On the other hand, we do not give and are unable to do so since we are neither good nor gods."[155] The relationship to this God, from whom alone "one receives all good things and is delivered from all evil,"[156] is defined in a strictly personal manner. Here Luther urges the inner attitude of the heart. No less is at stake than universal aid and

---

150   *BSLK*, 565.25.

151   *BSLK*, 563.13.

152   The members of the chain in *BSLK*, 565.29–32 are taken up there. Cf. the commentary on the First Article of the Creed and the Fourth Petition of the Lord's Prayer.

153   Cf. *BSLK*, 565 n. 6, and "Aliquod nomina propria Germanorum ad priscam etymologiam restituta, 1537," WA 50:150.12–18; "Pred. über Dtn. 6 vom 29.8.1529," WA 28:621.19–26, 617.26–33; "Ausl. d. ersten 25 Psalmen,1530," WA 31.1:325.29.

154   *BSLK*, 565.36–566.2. Cf. *BSLK*, 560.36–41, 563.16–18, 566.49–567.3. "Op. in Ps., 1518–21," WA 5:602.15: "However, God is life, light, wisdom, truth, righteousness, goodness, power, joy, glory, peace, happiness, and every good thing." Thomas Aquinas, *Duo praecepta* § 1200: "And this is conveyed by this name God, that it is said after distribution, that is, giver of things, because He fills everything with His goodness."

155   "Kat.-Pred. zum 1. Gebot vom 18.5.1528," WA 30.1:3.32.

156   *BSLK*, 565.35.

ultimate comfort.[157] In this earthly help is active the eternal God Himself, who lifts up our eyes from what is earthly to what is heavenly.[158]

2. CERTAINTY OF THE UNIVERSAL RULE OF THE CREATOR AND PROPER RECEPTION OF HIS GIFTS IN OBEDIENCE TO THE COMMANDMENTS

Faith goes beyond the earthly gifts of the Creator and takes shelter in the devotion afforded by the transcendent God Himself. However, in doing so it does not drop the Creator's blessing, since it is the bodily sign of God's promise of grace. Yet God's blessing in creation discloses itself only in the antagonism between daily experience and believing trust. This antagonism is not "objectively" solvable. Our human observation and experience must stand the test in the tension between God and Satan. One has to sustain faith's confidence in God's goodness in creation and His powerful blessing against the superficial appearance of the opposite. In this, Luther turns our attention to God's zeal for His sovereignty over all men and focuses narrowly on the problem of our being certain of God.

In "Sermon von den guten Werken" ("Sermon on Good Works"), Luther targeted the First Commandment as the center of the Reformation's certainty of faith. He demanded that this certainty regarding God's gracious promise not only should be maintained in the daily life on earth with its small cares and deep suffering but also should not be surrendered in the extreme satanic afflictions of doubt at life's end: "Above everything else concerning faith is that of the first order, when God does not punish consciences with temporal suffering, but with death, hell, and sin, and withdraws grace and mercy, as if He wanted to damn and be angry eternally, which is something few men experience. . . . To believe here that God in His grace is well pleased with us, this is the highest work that can take place by and in a creature."[159] Since only few individuals have to endure these struggles, Luther did not touch on them in the catechisms. In the catechisms, it is not God against God; here, it is God against Satan.

---

157 See the multitude of phrases: help and comfort (*BSLK*, 564.23); comfort and confidence (*BSLK*, 563.31); help, comfort, and blessedness (*BSLK*, 565.2); good things and help (*BSLK*, 567.5); good things, help, and comfort (*BSLK*, 563.41); faith and confidence of the heart (*BSLK*, 560.31); a hearty confidence of all good things (*BSLK*, 571.44); God's fear and trust (*BSLK*, 643.10); fear, love, and trust (*BSLK*, 643.38).

158 Cf. *BSLK*, 571.40–572.22. Luther takes these insights up in his elaborations on the arrangement of the Lord's Prayer.

159 "Von den guten Werken, 1520," WA 6:208.34 (see also AE 44:15–114). "Eine kurze Form, 1520," WA 7:216.8: "I do not believe any less, though I am a sinner. For this my faith shall and must hover above all that there is and is not, above sin and virtue and above everything, so that it may keep itself pure and unpolluted, as the First Commandment urges me."

In view of the First Commandment, Luther demands in the third explanation[160] and in the two interpretations of the word of threat and promise[161]
a threefold certainty: (1) We should believe, know, and acknowledge that
the Creator God, being zealous for His First Commandment, rages through
the history of the nations and individuals like a windstorm to wipe out all
self-aggrandizement and idolization of creatures. (2) We should believe,
know, and acknowledge that our life is well-pleasing to God only if we obey
His Commandments with heart and body in the estate and calling in which
He has placed us. (3) We should believe, know, and acknowledge that we
receive the good out of His hand rightly only if we accept it according to
His command and order by means of the cooperation of His creatures. In
these three items the direction of impact of the interpretation of the First
Commandment becomes concrete: turning away from trusting in creatures
and turning to the Creator. Our heart should not "gawk elsewhere,"[162] not
"make [its own] made-up thoughts and dreams of God into an idol,"[163] not
"presumptuously seek other manner and ways . . . than the ones God has
commanded,"[164] not think up "sundry special time, place, manner, and
gesture"[165] to serve God according to its own mind.[166] In these different relations and dimensions we can receive sure certainty only by means of God's
Word. The reformer unrelentingly demands this certainty.

Luther's attack on every form of self-righteousness before God throws
the hitherto naïve, precritical participation in the Christian ethos into tur-
moil. The question of certainty becomes consciously raised; the retreat of
our existence to the Word of God receives critical reflection. In this, it is
thinking insight, the quest for certain conclusions and consistent argumentation, that affords important help. Critical reason is not eliminated; rather,
it is at work in super-lucid consciousness.[167] Listening to Scripture, reflect-
ing on our experience in the world, and concluding insight interlock in all
three directions of thought.

---

160 *BSLK*, 566.12–43.
161 *BSLK*, 568.8–571.39, 639.11–641.37.
162 *BSLK*, 564.22.
163 *BSLK*, 564.16.
164 *BSLK*, 566.33.
165 *BSLK*, 639.33.
166 "Dtn.-Vorl., 1523/24," WA 14:648.13 (see also AE 9:1–311): "We have often said, and say again, that 'other gods' not only denotes that external idol but also much more the erroneous opinion or conscience contrived concerning the true God. However conscience is, such is God." Cf. "Pred. über Dtn. 5f. vom 29.8.1529," WA 28:609.25–614.20.
167 On reason's relationship to faith according to Luther, see Gerrish, *Grace and Reason*; Häg-glund, *Theologie und Philosophie bei Luther und in der occamistischen Tradition*; Lohse, *Ratio und Fides*; Joest, *Ontologie der Person bei Luther*.

1. The God who shows zeal for His sovereign Law proves Himself to be the Lord of history. He has "completely wiped out all idolatry from the beginning . . . and for its sake overthrown heathen and Jews, as well as all false worship today, so that finally all who remain therein must perish."[168] The witness of Scripture, the experiential wisdom of the nations, and the observations of reflective man himself are here together called to the witness stand.[169] Scripture confirms this from its first to its last page, because it is nothing else than a number of episodes of that watching of God over His First Commandment. Out of these, Luther picks the antagonism between Saul and David as an example.[170] Besides this first and decisive witness, there is the experience of humankind, of which "histories and stories"[171] represent a distillate.[172] As a third witness, Luther adds the wisdom of "old, experienced people"[173] and calls upon the reader to make his own observations.[174] The history of the world as well as the fate of the individual is revealed in the bright light of the Word of God. God's zeal for His sovereign Law can be demonstrated in very impressive examples. They are concentrated in the proverbial wisdom of the nations and have put the stamp of those typical traits on the historical accounts.[175]

On the other hand, the reformer as a perceptive reader of the Psalms and observer of the ways of the world knows that the calculations do not simply arrive at the answer. God's ways in the world are not always clearly seen; rather, God's acting in the world participates in the cross of Christ.[176] Those hints at God's sovereign acting for the good of the just are countered by experiences of God's silence and waiting:[177] "In the world's perception, it appears as if God were a complete dolt who only stands there with his mouth gaping or a cuckold, a good man who lets another sleep with his wife and

168   BSLK, 568.24.
169   BSLK, 568.21–24. See also, for example, "Kat.-Pred. zum 1. Gebot vom 14.9.1528," WA 30.1:28:32–35; and "Dtn. Predigten, 1529," WA 28:560.17–29, 562.12–16, 566.30–34, 573.11–21, 581.21–584.30, 638.10–19, 698.25–699.32.
170   BSLK, 571.7–17. Cf. "Kat.-Pred. zum 1. Gebot vom 14.9.1528," WA 30.1:29.16–22; "Pred. über Ex. 20 vom 1.10.1525," WA 16:448.21–449.10.
171   BSLK, 568.21.
172   Cf. "Dtn. Predigten, 1529," WA 28:562.17–33, 642.9–644.22, 680.18–681.16, 686.20–688.24, 699.16–29, 707.26–711.29.
173   BSLK, 571.5.
174   BSLK, 570.45ff.
175   Cf. von Rad, Weisheit in Israel, 229–39; "Der Anfang der Geschichtsschreibung"; "Die deuteronomistische Geschichtstheologie."
176   Cf. Bandt, Luthers Lehre vom verborgenen Gott.
177   BSLK, 570.17–30.

pretends he does not see it."[178] Seduced by satanic blinding,[179] the worldly person rejects God's word of threat and promise.[180] He says, "Do you think there's still a real manly man within this old boy?"[181] The believer will, on the contrary, cling to God's promise and overcome the "appearance"[182] of the rule of the world and of Satan in perseverance against all external enmity and internal affliction until God's Word will prove true. In the inner wrestling with the worldly people all around him, just as much as in his own heart, he pawns his own existence.[183]

In these constantly repeated calls and deliberations, the reformer shows that reason's duty to know and understand our human condition cannot be divorced from existence before God, from God's eschatological zeal for His right concerning His creatures struggling against the forces of death. Following Scripture's words of threat and blessing, our understanding feels its way into the darkness of history and is able to perceive something of God's intervention, insofar as it presses on through the superficial appearance of satanic seduction to believing trust.[184] These insights are based on concrete experiences; in their superficial aspects, they can be formed into manageable sayings, as the wisdom of all nations confirms. Yet they cannot be lifted out of the floods of affliction like a protected possession. Hegel's endeavor to comprehend, as it were, and stabilize daring trust by means of discerning insight must always fail.[185] As long as we do battle here on earth, these insights remain on the battlefield between faith and doubt, trust and affliction, God and idol. To be sure, the believer sees God's threats and promises come true quite manifestly already in this world. Yet history still does not fully add up, which is why we are instructed to rush in believing hope through life and death toward the final establishment of God's kingdom.

2. God, our gracious Creator and good Giver of blessings, is close to us under the masks (*larvae*) of His creatures and institutions in nature and history. The entire interpretation of the Decalogue looks tirelessly to God's

---

178 "Pred. über Dtn. 4 vom 20.6.1529," WA 28.559.16. Cf. also, e.g., "Ausl. v. Mt. 5–7, 1530/32," WA 32:315.12–26 (see also AE 21:1–294); and "In quindecim psalmos graduum commentarii, 1532/33," WA 40.3:144.34–145.30.

179 *BSLK*, 571.19ff.

180 "Pred. über Dtn. 4 vom 20.6.1529," WA 28:560.10: ". . . consider also our Lord God to be no more than a straw man that is set up in the hemp to scare away the birds. But when He will come at His time and turn everything into powder and ashes, then they will see."

181 "Ausl. v. Ps 101, 1534/35," WA 51:236.34 (see also AE 13:143–224).

182 *BSLK*, 570.28, 571.20.

183 *BSLK*, 622.49: "If this works out for you and you do well, then you should call God and me a liar before the whole world."

184 Cf. also Krumwiede, *Glaube und Geschichte in der Theologie Luthers*, and Zahrnt, *Luther deutet Geschichte*.

185 See Wittram, "Möglichkeiten und Grenzen der Geschichtswissenschaft."

creative commanding as well as commanding creating.[186] At the center is not the Redeemer God who saves us from the fall, but the Creator God who is near to us in our being as creatures even apart from the good news of our deliverance in Christ. After all, the "creatures [are] only the hands, pipes, and means through which God gives everything."[187] Luther here seems to point in the direction that Grundtvig classically expressed this way: "Man first, Christian thereafter."[188] Yet in light of the First Commandment, the salvific revelation here shines into humanity's original knowledge of God. The First Commandment tells the believer not only who this God is that meets him in blessing through the "hands, pipes, and means" of the creatures, but it also tells him how to behave appropriately before this Creator God. God is not merely a *causa prima*, some primal being that causes everything else. He approaches man in the Creator's glory of His blessing and commanding Word,[189] which is why even our creaturely relationship to the Creator is related to and permeated by the Word. This relation has three aspects: (a) God bestows on us the gifts of His blessing as a Creator directly and immediately in, with, and under the *larvae* of His creatures because He alone as the Creator is Lord over life and death. The creatures, to be sure, are *cooperatores*, but they are never *concreatores*, as Luther demonstrates in the First Article.[190] "It has to be baked and spun out of the First Commandment. If you are to have thread on your skin and a piece of bread in your mouth, the First Commandment has to give it to you, otherwise you will never get anything."[191] (b) At the same time, God has disclosed His acting as Creator to us in the Word and has integrated us, His reasonable creatures, into His creative orderings. As part of these "holy orders and true foundations"[192] of His, we have the commission to do good to our neighbor as God's cooperators. Out of these foundations and estates[193] protected by God Himself in the Commandments, the reformer here only mentions that of parents and

---

186 Cf. Gülhoff, *Gebieten und Schaffen*, and Surala, *Gottes Gebot bei M. Luther.*

187 *BSLK*, 566.20. "Fastenpost. zu Mt. 4:1–11, 1525," WA 17.2:192.28: "And in summary, all creatures are God's *larvae* and masks that He wishes to cooperate with Him and help Him to create many things that He can and does do without their cooperation so that we might hang on His Word alone."

188 Prenter, *Schöpfung und Erlösung*, 1:264 n. 94: "Man first and Christian thereafter, that is the main thing. We receive Christian faith for free. It is sheer luck, but a kind of luck that only strikes him who is basically already God's friend, from the noble stem of truth!" (according to Grundtvig).

189 On the blessing of the Creator, see "Gen.-Vorl. zu Gen. 27:24ff., 1535–45," WA 43:521–29 (see also AE 5:1–386).

190 Cf. the commentary on the First Article of the Creed.

191 "Pred. über Dtn. 7f. vom 28.11.1529," WA 28:722.20.

192 "Vom Abendmahl Christi, 1528," WA 26:504.30 (see also AE 37:151–372).

193 Cf. *BSLK*, 640.33f., 641.12.

"authorities"[194] comprehended in the Fourth Commandment and adds the "common order of Christian love"[195] that permeates all the commandments of the Second Table. We pass on His blessing as Creator in these divinely ordered foundations and estates. (c) Out of this grows the third aspect: We faithfully have to remain at the place where God has put us and must not think up self-designed estates; "remain in whatever condition the Gospel and His calling find you."[196] At this place we have to receive God's blessing in thanksgiving and in the ways prescribed by God and to pass it on in the manner commanded by Him.[197]

This threesome—God's blessing as Creator, God's foundations and callings, and God's Commandments—bestows on the Christian ethos a sacramental dimension, as it were. As the all-sovereign Redeemer reveals Himself for our salvation only under Word and Sacrament, so the omnipotent Creator wants to be found in His institutions and Commandments. Because these institutions and Commandments of His include the salvific mystery of the First Commandment, we, under the *larvae* of the creatures, not only take hold of the blessing hand of the Creator but also of the gracious hand of the Redeemer.[198] Whoever wants to approach God's blessing as Creator in an autonomous way falls under the judgment of the eternal wrath of God. In the horizon of creation, Luther touches on the certainty of Christian obedience: "Behold, as there is no one without order and calling, so there is no one without work, if he wants to do right. Everybody ought to take care to remain in his estate, mind his own business, carry out his orders, and serve God therein and keep His commandment. This is how he will get so much to do that all of time will be too short, all places too small, all powers too weak."[199]

3. The reformer underlines this interpretation of the Decalogue, as well as of the divine institutions protected by it, in the conclusion of the Decalogue's interpretation.[200] All of God's instructions are comprehended in the Decalogue; it is a "summary of divine doctrine,"[201] which is why "outside of the Ten Commandments no work or being can be good and pleasing to

---

194   *BSLK*, 566.16. Cf. the interpretation of the Fourth Commandment.

195   "Vom Abendmahl Christi, 1528," WA 26:505.11 (see also AE 37:151–372).

196   "Das 7. Kap. S. Pauli zu den Korinthern, 1523," WA 12:132.28 (see also AE 28:1–56). Regarding the interpretation of the word κλῆσις in 1 Cor. 7:17–20, see WA 12:126–33 (see also AE 28:1–56); "Weihnachtspost. zu Joh. 21:19–24, 1522," WA 10.1.1:305–24.

197   *BSLK*, 566.26–31.

198   "Ausl. v. Mt. 5–7, 1530/32," WA 32:491.38 (see also AE 21:1–294): ". . . that you may be certain that your faith, Gospel, and Christ is right and your estate pleases God." Cf. "Gen.-Vorl., 1535/45," WA 42:632.6–14 (see also AE 3:1–365).

199   "Weihnachtspost. zu Joh. 21:19–24, 1522," WA 10.1.1:309.14.

200   *BSLK*, 639.11–641.29, 645.30–52.

201   *BSLK*, 639.12.

God, however great and precious it may be in the world's view."[202] Every autonomous attempt to serve God in an immediate way is humbled under the "common daily housework one neighbor can do for the other."[203] The showy glitter of the priest as well as the much-admired devotion to prayer of the monk must give way to the despised service of a maidservant taking care of children. "The Ten Commandments justify the day to day of secular vocations lived in faith against the super-spirituality of monasticism and enthusiasm."[204] Only the Decalogue calls for the whole man and gives us the certainty of being pleasing to God because it leaves behind all self-chosen and autonomous service to God and thereby also all the uncertain, anxious works of self-justification.

The reformer, by tying all works of love in service of the neighbor back to the fear, love, and trust in the invisible Creator God, at the same time accentuates the certainty that we truly meet God in daily life.[205] Out of this grows, on the one hand, the demand that we perform our daily obedience in the Commandments alone for the sake of God's will and, on the other hand, the promise that we receive His blessing in our estates and callings through both the people assigned to us by God and also through nonhuman creatures. This is how the First Commandment as God's creative commanding and creating via blessing rises above all other commandments and permeates them as their "head and wellspring."[206] At the same time, the interpersonal orders that the commandments of the Second Table sanction and protect become stronger. Since we should not choose for ourselves our place in the estates and callings autonomously,[207] these gain a higher significance. God's good blessing as Creator and the zealous and holy eye of God the watcher rests on them. This obedience of ours is sustained by the recognition: "Cursed and damned is all life that is lived and sought for its own use and benefit; accursed all works that do not walk in love. For they walk in love, however, when they do not arise from one's own lust, use, honor, comfort, and salvation, but wholeheartedly arise on behalf of somebody else's use, honor, and salvation."[208]

---

202 *BSLK*, 639.16.

203 *BSLK*, 639.15.

204 Schott, "Luthers Verständnis des ersten Gebots," 203f.

205 "Von den guten Werken, 1520," WA 6:206.9 (see also AE 44:15–114): ". . . if he finds his heart in the confidence that it pleases God, the work is good, be it ever so insignificant as picking up a piece of straw. If the confidence is not there or in doubt, the work is not good, even if it raised all the dead and the man let himself be burned (Rom. 14:23)."

206 *BSLK*, 644.18.

207 By this, Luther does not wish to rule out, in principle, rising socially; cf. Elert, *Morphologie*, 2:71ff.

208 "Von weltlicher Oberkeit, 1523," WA 11:272.1 (see also AE 45:75–129).

3. Fear of God Out of His Threat of Punishment — Love of God Out of His Promise of Grace

In this vein of thought, we have to answer the question that was in-tensely debated in the Luther research and catechetics between World War I and World War II:[209] How is the motif of fear of God related to that of love of God when it comes to the fulfillment of the Commandments? In the cat-echisms, does Luther interpret the Decalogue as God's externally imposed yoke of the Law or as Christ-shaped *usus practicus Evangelii*?

Three observations seem to confirm that Luther has in mind chiefly the *crassus usus praeceptorum*[210] in the catechisms; the Decalogue works like the yoke imposed by God through Moses on His recalcitrant people.

1. In his Decalogue interpretations in the context of the Sinai cov-enant, Luther had inserted for us Christians God's entire salvific work in all three articles into the preamble to the Decalogue.[211] In the catechisms, the reference to the preceding covenant is miss-ing, since Luther, following late medieval memory texts, left out the preamble. Already in the "Sermon on Good Works," Luther moved "faith in Christ" to the top and praised it as that good work in which all the other works have to walk and "receive from it the infusion of their goodness as a vassal from a lord."[212] Faith is thus the "master craftsman and captain" in all other works.[213] To be sure, the catechisms do show how the obedience to all the other commandments is based on the fear and love of God de-manded by the First Commandment, but Luther does not insert Christ's work of salvation into the First Commandment. Not only does he omit the name of Christ, but he also describes God in conscious fashion only as the "eternal wellspring"[214] of all good things. He limits the relation to God to the *homo huius vitae*,[215] to the daily life on earth as lived by contemporary craftsmen and citizen-peasants.

2. The reformer, in the course of the 1528 catechism sermons, ac-centuates more and more the correlation of fear and trust of God:

---

209 An overview of the controversy is offered by Gülhoff, *Gebieten und Schaffen*, 53-64; cf. also Fraas, *Katechismustradition*, 31–41, 226–30, 286–92, 307–9.

210 "Pred. zum 1. Gebot vom 24.2.1523," WA 11:31.8.

211 Cf. especially "Pred. über Ex. 19:14ff., 20 vom 17.9.1525," WA 16:425.22–35, 426.27–33, 429.10–18; and "Wider die Sabbather, 1538," WA 50:331.30–36 (see also AE 47:57–98).

212 WA 6:204.26, 204.31 (see also AE 44:15–114).

213 WA 6:213.14 (see also AE 44:15–114).

214 *BSLK*, 565.41.

215 "Disp. de homine, 1536," WA 39.1:175.7 (see also AE 34:133–44).

"Fear is on the left side, trust is on the right. . . . Fear no one but Me, because I can slay you, and trust because I can help you."[216] The bare fear of God's zealous wrath pushes forward to first place. Does not Luther, along with Melanchthon's "Visitations-unterricht" ("Instruction of Visitors"), steer back into the Old Testament, falling behind the salvation in Christ? Does he not again call for a legalistic form of obedience that already Augustine and Thomas rejected,[217] for servile obedience out of fear of punishment and out of longing for earthly reward? Is the "eudemonist principle," which Luther exposed and pursued into its finest details, not reinstated here in its former privileges?

3. In his 1518 "Short Explanation" and, respectively, in the 1520 "Short Form,"[218] Luther still left the Decalogue to be concentrated in the Golden Rule (Matt. 7:12), as well as in the double commandment of selfless love of God and neighbor. Already in the sermons of 1523,[219] this New Testament connection recedes. In the sermons of 1528, the Old Testament threat of punishment and promise of blessing (Exod. 20:5f.) takes the place of the New Testament double commandment and comprehends the Decalogue in the catechisms like an iron clasp.[220]

This threefold observation confirms what has been said concerning the arrangement of the three central chief parts:[221] In the catechisms, the reformer has moved the Decalogue and the First Article quite far away from the Christ-center of the Second Article. His interpretation bears Old Testament features. Its spiritual place is markedly "before" the Second and Third Articles and "before" the Lord's Prayer. At the same time, Luther opens the Decalogue up toward the Creed's Christ-center and lets it be hinted at already in the First Commandment, albeit in a hidden way. He takes the

---

216 "Kat.-Pred. zum 1. Gebot vom 10.11.1528," WA 30.1:60.14 (see also AE 51:137–41). Cf. "Kat.-Pred. zum 1. Gebot vom 10.11.1528," WA 30.1:59.17f. (see also AE 51:137–41); "Kat.-Pred. vom 18.5.1528," WA 30.1:4.21f.; "Kat.-Pred. zum 3. Gebot vom 1.12.1528," WA 30.1:65.16 (see also AE 51:141–45); furthermore "Pred. über Dtn. 4 vom 27.6.1529," WA 28:578.21–32; "Pred. über Dtn. 5f. vom 29.8.1529," WA 28:614.10–615.3, 616.16f.; "Pred. über Dtn. 6 vom 12.9.1529," WA 28:650.19–26, 657.29–34; "Pred. über Dtn. 7 vom 31.10.1529," WA 28:675.26f.; "Pred. über Dtn. 7 vom 7.11.1529," WA 28:689.24–32.

217 Cf. already Irenaeus, *Adversus haereses* 4:11–16; Augustine, *De spiritu et littera*, pass.; Thomas Aquinas, *In Rom.* VIII, lect. 1; *Summa theologiae* I/II, q. 106, a. 2; *Duo praecepta* §§ 1133ff.

218 The Golden Rule is alluded to in "Eine kurze Erklärung, 1518" (WA 1:251.24–33); "Instructio, 1518" (WA 1:259.13–18); "Eine kurze Form, 1520" (WA 7:207.8–16). The double commandment is taken up in "Eine kurze Erklärung" (WA 1:254.10–14, 255.19–23); "Instructio" (WA 1:262.31–33, 264.5–8); "Eine kurze Form" (WA 7:212.4–11, 214.4–22).

219 WA 11:36ff.

220 See the outline on pp. 108–10.

221 Cf. pp. 40–51.

believer into the salvation-historical movement from Mount Sinai to Jeru-salem.[222] A more detailed analysis of the three characteristics mentioned before confirms this.

(a) The earthly/bodily threats and promises are opened toward the tran-scendent God. God's "terrible threatening" as well as the "beautiful, comfort-ing promise"[223] looks first to our temporal, worldly fate. This is why the historical knowledge of the nations as well as the daily experience of the addressees can stand as witnesses right next to Scripture.[224] It is in this world on earth that God shows zeal for His sovereignty. He does so in concrete punishments and blessings. How does this Old Testament vision compare to Luther's insight that the "holy, Christian people is known by the relic of the holy cross"?[225]

In his sermons on Exodus, Luther distinguishes between the two Testa-ments. In the old covenant, God punishes and rewards externally and bodily. "Yet in the New Testament we have a different threat, for here we are threat-ened by eternal death, by God's wrath with the Last Day, by hell, and eternal damnation. . . . Likewise, we again have in the New Testament not a bodily but a spiritual and eternal promise."[226] Jesus Christ has entered into the Jews' fear of human shame and bodily death and has changed both into honor and eternal life before God by carrying the cross. In a deepening thought the reformer adds: God, by those bodily-earthly threats and promises, did not mean to steer even the Jews toward what is perishable, as if they could in these things get a handle on their Creator and Lord. Rather, He meant to remove them from clinging to what is tangible and guide them to Himself as the Lord and Giver of temporal and eternal life.[227]

In his interpretation of the Decalogue in the Large Catechism, Luther as a preacher steps into God's Old Testament zeal for His covenant people but does not drop the insight gained in 1525: "Yet God has laid before this bodily, coarse people bodily promises; but they should have understood thereby the spiritual promises. He thus wanted to accustom them to Him-self and thus teach them that they should expect from Him that He would certainly feed and care for them temporally and eternally. Thus He mingled both promises, the bodily and the spiritual ones, though this is not clearly

---

222 The classic interpreters of the Small Catechism, such as Steinmeyer, Albrecht, Bachmann, and Meyer, rightly insist on this irreversible dynamic. They underline the "divine pedagogy with organic development" (Knoke, quoted by Fraas, *Katechismustradition*, 261).

223 *BSLK*, 567.17.

224 *BSLK*, 568.21–32.

225 "Von den Konziliis und Kirchen, 1539," WA 50:641.35 (see also AE 41:3–178).

226 "Pred. über Ex. 20 vom 1.10.1525," WA 16:449.23, 449.31. See on this Hardeland, *Katechismus-gedanken*, 179f.; and Meyer, *Historischer Kommentar*, 179f.

227 Cf. "Pred. über Ex. 20 vom 1.10.1525," WA 16:448–62.

expressed and stated; but He connected the spiritual promises to the bodily ones so as to make it impossible for them to be separated."[228] Luther sees the worldly promises as necessarily connected to the otherworldly ones, because everyone who, in accepting what is earthly, takes hold of the invisible hand of God, hides himself in the Lord of life and death and thereby leaves this earth behind and below.[229] Luther lets what is eternal be present in what is earthly in the same indefinite and vague way in which the former is present in the Old Testament promises, for example, in phrases such as these: ". . . who gives us body, life, food . . . and everything we need of temporal and eternal goods,"[230] or in the words: ". . . if we desired to have all good things in time and eternity."[231]

At the conclusion of the interpretation of the First Commandment,[232] Luther makes conscious that process of penetrating the world to God. Following Augustine, we should not enjoy (*frui*) but only use (*uti*) all earthly goods. They cannot afford final anchorage for our heart, since our citizenship is with God in the eternal homeland. As our heart does not let itself be caught but remains pure "of greed, of clinging to all things and finding comfort and confidence in them,"[233] we walk "rightly and straightly before us"[234] through this earthly world toward God Himself.

(b) All commandments are established on the First Commandment of fear and love of God. The Deuteronomist preachers, when they give their reasons for the Commandments, demand a free and understanding obedience, not for the sake of the fixed wording of the instructions but looking toward the Lord of the covenant. This is how the composite of the Commandments gains an inner dynamic. The "Hear, O Israel" removes itself, as the primal command corresponding to the making of the covenant, from the multitude of individual commandments: "Hear, O Israel: the Lord, our God, is one Lord. And you shall love the Lord, your God, with all your heart, with all your soul, and with all your strength" (Deut. 6:4f.). In the unqualified *yes* of the covenant people to its covenant God lies Israel's heartbeat. Luther

---

228 "Pred. über Ex. 20 vom 1.10.1525," WA 16:453.21.

229 "Enarratio in psalmi XC, 1534/35," WA 40.3:493.1 (see also AE 13:73–141): "Wherever the First Commandment is treated, you are to understand that in a hidden yet certain way eternal life and the resurrection of the dead is indicated." Similarly also "Enarratio in psalmi XC, 1534/35," WA 40.3:494.12ff., 569.15ff. (see also AE 13:73–141); and the beautiful "Confitemini, 1530," WA 31.1:154.8–155.9 (see also AE 14:41–106).

230 *BSLK*, 565.29.

231 *BSLK*, 569.41. Further texts in Peters, *Glaube und Werk*, 119f.

232 *BSLK*, 571.40–572.14.

233 According to "Ausl. von Mt. 5–7, 1532," WA 32:309.14ff. (see also AE 21:1–294); similarly also "Ausl. von Mt. 5–7, 1532," WA 32:308.5–16, 457.23–32 (see also AE 21:1–294).

234 *BSLK*, 571.45.

concentrates this in the classic formula: "We should fear, love, and trust in God above all things."[235]

Yet this turning of the core of the believer's heart to the living God does not remain in isolation from the concrete obedience in all other commandments. Rather, it proves itself to be the inner force of that obedience. The will, which lies at the basis of the Decalogue itself and which manifests itself in sermonlike reasons for the First Table of commandments, presses onward all the way to founding all individual commandments in the basic commandment to love and fear God. This intention is made conscious and carried out all the way to the last commandment in Luther's interpretive outline of the Second through Tenth Commandment in the Small Catechism: "We should fear and love God, so that we do not . . . but . . . ." This basic arrangement is hinted at before Luther only here and there vaguely,[236] but it is reflectively carried out first by him, beginning already in his preliminary interpretations.

Already in "Preaching of the Ten Commandments," Luther formulates: "The First Commandment contains all the other ones in it. For who observes it, observes all; and who does not observe one of them, does not observe it, because his heart regards something other than God only."[237] In "Sermon on Good Works," he restates this insight: "And as this commandment is of all the first, highest, best, out of which all the others flow, so also its work (that is, faith and confidence in God's grace at all times) is of all the first, highest, best, out of which must flow, go, remain, and be judged and tempered all the others. And compared to this one work, the other works are just what the other commandments would be without the first and without God being there."[238] In ever-changing formulations Luther reflects on the relation between the First Commandment and the others[239] against the backdrop of the coordination of works to faith, since "faith in God is the first, highest, and noblest good work in this commandment,"[240] in which alone our doing and leaving undone before God is accepted and, at the same time, made

235 *BSLK*, 507.42.

236 Hints given by Meyer, *Historischer Kommentar*, 170f. This arrangement follows the example of Augustine, who bases love of neighbor and self on the love of God: "For out of one and the same love do we love God and the neighbor, but God we love because of God, but ourselves and the neighbor because of God" (Peter Lombard, *Sent.* III, dist. 26:3).

237 WA 1:438.7.

238 WA 6:209.35 (see also AE 44:15–114).

239 "Op. in Ps., 1518–21," WA 5:392.26–31, 395.4–10; "Kirchenpost. zu Mt. 2:1–12, 1522," WA 10.1.1:675.6–676.28 (see also AE 52:159–286); "Dtn.-Vorl., 1523/24," WA 14:610.12f. (see also AE 9:1–311); "Pred. über Dtn. 1 vom 21.2.1519," WA 28:510.21–25; "Pred. über Dtn. 4 vom 20.6.1529," WA 28:551.13–16; "Pred. über Dtn. 4 vom 1.8.1529," WA 28:586.15–19; "Pred. über Dtn. 5 vom 15.8.1529," WA 28:601–5; "Kat.-Pred. vom 7.12.1528," WA 30.1:85.7f. (see also AE 51:155–61); "Ausl. von Ps. 101, 1534," WA 51:204.16f.

240 "Pred über Ex. 20 vom 1.10.1525," WA 16:463.3.

meaningful and directed. "Where the heart is on good terms with God and this commandment is kept, there all the others follow."[241]

In the final summary of the Large Catechism,[242] Luther carries this thought out for individual commandments to enjoin in an unforgettable way "how the First Commandment is the head and wellspring that goes through all the others and how, again, all refer back to, and hang on, this one, so that end and beginning are all well tied together."[243]

The anthropological-existential reference of all doing and leaving undone to the relationship with God is thereby unequivocally demonstrated by the reformer also and especially in the catechisms. On the other hand, the insight that with the First Commandment all true obedience is based in the preceding promise ("I am the Lord, your God") is not clearly formulated. Therefore Johannes Meyer asserted[244] that the reformer had come to a new understanding of the prohibition of idolatry based on the Christologically interpreted preamble and had thus worked out the evangelical character of the First Commandment in a pure way only in 1530 at Coburg Castle as a "new student of the Decalogue."[245] To support this thesis, he points to, among other things, the 1530 draft "De iustificatione" and its brief formulation: "The First Commandment is the promise that He wants to be God, and He demands faith before all works that are demanded in the following commandments."[246] However, in these sentences Luther merely expressed concisely what characterized his understanding of the Commandments, especially since the "Sermon on Good Works," and what he enunciated frequently: Only the man to whom God the Father through the Son in the Holy Spirit has given Himself completely to be His own and to whom He has given true saving faith—only He truly lives as a free child of God in the First Commandment and therein also begins to fulfill all the other commandments. As far as this goes, the insight "that in the unconditional *promissio* the entire Gospel is seen in a nascent form since the prologue—understood in light of the revelation of Christ—characterizes man's entire relationship

---

241   *BSLK*, 572.12.

242   *BSLK*, 643.24–644.35.

243   *BSLK*, 644.17.

244   Meyer, *Historischer Kommentar*, 163–66.

245   "Brief an Jonas vom 30.6.1530," WABr 5:409.26: "I have been made here a new student of the Decalogue. Becoming a boy again, I have learned it verbatim and see that it is true that its wisdom is beyond measure. I have also begun to judge the Decalogue to be the dialectic of the Gospel and the Gospel the rhetoric of the Decalogue, and that Christ has everything Moses had, but Moses not everything Christ has . . . ."

246   WA 30.2:663.37. Additional texts in Meyer, *Historischer Kommentar*, 163f.; cf. also Heintze, *Luthers Predigt von Gesetz und Evangelium*, 110–21; and Fraas, *Katechismustradition*, 32ff., 288f., 307ff.

to God as one of pure grace"[247] was always on Luther's mind.[248] In the Large Catechism, this insight is not used because Luther, from the First Commandment onward, aims at God only as the "eternal wellspring" of all good in the horizon of creation and hints at our redemption in Christ through the Spirit first at the end[249] to furnish this aspect in the Creed and the Lord's Prayer.[250]

(c) The relation between the fear and love of God in Christian obedience.
This attempt of ours to open Luther's Decalogue interpretation to the Creed seems to fail because of Luther's reference to fear as a motive of our obedience. Does the reformer not thereby direct us unambiguously back under the Law, especially since he moves fear so emphatically to the first place? The experiences during the visitation,[251] as well as Luther's solidarity with Melanchthon against Agricola's attacks,[252] might have given more weight to these accents; however, the ordering of fear, love, and faith (trust) in this sequence is not unusual for Luther.

In his 1516 sermons on the Decalogue, the reformer still summarized the First Commandment following Augustine by means of the Pauline triad: faith—hope—love.[253] Already in the 1518 "Short Explanation" the new, still quite loosely knit triad of fear—love—faith (trust) replaced the Pauline-Augustinian one.[254] In the "Short Form," the reformer ties both triads together. They paraphrase the inner Sabbath of contented man to which Scripture calls

---

247 Meyer, *Historischer Kommentar*, 165.

248 Meyer himself indicates that this perspective only opens up where we take the entire Decalogue out of its connections to the Sinai covenant and place it into the light of the Christ revelation. This begins in the "Sermon on Good Works" (WA 6:204–16 [see also AE 44:15–114]) and in the "Kirchenpostille" (WA 10.1.1:675.6–15, 684.6–16 [see also AE 52:159–286]), is thoroughly reflected in the 1525 sermons on Exodus (WA 16:424–34), and is reformulated in the 1529 sermons on Deuteronomy, where Luther connects the dimensions of creation and redemption and ties both together in the First Commandment under the head: "And Christ is comprehended equally in the First Commandment as God" (WA 28:604.11; cf. WA 28:600.7–601.9, 621.3–7, 751.13–752.4).

249 *BSLK*, 640.39–43.

250 See the commentaries on the Creed and the Lord's Prayer.

251 Cf. Meyer, "Dekalogerklärung 1528."

252 Melanchthon had formulated in the "Unterricht der Visitatoren" ("Instruction for Visitors"): "The First Commandment of God teaches to fear God. . . . It also teaches to believe and trust in God" (Melanchthon, *Studienausgabe*, 1:224.15). Cf. also *Catechesis puerilis*, 1540: "True worship consists of fear and faith and perfect love" (Reu, *Quellen*, 1.2.2:18, 13).

253 "De fiducia, Pred. über Joh. 12:24," WA 1:74.11: "The Lord says and mandates: 'You shall have no alien gods,' that is, so that we might trust in God with pure faith, firm hope, true love . . . ." Cf. Augustine, *De cat. rud.* 1:8; *Enchiridion* 7f., et pass.; and "Von den guten Werken, 1520," WA 6:210.3–9 (see also AE 44:15–114).

254 WA 1:254.17: "Fearing and loving God in true faith and firm trust, entirely alone, purely in all things confidently, be they evil or bad." "Instructio, 1518," WA 1:263.4: "Fear and love of God in full faith and hope that is perfect self-denial and resignation—that is grace by Jesus Christ our Lord."

us: "God's fear and love in true faith, and always in all works firmly trusting, to stand entirely alone, purely, confidently in all things, be they bad or good. Here belongs everything that is written in all of Scripture about faith, hope, and love of God, which is all included briefly in this commandment."[255]

The triad fear—love—trust[256] is found in the Large Catechism only at the conclusion of the Decalogue.[257] In the Small Catechism, Luther summarizes by it the content of the First Commandment.[258] In this triad, the fear of God stands on the left side; on the right side stand trust and love. In the 1528 catechism sermons, that counterposition gains its terminological contours. In the first sermon series, Luther compresses the interpretation in this sentence: "Thus in the First Commandment fear and faith are taught."[259] In the second series, he elaborates in great detail on God's zeal in threat and promise[260] without presenting a summarizing phrase. In the third series, he unequivocally establishes the counterposition of fear and trust, especially in the conclusion of the First Commandment: "This is why the First Commandment takes both parts of your heart for itself, fearing and trusting God."[261] The concluding interpretation of the word of threat and promise in the Large Catechism goes back to that sermon and summarizes it,[262] which the Small Catechism takes up. The question *What does God now say about all these commandments?*[263] places all commandments under the basic commandment to fear and love God by means of the epilogue.[264]

It appears, however, that in the Small Catechism Luther accentuates differently than in the 1528 sermon and in the Large Catechism. Time and again in the explanations he juxtaposes fear and trust. The entire Scripture seems to be focused "on the two parts, fear and trust in God."[265] Love of God is grouped with trust.[266] However, in the Small Catechism the basic formula for all commandments reads: "We should fear and love God." Only in the interpretation of the word of promise is trust added to love, which links this

---

255 WA 7:212.14. Further texts given by Hardeland, *Das erste Gebot*, 161–84; cf. also Heintze, *Luthers Predigt von Gesetz und Evangelium*, 128–37.

256 *BSLK*, 643.38.

257 *BSLK*, 643.1: "You shall fear, love, and trust in Me as your one true God." See furthermore the phrases compiled in p. 121 n. 157.

258 *BSLK*, 507.42.

259 WA 30.1:4.21. The sequence is not unequivocal; cf. the note.

260 WA 30.1:28.22–29.34. Cf. WA 30.1:28.31: "This shows the word 'zealous one,' that He is envious; He cannot stand it; it ought not to be so."

261 WA 30.1:59.17 (see also AE 51:137–41); cf. WA 30.1:59.4–61.22, 65.16–19, 66.8f.

262 *BSLK*, 641.46–643.23.

263 *BSLK*, 510.5.

264 *BSLK*, 564.40–565.17.

265 *BSLK*, 643.8.

266 Cf. *BSLK*, 642.28, 643.6.

part back to the First Commandment.[267] It appears that Luther juxtaposed fearing and loving for linguistic reasons only, since both verbs in German have an accusative object and therefore can be parallelized without much ado. Therefore not the tension between fear and love is foundational for the reformer but that tension between fear and trust. Christian obedience in all commandments is founded first and last on the fear of God and on the trust of God.

Yet this makes the question all the more pressing: How is the fear of God to be understood as an independent motif of Christian ethics? "God threatens to punish all who transgress these Commandments; therefore we should fear His wrath and not do anything against such Commandments."[268] We should fear God lest we transgress His Commandments; for Luther, this is the clear scope of all biblical prohibitions. In the 1523 sermons, Luther calls this the *usus crassus* of the Commandments,[269] and he distinguishes it from the *usus spiritualis*.[270] Also behind this basic and concrete use of the Commandments stands God Himself. As Lord of all creation, He watches over His honor among His reasonable creatures as well as over interpersonal community. No one will escape His judgment. Already here on earth, the Lord will know how to find and punish him, be it by means of the rod of the legitimate authorities, as Luther points out especially on the Fourth Commandment,[271] or by means of the forces of chaos unleashed by the evildoer himself, as Luther graphically points out especially on the Seventh Commandment.[272] God is the Lord and Guarantor of all true order; the preachers are to drum this into the adolescents by means of Scripture and the experiences of past generations. And the parents are to raise their children "in the discipline and training of the Lord" (Eph. 6:4).[273] In this way, the adolescents are to comprehend the nature of the world "as in a mirror, from which they might

---

267 The phrase "this is why we should also fear and trust in Him" is, grammatically speaking, as daring as the triad on the First Commandment: "We should fear, love, and trust in Him above all things." The phrase in the Large Catechism (*BSLK*, 643.2) avoids this problem.

268 *BSLK*, 510.15.

269 "Pred. zum 1. Gebot vom 24.2.1523," WA 11:31.6: "First, let us accept the Commandments of God, which are given for a double purpose: first, that our outward life be good, that man outwardly abstain from and not worship an idol. This is the gross use of the Commandments."

270 "Pred. zum 1. Gebot vom 24.2.1523," WA 11:31.12.

271 See pp. 201ff.

272 See pp. 280–83.

273 Luther references Eph. 6:4 already in "Preaching on the Ten Commandments" and gets the tension between *amor* and *timor* from here, WA 1:450.23: "For in these two the Lord wants to be worshiped: to be loved as Father based on past, present, and future benefits; feared as Judge based on past, present, and future punishments. Thus He says: If I am the Father, where is love of Me? If I am the Lord, where is fear of Me? Therefore this is how the sons learn to sing mercy and judgment to the Lord (Ps. 101:1)."

get their senses and arrange themselves in this world with fear of God."[274] In the Law, God shows zeal for His sovereignty over the interpersonal community and protects our neighbors' space to live against our attacks. This is the Creator's and Sustainer's dimension of the *usus crassus legis*.

Yet the impulse of the Commandments goes beyond our earthly fate insofar as in it God is present not only as Creator and Sustainer but also as eternal Judge. This is why not only the word of blessing affects man's existence before God, but also in the threat of divine wrath Luther lets the earthly punishments expand the vista to eternal condemnation. "To you apply either eternal blessing, fortune, and blessedness or eternal wrath, misfortune, and heartache."[275] This inclusion of eternal judgment in temporal punishment is enunciated in various formulations[276]—in the most drastic way perhaps in the 1530 "Schulpredigt" ("School Sermon"): "Thus, again, you shall now be cursed and suffer, both in your children and for yourself, plain shame and weeping, or at least be harassed in such a way that you will be condemned with them not only here on earth but also eternally in hell."[277] The transition from temporal misfortune and heartache to God's eternal wrath is understood specifically and concretely: Whoever is caught by death in the impenitent breaking of God's Commandments falls immediately into final condemnation. One should teach in this manner: God uses the *usus crassus praeceptorum* to sustain and preserve His rational creation against the breaking in of chaos. By proclaiming the temporal and eternal judgment of God, the preacher points to the holy, wrathful zeal of the Creator and Lord.

Alongside the defensive side of the threat of punishment stands the enticing promise of grace. "Yet He promises grace and all good things to all who keep these Commandments. *This is why* we should also love and trust in Him and gladly do according to His Commandments."[278] God is not satisfied with the *usus crassus*; He wants the *usus spiritualis*. Whoever fulfills the Law merely because of the punishment threatened or because of the graces promised, but nevertheless sighs in his heart under the hard yoke of the Commandments and seeks to cast them aside, remains under

---

274 "An die Ratherren . . . daß sie christliche Schulen, 1524," WA 15:45.18 (see also AE 45:339–78). The image of the mirror Luther takes out of the medieval confessional manuals. Cf. "Decem praecepta, 1518," WA 1:438.2: "Therefore the Decalogue of commandments is like a mirror in which a man considers himself, in what and how much he fails or accomplishes."

275 *BSLK*, 570.10.

276 E.g.: ". . . firstly, plain wrath and disfavor from God, no peace in the heart, followed by all torture and misfortune" (*BSLK*, 598.15); "wrath and condemnation" (*BSLK*, 610.29); "God's wrath and punishment" (*BSLK*, 619.43, 623.18, 645.38): "wrath and misfortune" (*BSLK*, 624.13). Cf. *BSLK*, 605.10–19.

277 "Eine Predigt, daß man die Kinder zur Schule halten solle, 1530," WA 30.2:532.23.

278 *BSLK*, 510.18.

God's holy curse upon the breakers of the Law.[279] This is why the reformer carries out the inner movement from the negative prohibition to the positive commandment and places trusting love next to fear. Already fear no longer looked to the punishment threatened but to the wrathful Lord Himself; thus also loving trust turns to the gracious Father. To the heart that "fears God alone and has only Him before its eyes and out of this fear omits everything that is against His will lest it anger Him" comes the heart that "trusts in Him alone and to please Him does what He wants because He makes Himself heard so kindly as a father and offers us all grace and good things."[280]

Yet in one and the same heart, love of the gracious Father combines with fear of the angry Judge. How does the reformer interpret this combination of "*Timor* . . . on the left-hand side" and "*fiducia* on the right"?[281] Does not perfect love drive out fear (1 John 4:18)? In the catechisms, Luther merely described the combination in a sermonlike manner without systematically penetrating it. He unfolds the proper coordination between the two already in an early sermon.[282] The true Christian constantly finds himself in an eschatological transition from the stained fruit of the servants of God to the pure and reverent love of the children of God. The servants fear God the Lord only because of something that is extrinsic to Him, namely, on account of the temporal or even the eternal punishment threatened by Him. The servants also do not properly love God; they seek from Him the promised earthly or even the eternal reward. The true children, on the other hand, love and fear God the Father only for His own sake.[283] Obedience for the sake of the punishment threatened is thus a first step on the eschatological

---

279 Cf. Hardeland, *Das erste Gebot*, 31ff.

280 *BSLK*, 642.24. "Pred. über Dtn. 5f. vom 29.8.1529," WA 28:617.19: "This is why the true core and understanding of the First Commandment is to *fear* God, lest one seek another one, and trust Him who wants to give you all good things. Fear serves the purpose of keeping us with Him, lest we choose another god. *Trust* brings along with it all help so that in all needs you might look into His hands alone and be certain that He will do the best for you, give you counsel and aid, since He has promised it to you and does not lie while you do not cling to any other." Cf. "Op. in Ps., 1518–21," WA 5:400.38ff.; "Weihnachtspost. zu Tit. 2:11–15, 1526," WA 10.1.1:37.15–18; "Dtn.-Vorl., 1526," WA 14:606.17ff., 613.30ff. (see also AE 9:1–311); "Jona-Ausl., 1526," WA 19:220.32f. (see also AE 19:33–104); "Eccl.-Vorl., 1526," WA 20:40.13 (see also AE 15:1–187); "Ausl. d. ersten 25 Pss., 1530," WA 31.1:286.31, 278.24; "Arbeiten zu Ps. 1–8, 1530–32," WA 31.1:496.25; "Enarratio psalmi, 1546," WA 40.2:293.10; and passim.

281 "Kat.-Pred. zum 1. Gebot vom 30.11.1528," WA 30.1:60.14.

282 Cf. "Pred. über Sir. 15:1 vom 27.12.1514," WA 1:37–43; and WA 4:65–66 (see also AE 11:1–553). Luther defends this coordination in the "Leipziger Disputation" against Eck (WA 2:359–72 [see also AE 51:53–60]). Further parallels compiled by Hardeland, *Begriff der Gottesfurcht*, 6–12.

283 Luther distinguishes between the "holy, filial, free, instrinsic fear," on the one hand, and the "impure, servile, forced, extrinsic fear," on the other hand. The former he also calls simply "fear," while the latter he calls "horror." "Fear is a fruit of love, but horror is a seedbed of hatred" (WA 1:29.17; "Pred. über Sir. 15:1 vom 27.12.1514," WA 4:661.10). Cf. Peter Lombard, *Sent.* III, dist. 34.

way; at the same time it is as *terminus a quo*, the place that absolutely must be left behind. Whoever fears or loves God only for the sake of earthly goods might perhaps receive these things from Him, but the Lord, for His part, will reject him and let him sink into eternal damnation. Whoever fears God because of hell or loves Him because of heaven will go down to the pit. We must leave the servile fear and the hypocritical love of the old man behind.

Coming from himself, based on his own reason and power, no one can change the servile fear into filial love. God's Spirit Himself must come from on high and has to drive out the lowly servile fear by means of the trust in God enabled by Him. We do not purify ourselves here in a harmonious ascent from what is below to what is on high. The movement does not push from below to the top; rather, the light of grace breaks in from above and drives back the dissipating darkness. The servant's fear is not changed into the son's fear but is overcome by it; the servant's love is not changed into the love of the children of God, but the pure trust of the child of God overcomes the old Adam's hypocritical appearance of trust.[284] We have to place the antagonism between the old and new man into the sermonlike parenesis of the catechisms. "In a real person there must always be the fear of God's judgment, due to the old man whose enemy and opponent is God, and beside this fear there must be hope of grace from the mercy that looks favorably on the fear for the sake of the new man, who is also an enemy of the old man and thus agrees with God's judgment."[285]

The Decalogue interpretation of the catechisms does carry out this eschatological transition from fear to love, from external to internal obedience of the Law, which, however, is only possible out of the grace of the Spirit of Christ.[286] Luther's interpretation is not easily translated into the schematic of the threefold use of the Law. The antagonism between Law and Gospel recedes. At the center is God's creative commanding and commanding

---

284   "Pred. über Sir. 15:1 vom 27.12.1514," WA 1:42.20 and WA 4:664.25: "For beginning love and great servile fear coexist, but fear decreases while love increases." Cf. "Pred. über Sir. 15:1 vom 27.12.1516," WA 1:116.3–7. This is anticipated by Augustine, to whom Peter Lombard refers, *Sent.* III, dist. 34, a. 6: "Fear prepares a place for love, as it were. But when love begins to dwell, the fear that prepared the place is thrown out. For when the one grows, the other decreases; and to the extent love becomes internal, fear is thrown out."

285   "Weihnachtspost. zu Gal. 3:23–29, 1522," WA 10.1.1:462.4.

286   See furthermore "Brief Luthers an Melanchthon vom 27.10.1527," in which he comments on Agricola's attacks: "For how fear of punishment and the fear of God differ is more easily said in syllables and letters than known in reality and affection. All unbelievers fear punishment and hell. God will be with those who are His so that they fear God and punishment simultaneously. There can be no fear of God in this life without fear of punishment, as there can also be no spirit without flesh, though the fear of punishment is useless without fear of God" (WABr 4:272.16). "Enarratio Psalmi, 1546," WA 40.2:290.8: "As here the Holy Spirit (says): to fear and to exult. This is Christian wisdom. Many argue over fears—filial and servile. It is true, in a son one can see this mixed fear. When the father punishes, it hurts the son, but he does not cast away all hope."

creating[287] in which the triune one is present as our Creator, Redeemer, and Re-Creator and asserts His holy Law as well as His gracious will among us.

This working of God through His Commandments can be divided into four aspects, at which Luther hints in an anthropological horizon in the "Sermon on Good Works"[288] and which later Melanchthon and Calvin unfold doctrinally.[289]

(a) The defensive function of the *usus crassus praeceptorum* grows out of God's zeal for His sovereignty over the human community. The negative prohibitions protect the orders of the worldly government of God.

(b) The pedagogically guiding function of the *usus puerilis praeceptorum*[290] is meant to instruct in joyous obedience.[291] In contradistinction from the forced external obedience of those rebelling against the Law and from the inner hypocrisy of the Pharisees, the playful growing into the Commandments is not connected to an inner hatred of Law and God but is opened for the filial fear and child's love toward the Creator and Father.

(c) The full *usus spiritualis* of the Commandments is, as genuine *usus practicus Evangelii*,[292] deepest obedience of the heart for the sake of God alone, "because He makes Himself heard in such a kind manner as a father and offers us all grace and goods."[293] This free obedience of the Commandments has the accusing function of the Law always in it; however, in the catechisms it is focused on the blessing Creator in whom the gracious Redeemer and the consummating Sanctifier are secretly present.[294]

---

287 Siirala, *Gottes Gebot bei M. Luther*, 66 n. 40: "By means of God's commanding, man constantly is given a share in God's grace." Siirala, *Gottes Gebot bei M. Luther*, 72: "The God of the Bible is the God whose command bears the entire being of man."

288 WA 6:213f. (see also AE 44:15–114).

289 Melanchthon in the *Loci* since 1535, *Studienausgabe* 2.1:321–26; Calvin, *Inst.* 2:7.6–15. Cf. also FC VI.

290 Cf. "Op. in Ps., 1518–21," WA 5:405.6–408.13; "Von den guten Werken, 1520," WA 6:214.2–11 (see also AE 44:15–114); "Pred. zum 1. Gebot vom 24.2.1523," WA 11:31.8–11; *BSLK*, 644.36ff., 579.18–37; and the interpretation of the prefaces above.

291 Luther underlines the willing obedience, especially in "Coburger Vorrede" ("Coburg Preface"); cf. p. 31.

292 Joest, *Gesetz und Freiheit*, 132. Cf. Althaus, *Theologie Luthers*, 119f.

293 *BSLK*, 642.29.

294 "Von den guten Werken, 1520," WA 6:213.23 (see also AE 44:15–114): "For the just (that is, the believer), there is no law given (1 Tim. 1:9), but such do willingly what they know and like, only beholding in firm confidence that God's good pleasure and favor hovers over them in all things."

(d) The convicting function, the *usus elenchticus*, which Luther called the *usus theologicus* and *usus praecipuus* in "Großen Galaterbrief-Kommentar" ("Great Galatians Commentary"),[295] is practiced only indirectly in the entire Decalogue interpretation and is addressed immediately in the conclusion.[296]

These distinct functions of the Decalogue are concentrated in the First Commandment and are unfolded by means of the word of threat and grace.

APPENDIX: THE PROHIBITION OF IMAGES[297]

Luther, along with the medieval tradition shaped by Augustine, skips over the prohibition of images in the Small Catechism. In the Large Catechism he touches on it only in one sentence: Idolatry "does not only consist in setting up an image and worshiping it, but above all in the heart that gawks elsewhere."[298] The prohibition of images is no independent prohibition; as a special case, it is part of the general prohibition of idols. In this, Luther follows the Deuteronomist preachers who assigned the prohibition of images to the prohibition of idols.[299]

Within Christendom, the prohibition of idols has been embattled repeatedly.[300] Seen schematically, one can point out three positions:

(a) The Eastern Church argues for the veneration of images based on the Christological dogma and the Neoplatonic notion of idea and reflection. From the vantage point of intellectual history, this might be interpreted "as a victory of Greek thinking over the formlessness of the Orient."[301] The Eastern Church interprets it theologically as triumph of Christianity over Judaism. "First, when the Son of God became man in time and the image of man was renewed by Him, the making of images became a new truly

---

295 WA 40.1:480.13 (see also AE 26:1–461): "holy use"; WA 40.1:482.3 (see also AE 26:1–461): "the Law's proper and absolute use"; WA 40.1:481.4 (see also AE 26:1–461): "the true office of the Law and its proper use"; WA 40.1:490.5 (see also AE 26:1–461): "the best and most perfect use of the Law"; WA 40.1:509.1 (see also AE 26:1–461): "the legitimate use of the Law."

296 *BSLK*, 640.38ff.

297 Texts on the prohibition of images on pp. 147–48.

298 *BSLK*, 564.20. "Pred. über Dtn. 4 vom 20.6.1529," WA 28:586.25: "True idolatry is in the heart, that one neither fears nor trusts God but sets it on other things. External images are not true idolatry; external idolatry is a coarse thing." "Dtn.-Vorl., 1523/24," WA 14:593.16 (see also AE 9:1–311): "These gross forms of idolatry over the course of time came from the inner idolatry in which we, out of our impiety, want to worship God in human form and some idea. Out of this followed that external worship."

299 See the literature given on p. 90 n. 9.

300 See the articles by Beck, Baus, and Iserloh on the image controversy.

301 Von Campenhausen, "Die Bilderfrage als theologisches Problem der alten Kirche," 249.

human and holy possibility."[302] Here the prohibition of images appears as being abrogated by salvation history itself.

(b) Occidental Christendom did not appropriate the Christological foundation. It interprets the images more from a pedagogical-didactic perspective as *biblia pauperum*. The Middle Ages use images (1) for the instruction of the ignorant, (2) to strengthen the memory, and (3) to stir up the affection of devotion.[303]

(c) However, the rejection of images has sounded forth repeatedly in Christendom. Very different motives were in play here: The Old Testament prohibition of images was connected to a rationalizing struggle against anthropomorphisms. The *no* of the martyrs' Church against sacrifices before pagan idols was connected to the spiritualist-ascetic flight from the world in ancient Christendom. The Antiochene separation between the divine and human natures in Christ was amplified in the Reformed tradition to the point of divorcing a religious realm that was iconoclastic from a worldly realm that was open to images.[304]

Luther takes up the basic ideas behind these three positions and focuses them on his understanding of justification: "Works-righteousness is the source and origin of all external idols."[305] Looking at the donation and care of images, he points out: the core of sinning against the First Commandment does not consist in erecting and outwardly venerating images but in the heart's opinion that it is doing a meritorious work by doing so. Again Luther consciously focuses on the relation of trust of the inner man. In it, the decision between true worship of God and prohibited idolatry takes place. After all, one cannot "grasp and catch [God] with fingers, or put Him in a bag or lock Him up in a chest. . . . This is what it means to grasp Him, when the heart grasps Him and hangs on Him."[306]

According to Luther, the key idolatry grows out of fallen man's basic will to enclose the superior divine power in the things of the creaturely world. "All sons of Adam are idolaters because he takes something up by which he wants to imprison God."[307] In this, men rarely identified the images with

302 Von Campenhausen, "Die Bilderfrage in der Reformation," 407. Cf. von Campenhausen, "Die Bilderfrage als theologisches Problem der alten Kirche," 251f.

303 Cf. von Campenhausen, "Die Bilderfrage in der Reformation," 364.

304 Cf. the "Erlauthaler Bekenntnis" (Müller, *Bekenntnisschriften der reformierten Kirche*, 320): "We approve of secular images in political uses made by artists."

305 "Jes.-Vorl. über Jes. 44, 1527/30," WA 31.2:345.33.

306 BSLK, 563.4. "Kat.-Pred. zum 1. Gebot vom 14.9.1528," WA 30.1:28.13: "Non potes deum habere in loculo, arca, manu, sed corde, et hoc tum, quando fidis et credis ei."

307 "Pred. zum 1. Gebot vom 24.2.1523," WA 11:33.10. "Eine Vermahnung Luthers an alle Pfarrherrn, 1539," WA 50:478.39: "And all hope that the devil is beyond the sea and God is in our

the godhead; rather, they sought to guarantee the presence of the numen among them by means of the cultic image.[308] This basic will in pagan as well as Christian veneration of images is to be exposed and bent under the judgment of the Creator God who is zealous for His honor. It does not help to ban the images from our eyes and leave them standing in our hearts; they have to be ripped out of the heart, then also the external ones may fall or remain as a true *biblia pauperum* under God's Word. "Where hearts are instructed that one is pleasing to God by faith alone and that He is not pleased with images, that they are rather a lost service and expense, then the people will willingly fall away from them, despise them, and no longer have any made."[309] In this, Luther takes up the Old Testament prohibition of images.

The Reformed tradition has supported this basic idea of Luther's in a biblicist manner and, in a rationalizing way, made it one-sided. God as invisible Spirit is strictly opposed to any earthly/bodily form. "Since God is invisible Spirit and infinite Being, He cannot in any way and by any image be represented, which is why we are not ashamed of calling images of God pure lies with Holy Scripture. Therefore we reject not only the idols of the pagans but also the images of the Christians."[310] As already our immortal soul is beyond all that is corporeal/earthly, so all attempts to capture God's eternal Spirit in the perishable image are to be rejected as illegitimate. "These images deceive us regarding the immense chasm that has been established between the created nature and the supernatural-eternal God. God is not to be found in external matter but only within man, and by turning toward the images, we necessarily turn away from Him and His true being."[311]

At the opening of his *Glaubenslehre*, Schleiermacher has summarized all of religious history under the main thought hinted at here. He understood

---

pocket." Calvin, *Inst.* 1:11.8 (*Opera Selecta* 3:97.11): "This is the origin of idolatry: that men do not believe God to be with them unless they carnally show Him to be present, as the example of the Israelites shows (Exod. 32:1)."

308 "Gen.-Vorl. zu Gen. 31, 1535–45," WA 44:36.5 (see also AE 6:1–607): "For no nation was ever so stupid as to worship wood, rocks, gold, silver, out of which the statues were made. But they added the First Table and pretended that God in heaven regarded this worship and heard the invocation made to this statue." "Invokavitpred. vom 12.3.1522," WA 10.3:31.7 (see also AE 51:84–88): "For I think that there is no one, or only very few individuals, who does not know: the crucifix that stands there is not my God—for my God is in heaven—but only a sign."

309 "Wider die himmlischen Propheten, 1525," WA 18:67.18 (see also AE 40:73–223). "Pred. über Dtn. 4 vom 20.6.1529," WA 28:555.14: "I would also like to destroy images, if one first let the destruction of the heart take place."

310 *Conf. helv. posterior* IV: "Quoniam vero Deus spiritus est invisibilis et immensa essentia, not potest sane ulla arte aut imagine exprimi, unde non veremur cum scriptura, simulacra Dei, mera nuncupare mendacia. Reiicimus itaque non modo gentium idola, sed et Christianorum simulacra" (Niesel, *Bekenntnisschriften und Kirchenordnungen*, 226.15; or Müller, *Bekenntnisschriften der reformierten Kirche*, 174.5). Cf. Geneva Catechism, quest. 145–48; Calvin, *Inst.* 1:11f.; 2:8.17; 4:9.9; Scottish Conf., Art. XIV; Heidelberg Catechism, quest. 97f.

311 Von Campenhausen, "Die Bilderfrage in der Reformation," 375. Von Campenhausen also offers proofs from Zwingli; see "Die Bilderfrage in der Reformation," 365–80.

it as the gradual turning away of our consciousness of utter dependence, which is aimed at the divine and transcendent, from the sensual consciousness of the world.[312] All anthropomorphisms thus appear to be clouding that pure spiritual feeling of dependence.[313]

Luther fights these rationalizing consequences by pointing, with the Alexandrine tradition of the early Church, to God's condescension. Without question, God in His transcendent majesty remains hidden to us.[314] Yet because He has created us into this corporeal/earthly world and because He has thrown us into this life with our five senses, this is also why He, the eternal and transcendent Lord, lets Himself down into what is earthly/corporeal. He comes near and discloses Himself to us in His concrete acting in history, in the prophetic Word, and under sacramental signs that are permeated by the Word. For us, these become instruments and protective coverings by means of which He saves us out of what is worldly/earthly to what is transcendent/heavenly.[315] Herein Luther takes up the intention of the Eastern Church. However, he develops this Christological approach not based on vision by means of the Platonizing idea/reflection motif, but based on hearing, by pointing to the word of promise and the faith corresponding to it. Along with the occidental tradition, he subordinates images and also music to the Word.[316] By doing so, he renews the idea of the *biblia pauperum*.[317]

In his writings on the Lord's Supper, Luther paradoxically turns the prohibition of images directly against the ideal of a spiritual/imageless worship of God.[318] Our old Adam does not want merely to capture God in manageable images; he no less tries to grasp Him in His exalted spiritual ideas of God. In this, we rely on our ability to transcend ourselves and approach God in the imagelessness of mystical ascent. Luther sets the *theologia crucis* directly against this negative mystical theology of the Neoplatonic tradition.[319] Precisely in these exalted spiritual ideas of God the old carnal man is at work. The Lord must let the old man run up and stumble over those despised forms of encounter in which the Exalted One approaches us, hidden

---

312   Cf. Schleiermacher, *Der christliche Glaube*, §§ 7–10.

313   Cf. Schleiermacher, *Der christliche Glaube*, § 5, Addition.

314   "Dtn.-Vorl. zu Dtn. 9ff., 1523/24," WA 14:593.21 (see also AE 9:1–311): "He removes every human idea about God; He cannot be pictured to be anything; only with His voice we ought to be content, not to conceive, contrive various ideas or forms of Him."

315   Cf., e.g., "Pred. über Ex. 19:14ff. und 20 vom 17.9.1525," WA 16:424.35–425.10; "Pred. über Dtn. 4 vom 27.7.1529," WA 28:576.14–31; "Pred. über Dtn. 5 vom 15.8.1529," WA 28:600.11–37. Further proofs found in von Campenhausen, "Die Bilderfrage in der Reformation," 395–401.

316   Cf. "Vorrede zum Passional, 1529," WA 10.2:458.14–459.11 .

317   Cf. Grüneisen, "Grundlegendes für die Bilder in Luthers Katechismus."

318   Cf. Peters, "Gegenwart Gottes—Wort Gottes."

319   Cf., e.g., "Scholien zur Röm.-Vorl., 1515/16," WA 56:371.17–27 (see also AE 25:1–524); "Op. in Ps., 1518–21," WA 5:163.17–29; "De captivitate Babylonica, 1520," WA 6:562.3–563.9 (see also AE 36:3–126); and passim.

under the lowly cross of Christ. Only in this way does the Lord want to fashion the new man of God who, against all autonomous self-transcending, finds shelter in those concrete forms of God's turning to man so as to risk, in believing hope, the death leap into nothingness. This is the paradox of the free majesty of the self-humbling God. To it corresponds what Luther enunciated as well: it is God's mercy that He does not break into our humanity in His unveiled majesty; we would perish in the consuming fire of His holy zeal. Thus the reformer consciously places Jesus of Nazareth, the image of the invisible Father given by God Himself, into the prohibition of images and thereby again assigns it to the basic commandment of fearing and trusting God.

In this, Luther confronts the biblicist argumentation of Carlstadt and Zwingli in a surprisingly unconcerned and free manner. The order of God's people given at Sinai, for him, is abrogated by God's new salvific act in Jesus Christ. The cultic order of Israel, which reaches into the Decalogue by means of the prohibition of images and the Sabbath commandment, is abrogated for Christendom. The prohibition of images is binding for the Church only insofar as in it the basic commandment of undivided devotion to God is at stake, since, according to the reformer, only the double commandment of selfless love of God and neighbor is engraved on man's heart by the Creator.

Contemporary exegesis shows that already the Old Testament understanding of the prohibition of images is not homogeneous.[320] On the one hand, a rationalizing rejection of anthropomorphisms can only draw upon Scripture insofar as the prohibition of images with God's exaltation over all that is created is established already at the margins of the Old Testament. On the other hand, the prophets and seers all the way into the Revelation of St. John unabashedly describe their visions of God.

The scriptural proof text Deut. 4:9–20, probably written during late exilic times, bases the prohibition of images on the fact that Israel did not see any form of Yahweh at Sinai but only heard His voice.[321] Deutero-Isaiah's "satirical tract" (Isa. 44:9ff.) on the fabrication of idols directs the attention to the worldly stuff used and to the feeble fabricators. According to the Legend of Bel in the apocryphal additions to Daniel, the pagan priests are stupid yet cunning impostors. At the same time, however, that "enlightening rationalism that makes fun of the idol 'that totters' (Isa. 41:7) . . . [begins] to transcendentalize Yahweh."[322] This late marginal strand of Old Testament

---

320 Cf. Bernhardt, *Gott und Bild*; Hempel, *Das Bild in Bibel und Gottesdienst*; von Rad, *Theologie des Alten Testaments*, 1:211–18; *Weisheit in Israel*, 229–39; Schrade, *Der verborgene Gott*; Zimmerli, "Das zweite Gebot."

321 Luther's interpretation is found in "Dtn.-Vorl., 1523/24" (WA 14:593.8–23 [see also AE 9:1–311]) and "Pred. über Ex. 19:14ff. und 20 vom 17.9.1525" (WA 16:422.3–5, 122.17–19).

322 Von Rad, *Theologie des Alten Testaments*, 1:217.

interpretation of the prohibition of images follows antiquity's philosophical critique of the cultic worship of God.[323]

It is countered by "Yahweh's grossly anthropomorphic self-introduction as the Zealous One,"[324] which is supported by the prophetic visions of God in human form as well as the cultic/priestly signs of revelation. The New Testament does not diminish anything here, since it bears witness to the Revealer as the Word of Life whom the disciples saw with their eyes and touched with their hands (1 John 1:1). This is the main strand of the whole Bible.

Referencing it, Walther Zimmerli writes against Paul Volz:[325] "The antithesis spiritual-invisible sensual-visible, by which one . . . attempts to understand the Second Commandment, originates in idealistic, not biblical, thought. Biblical thought knows of the gracious condescension of the God-event into the corporeality that is accessible to the senses."[326] In all this, God's free sovereignty shows itself in this His gracious self-binding. Unlike the other nations, Israel is not directed to a cultic image but to Yahweh's word-driven action in history. Thus the prohibition of the image of God first gains its meaning in the context of the all-inclusive zeal of Yahweh for His sovereign freedom in His condescension. "There is a perhaps hidden, but in reality close, theological connection between the irreverent breaking apart of ideas of God that had grown dear to the people in which we see the pre-exilic prophets engaged and the prohibition of images."[327] Luther worked out exactly this zeal of God for His holy and merciful sovereignty among us men as the scope of the prohibition of images.

SOME CENTRAL TEXTS ON THE FIRST COMMANDMENT

WA 1:74–77: De fiducia in Deum, secundum praeceptum I; Predigt über Joh. 12:24 vom 10.8.1516

WA 1:398–430: from Decem praecepta Wittenbergensi praedicata populo, 1518

WA 5:392–401: Operationes in Psalmos, zu Ps. 14:1, 1518–21

WA 6:204–16: from Sermon von den guten Werken, 1520 (see also AE 44:15–114)

WA 10.1.1:674–86: from Kirchenpostille zu Mt. 2:1–12, 1522 (see also AE 52:159–286)

WA 10.2:458–59: Vorrede zum Passional, 1529

WA 16:421–64: Predigten über Ex. 20, 1. Gebot, 1525

---

323 Cf. Geffcken, "Der Bilderstreit des heidnischen Altertums"; Baynes, "Idolatry and the Early Church."

324 Zimmerli, "Das zweite Gebot," 244.

325 Volz, Mose und sein Werk, 40: "This prohibition, which declares God to be Spirit, also makes man into spirit and elevates him to his highest dignity. In his innermost motions and actions, in religion, man departs from the earthly sphere, from everything that is made, what is seen and touched and what can be pictured, and elevates himself into a totally different realm."

326 Zimmerli, "Das zweite Gebot," 244f.

327 Von Rad, Theologie des Alten Testaments, 1:217.

WA 28:509–763: Wochenpredigten über das Dtn., 1529

WA 30.2:663f.: from De loco iustificationis, 1530

WA 40.3:492–97, 569f.: from Enarratio in psalmi XC, 1534/35 (see also AE 13:73–141)

WA 42:436–51, 550–67, 631f.: from Genesisvorlesung 1535–45, zu Gen. 12:1ff.; 15:1ff.; 17:7f. (see also AE 2:1–399; 3:1–365)

LITERATURE ON THE FIRST COMMANDMENT

Albrecht, "Streiflichter auf Luthers Erklärung des ersten Gebots im Kleinen Katechismus"

Bornkamm, *Luther und das Alte Testament*, 139–51

Gühlhoff, *Gebieten und Schaffen Gottes in Luthers Auslegung des ersten Gebotes*

Hardeland, *Luthers Katechismusgedanken in ihrer Erklärung des Kleinen Katechismus Dr. Martin Luthers*, 6–53, 178–86; *Der Begriff der Gottesfurcht in Luthers Katechismen*; *Das erste Gebot in den Katechismen Luthers*; "Luthers Erklärung des ersten Gebotes im Licht seiner Rechtfertigungslehre"

Heintze, *Luthers Predigt von Gesetz und Evangelium*, 102–46

Lau, "Erstes Gebot und Ehre Gottes als Mitte von Luthers Theologie"

Meyer, "Fürchten, lieben und vertrauen: Eine geschichtliche Erörterung zu Luthers Katechismen"; "Luthers Dekalogerklärung 1528 unter dem Einfluß der sächsischen Kirchenvisitation"

Müller, "Der christliche Glaube und das erste Gebot"

Schott, "Luthers Verständnis des ersten Gebots"

Siirala, *Gottes Gebot bei M. Luther*, 53–104

TEXTS ON THE PROHIBITION OF IMAGES

WA 10.2:33ff.: from Von beider Gestalt des Sakraments zu nehmen, 1522 (see also AE 36:231–67)

WA 10.3:26–36: from 3. und 4. Invokavitpredigt, 11. und 12.3.1522 (see also AE 51:79–88)

WA 14:620–22: from Dtn.-Vorlesung, 1523/24 (see also AE 9:1–311)

WA 15:219f.: from Brief an die Fürsten zu Sachsen von dem aufrührerischen Geist, 1524 (see also AE 40:45–49)

WA 15:393–95: from Brief an die Christen zu Straßburg wider den Schwärmergeist, 1524 (see also AE 40:61–71; 49:94–96)

WA 16:437–43: from Predigt über Dtn. 4 vom 20.6.1525

WA 18:67–84: from Wider die himmlischen Propheten, 1525 (see also AE 40:73–223)

WA 28:551–61: from Predigt über Dtn. 4 vom 20.6.1529

WA 31.2:344–51: from Jes.-Vorlesung über Jes. 44:9–20, 1527/30

WA 25:285–87: Scholien zu Jes. 44, 1532–34 (see also AE 17:1–416)

WA 44:31–40: from Gen.-Vorlesung zu Gen. 31:26ff., 1535–45 (see also AE 6:1–607)

LITERATURE

Von Campenhausen, "Die Bilderfrage in der Reformation"

Grüneisen, "Grundlegendes für die Bilder in Luthers Katechismus"

Preuss, *Martin Luther: Der Künstler*

THE SECOND COMMANDMENT[1]

WORDING OF THE COMMANDMENT
AND ARRANGEMENT OF THE INTERPRETATION

The wording of the prohibition against abusing the divine Name varies greatly. In the Large Catechism, it reads: "You shall not use the name of God (God's name) in vain."[2] In the Small Catechism, Luther adds from Exod. 20:7 "your God"[3] and translates *in vanum* again with "uselessly."[4] He did struggle with the translation of *assumere*; via *antziehen*[5] ("draw in"), *annehmen*[6] ("assume"), and *brauchen*[7] ("employ"), he came through Melanchthon's *Enchiridion* to *führen*, as in "im Munde führen" ("mention, use"). In the interpretation of the Large Catechism[8] and in "Eine einfältige Weise" ("Simple Way"),[9] he uses *mißbrauchen* ("abuse or misuse"), which entered into the text of the Small Catechism between 1536 and 1540.[10] The word of threat is added merely in the interpretation of the Large Catechism: ". . . for the Lord will not hold guiltless him who uses His name in vain."[11] The Nürnberg prints of 1531 and 1538 also insert it into the text of the Small Catechism.[12]

The interpretation in the Small Catechism grows out of the summarizing formulations of the third sermon series, which are already foreshadowed

---

1   For texts on the Second Commandment, see pp. 164–65.

2   *BSLK*, 555.16, 572.24.

3   Thus in many medieval texts; cf. Meyer, *Historischer Kommentar*, 88.

4   Thus already "Eine kurze Erklärung, 1518," WA 1:250.8; "Von den guten Werken, 1520," WA 6:217.7 (see also AE 44:15–114); "Eine kurze Form, 1520," WA 7:205.25; "Kat.-Pred. zum 2. u. 3. Gebot vom 15.9.1528," WA 30.1:30.

5   "Eine kurze Erklärung, 1518," WA 1:250.8.

6   "Eine kurze Form, 1520," WA 7:205.25.

7   "Von den guten Werken, 1520," WA 6:217.7 (see also AE 44:15–114).

8   *BSLK*, 572.40, 573.1, 573.13, 575.43.

9   "Eine einfältige Weise zu beten, 1535," WA 38:365.30 (see also AE 43:187–211). Cf. already "Eine kurze Unterweisung, wie man beichten soll, 1519," WA 2:61.20.

10   See Ebeling, "Das zweite Gebot in Luthers Kleinem Katechismus," 229f.

11   *BSLK*, 574.27. Cf. already "Pred. über Ex. 20:7 vom 22.10.1525," WA 16:464.21.

12   Cf. *BSLK*, 508 n. 1.

in "Sermon von den guten Werken" ("Sermon on Good Works").[13] Loosely following late medieval tradition,[14] the reformer summarizes the negative portion: "You shall not swear, curse, do magic, blaspheme, lie, deceive, teach falsely by His name."[15] Luther independently adds the positive portion in which he takes recourse to his earlier interpretations: "call upon Him in every need with trust, praise, honor."[16]

The Large Catechism does not unfold the abuse, much less the right use, of God's name by stringing verbs together.[17] Following the second sermon series,[18] it seeks to enjoin the either/or: Either to abuse God's name for lies, evil, and vice[19] or to use it rightly for truth and all that is good.[20] In its progression of thought, the Large Catechism follows the sermon on Sept. 15, 1528. The admonition to raise the young in the fear and honor[21] of God reaches back to the sermon on May 19.[22]

The arrangement of the section in the Large Catechism shows a Johannine influence. The entire context remains continuously present and it simultaneously unfolds according to its individual dimensions. The catechetical

---

13   Cf. "Kat.-Pred. zum 2. Gebot vom 1.12.1528," WA 30.1:62.19ff., 63.12ff. (see also AE 51:141–45); "Von den guten Werken, 1520," WA 6:218.2, 225.32 (see also AE 44:15–114).

14   See the compilation in Geffcken, *Bildercatechismus*, 59–63, as well as the texts in Weidenhiller, *Untersuchungen*, 46, 70, 113, 182f., 192, 229ff.

15   WA 30.1:63.12 (see also AE 51:141–45). Cf. "Kat.-Pred. zum 2. Gebot vom 1.12.1528," WA 30.1:62.19 (see also AE 51:141–45): "I should not curse, swear, do magic by His name." "Kat.-Pred. zum 2. Gebot vom 1.12.1528," WA 30.1:63.26 (see also AE 51:141–45): "In sum, not cursing, swearing, doing magic, lying, and deceiving." "Von den guten Werken, 1520," WA 6:225.32 (see also AE 44:15–114): "this commandment's work that we do not swear, curse, lie, deceive, or do magic with God's holy name." "Pred. zum 1. u. 2. Gebot vom 26.2.1523," WA 11:36.30: "Externally: you should not curse and swear, lie and deceive." "Pred. über Ex. 20:7 vom 22.10.1525," WA 16:466.20: "That we should not swear, curse, lie, deceive, do magic with the name of God nor commit other abuses." "Eine einfältige Weise zu beten, 1535," WA 38:365.31 (see also AE 43:187–211): "not swear, curse, lie by it."

16   WA 30.1:62.20 (see also AE 51:141–45). Cf. "Kat.-Pred. zum 2. Gebot vom 1.12.1528," WA 30.1:63.2 (see also AE 51:141–45): "Who trusts in Him calls upon Him in every need, praises and thanks Him." WA 30.1:63.14 (see also AE 51:141–45): "On the contrary, he should fear God, etc., call upon Him in every need, praise, and honor Him." "Von den guten Werken, 1520," WA 6:218.2 (see also AE 44:15–114): "honor, call upon, praise, preach, and laud His name." "Pred. zum 1. u. 2. Gebot vom 26.2.1523," WA 11:37.37: "When you are in time of death, in dangers, then call upon the name with mouth and heart. Then His name is glorified and the world becomes better." "Eine kurze Erklärung, 1518," WA 1:254.20: "Laud, honor, blessing, and calling on God's name."

17   An exception is found in *BSLK*, 575.44ff.

18   "Kat.-Pred. zum 2. und 3. Gebot vom 15.9.1528," WA 30.1:31.34: "Do not use the name of God for lying, evil, harm, but for truth and your and your neighbor's good."

19   *BSLK*, 572.42, 573.2, 574.13, 574.36, 575.44, 576.11, 577.3.

20   *BSLK*, 576.3, 576.7, 576.12, 576.23.

21   *BSLK*, 577.33–580.9.

22   "Kat.-Pred. zum 2. praeceptum vom 19.5.1528," WA 30.1:4.30–5.15. The sermon from Dec. 1, 1528 (WA 30.1:63.18–64.4 [see also AE 51:141–45]) clarifies this admonition by means of the negative counterimage of a bridge builder who falls into his damnation cursing.

movement includes the simple exposition of the commandment, coverage of its realm of application, and exercise in concrete obedience. These three steps are applied to both the negative prohibition and to the positive commandment, as well as being connected simultaneously to the threat. First, Luther concentrates on the abuse of God's name,[23] then he unfolds the proper use of the divine name.[24]

I.   In a first address, the abuse is (a) enunciated "in a simple way."[25] It takes place where the Lord's name is mentioned "for lying or all sorts of vice."[26] (b) Then, Luther briefly describes the possible forms of abuse.[27] First, he differentiates between (1) the "worldly dealings and matters that affect money, goods, honor"[28] and (2) the "spiritual matters that affect conscience."[29] In both realms one seeks to counterfeit truth under the protection of God's name. This is the central abuse of the name in comparison to which open blaspheming is easily spotted; therefore Luther mentions the latter (3) only briefly.[30] (4) The result is summarized concisely:[31] The abuse of the name is the "greatest sin that can take place outwardly."[32] (c) Against this abuse the zealous holy God asserts His word of threat.[33] In this, Luther confronts both (1) our machinations to cover our disgrace with God's name and (2) God's punishment within the world. (d) At the end, Luther draws the conclusion and summarizes the transgressions in which, in a relatively abrupt manner, the triad "curse, swear, employ magic"[34] stands next to the lie, perhaps as a short insertion from the sermon on December 1 or from the Small Catechism.[35] Yet he first demands that this commandment is to be drummed

---

23   *BSLK*, 572.26–576.6.

24   *BSLK*, 576.7–580.9.

25   *BSLK*, 572.26–573.10. Following "Kat.-Pred. zum 2. u. 3. Gebot vom 15.9.1528," WA 30.1:30.9–17.

26   *BSLK*, 572.42.

27   *BSLK*, 573.11–574.24. Following "Kat.-Pred. zum 2. u. 3. Gebot vom 15.9.1528," WA 30.1:30.17–28.

28   *BSLK*, 573.17.

29   *BSLK*, 573.26.

30   *BSLK*, 573.34ff.

31   *BSLK*, 574.8–24.

32   *BSLK*, 574.12.

33   *BSLK*, 574.25–575.31. According to "Kat.-Pred. zum 2. u. 3. Gebot vom 15.9.1528," WA 30.1:30.29–31.2.

34   *BSLK*, 575.46.

35   *BSLK*, 575.42–576.6. This recapitulation is identical with the first three topics of what is prohibited in the Small Catechism, as well as in the third sermon series ("[Kat.-Pred.] zum 2. Gebot vom 1.12.1528," WA 30.1:62.13, 62.21, 63.13, 63.26 [see also AE 51:141–45]). From this,

into the young.[36] He describes how this is to be done after unfolding the positive dimension of the commandment.

II. The proper use of the name of God[37] is (a) in an initial address deduced from the negative,[38] in which the truth replaces the lie and the good replaces the vice. This yields the phrase: to use God's name "for the truth and all good things."[39] (b) The unfolding is only hinted at in four directions:[40] swearing rightly, teaching rightly, calling upon God in all needs, thanking God in good fortune (Ps. 50:15), whereby the First Petition of the Lord's Prayer is hinted at in advance.[41] (c) An insertion[42] reflects, along with tradition,[43] on the permitted oath and again points to God's zealous holiness that sets justice apart from injustice.[44] (d) Practicing what has been recognized follows.[45] In a way reminiscent of his preface to the "Deutschen Messe" ("German Mass"), Luther shows how one could and should "raise the youth in a childlike and playful way," "in God's fear and honor, so that the First and Second Commandment would always be about and in constant practice."[46]

THE PROHIBITION OF ABUSING THE HOLY NAME IN THE OLD TESTAMENT DECALOGUE[47]

The prohibition of abuse of God's name is, by means of the sermonlike transition, immediately tied back to the basic commandment. Yahweh denies the cultic image to Israel; "where the cultic image stood in the pagan religions,

---

Meyer has drawn important conclusions for the relative chronology of the Large and Small Catechisms (Meyer, *Historischer Kommentar*, 59; *Luthers Großer Katechismus*, 19).

36 *BSLK*, 575.32–41.

37 *BSLK*, 576.7–580.9.

38 *BSLK*, 576.7–22.

39 *BSLK*, 576.13. "Kat.-Pred. vom 15.9.1528," WA 30.1:31.14: "for justice, truth, for improvement for me and my neighbor."

40 *BSLK*, 576.15–36.

41 *BSLK*, 576.24f.

42 *BSLK*, 576.37–577.32.

43 *BSLK*, 576.37–577.32, going back freely to "Kat.-Pred. vom 15.9.1528," WA 30.1:31.16–27.

44 Luther here mentions the specific needs of those years; cf. *BSLK*, 575 nn. 4–7.

45 *BSLK*, 577.33–580.9.

46 *BSLK*, 579.18, 577.33–580.9, going back to "Kat.-Pred. vom 15.9.1528," WA 30.1:31.27–34. Cf. "Vorrede zur Deutschen Messe, 1526," WA 19:75–78 (see also AE 53:51–90).

47 See on this Hans Bietenhard, ὄνομα, *TWNT* 5:242–83. Grether, *Name und Wort Gottes im Alten Testament*; Stamm, "Dreißig Jahre Dekalogforschung," 281–90.

there was Yahweh's word and name."[48] The name is the divine revelatory power facing man. In it the revelation, as well as the salvific activity, is present in such a way that believers can secure them by means of the name. As an originally cultic expression, qar'a b^{e}šēm yhwh means "to call upon Yahweh by means of His name."[49] This took place in the cult during sacrifice and prayer, in blessing as well as in cursing.

Only this cultic use is legitimate. It is protected by the prohibition that is given to the pilgrims gathered at the sanctuary for their daily lives in which cultic rites were absent. The clans are not to "lift up [Yahweh's name] to what is vain." The word šaw', "to abuse blasphemously," originally might have meant the "mischief-causing spell"[50] or magical practices in general, since it is not surprising "that also people in Israel were vulnerable to using Yahweh's name for dark and dangerous practices."[51] In those concrete abuses is concentrated the human will to grab that mysterious supreme power that disclosed itself by the revealed name and thus to claim it for itself, to wrest the blessing from it. "This is why man wants to know the name of the god: first, then, can he use the latter, live with him, argue with him, and possibly—by magic—control him."[52] This primeval grasping for the name we can observe in Manoah's question for the angel: "What is your name?" (Judg. 13:17), as well as in Jacob's wrestling with the God-man for the blessing (Gen. 32:27).

Just as Moses' call is marked with the Elohistic interpretation of the Lord's name (Exod. 3:14)—the one-time 'ehyeh 'ašer 'ehyeh, "I will show Myself as the one I will show Myself"[53]—so these accounts, too, are marked by the tension between God's turn to man by which He exposes Himself and His sovereign freedom. As He reveals His name, God gives Himself completely into our human world, yet He remains, precisely in His self-exposure, the sovereign Lord who is tied to His own promise in faithfulness alone and who rejects, even strikes down, the lustful grasp of man.[54]

---

48   Von Rad, Theologie des Alten Testaments, 1:218.

49   Gen. 12:8; 13:4; 21:33; 1 Kings 18:24.

50   Mowinckel, Psalmstudien, 1:50ff.

51   Von Rad, Theologie des Alten Testaments, 1:185. Stamm, Der Dekalog im Lichte der neueren Forschung, 47: "Magical texts hold an important place in ancient oriental literature. Contrariwise, they are entirely absent in the Old Testament because magic and spells are excluded here."

52   Van der Leeuw, Phänomenologie der Religion, 157. Volz, Mose und sein Werk, 42: "Name and existence are intimately connected in antiquity, name and appearance are related, name is power; who knows the name of a numen has power over the numen . . . who calls out the name of the numen summons the numen and works the power that lies in the numen. This is why especially magic and enchantment are connected to the name."

53   Vriezen, " 'Ehje 'aser 'ehje." Cf. also Grether, Name und Wort Gottes im Alten Testament, 9ff.

54   Cf. Buber, Moses, 150ff.; Noth, Das zweite Buch Mose, 29ff.; Zimmerli, "Das zweite Gebot," 246.

The Second Commandment bends us under Yahweh's zealous, holy watching over the salutary use of His name. This is why it alone and exclusively has a threat added to it. By this threat, the Lord fences in His name, even as He lets it dwell in the midst of His people. The holy walk in God's name,[55] as well as the unholy abuse of it, takes place in three directions: (1) God's name separates between the vain idols and the living God. His name is hallowed where He dominates the cult; it is desecrated where other gods are worshiped and offered sacrifices,[56] as this has already been shown regarding the First Commandment. (2) God's name separates what is good from what is evil. It is hallowed wherever it is called upon in all needs in a ritually correct way and praised for its demonstrations of salvation; it is desecrated wherever it is abused for dark practices, wherever it is subjected to the lie and the evil or even cursed.[57] (3) God's name is the foundation and guarantee for the community among people.[58] It is hallowed where, for example, God's Law is corroborated and confirmed before the community by an oath; it is desecrated where an evil deed is to be covered by it.[59]

CHARACTERISTICS OF LUTHER'S INTERPRETATION

1. HONORING GOD'S NAME IN LUTHER'S EARLY INTERPRETATIONS

In his interpretations, Luther moves the Second Commandment increasingly into the light of the First. By doing so, he moves away from the traditional interpretation. In "Decem praecepta Wittenbergensi praedicata populo" ("Preaching of the Ten Commandments"), Luther still follows the medieval confessional manuals that, above all, refer to frivolous swearing, to perjury, and to broken vows.[60] In his "Kurzen Erklärung" ("Short Explanation"),[61] he takes this triad together as well. In the "Sermon on Good Works," Luther pushes beyond the gross fleshly abuse and aims at the subtle and spiritual one.[62] At the same time, he places the commandment, based on

---

55   Mic. 4:5.

56   Lev. 18:11; 20:3.

57   Exod. 22:28.

58   Gerstenberger, *Wesen und Herkunft*, 141ff.

59   Cf. F. Horst, "Der Eid im AT," *Evangelische Theologie* 17 (1957): 366–84; Johannes Schneider, ὀμνύω and ὅρκος, *TWNT* 5:177–85, 458–67.

60   See the overview in Geffcken, *Bildercatechismus*, 59–63, as well as Weidenhiller, *Untersuchungen*, 46, 70f., 113. Cf. "Decem praecepta, 1518," WA 1:432.16–435.10.

61   WA 1:252.17: "Whoever swears frivolously or out of habit; whoever commits perjury or also breaks his vow." WA 1:260.14: "Who swear out of bad habit and without cause. Who swear falsely or vow evil or violate good vows."

62   WA 6:225.32–226.3 (see also AE 44:15–114).

its positive core, into the situation of the incipient persecution of the Protestants.[63] In this controversy regarding God's honor, every Christian must take sides with the prophets and apostles and bear with them the enmity of the world.[64] Luther concludes his comments with these words: "It is high time that we ask God that He would hallow His name, but it will cost blood."[65]

In the Large Catechism, Luther returns to the gross abuse, but not without hinting at the inner spiritual aspect and, by doing so, accentuating the positive use of God's name. This is why our interpretation will keep those deeper references in view.[66]

In the Large and Small Catechisms, Luther uses the code word of God's name like a coin—without examining its value. Following Augustine and Bonaventure,[67] the reformer had, in his early commentary on the Psalms, identified God's name by and large with Christ. For Luther, Christ is essentially God's name because He is the Word of the invisible Father.[68] In Christ, God has revealed Himself to us, which is why the Church returns through Him in prayer to the Father. The Old Testament insight is that God's saving activity is concentrated in God's name; indeed, God has "deposited" His name here on earth so that we would have a place to find refuge. Yahweh wants to hear and save us "for His name's sake."[69] For Christendom, this Old Testament connection between God's name and His self-disclosure is filled by the suffering, death, and resurrection of Jesus of Nazareth; He is that name in which alone salvation is promised us (Acts 4:12).

This identification is not found in the catechism. Following the First Commandment, God's name is addressed primarily in the horizon of creation as the source of all goods[70] and as helper in all needs.[71]

---

63   WA 6:228.33–229.14 (see also AE 44:15–114).

64   WA 6:226.5f. (see also AE 44:15–114). Cf. "Pred. über Ex. 20:7 vom 22.10.1525," WA 16:472.27–473.24.

65   WA 6:229.11 (see also AE 44:15–114).

66   The eschatological struggle for the sanctification of God's name is taken up with the First Petition of the Lord's Prayer.

67   See in Augustine, e.g., C. Faust. M., I:XV, c. 6ff.; Serm. 8:5; 9:2. Augustine here follows ecclesiastical usage that referred dominus to Jesus Christ. In Bonaventure, e.g., Collationes de decem praeceptis 3:2; 2:9ff.

68   "Dict. super Psalterium, 1513–16," WA 3:158.18 (see also AE 10:1–464): "But the divinity is mostly in the Person of the Son, because He is the Name and Word of the Father." "Dict. super Psalterium, 1513–16," WA 3:461.10 (see also AE 10:1–464): "The name of His majesty, which is Jesus Christ, the Son of God." Additional texts given by Hardeland, Katechismusgedanken, 53f.

69   Proofs in Bietenhard, ὄνομα, TWNT 5:242–83; for Luther, e.g., "Eine kurze Form, 1520" (WA 7:205.22f.); "Pred. über Lk. 10:23ff. vom 22.8.1529" (WA 29:529.18f.); "Eine einfältige Weise zu beten, 1535" (WA 38:365.33–38 [see also AE 43:187–211]).

70   BSLK, 565.41.

71   "Kat.-Pred. zum 2. praeceptum vom 19.5.1528," WA 30.1:4.32: "The honor of His name consists in that I expect all good from it, that He is present in all need."

However, the early Christological focus and the later limitation to the Creator have in common the rather anthropocentric connection between name and honor. As in some Old Testament texts,[72] Luther also uses the name frequently as a code word for laud, honor, and praise. Thus in the 1517 "Auslegung der Bußpsalmen" ("Interpretation of the Penitential Psalms"), he writes on Ps. 102:22: "Laud, name, and honor are one thing—for to whom belongs the essence, to him belongs also the work—yet to whom belongs the work, to him belongs justly also the name."[73] And in the "Short Explanation," he adds: "Of God are these too: truth, goodness, power, and the name of all good things is His name."[74] In "Operationes in Psalmos" ("Operations in the Psalms"), Luther unfolds this understanding and heaps all laud on God: "Since, however, only God works all in all, the conclusion is certain: Only to God is owed the name of all works. Therefore only He is good, wise, just, truthful, merciful, gentle, holy, strong, Lord, Father, Judge—finally, whatever He can be named or whatever can be predicated of Him in praise."[75]

In these early interpretations, Luther emphasizes God's honor against human self-glorification. Following Augustine, he shows tirelessly that the destruction of man has to correspond to the praise of God. Thus the fulfillment of the commandment reads according to the "Short Explanation": "Laud, honor, praise, and calling upon God's name and totally destroying one's own name and honor so that God alone might be praised who alone is and works all things."[76] In great detail in "Operations in Psalms," Luther shows the correspondence between praising God and self-annihilation: "Hallowed be Your name, but profaned be my name and everything."[77] Tirelessly he

---

72 E.g., Exod. 9:16; Josh. 9:9; Isa. 26:8; 55:13; 59:19; Ps. 48:11; 102:16; 106:47; 145:21. Cf. Bietenhard, ὄνομα, *TWNT* 5:256.21–39.

73 WA 1:204.6. In the 1525 edition of the "Bearbeitung der Bußpsalmenauslegung," WA 18:514.36 (see also AE 14:137–205): "Whose work it is, to him belongs justly the name; whose name it is, to him also belongs laud; and the honor belongs to him to whom belongs laud."

74 WA 1:250.9. Cf. "Instructio, 1518," WA 1:258.10; "Ausl. dtsch. d. Vaterunsers, 1519," WA 2:94.12 (see also AE 42:15–81); "Eine kurze Form, das Paternoster zu verstehen u. zu beten, 1519," WA 6:12.29 (see also AE 44:15–114); "Ausl. d. Magnificat, 1521," WA 7:575.30 (see also AE 21:295–355); *BSLK*, 670.18, 671.18, 672.11, 672.40.

75 WA 5:187.35. Cf. WA 5.184.14–31, 248.3–27, 657.1–659.3; "Dict. super psalterium, 1513–16," WA 3:158.12–17 (see also AE 10:1–464); "Pred. vom 9.3.1523," WA 11:57.7: "He is what is called 'God,' 'Lord,' 'merciful,' 'just,' 'truthful,' love,' 'prudence,' 'strength.' Who takes up these names blasphemes God." Similarly, the "Nürnberger Katechismuspredigten" (Reu, *Quellen*, 1.1:469.41–470.2).

76 WA 1:254.20. "Instructio, 1518," WA 1:263.7: "Invocation, laud, glorification of God's holy name and of the name of the neighbor, and contempt of vainglory—that is God's grace through Jesus Christ." Cf. "Eine kurze Erklärung, 1518," WA 1:250.9f.; "Eine kurze Unterweisung, 1519," WA 2:61.23f.; "Eine kurze Form, 1520," WA 7:212.21ff.; "Eine einfältige Weise zu beten, 1535," WA 38:365.30ff. (see also AE 43:187–211).

77 WA 5:183.2. Cf. WA 5:188.5–21, 191.12–192.23, 250.18–39, 542.7–543.34, 657.1–659.23 and passim.

sharpens the penetrating sword of the Thesis 95 against scholastic theology: "To love God means to hate oneself and to know nothing besides God."[78]

In the "Sermon on Good Works," Luther advances this alternative against the extraordinary moral feats of man, emphatically referencing Augustine.[79] By means of this Second Commandment, God enforces His honor against every self-glorification of man. God thereby condemns not only any verbal abuse of His name, but He also rejects striving for glory.[80] Especially in his purest works—in the sacrificial death for one's land, in dedication to wife and child, in enduring superhuman hardships—man seeks his glory. The nations have unabashedly articulated this in their songs and poems, especially the Romans but also the Greeks and the Jews.[81] On the level of interhuman ethics, a praiseworthy deed took place; on the level of how the person in this deed related to God as his Creator and Savior, sinful defilement took place. Here the ego held on to itself in its honor before fellow men and did not hide itself in God's omnipotence. "Therefore God's holy name, which alone should be honored, is abused and dishonored by our cursed name, by our self-pleasing and seeking of honor. This sin is more serious before God than murder and adultery, but its evil nature is not as easily perceived as that of murder because of its subtlety, because it is committed not in gross flesh but in the spirit."[82]

In this way also, the prohibition against misusing the name uncovers the original sin of man: We refuse to honor the God who discloses Himself to us in His name and Word, that is, in Jesus Christ. In view of the God who in creation and redemption showers His blessing on us, we go on our self-chosen paths and pursue our own honor. Yet we can gain and preserve true honor before God and man only by subjecting it to the cross of Christ and carrying it home to God.[83] Luther illustrates the obedience under the

---

78   WA 1:228.29.

79   Augustine, *De spir. et lit.* 27:48, and the Augustine citation in Prosper of Aquitaine (PL 45:1863): "All vices only prevail in evildoers; only hubris is to be feared also in those who act rightly."

80   Cf. especially "Röm.-Vorl., 1515/16," WA 56:157.11–19 (see also AE 25:1–524); "Von den guten Werken, 1520," WA 6:220.10–33 (see also AE 44:15–114); "De servo arbitrio, 1525," WA 18:742.31–743.15 (see also AE 33:3–295); "Gal.-Komm., 1535," WA 40.1:461.6–9 (see also AE 26:1–461).

81   "De servo arbitrio, 1525," WA 18:743.8 (see also AE 33:3–295): "Yet how they acted for the glory of God while they were ignorant of God and His glory, not because it did not appear but because the flesh did not allow them to see the glory of God before all that raging and madness for their own glory."

82   "Von den guten Werken, 1520," WA 6:220.28 (see also AE 44:15–114). Cf. "De votis monasticis, 1521," WA 8:618.1–619.26 (see also AE 44:243–400); "Pred. über Ex. 20:7 vom 22.10.1525," WA 16:466.26–470.25.

83   "De votis monasticis, 1521," WA 8:619.17 (see also AE 44:243–400): "For who says, 'I will be saved by my own works,' says nothing else than, 'I am Christ,' since only Christ's works save as many as are saved."

Second Commandment by means of Mary, who in the Magnificat is fully absorbed in praising the exalted God who has come down to her lowliness.[84] "She did not want anybody to think anything of herself, but God alone she makes great. To Him she gives all praise. She takes everything off and offers everything again up to God from whom she had received it."[85]

Again the reformer has penetrated the gross carnal understanding of the commandment to arrive at the subtle spiritual understanding. No longer is he wrestling with young students and simple Christians but with monks and spiritually awakened believers. This struggle on the part of Christians against the inner Pharisee goes right through those who wish to be Christians in earnest. The difficult choice—either praising God or praising self—marks the front line.

This holds true in view of the individual Christian. In view of the whole Church there is the battle for God's honor between true and false proclamation and doctrine. This is the latest instance of Yahweh's battle against the idols. In his "Sermon on Good Works" and in his sermons on Exodus, Luther calls the struggle for right preaching the proper work of this commandment: "The greatest and most difficult work of this commandment is to protect the holy name of God against all who abuse it spiritually and to spread it among all of them."[86] The Lord demands readiness for martyrdom; for His name's sake we have to endure the enmity of the world. "Whenever a person accepts the Word of God, the Gospel, let him only think that from that time on he is in danger of losing all his goods, house, farm, fields, pastures, wife, children, father and mother, even his own life."[87]

While the first tension between love of God and self was not mentioned in the Large Catechism, the struggle for right preaching is hinted at.[88] The false preachers who "offer their cheap lies as word of God"[89] appear in a

---

84   Cf. especially "Ausl. d. Magnificat, 1521," WA 7:568.4–8, 573.24–30, 574.3–575.27, 576.13–32 (see also AE 21:295–355).

85   "Ausl. d. Magnificat, 1521," WA 7:555.14 (see also AE 21:295–355). WA 7:555.25 (see also AE 21:295–355): "In such a complete manner she has not taken on all these things and has left to God His goods for Himself freely and without any strings. She was no more than a joyous inn and willing host of such a guest. This is why she has also retained all these things forever. Behold, this is what it means to magnify God alone: only think of Him greatly and take on nothing for ourselves."

86   "Von den guten Werken, 1520," WA 6:226.1 (see also AE 44:15–114); "Pred. über Ex. 20:7 vom 22.10.1525," WA 16:472.27. Cf. "Von den guten Werken, 1520," WA 6:228.27–229.14 (see also AE 44:15–114). This is taken up in the "Nürnberger Katechismuspredigten" (Reu, Quellen, 1.1:472.43–473.9).

87   "Pred. über Ex. 20:7 vom 22.10.1525," WA 16:473.14.

88   BSLK, 573.25–29, 573.39–42.

89   BSLK, 573.27.

negative light, while the positive of right teaching is only touched upon.[90] In this dimension, everything is at stake, which is why the greatest care is required. "In matters affecting the salvation of souls, nothing but God's Word is to be taught and accepted."[91] In his Exodus sermons, Luther mentions the pope and the enthusiasts as the two opponents;[92] reminds his hearers that the devil "makes himself out to be the angel of light" (2 Cor. 11:14);[93] and comfortingly points to God's final action: "To be sure, God looks on for a while, but He is a zealot. He is jealous, unable to endure it for long. This is why He finally strikes, and really roughly too."[94]

2. Misusing the Name and Swearing an Oath According to the Catechisms

In the catechism, Luther concentrates the interpretation on the interhuman level. God's worldly rule moves to the center. The struggle for the right proclamation in God's spiritual rule is assigned to the First Petition of the Lord's Prayer.[95] Here, in the realm of the sociopolitical common human life, should God's name serve to to cover up lies and evil,[96] then the breaking of human fellowship is made worse as its divine Guarantor Himself is drawn into committing evil. Almost in a naïve manner, lacking reflection, Luther here presupposes what Calvin and Melanchthon unfold and prove,[97] namely, that these interhuman orders are not secular but have in God Himself their Guarantor and Lord Protector. In this sense, the First Commandment really is at stake even in the interhuman realm. Luther shows this by the way he makes connections. While the First Commandment was about the relation of man's heart to God, the Second Commandment focuses our mouth and tongue on God.[98] The heart gives God His honor by faith; the mouth

---

90   *BSLK*, 576.16. "Kat.-Pred. zum 2. Gebot vom 1.12.1528," WA 30.1:64.8 (see also AE 51:141–45): "I now speak about childish and domestic matters. I will not now speak also about our abuse of God's name in preaching."

91   "Von weltlicher Oberkeit, 1523," WA 11:263.5 (see also AE 45:75–129).

92   Cf. "Pred. über Ex. 20:7 vom 22.10.1525," WA 16:466–70.

93   "Pred. über Ex. 20:7 vom 22.10.1525," WA 16:468.8.

94   "Pred. über Ex. 20:7 vom 22.10.1525," WA 16:470.9.

95   Cf. the commentary on the First Petition of the Lord's Prayer.

96   *BSLK*, 574.8–24.

97   Calvin, *Inst.* 4:20.9 (*Opera Selecta* 5:479.34): "If Scripture did not teach the extension (of the authority of the magistrate) to both Tables of the Law, one would have to learn it from the secular writers, for not one of them talked about the office of magistrates, the enacting of laws, and the public estate that did not begin with religion and divine worship." Melanchthon, *Loci*, in *Studienausgabe* 2.2:727.20–730.5.

98   *BSLK*, 572.29. "Decem praecepta, 1518," WA 1:430.10: "Therefore, in the First Commandment, the heart and the inner man are established toward God; in this one, the mouth is established likewise."

does the same by the doctrinal confession.[99] In this, our mouth points back to our heart, as the former shows what is in the latter. This is how, even in interhuman matters, God is first and last. The word of threat underlines this,[100] as this prohibition means to prevent "the greatest sin that can be done externally."[101]

The relation between the *coram hominibus* and the *coram Deo* is centered in the oath.[102] In it the divine numen is directly invoked over the human community. Here the highest stake is demanded and given. This is why making an oath is a dangerous and controversial field.[103] Already tradition had connected the question of the permitted oath with this commandment,[104] and Luther, too, deals with it prominently in "Preaching of the Ten Commandments."[105] Already in this first interpretation, Luther asks for the true meaning of the words of Jesus in Matt. 5:33–37[106] and thus aligns the basic tension in his tract on civil authority: I look either to myself or to my "sick neighbor."[107] We should not and may not swear spontaneously and based on our own desires, but we should and may do so to help the neighbor, forced and urged by his need.[108] Luther is conscious of the fact that by means of this distinction he has reached a new level of clarity.[109] Yet looking to the neighbor and his need in this way is prepared by the accentuation of the common good, when, for example, Bonaventure states that the oath is right where it takes place "to promote good, to preserve fidelity, and

---

99 *BSLK*, 578.1–3.

100 *BSLK*, 574.25ff.

101 *BSLK*, 574.12. Cf. "Von den guten Werken, 1520," WA 6:219.16–21, 228.31 (see also AE 44:15–114).

102 *BSLK*, 576.37–577.32.

103 On the oath: Hermann Strathmann, "Eid," *EKL* 1:1027–33; Günther Wendt, "Eid IV," *RGG* 2:351–54; Georg Holzherr, "Eid III," *LTK* 3:728–29; Bauernfeind, *Eid und Frieden*; Elert, "Zur Frage des Soldateneides"; Thielicke, *Ethik* 2.1, §§ 749–58, 2569–90. Luther texts: "Decem praecepta, 1518," WA 1:432.21–433.2, 435.11–436.10; "Pred. zum 1. u. 2. Gebot vom 26.2.1523," WA 11:37.15–38.3; "Pred. über Ex. 20:7 vom 22.10.1525," WA 16:473–76; "Kat.-Pred. zum 2. u. 3. Gebot vom 15.9.1528," WA 30.1:31.16–34; "Ausl. v. Mt. 5–7, 1530/32," WA 32:381–86 (see also AE 21:1–294). Texts from the Confessions: AC XVI, XXVII (*BSLK*, 116.21–28); Ap XVI; Ep XII (*BSLK*, 824.16–20); SD XII (*BSLK*, 1095.27–31). Additionally Calvin, *Inst.* 2:8.23–27; Geneva Catechism, quest. 161f.; Heidelberg Catechism, quest. 101f.

104 From tradition: Augustine, *De mendacio* 15:28; *De sermone Domini in monte* 1:17.51; Serm. 180.3; Peter Lombard, *Sent.* III, dist. 38f.; Thomas Aquinas, *Summa Theologiae* I/II, quest. 89; Bonaventure, *In sent.* III, dist. 39, c. 4, t. III; Geffcken, *Bildercatechismus*, 59f.

105 WA 1:432.21–433.2, 435.11–436.10.

106 Cf. also Matt. 23:16–22; 2 Cor. 1:17; James 5:12.

107 "Von weltlicher Oberkeit, 1523," WA 11:254.17 (see also AE 45:75–129).

108 "Decem praecepta, 1518," WA 1:435.26: "For now he does not swear because he does not act on his will, but serves in humility somebody else's will or, in love, somebody else's need."

109 "Pred. zum 1. u. 2. Gebot vom 26.2.1523," WA 11:37.35: "Not even Augustine was able to explain it well, since they did not consider faith and love and that all works are to be done for the sake of the neighbor, but considered one's own matters."

to enter mutual peace."[110] In his sermons on Exodus and his 1532 exposition of the Sermon on the Mount, Luther adds the distinction of the two realms and states: "When the civil authorities mandate it and your neighbor desires it and it is useful for him, then swear at last. It is right, for you pledge God to him."[111]

However, here it becomes apparent that the question regarding the right or the illegitimate oath embraces both realms. The examples of Christ, of prophets and apostles, especially that of Paul,[112] shows that here, too, the all-embracing battle between good and evil, God and Satan is at stake. The oath is rightly demanded and given when it unequivocally stands on the side of the good and separates it from the evil in this battle, when it is necessary for the sake of this battle.[113] By means of His two realms, God breaks into the kingdom of Satan. In the Large Catechism, Luther merely turns our attention to this general meaning of the right oath; in it God Himself steps "into the fray"[114] and establishes among us His sacred divine right.[115] Thus it is the purpose of this commandment "to protect [His] right and defend the holiness of His name."[116]

By this, the meaning of the verb "swear" in the Small Catechism is delimited. Luther connects it closely to "cursing" in his compilations; "lying and deceiving" typically follow.[117] From this context it gains a pejorative

110   Bonaventure, *Collationes de decem praeceptis* 3:21–23; Thomas Aquinas, *Duo praecepta* § 1206: "For no society can last among people unless one believes another." Cf. Peter Lombard, *Sent.* III, dist. 39.3.

111   "Pred. über Ex. 20:7 vom 22.10.1525," WA 16:475.33. Similarly, "Ausl. v. Mt. 5–7, 1530/32," WA 32:385.3–30 (see also AE 21:1–294). The "Nürnberger Katechismuspredigten" simultaneously condemn the frivolous mandating of oaths by the authorities (cf. Reu, *Quellen*, 1.1:470.28f., 35ff.), thereby struggling against the "plague of perjury" (Strathmann, "Eid," EKL 1:1032).

112   BSLK, 576.42f. Cf. "Decem praecepta, 1518," WA 1:432.25f.; "Pred. zum 1. u. 2. Gebot vom 26.2.1523," WA 11:37.16f.; "Pred. über Ex. 20:7 vom 22.10.1525," WA 16:475.3ff.; "Ausl. v. Mt. 5–7, 1530/32," WA 32:385.22ff. (see also AE 21:1–294).

113   "Decem praecepta, 1518," WA 1:432.33: "The reason why this swearing pleases God is this: by it, His truth is invoked and one believes in Him, and because of Him there is peace and concord among those who swear. This is why He is worshiped in a holy manner in this work, because the work of the devil is destroyed, namely, dissention and quarrel." "Ausl. v. Mt. 5–7, 1530/32," WA 32:385.28 (see also AE 21:1–294): "For all this is what it means to use God's name well, for God's honor and for the truth and for the neighbor's salvation and blessedness."

114   BSLK, 577.11.

115   Bauernfeind, "Eid III," 350: "Who calls upon God to be witness to facts or promises that are not unambiguously defined by His revelation and His will goes, according to Matt. 5:33f., back behind that line that separates Jesus from 'those of old.'"

116   Calvin, *Inst.* 2:8.22 (according to the Weber Edition, p. 232). According to Luther, cursing in the name of the zealous holy God can also be done rightly; cf. "Ausl. v. Mt. 5–7, 1530/32," WA 32:383.17–384.8 (see also AE 21:1–294). This reference to the eschatological establishment of the kingdom of God does not receive its due in the literature on the oath.

117   See the compilation on p. 150 n. 15.

meaning.[118] For example, in the sermon on December 1, 1528, it means to perjure oneself blasphemously by God's name.[119] The Large Catechism adds the prohibition of the frivolous oath and thereby summarizes "in a brief manner" also the "meaning" of the Small Catechism: "One ought not to swear for bad, that is, for lying and where it is not needed or useful. But one is to swear for good and for the neighbor's improvement."[120] As "swearing" goes beyond the formal oath and still includes the Middle High German connotation of *sweren*, that is, "to make weighty,"[121] and thus moves close to "cursing," so "lying and deceiving" also goes beyond "perjury." According to the Large Catechism, the former embraces all attempts to abuse God's name for lie and evil; the latter is concentrated more on the deceit, "to allege something under the name that is not."[122] Both verbs are always connected to each other; they circumscribe what is common with their respective accents. In the Large and Small Catechisms and in the sermon on December 1, the notion "engage in magic"[123] Luther apparently picks up from his early compilations without here giving it any further explanation.

3. Practicing the Right Use of the Holy Name

As our Creator and Lord, God Himself enforces His Second Commandment among us. He places His name on our lips. Seemingly, He thereby gives Himself totally into our power and still remains the Lord of history, in which fortune and misfortune, damnation and salvation are decided by His name.[124] As in the First Commandment the reformer taught us to understand world history under the word of threat and blessing as God's campaign against idolatry, so he now interprets world history in the Second Commandment as God's warfare against the abuse of His name for the purpose of lies and deception. In this name God Himself is hidden with His omnipotence and He wars against the prince of this world. "The name of God is powerful and strong."[125]

---

118 In "Decem praecepta, 1518," Luther compiled such frivolous forms of swearing that we use habitually (*ex consuetudine*). He calls on fathers and mothers to resist this evil habit (WA 1:433.5–11). Similarly, see also the "Nürnberger Katechismuspredigten" (cf. Reu, *Quellen*, 1.1:471.5–15).

119 Cf. "Kat.-Pred. zum 2. Gebot vom 1.12.1528," WA 30.1:63.8ff. (see also AE 51:141–45); "Kat.-Pred. zum 2. u. 3. Gebot vom 15.9.1528," WA 30.1:31.30.

120 *BSLK*, 577.2.

121 In the sense of "solemnly affirming." See the proofs given by Ebeling, "Das zweite Gebot in Luthers Kleinem Katechismus," 237ff., and by Meyer, *Historischer Kommentar*, 197f.

122 *BSLK*, 575.45.

123 *BSLK*, 575.46; "Kat.-Pred. zum 2. Gebot vom 1.12.1528," WA 30.1:62.13, 62.21, 63.13, 63.26 (see also AE 51:141–145). Cf. p. 150 n. 15.

124 *BSLK*, 574.45–575.31.

125 "Kat.-Pred. zum 2. praeceptum vom 19.5.1528," WA 30.1:4.34. "Kat.-Pred. zum 2. praeceptum vom 19.5.1528," WA 30.1:5.1: "And Satan does not like to hear it, because he is terrified by it

This name is to be called on as a life-giving force. Yes, it is to be used like a weapon against the cunning assaults of the foe. The devil fears this name; it is the "little word" that can fell him. Luther is not ashamed to point to concrete instances of answered prayer.[126] God's name is our fortress of refuge.[127] Where somebody despises the name, he remains under the rule of Satan. In the third series of sermons, Luther describes, quite in the style of late medieval examples, the death of a master builder who was accustomed to begin his daily work with the curse: "Onward, then, in the devil's hundred thousand names!" When somebody pointed out the foolishness and danger of that manner of speaking, he replied that he would call on God in time of need. One day he fell off a bridge. Out of his old habit, this curse again came from his lips. Thus he died frivolously while calling on the destructive forces.[128]

To prevent this from happening, Luther wants to teach the youth "playfully" in the "blessed useful habit"[129] of calling on God. The defensive discipline of the rod,[130] the *crassus usus praeceptorum*,[131] can at first only govern the abuse and make the bodily turning toward God a habit. Yet if the loving heart were not added, then everything would remain under the curse of the Law. In "Operations in the Psalms," Luther rejects a superstitious worship of God's name that only takes place as an *opus operatum*. He formulates crisply: "Not the name, but faith in the name of the Lord does everything."[132]

In the catechisms, the accent lies on the positive side of the practice, on the morning and evening blessing as well as on the table prayers, on the good habit of making the sign of the cross, of calling on God in fear and gratitude.[133] However, the former delimitation is thereby not revoked.

---

and forced to flee."

126 Cf. *BSLK*, 578.18–34. "Gen.-Vorl., 1535–45," WA 43:510.18 (see also AE 5:1–386): "There, then, I will be forced to fall on my knees and implore help and counsel from God, who is strong and who, while we sleep, turns a tragic convulsion into a comical conclusion." Cf. "Gen.-Vorl., 1535–45," WA 43:510.13–30, 519.18–34 (see also AE 5:1–386); "Kat.-Pred. zum 2. Gebot vom 1.12.1528," WA 30.1:64.4–9 (see also AE 51:141–45).

127 "Eine einfältige Weise zu beten, 1535," WA 38:365.37 (see also AE 43:187–211): ". . . that His name is a refuge like a mighty fortress (as Solomon says, Prov. 18:10), to which the righteous flee and are protected."

128 "Kat.-Pred. zum 2. Gebot vom 1.12.1528," WA 30.1:63.18–64.6 (see also AE 51:141–45). But Luther says that he knew this man.

129 *BSLK*, 578.18.

130 *BSLK*, 575.35ff.

131 "Pred. zum 1. Gebot vom 24.2.1523," WA 11:31.8.

132 WA 5:184.15: "Without the piety of faith all things are superstitious and damnable to the point that neither Christ nor God is salutary for anyone unless He is had by faith. This is why every name of God, in fact, every word of God, is of omnipotent force to save body and soul if it is seized by the reverence of faith. Therefore not the name but faith in the name does everything." Cf. "Decem praecepta," WA 1:431.16–19.

133 *BSLK*, 578.43–579.17.

Adolescents are drilled to use God's name rightly not only by means of rods and beatings—this would not overcome the heart's hatred of God. Rather, everything depends on the fear and love of God taking root in the heart and on the heart becoming free from fear of men or the mere habit. Quite consciously the reformer wants to lead the external practice over into the inner willingness of the heart. This would be the *sensus puerilis praeceptorum* that is deepened in the *usus spiritualis*.[134] In the preface to the "German Mass," Luther remembers the example of the Lord Himself: "Christ, since He wanted to draw men, had to become a man. If we are to draw children, we also have to become children with them."[135] This condescension of parents, pastors, and teachers to the adolescents appears in light of Phil. 2:5–12.[136]

By means of these childlike exercises, the way to the Lord opens up for little ones. They are not seen primarily (let alone exclusively) as depraved people who "have to be forced with laws spiritually and in the way of the world," like wild beasts; they also are not seen as those who abuse their freedom as a cover for their evilness (1 Pet. 2:16), even if God will enforce His prohibition also against them. First and foremost, Luther thinks of the young and simple people as those who have to be led to the inner obedience of faith by means of bodily gestures and outwardly spoken words.[137] This pedagogical accent is clearly made. However, we must not overlook that Luther is not talking here about the pedagogic of a humanist master teacher but about the practice of God the Father through Jesus Christ in the Holy Spirit.[138] In this sense also the reformer, as a student of the catechism, submits to this childlike exercise,[139] since no one here on earth has ever gone beyond it. Among those who "wish to be Christians in earnest and confess the Gospel with hand and mouth,"[140] this exercise could be concentrated on the center, on a good, brief catechism. Desiring to overcome this exercise would be tantamount to enthusiasm.

TEXTS ON THE SECOND COMMANDMENT

WA 1:430–36: from Decem praecepta Wittenbergensi praedicata populo, 1518

---

134 "Pred. zum 1. Gebot vom 24.2.1523," WA 11:31.10, 31.12. Cf. *BSLK*, 575.39f., 579.27, 579.33ff.

135 WA 19:78.13 (see also AE 53:51–90).

136 Cf. "Sermo de duplici iustitia, 1519," WA 2:147.19–150.31 (see also AE 31:293–306); and "Fastenpost. zu Phil. 2:5–12, 1525," WA 17.2:237–45.

137 See the comments on the prefaces, pp. 31ff., and on the *usus praeceptorum*, p. 141.

138 These insights confirm that the reformer sought to gain his pedagogical-didactic consequences directly from his spiritual-theological insights. This is why it is not good to bring the alternative between "methodical aid" and "theological principle" to the catechisms (against Fraas, *Katechismustradition*, 28).

139 *BSLK*, 548.4ff.

140 "Vorrede zur Deutschen Messe, 1526," WA 19:75.5 (see also AE 53:51–90).

WA 6:217–29: from Sermon von den guten Werken, 1520 (see also AE 44:15–114)

WA 7:544–604: Das Magnificat verdeutscht und ausgelegt, 1521 (see also AE 21:295–355)

WA 8:617–23: from De votis monasticis iudicium, 1521 (see also AE 44:243–400)

WA 16:464–77: from Predigt über Ex. 20:7 vom 22.10.1525

WA 18:739–55: from De servo arbitrio, 1525 (see also AE 33:3–295)

WA 32:381–86: from Auslegung zu Mt. 5–7, zu Mt. 5:33ff., 1530/32 (see also AE 21:1–294)

WA 47:472–82: Predigt über Mt. 23:16ff. vom 9.7.1539

LITERATURE[141]

Ebeling, "Das zweite Gebot in Luthers Kleinem Katechismus"

Hardeland, *Luthers Katechismusgedanken in ihrer Entwicklung bis zum Jahre 1529,* 53–74

Meyer, *Historischer Kommentar zu Luthers Kleinem Katechismus,* 192–205

---

141 Cf. the literature on the First Petition of the Lord's Prayer.

THE THIRD COMMANDMENT[1]

THE WORDING OF THE COMMANDMENT
AND THE ARRANGEMENT OF THE INTERPRETATION

Luther consistently translates the commandment as: "You shall sanctify the feast day."[2] With one class of medieval mnemonic texts, he follows Exod. 20:8; the accent lies on the sanctifying, not on the resting. Other texts, with Exod. 20:9f., emphasize more the rest and the religious observance.[3] Using *Feiertag* ("feast day"), Luther wishes to express the meaning of the Hebrew *šabbat*.[4] That Luther does not want to place emphasis on the command to rest but on the sanctification of the day is something that he first unfolds step by step[5] so he can express it unambiguously in the Large Catechism.[6] In his earlier interpretations, he looked instead to the inner Sabbath rest of the soul.[7] Only little by little does the hearing of the Word of God move to the center and finally eliminate all other aspects,[8] so that the interpretation in the

---

1   For texts on the Third Commandment, see pp. 183–84.

2   *BSLK*, 508.12, 555.18, 580.11. "Eine kurze Erklärung, 1518," WA 1:250.12; "Von den guten Werken, 1520," WA 6:229.20 (see also AE 44:15–114); "Eine kurze Form, 1520," WA 7:205.28.

3   Cf. the proofs offered by Meyer, *Historischer Kommentar*, 89, 207; Weidenhiller, *Untersuchungen*, 46, 67, 71, 183f., 191f.; on Augustine, cf. Rentschka, *Dekalogkatechese*, 128.

4   *BSLK*, 580.12f. "Pred. über Gen. 2 vom 19.4.1523," WA 14:116.14: "'Sabbath,' 'religious observance' *(feir)*, 'rest,' that is the cessation of and desisting from all [human] work and waiting upon the work of God [*quia quiescendum et desistendum ab omnibus operibus, et gewarten dei operibus*]." "Pred. über Gen. 2, 1527," WA 24:61.14: "*Sabbath*, the Hebrew word, means rest or religious observance (*Feier*), so that one might be still and rest of all words and works and cling to God's Word alone."

5   The transition is found in "Eine kurze Form, 1520," WA 7:212.26–213.3.

6   *BSLK*, 584.17–20.

7   "Eine kurze Erklärung, 1518," WA 1:250.13: "The best feast [*Feir*] is that the soul with all deeds on this day wait for Him who fills those who are hungry and free of good things (Lk. 1:53), for 'Feier' means to be free." Cf. "Eine kurze Erklärung, 1518," WA 1:254.24–28; "Instructio, 1518," WA 258.14–16, 263.10–14; "Decem praecepta, 1518," WA 440.23–32; "Von den guten Werken, 1520," WA 6:243.6–13 (see also AE 44:15–114); "Scholia in Gen., 1519–21," WA 9:331.10–17.

8   This concentration is characteristic of "Katechismuspredigt zum 3. Gebot vom 1.12.1528" (WA 30.1:64.10–65.15 [see also AE 51:141–45]), which only hints at the physical rest (WA 30.1:64.10f. [see also AE 51:141–45]) before dedicating itself wholly to the tension between

Small Catechism reads: "We should fear and love God, so that we do not despise the sermon and His Word but hold it sacred, gladly hear and learn it."[9]

Peculiar is the phrase "the sermon *and* His Word." It forms a certain parallel to the strange "and" of the Second Article[10] and means to say: the sermon, and that is, His Word in it. This is why the positive statement refers to the Word: the Word of God is not to be despised in the sermon but held sacred. The parallel section of the Large Catechism[11] equally concentrates on the Word of God. It interprets the despising as unwillingness to hear and learn,[12] and it places those who go to the sermon "only out of habit,"[13] who hear the Word without seriousness and care and do not learn anything from it, next to those who do not come to the Divine Service at all, be it out of greed or carelessness. Both groups desecrate the Word. The more precise use of "despising" confirms in a negative manner that Luther is paraphrasing the positive phrase "keep it holy" with the phrase "gladly hear and learn it":[14] we sanctify the feast day in that we deal with God's Word and practice it,[15] overcome the mortal sin of ἀκηδία (*acedia*),[16] hear the Word with open ears, and lay hold of it with ready hearts.

Luther's analysis of the commandment of the feast day in the Large Catechism states more precisely what he set forth in the Sept. 15, 1528, sermon,[17] and it adds the warning against *acedia* and the function of the Word in the battle between God and Satan from the May 19 sermon.[18] The December 1 sermon adds the struggle against bad habits.[19]

Luther structures the interpretation according to the three key words: feast day,[20] sanctifying,[21] practice.[22] In the practical execution, however, his thoughts circle around the tension between physical rest and spiritual

---

despising and hallowing God's Word. See also the prayer in "Eine einfältige Weise zu beten, 1535," WA 36:366.16–367.14 (see also AE 51:257–87).

9   *BSLK*, 508.14.
10   *BSLK*, 511.28.
11   *BSLK*, 584.17–586.33.
12   *BSLK*, 584.35.
13   *BSLK*, 584.45.
14   *BSLK*, 585.12: "how you have heard, learned, and honored His Word."
15   Cf. *BSLK*, 582.29, 582.37.
16   *BSLK*, 585.30–41, with nn. 5–6.
17   *BSLK*, 580.13–584.16, follows primarily "Kat.-Pred. zum 2. u. 3. Gebot vom 15.9.1528," WA 30.1:31.37–33.10.
18   *BSLK*, 585.30–586.33, freely takes up "Kat.-Pred. zum 3. praeceptum vom 19.5.1528," WA 30.1:5.25–37.
19   *BSLK*, 584.41–585.29, hints at "Kat.-Pred. zum 3. Gebot vom 1.12.1528," WA 30.1:65.19–66.5 (see also AE 51:141–45).
20   *BSLK*, 580.13–582.20.
21   *BSLK*, 582.21–584.16.
22   *BSLK*, 584.17–586.33.

submission under God's Word. This is why a progression of insights is hard to grasp.

Section I on "feast day" clarifies (a) the meaning of the word as a rendition of the Hebrew *šabbat*.[23] Then it (b) points out that the legalistic Old Testament commandment, as well as its Jewish narrowing on the physical rest, is abrogated for us Christians[24] and juxtaposes it (c) with God's gift of the Christian feast day that is to be observed not only for the sake of the needs of the body but also first and foremost for the sake of God's Word in true freedom.[25] Finally, the "simple meaning" of the commandment is summarized.[26]

Section II on the verb "to hallow" is the central section and first paraphrases again (a) the meaning of the word as dealing with God's Word and practicing it.[27] (b) For true Christians this dealing is to take place constantly. For the sake of the youth and the common crowd, however, certain days and hours have to be set aside for the Word,[28] since (c) only God's Word sanctifies our whole life.[29]

Section III puts forward in more precise terms, in view of the interpretation in the Small Catechism, the "certain holy practice."[30] (a) Here, too, Luther first explains the key word.[31] (b) Then he interprets under God's zealous holy watch the gross abuse of despising the sermon out of greed or carelessness and the more subtle abuse of fruitlessly hearing out of mere habit, and he adds the warning against the mortal sin of ἀκηδία.[32] (c) Clinging to the life-giving Word of God in the battle against Satan forms the positive conclusion.[33]

THE COMMANDMENT OF THE FEAST DAY IN THE OLD AND NEW TESTAMENTS[34]

A different rationale is given for the Sabbath commandment in the two versions of the Decalogue (Exod. 20:8–11; Deut. 5:12–15). Each version is

---

23   *BSLK*, 580.13–16.

24   *BSLK*, 580.16–581.5.

25   *BSLK*, 581.5–582.10.

26   *BSLK*, 582.10–20.

27   *BSLK*, 582.21–41.

28   *BSLK*, 582.42–583.25.

29   *BSLK*, 583.26–584.6.

30   Cf. "Kat.-Pred. vom 1.12.1528," WA 30.1:64.15 (see also AE 51:141–45); "Kat.-Pred. vom 15.9.1528," WA 30.1:33.3f.

31   *BSLK*, 584.17–30.

32   *BSLK*, 584.31–585.45.

33   *BSLK*, 585.46–586.33.

34   For literature on this, see p. 184.

structured in a threefold manner: commandment—prescriptions for execution—motive. The commandment is, as is the one concerning honoring
parents, already formulated positively. Perhaps it originally read negatively:
You shall not work on the Sabbath day.[35] Perhaps the verbs "remember" and
"observe" suggest that it had its place of origin in priestly tradition and that
it was formulated positively from the beginning.[36]

The origin of Sabbath is shrouded in darkness;[37] apparently it already
was observed by the nomadic ancestors of Israel.[38] There might have been
at one point a connection to the Babylonian-Assyrian days related to the
moon phases. However, they remained tied to the lunar orbit and were
characterized as days of taboo and repentance.[39] The emergence from the
constraints of the lunar orbit and the positive filling with Yahweh's salvific
zeal set the Sabbath apart from these possible protodevelopmental stages.
Even more unlikely seems the hypothesis according to which the Sabbath
built on a regular cycle of market days, since there is no evidence for this
among Israel's neighbors, and trading on the Sabbath is prohibited according to Amos 8:5.[40]

Regardless of evidence of historical roots, the Sabbath day's peculiarity
cannot be grasped apart from Israel's relation to Yahweh. "If we correctly
understand the Sabbath year, the year of a sacred fallow proclaimed every
seven years, as an act of confession by which Yahweh's original property
right to the ground was made visible, then one could analogously consider
the Sabbath day to be a day that was kept free from all human economiza-
tion and returned to Yahweh as a kind of normal day."[41] In this context, the
"absolute system of seven days [might come] from the general importance
of the number seven in the priestly Torah that also determines the festal
calendar."[42] Two things remain remarkable in this order: (1) The rhythm of
seven days is disconnected from the world of the stars and revolves through
the times as something rational. (2) The Sabbath is free from daily care and

---

35   Cf. Exod. 34:26; Amos 8:5.

36   Thus von Reventlow, *Gebot und Predigt im Dekalog*, 54ff., 63.

37   For an alternate reading, see John W. Kleinig, *Leviticus*, Concordia Commentary (St. Louis:
Concordia, 2001). See also the publisher's introduction, pp. 10–11.

38   On the so-called Kenite hypothesis, see Stamm, "Dreißig Jahre Dekalogforschung," 292f.

39   See the literature given by Kutsch, "Erwägungen zur Geschichte der Passafeier," 25ff., and Eduard Lohse, σάββατον, *TWNT* 7:2f.

40   The remarks by Jenni, *Die theologische Begründung des Sabbatgebotes*, 12f., suggesting this are
generally rejected; cf. Lohse, σάββατον, *TWNT* 7:3 n. 10, and Ernst Kutsch, "Sabbat," *RGG*
5:1259.

41   Von Rad, *Theologie des Alten Testaments*, 1:25 n. 2; cf. Ernst Kutsch, "Erlaßjahr," *RGG* 2:568–
69; Wildberger, "Israel und sein Land."

42   Von Reventlow, *Gebot und Predigt im Dekalog*, 55.

labor, as well as from ritual sacrifice and cultic observance. It is a space free for God.

This rather negative disconnectedness of the day from everything else is filled with Yahweh's salvific acts in the theological motive clauses.[43] The motivation has a dual direction. The priestly tradition grounds the Sabbath as an eternal covenant order on the Creator's rest after the creation of the world.[44] As a kind of "gift of consecration," the Sabbath for Israel becomes a sign of participating in God's covenant.[45] The Decalogue version in Exod. 20:11 adopts this view from priestly wisdom: "For in six days Yahweh made the heaven and the earth, the sea, and everything in them, but on the seventh day He rested; *this is why* Yahweh blessed and sanctified the seventh day."

The Deuteronomist tradition bases the Sabbath on the central salvific event of the exodus from Egypt and hereby simultaneously underlines the social and humanitarian dimension of the commandment of rest (Deut. 5:14f.).[46] While the chain of prescriptions for the execution of the commandment[47] lists all the living beings belonging to the house (except for the mother of the house) and places them under the commandment, the Deuteronomistic preacher emphatically focuses this participation in the Sabbath's blessings to the stranger in the gate and to the slave, "so that your male and female slaves might be able to rest like you. And remember that you were a slave in the land of Egypt and that Yahweh, your God, led you out of there with a strong hand and an outstretched arm. *This is why* Yahweh commanded you to keep the day of rest" (Deut. 5:14f.).[48]

Both versions unfold the one center of this divine institution. God singles out this day from all other days. He takes hold of it and sequesters it for Himself and blesses it. He places His covenant people into the blessing of this day.[49] The Deuteronomistic preachers look more closely at the

---

43   This is a characteristic of Israel's law. Cf. Gemser, "Importance of the Motive Clause in Old Testament Law."

44   Cf. Jenni, *Die theologische Begründung des Sabbatgebotes*, 19–29; von Reventlow, *Gebot und Predigt im Dekalog*, 58f.; Westermann, *Genesis*, 236ff.

45   Friedrich Nötscher, "Sabbat," *LTK* 9:189.

46   Cf. Jenni, *Die theologische Begründung des Sabbatgebotes*, 15–19; von Reventlow, *Gebot und Predigt im Dekalog*, 57f.

47   Perhaps here, in analogy to the last double commandment, a chainlike catalog was adopted from priestly tradition.

48   Cf. Exod. 23:12.

49   Westermann, in *Verlorener Sonntag?* (ed. F. Karrenberg and Kv. Bismarck, Kirche im Volk 22 [Stuttgart: Kreuz, 1959]), 20f.: "God had sanctified the Sabbath day before a human ear heard the commandment to sanctify it. At the same time, He also blessed it as a source of life for the people." Westermann, *Genesis*, 237: "The holy day that is set apart as a day of rest receives in the blessing the prospering, enlivening force that enriches and fills the existence. This means what is blessed is not really the seventh day as an entity by itself. What is blessed, rather, is the day in its significance for the community or here in relation to creation: the day in its significance for the world and humanity. The force of blessing, that is, the force of prosperity

horizontal dimension of interhuman relations. Because the Lord has delivered those who were enslaved and has brought to rest those who were going astray, this is why they are to give the outlaws and strangers a share in the joy before His face. The servants and the cattle are set free from the yoke of labor and returned to their Lord and Creator. The priests committed to the cult look primarily at the eternal workings of God, whereby the all-embracing vertical dimension of the Sabbath comes to the fore. The seventh day, set apart, filled to the brim with the joy and blessing of God the Creator, stands as a divine sign of blessing above the entire history of the world and of mankind and proclaims the covenantal faithfulness of the Creator.[50] Israel is accepted in this covenant and has received the Sabbath as an earthly analogy to the eternal rest of Yahweh. It is the sacrament-like "sign of guarantee"[51] for the eternal duration of this covenant. At the same time, however, the people with their obedience enter into this space of blessing; the Sabbath observance becomes the pledge of salvation.[52] Desecration of the Sabbath separates the individual from the community of salvation and results in the death penalty;[53] it drives the people into disaster by provoking God's judgment of wrath.[54]

The Sabbath is permeated by God's holy zealous force of blessing. On the one hand, it petrifies in the minutiae of postexilic Judaism's prescriptions.[55] On the other hand, it penetrates the noneschatological horizon of the priestly code and of Deuteronomy and, in the salvific gift of rest, grows beyond this earthly world. Third Isaiah promises the eschatological inclusion of all people in the worship of God (Isa. 66:23),[56] and the Epistle to the Hebrews witnesses in its interpretation of Psalm 95 that the wandering people of God still wait for the Sabbath rest of the Creator (Hebrews 3f.).[57]

Jesus broke through the Jewish legalism attached to the Sabbath. He showed Himself to be the Lord by anticipating the promised salvation without, however, abrogating the order of the feast externally.[58] The Jewish-

---

and success, will emanate from this day." See also Westermann, *Der Segen in der Bibel und im Handeln der Kirche*, 58–61.

50   See Quervain, *Die Heiligung*, 353–56; Barth, *Kirchliche Dogmatik*, 3.4:55–57, 60; Westermann, *Genesis*, 236ff.

51   Keller, "Das Wort OTH als 'Offenbarungszeichen Gottes,'" 145.

52   Isa. 56:4–7; 58:13f.; cf. Exod. 31:12–17; Ezek. 20:12.

53   Exod. 31:14f.; 35:2; Num. 15:32–36.

54   Neh. 13:17f.; Jer. 17:19–27.

55   Cf. the compilation by Lohse, σάββατον, *TWNT* 7:5–18.

56   Zechariah expected all people to gather for the Festival of Booths in the end times (Zech. 14:16).

57   Cf. von Rad, "Es ist noch Ruhe vorhanden dem Volke Gottes."

58   See Lohse, σάββατον, *TWNT* 7:21–29; Lohse, "Jesu Worte über den Sabbat"; Rordorf, *Der Sonntag*, 55–79.

Christian congregation submitted itself under the traditional orders of the Sabbath and of the temple prayer until the destruction of the temple[59] while bearing witness to its eschatological freedom.[60] The apostle to the Gentiles did not want his congregations to be burdened by the Jewish ceremonial law;[61] Christ is the end of the Law (Rom. 10:4).

By means of the resurrection of Jesus and the appearances of the Risen One, God Himself has set apart the first day of the week. Early Christendom observes it as the Lord's Day (Rev. 1:10; *Barnabas* 15:9) by celebrating the Lord's Supper with the One who is risen and exalted to the right hand of the Father.[62] By God's eschatological intervention, both Jewish and pagan observances of the feast are abrogated. "But the Christ event makes possible the Easter memorial and thereby the cult that makes present the eschatological salvific event in the observance of Sunday."[63] The Christian Sunday does not simply succeed the Jewish Sabbath. "During the first three centuries, it is nowhere understood as the Christian Sabbath, its observance is nowhere grounded on the Third (Fourth) Commandment of the Decalogue."[64] Rather, the early Church struggles against "sabbathizing."[65]

Sunday rest as a civil ordinance is first put in place in AD 312 by Constantine: "All judges, the population of the cities, and the entire business life is to rest on the venerable day of the sun. The peasants, however, shall be free and unhindered as they work their fields."[66] The emperor applies the Roman order for religious observances to Sunday; he might also have been influenced by the sun worship of the Mithras cult, which was popular especially among soldiers.[67] The Christian Church begins to ground the Sunday rest on the Sabbath commandment. In the transition to the Middle Ages, the Church increasingly adopts the Jewish prescriptions. A Christian Sunday casuistry emerges[68] under the motto: "Let him be cursed who does anything on the holy Lord's day except the things that foster the soul and the care of the animals."[69]

---

59   Cf. Matt. 24:20; Acts 2:46f.; 3:1; 5:12.

60   Cf. Matt. 17:26f.; 12:1–11.

61   Col. 2:16f.; Gal. 4:10; cf. Bornkamm, "Die Häresie des Kolosserbriefes."

62   Acts 20:7; 1 Cor. 16:2; *Didache* 14:1; cf. Rordorf, *Der Sonntag*, 173–288, esp. 218, 270.

63   Heinz-Dietrich Wendland, "Feste und Feiern III," *RGG* 2:918.

64   Erich Hertzsch, "Sonntag," *RGG* 6:140.

65   E.g., Gregory of Nyssa, *De castigatione* (PG 46:309); the Synod of Laodicea, c. 29; John Chrysostom, *Adv. Iul.* 1:1; 8:8; Gregory the Great, *Epist.* 13:1.

66   Codex Iustinianus XII, de feriis 2 (*Corpus Iuris Civilis*, 2:127).

67   See the literature in Rordorf, *Der Sonntag*, 160ff.

68   See for this Huber, *Geist und Buchstabe der Sonntagsruhe*; Pettirsch, "Das Verbot der opera servilia"; Thomas, "Der Sonntag im frühen Mittelalter."

69   TU 20:4b, 5 (ed. C. Schmidt); the author of this discourse on Sunday rest is unknown. Exodus 12:16 (LXX) and Luke 13:15 stand in the background.

CHARACTERISTICS OF LUTHER'S INTERPRETATION

1. RECEPTION OF THE TENSION BETWEEN AN EXTERNAL CASUISTRY OF SUNDAY AND THE INNER SABBATH OF THE SOUL

Luther receives from the Church's tradition primarily, on the one hand, the Sunday casuistry. In "Decem Praecepta" ("Preaching of the Ten Commandments"), he examines the works permitted on Sunday even to the extent of the shooting festival and the military exercises of the town of Wittenberg.[70] On the other hand, there stands, without any real connection, the mystical Sabbath rest of the inner man, which is to endure throughout the entire life of the Christian. Here, too, Luther connects with a tradition that was shaped primarily by Origen and Augustine. Thus Origen writes against Celsus: "The perfect One (Christ), who always walks in the words and works and thoughts of God's Logos, the natural Lord, lives constantly on the day of the Lord and observes Sunday constantly."[71] And Augustine tirelessly offers variations of the insight: "Within, in the heart, there is our Sabbath!"[72] Only the good conscience can desire it rightly and in a God-pleasing manner.[73] This explanation of the *otium spirituale* ("spiritual leisure" or "tranquility") is handed down in the medieval interpretations[74] and is received by Luther.[75] Going beyond Augustine, the reformer interprets this spiritual Sabbath as

---

70   WA 1:440.35–442.29. Cf. Geffcken, *Bildercatechismus*, 63–68.

71   Origen, *C. Celsum* 8:22 (GCS Origen 2:239.13ff.); similar words in Rordorf, *Der Sonntag*, 102ff.

72   Augustine, *C. Faustum* 19:9f.; *Enarr. in Ps.* 91:2; *Serm.* 8:6; 270:5; *In Joan.* 20:2; *De Gen. ad Litt.* 4:16.

73   Augustine, *Serm.* 8:4 (CCSL 41:85): "The rest of the heart, the tranquility of the mind that a good conscience makes." Cf. *Serm.* 9:3f.

74   This reference to the Sabbath rest of our hearts, which Augustine highlighted against the attacks of the Manichaeans (Rentschka, *Dekalogkatechese*, 65), emerged from Augustine's catecheses into the occidental tradition. A reference to the *otium spirituale* ("spiritual leisure") is also found, e.g., in Isidore of Seville (*Quaest. in Exod.* 29:7 [PL 83:302B]), in Peter Lombard (*Sent.* III, dist. 37:2), in Albert the Great (*Compendium theol.* 5:59ff.), as well as in Bonaventure (*Collationes de decem praeceptis* 5:6ff.) and in Thomas Aquinas (*Duo praecepta* §§ 1221f., 1234ff.). The eschatological dimension of this spiritual Sabbath is underlined by Alcuin (*De decem verbis legis* [PL 100:568C/D]): "Therefore the Sabbath is sanctified when we are promised eternal rest after the good works of this life. Therefore whatever we do, if we do it because of the rest of the coming age, then we truly observe the Sabbath day."

75   "Decem praecepta, 1518," WA 1:440.21: "Mysteries. The bodily rest signifies the spiritual rest, that it may cease from desires and evil thoughts, that it may be capable of God's Word, which requires an empty soul." Cf. p. 167 n. 7 above. "Scholia in Gen., 1519–21," WA 9:331.12: "All these were done so that the Sabbath might be commended to us, that is, the rest of the soul, so that we may bear upward and downward whatever happens to us, hanging solely on God, trusting neither in our powers nor plans. Furthermore, the entire life of men and all of Christianity is nothing but a Sabbath."

the unconditional giving up of one's own will to the divine superwill,[76] thus Luther uncovers also in this commandment the center of justifying faith. At first, however, he does not manage to construe an unconstrained way of connecting it with the commandment of physical rest.

In "Von den guten Werken" ("Sermon on Good Works"); in the Feb. 27, 1523, Decalogue sermon; and in the Exodus sermons,[77] the spiritual observance of the Sabbath day continues to be the high point and the goal of the commandment: "The spiritual observance that God chiefly has in mind here consists not only in that we cease to do work and handiwork but also that we let God alone work in us and not do anything of our own by any of our abilities."[78] This spiritual Sabbath corresponds to the salvific activity of God in us by Law and Gospel, by His alien and His proper work.[79] It is nothing other than the dying of the old man and the rising of the new man, truly a "bitter feast day"[80] and simultaneously a highly comforting one.

The idea of this observance and the one who effects it is Jesus Christ.[81] On the Saturday before Easter, He "lay the entire feast day free from all His works"[82] and thereby fulfilled this commandment for us.[83] Following His observance of rest, He is raised from the dead, lives, and now rules in God over all creatures. He wants to take us into this His eschatological Sabbath and calls out to us:

"You shall hallow the Sabbath day,
That I may work in you."[84]

Whoever now wishes to observe the true spiritual Sabbath must completely die with Christ. No one will consider him right unless he be quite dead. But we begin to keep the right Sabbath here when our old Adam ceases

---

76 "Dtn.-Vorl., 1523/24," WA 14:605.4 (see also AE 9:1–311): "The killing of the old man means that he rests and that God works all things in us." Cf. Melanchthon, 1523 *Scholia* (MGP 20:78.13): "However, only the Sabbath is blessed and set apart by God, namely, when we do not work but God [works] in us."

77 WA 6:243.5–249.6 (see also AE 44:15–114); WA 11:38f.; WA 16:477–85.

78 "Von den guten Werken, 1520," WA 6:244.3 (see also AE 44:15–114). Cf. "Pred. zum 3. Gebot vom 27.2.1523," WA 11:39.13ff.; "Pred. über Gen. 2 vom 19.4.1523," WA 14:116.14ff.; "Pred. über Gen. 2, 1527," WA 24:61.14; and also Melanchthon, *Loci* from 1521, in *Studienausgabe* 2.1:47.28–48.4.

79 In "Von den guten Werken" (WA 6:248.5–15 [see also AE 44:15–114]), Luther points to Isa. 28:21.

80 "Von den guten Werken," WA 6:248.26 (see also AE 44:15–114).

81 Cf. "Von den guten Werken," WA 6:244.17, 248.32 (see also AE 44:15–114).

82 "Von den guten Werken," WA 6:248.33 (see also AE 44:15–114).

83 Cf. "Pred. über Ex. 20 vom 22.10.1525," WA 16:480.27–31; "Pred. zum 3. Gebot vom 27.2.1523," WA 11:39.14–19; "Pred. über Gen. 2 vom 19.4.1523," WA 14:118.8.

84 Hymn, "Mensch willst du leben seliglich," WA 35:429.11 (see also AE 53:280–81). Hymn, "Dies sind die heiligen zehn Gebot," WA 35:427.3 (see also LSB 581; AE 53:277–79): "Du sollst von deim Tun lassen ab / daß Gott sein Werk in dir hab."

with all his works, reason, will, desires, lust—all of which is to die and cease on the true Sabbath.[85]

In his Decalogue hymns, the reformer continues to allow to sound forth this interpretation of the commandment in relation to our dying and rising with Christ.[86] Thus it is also handed down in many other reformation catechisms.[87] However, in the Small and Large Catechisms, it is passed over. Its essential content is taken up in the question concerning the power, work, and significance of Baptism,[88] as well as in the interpretation of the Third Article in the Large Catechism.[89]

In "Preaching of the Ten Commandments," this spiritual interpretation was accompanied by the five works of sanctification, the *opera sanctificationis*,[90] which Luther took over from the medieval confessional manuals:[91] hearing Mass, not missing God's Word, praying, sacrificing, and propitiating God. Luther merely touches on the sacrifice and thereby deepens Sunday's customary atonement for the sins committed during the week to a searching of one's conscience and a confession in the heart, for the purpose of which he makes the Decalogue useful as a concise confessional manual and aligns the individual transgressions with original sin against the First Commandment.[92] Thus that fifth good work changes into the mortification of the old man.[93] In the "Sermon on Good Works," the contrition worked by God as the "spiritual meaning"[94] of the commandment accompanies the first three demands: participating in the Mass, listening to the

---

85   "Pred. über Ex. 20 vom 22.10.1525," WA 16:480.31. Cf. "Von den guten Werken, 1520," WA 6:248f. (see also AE 44:15–114).

86   See p. 175 n. 83 and the quotation in the text.

87   Melanchthon, 1523 *Scholia* (MGP 20:77.5): "For the Sabbath signifies the cessation of our works, or of the works of the free will, when not reason but God's Spirit works in us." Similarly, Hegendörfer, Bader, Agricola, Oecolampadius, Poltz, Gräter, Althamer, Brenz. Cf. the compilation in MGP 39:108–10, furthermore the "Nürnberger Katechismuspredigten" (Reu, *Quellen* a.1:476.20–36); Geneva Catechism, quest. 171–76; Calvin, *Inst.* 2.8:29.34; Heidelberg Catechism, quest. 103.

88   *BSLK*, 516.30–517.7, 704.19–707.45. Cf. the comments on the respective parts.

89   *BSLK*, 659.1–43. Cf. the comments on the Third Article.

90   "Decem praecepta, 1518," WA 1:443.8: "Yet, as one gathers from the decree, five things are to be done for the sanctification of the feast: namely, hearing Mass, hearing God's Word, praying, give according to some, and wearing oneself out on account of sins."

91   See Weidenhiller, *Untersuchungen*, 23. The ecclesiastical commandments are compiled by Bonaventure, *In Sent.* III, dist. 37, a. 2, q. 3, dub. III: "Which is why on those days they ought to frequent churches, hear Masses, remember God's benefits, hear the words of the sermon, and immerse themselves in spiritual writings. This is holding a Sabbath for God." Cf. Bonaventure, *Collationes de decem praeceptis* 4:12, as well as Thomas Aquinas, *Duo praecepta* §§ 1231–36.

92   "Decem praecepta, 1518," WA 1:438.2–439.31; cf. "Von den guten Werken, 1520," WA 6:236.21ff. (see also AE 44:15–114).

93   Cf. "Decem praecepta, 1518," WA 1:446.11–447.16.

94   WA 6:243.5 (see also AE 44:15–114).

sermon, praying. Prayer moves over to the Second Commandment,[95] where it ends up in the catechisms. Thus the demand to attend Mass and hear the sermon remains as the real source of the interpretation of the commandment in the catechisms. Already in "Preaching of the Ten Commandments," where Luther still struggles with the question of whether private Masses or Masses at the monastery are to be preferred over congregational services, the thought emerges that introduces the new development:[96] The Mass is, according to Christ's institution, indissolubly tied to the proclamation of the sacrificial death of our Lord. This is why preaching needs to take place in the Mass. In the "Sermon on Good Works," Luther accentuates this aspect:[97] As testament and institution of Jesus, the Mass is, along with Baptism, the only ceremony and exercise instituted by the Lord for the new people of God. It is to be proclaimed and interpreted by the sermon.[98] This is how the change is prepared that "Ein Sermon vom Neuen Testament" ("Sermon on the New Testament") unfolds and proves in great detail.[99] This change is so radical that not only in the short phrases of the Small Catechism but also in the exposition of the Large Catechism the Lord's Supper totally recedes behind the sermon and is treated with silence. As a basic form of the Gospel, it doubtlessly is meant here as well;[100] yet at the center is the Word passed on in teaching.

While Luther thinks about the entirety of public worship regarding the commandment to observe the feast day,[101] he does especially emphasize its doctrinal form.[102] For students, he points to catechism class and biblical

---

95 In the 1518 instructions for confession, prayer as calling on the name of God is unfolded in relation to the Second Commandment and only hinted at in the Third ("Eine kurze Erklärung," WA 1:252.28, 254.24; "Instructio," WA 1:263.11; "Eine kurze Unterweisung," WA 2:61.37). In the "Sermon on Good Works," on the other hand, Luther offers a brief instruction on prayer under the Third Commandment (WA 6:232.13–243.4 [see also AE 44:15–114]). In "Visitationsunterricht," Melanchthon inserts prayer under the Second Commandment (*Studienausgabe* 1:244f.).

96 WA 1:444.39: "This is why it is not permitted to carry out a Mass without the Gospel, the private Mass in private, the public one in public." "Instructio," WA 1:260.26: "who omit without reason divine offices, especially the Word of God." Cf. "Ausl. deutsch d. Vaterunsers, 1519," WA 2:112.8–34 (see also AE 42:15–81).

97 WA 6:230.10–232.12 (see also AE 44:15–114).

98 See the comments on the Fourth Petition of the Lord's Prayer and the commentary on the Sacraments.

99 Cf. "Sermon von dem Neuen Testament, 1520," WA 6:373.31–374.5 (see also AE 35:75–111); "De captivitate Babylonica, 1520," WA 6:525.36–39 (see also AE 36:3–126); "Von Ordnung Gottesdiensts, 1523," WA 12:37.26–35 (see also AE 53:7–14); "Formula missae, 1523," WA 12:211.6–11 (see also AE 53:15–40).

100 See *BSLK*, 449.5–14 (SA). The Heidelberg Catechism mentions the Lord's Supper in quest. 103.

101 *BSLK*, 584.17–30.

102 *BSLK*, 582.42–583.8.

instruction;[103] for the "entire crowd," he references the catechism services and sermons that, in addition to the special ember days, were held early on Sundays or for Vespers.[104] While under the Second Commandment he demanded the daily prayers of the individual in the community of the house,[105] when it comes to the Third Commandment, Luther urges the hearing, learning, and honoring of God's Word in the assembled congregation.

2. The Spiritual/Internal Meaning of Sanctifying the Holy Day

The second main section of the Large Catechism[106] interprets "holding sacred"[107] as "to conduct one's language, work, and life in a holy manner"[108] and takes as its starting point God's Word, "the Holy of Holies,"[109] the core sacrament. "But the sanctifying, that is, teaching and preaching God's Word, which is the true, pure, and simple meaning of the commandment, was from the beginning and remains forever in the entire world."[110] Luther moves the Word as the God-given means of sanctification into the center and in it connects the Third Commandment with the First.

Indeed, all the works of a person are holy only when the person himself has become holy. For its part, this sanctification of the person in his heart of hearts does not grow out of self-chosen works,[111] but out of God's ongoing work in us.[112] However, God only wants to work in us by means of His Spirit, who has tied Himself to the oral word of the message of Christ. Only in faith, created by the sermon, are we right before God. But if we are right before God, then we are also holy. Our works are right before God, first, when they

---

103   Cf. Hahn, *Die evangelische Unterweisung in den Schulen des 16. Jahrhunderts*, 9–52; Fraas, *Katechismustradition*, 58–83.

104   Cf. Jordahn, "Katechismus-Gottesdienst im Reformationsjahrhundert," as well as above on the prefaces, pp. 28–29.

105   *BSLK*, 578.43–579.17.

106   *BSLK*, 582.21–584.16.

107   *BSLK*, 582.24.

108   *BSLK*, 582.25.

109   *BSLK*, 583.26.

110   "Wider die Sabbather, 1538," WA 50.333.12 (see also AE 47:57–98). "Gen.-Vorl., 1535–45," WA 42:61.39 (see also AE 1:1–359): "This is the proper work of the seventh day: God's Word being preached and heard." "Pred. über Lk. 14:1ff. vom 22.9.1532," WA 36:330.8: "Therefore learn what it means to sanctify the Sabbath, namely, preaching, hearing, learning God's Word, and acting according to it." Cf. "Eine einfältige Weise zu beten, 1535" (WA 38:366.16–28 [see also AE 43:187–211]), referencing 1 Tim. 4:5.

111   *BSLK*, 583.42–584.16.

112   "Von den guten Werken, 1520," WA 6:216.34 (see also AE 44:15–114): "Therefore we never read that somebody was given the Holy Spirit when he did something, but always when they heard the Gospel of Christ and the mercy of God."

THE THIRD COMMANDMENT 179

partake in the person's being right.[113] Accordingly, for Luther everything depends on kindling the heart's inner joy in God's Word and overcoming the primal sin of *acedia*,[114] in which already ancient monasticism saw a mortal sin. Again, he places the struggle for God's Word into the eschatological struggle between God and Satan.[115] The inner Sabbath rest of the heart does not mean a mystical emptiness from all contents or spiritual idling.[116] Such rest is positively filled by remaining inwardly connected to the life-creating Word of God.[117] "Where one preaches God's Word, it follows consequently that a person during that hour or time necessarily must be observant and quiet and, without any other things to keep him busy, merely speak and listen to what God says and teaches us or says in conversation with us."[118] The day of rest is permeated by the proclamation of the salvific acts of God.

The legally delimited emptiness of the day of rest cannot grasp the actual divine meaning of the commandment; it breaks under its dynamic. The sanctification of our life by God's Word cannot be narrowed to one special day of the week. The setting apart of the Sabbath day by God and thereby the concrete wording of this Old Testament commandment is "given to the Jews alone."[119] It is thus only "a temporal addition and adornment, given only to this people led out of Egypt, which also was not meant to remain forever, as little as the entire Law of Moses."[120] In this sense, the Third Commandment does not bind us. By Christ it has been taken away from the hearts and consciences of the believers[121] and has been abrogated in its external Lawlike form. At the same time, in Christ it is disclosed in its inner spiritual meaning and given to us as a gift: "We Christians shall always keep such a feast day, do only holy things, that is, daily walk around with God's Word and carry

---

113 "Zirkulardisp. De vestenuptiali, 15.6.1537," WA 39.1:283.1: "Faith makes the person." "Disp. über Dan. 4:24, 16.10.1535," WA 39.1:69:16: "The person is prior to the works." "Entwürfe in librum de loco iustificationis, 1530," WA 30.2:659.32: "Faith does not anticipate works that it might justify by them, but the works anticipate faith that they might be justified by it, so that faith might be active in the righteousness of works and works be passive in the righteousness of faith."

114 *BSLK*, 585.30–586.33.

115 *BSLK*, 585.46–586.14. On the struggle between God and anti-god, see "Decem praecepta, 1518" (WA 1:521.15–32); "Ausl. von Ps. 117, 1530" (WA 31.1:223–28 [see also AE 14:1–39]); "Eine einfältige Weise zu beten, 1535" (WA 38:366.37–367.7 [see also AE 43:187–211]).

116 *BSLK*, 586.7f.

117 *BSLK*, 586.16.

118 "Wider die Sabbather, 1538," WA 50.332.30 (see also AE 47:57–98).

119 *BSLK*, 580.21.

120 "Wider die Sabbather, 1538," WA 50:333.10 (see also AE 47:57–98).

121 Cf. Isa. 66:23 in "Decem praecepta, 1518," WA 1:436.29–35; Col. 2:16f.; Gal. 4:10; 1 Tim. 1:9 in "Von den guten Werken, 1520," WA 6:243.25 (see also AE 44:15–114); Matt. 12:8; Gal. 4:10; Col. 2:16f. in "Pred. über Ex. 20 vom 22.10.1525," WA 16:477.33–478.18; and "Wider die himml. Propheten, 1525," WA 18:73.25 (see also AE 40:73–223): "I want to have the consciences and souls free from sins, which is a truly spiritual evangelical preaching office."

it around in heart and mouth."[122] This far Luther retains the spiritual inter-
pretation of the early Church fathers also in the catechisms. Being free for
God's Word and prayer is communicated to Christendom. This is how the
"Christians' feast day"[123] goes beyond Sunday and penetrates the entire life.
It is carried out in tireless meditation on the Word and in the constant prayer
of the heart.[124] As a sign for this, the "spiritual ones" [the pastors] are taken
out of daily work. They are permitted to dedicate themselves wholly to the
Gospel "and have a feast day every day."[125]

3. THE BODILY OUTWARD FORM OF THE COMMANDMENT OF REST

This all-embracing "Christians' feast day," however, does not totally absorb the specific day of rest for the "common crowd."[126] The commandment
of rest retains its rightful place under the spiritually unfettered commandment of sanctification. Christ has liberated us from the yoke of the Sabbath
law, consciences are no longer bound by the Old Testament commandment,
as especially Paul asserted against an encroaching Gnostic legalism.[127] Nonetheless, the *lex naturae* demands that, for a day, toiling man and also animals
retire, rest, and be refreshed.[128] In a sermon on Feb. 27, 1523, Luther ties this
together with God's curse on Adam. God gives and orders for us the day of
rest, lest the curse that because of us lies on the ground utterly destroy both
man and beast.[129] Thus the day of rest is also a sign of the goodness of the
Creator. Those who work with their minds, however, do not seem to participate in this sign, since their activity goes beyond what is tied to the earth.[130]

---

122 *BSLK*, 582.42. "Decem praecepta, 1518," WA 1:436.37: "For the truly righteous person is so shaped like God that he, like God, is indifferent about every day, every place, every person. Thus also for him every day is a feast."

123 *BSLK*, 583.8.

124 Cf. "Von den guten Werken, 1520," WA 6:234.34–235.7 (see also AE 44:15–114).

125 "Von den guten Werken, 1520," WA 6:234.31–244.2 (see also AE 44:15–114). Barth, *Kirchliche Dogmatik* 3.4:74: "Is the pastor not really the ideal case of the person who joyfully works on the holy day and who in this way and thereby keeps it holy?"

126 *BSLK*, 581.11.

127 See Lohse, σάββατον, *TWNT* 7:30f.

128 *BSLK*, 581.14. Cf. "Wider die himml. Propheten, 1525," WA 18:81.26–82.6 (reprinted 581 n. 12) (see also AE 40:73–223); hymn, "Dies sind die heiligen zehn Gebot," WA 35:427.1 (see also LSB 581; AE 53:277–79): "You are to hallow the seventh day / so that you and your house may rest."

129 "Pred. zum 3. Gebot," WA 11:38.7–21. Cf. also "Pred. über Gen. 2:2f. vom 19.4.1523" (WA 14:117f.), where the change of the paradisical Sabbath by sin and curse is described. Similarly, "Gen.-Vorl., 1535–45, zu Gen. 2:1ff.," WA 42:56–62 (see also AE 1:1–359).

130 "Kat.-Pred. zum 3. praeceptum vom 19.5.1528," WA 30.1:5.18: "Feasts . . . are observed not for me and the learned but for the masses." Against this stand Luther's insightful comments on sweat from "Gen.-Vorl., zu Gen. 3:19" (WA 42:157ff. [see also AE 1:1–359]), see especially WA 42:159.17 (see also AE 1:1–359): "It is the highest . . . stupidity that the fanatics urge manual

Perhaps this is a residue of the medieval understanding of servile works, the identification of the *opus servile* with the *opus corporale*.[131]

4. CORRELATION OF THE EXTERNAL FORM TO THE INNER MEANING OF THE COMMANDMENT

The rest from work, however, does not seem to have an inherent meaning for Luther. Tirelessly, it is aligned with the congregation's divine service.[132] The day of rest is sanctified rightly only by listening to God's Word, in prayer, and in praising God. Everything in Christendom is instituted and ordered so that the Word "might go about publicly on a regular basis."[133] To this corresponds Luther's instructions for the right form of Sunday rest.[134] All activity is right only when it is necessary for the use and support of the neighbor; all leisure and joy is blessed where it is focused on studying God's Word; all external carrying out of worship is salutary where it opens up the hearts for God and neighbor.[135] The entire existence of the individual, as well as that of the entire community, is to be reestablished and refocused by God's Word on the feast day. All that we need not be ashamed of before our eternal Judge and Savior may be used here. In this way, Luther coordinates the external Sunday work with the heart's inner life in God's Word.

Again the decrees from the "Sermon on Good Works" prove useful.[136] The "sensible and instructed Christians"[137] who constantly have their lives sanctified out of God's Word are free from the external commandment of the holy day; they do not need it. The holy day with the bodily carrying out of worship is prescribed for the young and the simple Christians in the servant estate, primarily as an exercise of faith; secondarily, also for the reinvigoration of the physical person. Here, too, the *usus puerilis praecepti* is understood as pedagogic toward Christ.

---

labor so much, while it is on the contrary these greatest political and ecclesiastical works that wear out the bodies and suck all sap out of the inmost marrow, as it were. Therefore we will distinguish sweat according to just proportion. Economic sweat is great, greater is political sweat, the greatest is ecclesiastical sweat."

131 Thomas Aquinas, *Duo praecepta* § 1227: "However, the servile work is the corporal work, because the free work is that of the soul, such as thinking and so forth."

132 *BSLK*, 581.5–26, 582.34–41, 584.17ff.

133 *BSLK*, 584.29.

134 "Decem praecepta, 1518" (WA 1:440.33–442.21), with the summary: "All these are excused as necessity, so long as by them the divine things are not neglected."

135 Quervain, *Die Heiligung*, 366: "The rest about which the congregation is concerned looks back on the deeds of God, takes place in praising His gifts, and expects the consummation of the ways of God in the kingdom of the resurrection."

136 Cf. pp. 140f. and 164f.

137 *BSLK*, 581.7.

5. CRITIQUE OF LUTHER'S UNDERSTANDING OF THE COMMANDMENT[138]

This distinction between the sensible Christians and the "common crowd"[139] is an aftereffect of the spiritualistic separation of the inner spiritual man from the external bodily man that already was present in the paraphrase of the spiritual Sabbath rest in Origen and Augustine.[140] By broadening the sanctification of Sunday to every true hearing of God's Word, Luther secondarily separates Sunday and the feast days from their specific ties to God's salvific activity. Thus they are placed into the equality of all the days of the Creator. The insight that God adorned and blessed Sunday by the resurrection of the Son[141] loses its weight.

Luther's *no* to a legalistic understanding of Sunday is biblically mandated and, therefore, cannot be given up. However, it is tied to a peculiar rationalism that we have to analyze critically. In the Large Catechism, Luther connects two propositions. On the one hand, all days as work and creation of God are holy and good[142]—no one day is better than the next.[143] On the other hand, Sunday has come upon us as the day of worship "from of old."[144] This is why we should leave it at that for the sake of love and unity.[145] Here the rational component, which we already encountered when the rhythm of seven was separated from the moon phases, is strengthened. It is justified and deeply necessary insofar as we are liberated by the Creator from all astral forces. At the same time, however, Sunday as a Christian holy day is based not simply on a rational decision that does justice to the needs of our earthly existence.[146] Rather, it ultimately grew out of the appearances of the Risen One. "The feast day as a divine sign totally recedes in Luther."[147] Where God's activity is spiritualized and internalized in this way, there ex-

---

138 Cf. Barth, *Kirchliche Dogmatik* 3.4:70f.; Quervain, *Die Heiligung*, 361–65; Thomas, *Erneuerung des Sonntags als Auferstehungstag.*

139 *BSLK*, 581.11.

140 Cf. p. 174 nn. 70ff.

141 "Pred. über Ex. 20 vom 22.10.1525," WA 16:479.3: "We have the Sunday on which Christ rose." Barth, *Kirchliche Dogmatik* 3.4:70: "The small interruption of our daily lives by the weekly holy day corresponds to the great interruption of the daily life of the world by Easter day."

142 *BSLK*, 582.26ff.

143 *BSLK*, 581.30.

144 *BSLK*, 582.1–6; WATR 5, nos. 6191, 6355. Luther traces it back to the apostles. Melanchthon, *Catechesis puerilis*, 1540 (Reu, *Quellen*, 1.2.2:28.12): "We have a divine precept concerning the works, but we do not have a precept concerning a certain day."

145 *BSLK*, 582.1–6.

146 *BSLK*, 581.32ff.; cf. *BSLK*, 581 n. 12 and Melanchthon, "Katechismuspredigten, 1528" (MGP 22:64.29): "And there are set certain days so that one might know when to gather, just as one sets certain hours at school for the lecture."

147 Quervain, *Die Heiligung*, 361. Cf. Barth, *Kirchliche Dogmatik* 3.4:70.

ternal statutes will have to replace and fill out what is missing. Where God's historical salvific acts are not taken as points of departure anymore, there is the Law again to fill the void. Therefore it is perhaps no accident that Protestant orthodoxy went back to medieval casuistry.[148]

Sunday regains the character of the Lord's Day as an eschatological sign when the celebration of the Lord's Supper is again at its center. Luther hints at the eschatological connection of Sunday only here and there,[149] but he does not unfold it as comprehensively as Augustine.[150] The public nature of Sunday's congregational assembly, which Luther first positioned against the Masses in private and in the monastery and later defended against enthusiastic conventicles, would need accentuation. In it, above all, God's Word goes about "publicly on a regular basis,"[151] calls people from all nations and tongues into the communion of saints, and places this congregation before God's face. In this congregation, God's Spirit does His global work of sanctification.

The Christological, ecclesiological, and eschatological connections of the commandment of the feast day are not sufficiently appreciated by Luther in the catechisms. The reformer places daily sanctification by God's Word as immediately as possible into the narrow world of his peasant citizens and craftsmen and thereby underlines the connection to the First Article.

TEXTS ON THE THIRD COMMANDMENT

WA 1:436–77: from Decem praecepta Wittenbergensi praedicata populo, 1518

WA 6:229–50: from Sermon von den guten Werken, 1520 (see also AE 44:15–114)

WA 14:116–18: from Predigt über Gen. 2 vom 19.4.1523

WA 16:477–85: from Predigt über Ex. 20 vom 22.10.1525

WA 18:67–84: from Wider die himmlischen Propheten, 1525 (see also AE 40:73–223)

---

148 Cf. Barth, Kirchliche Dogmatik 3.4:71f.

149 "Gen.-Vorl., 1535–45, zu Gen. 2:1ff.," WA 42:61.4 (see also AE 1:1–359): "For all things that God wants to be done on the Sabbath are evident signs of the other life after this life."

150 Augustine, Serm. 125; De civ. Dei 22:30. Augustine's intentions are taken up by, among others, Isidore of Seville, Quaest. in Exodum 29:7 (PL 83.302B); Pseudo-Beda Venerabilis, In Psalm. libr. exegesis (PL 93:481C–482A); Alcuin, De decem verbis legis (PL 100:568C/D); Hugh of St. Victor, Inst. in decalogum legis dominicae (PL 176:11D–12B). Cf. esp. Ps.-Beda Ven. (PL 93:481D–482A): "That person spiritually observes the Sabbath who, divinely inspired, does everything he does in this life's time to gain the coming rest . . . . Yet he observes the Sabbath carnally who, whether he works or rests, rushes solely toward earthly joy and rest." Harnack, Katechetik, 73: "If we look to this final goal, to the eternal rest of the saints that Christ has earned and guaranteed to us, then the Christian's life here on earth is surrounded by these two great points of rest: the one, the lost Sabbath at the beginning, accuses him, while the other, the regained and promised one in eternity, comforts and gives him bliss. Placed in between the two is the Old Testament Sabbath and the New Testament Sunday as a material prophecy of that abiding dwelling."

151 BSLK, 584.29.

WA 24:61–64: from Predigt über Gen. 2 (Genesis-Predigten, 1527)

WA 36:329–33: Predigt über Lk. 14:1ff. vom 22.9.1532

WA 37:571–77: Predigt über Mt. 12:1ff. vom 31.10.1534

WA 38:531ff.: from Annotationes in aliquot capita Matthaei, zu Mt. 12:1ff., 1538

WA 42:56–62: from Genesisvorlesung, 1535–45, zu Gen. 2:1ff. (see also AE 1:1–359)

WA 50:312–337: Wider die Sabbather, 1538 (see also AE 47:57–98)

Literature on the Feast-day Commandment

The articles "Sabbat" by Lohse (*TWNT*), Kutsch (*RGG*), Nötscher (*LTK*)

The articles "Sonntag" by Hertzsch (*RGG*), Koep and Stiegler (*LTK*)

The articles "Feste und Feiern" by Kutsch and Wendland (*RGG*)

Botterweck, "Der Sabbat im Alten Testament"

Huber, *Geist und Buchstabe der Sonntagsruhe*

Jenni, *Die theologische Begründung des Sabbatgebotes im Alten Testament*

Karrenberg, et al., eds., *Verlorener Sonntag?* (Stuttgart: Kreuz, 1959)

Kutsch, "Erwägungen zur Geschichte der Passafeier und des Massotfestes"

Lohse, "Jesu Worte über den Sabbat"

Peichl, *Der Tag des Herrn*

Pettirsch, "Das Verbot der opera servilia in der Hl. Schrift und in der altkirchlichen Exegese"

Rordorf, *Der Sonntag*

Schrenk, "Sabbat oder Sonntag"

Szabó, "Sabbat und Sonntag"

Thomas, "Der Sonntag im frühen Mittelalter"

Westermann, *Genesis*, 230–44

Westermann, *Der Segen in der Bibel und im Handeln der Kirche*

Zahn, *Geschichte des Sonntags, vornehmlich in der alten Kirche*

The Fourth Commandment[1]

Wording of the Commandment and Arrangement of the Interpretation

The wording of the commandment to honor the parents varies only slightly. Luther always uses "to honor" as a verb; the phrase "hold in honor" in the explanation in the Small Catechism[2] is found, following the memory verse,[3] in several late medieval texts.[4] From this verse likely also came the summary expression "parents," alongside which Luther, also following the tradition, places "lords" so he can insert into this commandment of God the secular and spiritual authorities.[5] In the translation, however, Luther always uses the phrase "father and mother."[6] Luther increasingly emphasizes the personal pronoun "your." In the preliminary text of the Large Catechism it is still absent,[7] as it is in most medieval texts.[8] In the Large Catechism, it is only given in relation to the father.[9] In the Small Catechism,[10] the commandment reads: "You shall honor your father and your mother."[11] Following the biblical text Exod. 20:12, the reformer accentuates the God-given assignment of children to their parents.

The explanation in the Small Catechism places the emphasis on the positive formulation of the commandment, that is, "holding in honor," which is unfolded by four verbs. Two positive verbs each correspond to a negative

---

1 For texts on the Fourth Commandment, see p. 213.

2 *BSLK*, 508.24.

3 *Habeas in honore parentes* ["Hold father and mother in honor"]!

4 Cf. Meyer, *Historischer Kommentar*, 89.

5 Cf. pp. 197–207.

6 Cf. "Eine kurze Erklärung, 1518," WA 1:251.2; "Von den guten Werken, 1520," WA 6:250.21 (see also AE 44:15–114); "Eine kurze Form, 1520," WA 7:206.8. Only "Eine kurze Unterweisung, 1519," WA 2:62.10: "You shall honor your parents."

7 *BSLK*, 555.20.

8 Proofs in Meyer, *Historischer Kommentar*, 89.

9 *BSLK*, 587.4.

10 *BSLK*, 508.19.

11 Thus already in "Eine kurze Erklärung, 1518," WA 1:251.2, and "Eine kurze Form, 1520," WA 7:206.8.

one: The attitude of despising is juxtaposed with loving and cherishing. Failure, angering the parents, is overcome by serving obedience. This results in a chiastic structure that is carefully worked out in detail, circling around the central phrase "holding in honor."

> Wir sollen Gott fürchten und lieben,
>> daß wir
>> unser Eltern und Herrn
>> nicht
> verachten noch erzürnen
>> sondern sie
>> in Ehren halten,
> ihnen dienen, gehorchen, (sie) lieb und wert haben.

> We should fear and love God,
>> so that we,
>> to our parents and lords,
>> [do] not
> [show] spite or anger,
>> but rather
>> hold them in honor,
> serve, obey, love them, and esteem them.

The exposition in the Large Catechism first identifies the place of the commandment to honor the parents between the First and Second Table.[12] It introduces the Second Table but stands above the remaining commandments because God set apart parents and other authorities and "placed them at the top, even in His stead on earth."[13]

The interpretation is divided into three sections. First, Luther interprets the commandment,[14] then he expands the obedience of parents to other "superior persons" in house, state, and Church.[15] In an appendix, he unfolds the dual duty of the "authorities" toward those who are entrusted to them.[16] In all three sections, Luther tirelessly drives home God's zealous holy watching, whereby He, according to the positive formulation of the commandment and the added promise, underscores both the earthly blessing as well as the good conscience that result from obeying the commandment.

For this interpretation, Luther weaved together the three sermon series. Section I follows the second series,[17] yet Luther works in the sermon

---

12   *BSLK*, 586.35–587.6.
13   *BSLK*, 592.40.
14   *BSLK*, 587.7–596.16.
15   *BSLK*, 596.17–603.16.
16   *BSLK*, 603.17–605.34.
17   "Kat.-Pred. zum 4. Gebot vom 17.9.1528," WA 30.1:33.12–34.31.

delivered on May 20.[18] The third sermon series reinforces tying the Fourth
Commandment to the First Commandment.[19] The reference to the authorities[20] connects thoughts found in the sermons on September 17 and
December 3.[21] The concluding section on the service of those in authority[22]
follows the sermon on December 4.[23]

I.   The interpretation of the commandment[24] outlines (a) its mean-
     ing: We should not only love parents but also honor them, be-
     cause God by His Word gives them a share in His power and
     glory.[25] This is unfolded in two threads of thought: (b) In a brief
     saying, Luther paraphrases the term "to honor"[26] as we should
     above all "esteem (the parents) glorious and worthy" in the heart;
     keep our words to them in check; and serve them with works
     and provide for them. The triad *corde—ore—opere* is hinted at.
     (c) In a relatively long explanation, Luther points to God as Lord
     and Giver also of this commandment.[27] First, against man's self-
     chosen works, it needs to be asserted that obeying one's parents is
     based on God's Word and commandment.[28] Second, obeying the
     commandment is a duty of thanks toward "the hand, pipes, and
     means"[29] of the Creator and Sustainer.[30] Third, on this obedience
     rests God's promise[31] that is observed by someone, whether in
     punishment or in blessing.[32]

II. The expansion of the commandment[33] shows how all divinely or-
     dered "authority" participates in the office of father and mother[34]

---

18   *BSLK*, 587.7–50 follows WA 30.1:6.5–18, and *BSLK*, 593.12–594.5 follows "Kat.-Pred. zum 4.
     Praeceptum vom 20.5.1528 (1. Reihe)," WA 30.1:6.25–32.
19   E.g., "Kat.-Pred. zum 4. Gebot vom 3.12.1528 (3. Reihe)," WA 30.1:67.13, 68.2–8 (see also AE
     51:145–50).
20   *BSLK*, 596.17–603.16.
21   WA 30.1:35.3–36.16, 69.2–72.4.
22   *BSLK*, 603.17–605.34.
23   WA 30.1:73.1–74.7 (see also AE 51:150–55).
24   *BSLK*, 587.7–596.16.
25   *BSLK*, 587.7–50.
26   *BSLK*, 588.1–34.
27   *BSLK*, 588.35–596.16.
28   *BSLK*, 589.40–593.6.
29   *BSLK*, 566.21.
30   *BSLK*, 593.7–594.5.
31   *BSLK*, 594.6–31.
32   *BSLK*, 594.32–596.16.
33   *BSLK*, 596.17–603.16.
34   Cf. *BSLK*, 613.10–32.

and how it becomes a sign of God's Fatherhood.[35] (a) Next to the "fathers of blood" there are those of the extended family as a community of life together[36]—the heads of the household, as well as (b) secular authority[37] and (c) the spiritual fathers[38]—who "govern and preside by God's Word."[39] By means of these fourfold fathers, God wants to sustain and govern us, bless and foster us. This is why we are to honor in them His fatherly majesty.

III. The application of the commandment to the office of the authorities[40] briefly hints at the dual duty of all those fathers. Not only are they to nourish their children, servants, and subjects and provide for their physical needs, "but above all they are to rear them for God's praise and honor."[41] Not only are they to gather money and goods, but they also are to maintain both kingdoms of God for their children and offspring and to equip them for serving in both kingdoms.

THE COMMANDMENT OF HONORING THE PARENTS IN THE DECALOGUE[42]

The mandate to honor the parents is older than Israel.[43] It holds true in every true human community and has its original place in the life of the clan, where all prohibitions of the Second Table originated.[44] The head of the family was the guardian and preserver of the clan's ethos—"vis-à-vis him stand son, grandson, nephew, in short, the male offspring in descending line, for the second person of the prohibitions likely is exclusively directed to the male members of the family."[45]

---

35   *BSLK*, 596.17–597.8.

36   *BSLK*, 597.9–598.38.

37   *BSLK*, 598.39–601.23.

38   *BSLK*, 601.24–603.16.

39   *BSLK*, 601.30.

40   *BSLK*, 603.17–605.34. A parallel is found in the preface to the Small Catechism (*BSLK*, 505.19–47).

41   *BSLK*, 603.36. Cf. *BSLK*, 604.24–30, 612.38–43.

42   Literature on this: Lorenz Dürr, *Die Wertung des Lebens im Alten Testament und im antiken Orient* (Münster: Aschendorffsche, 1926); Gerstenberger, *Wesen und Herkunft*, 110–17, 130–48; Kremers, "Die Stellung des Elterngebotes im Dekalog"; von Reventlow, *Gebot und Predigt im Dekalog*, 60–71.

43   See also the publisher's introduction, pp. 10–11.

44   Cf., e.g., Gräf, *Das Rechtswesen der heutigen Beduinen*, 34ff.; Gottlob Schrenk, πατήρ A, *TWNT* 5:948–59; Gottfried Quell, πατήρ B, *TWNT* 5:959–74; van der Leeuw, *Phänomenologie der Religion*, §§ 32–38.

45   Gerstenberger, *Wesen und Herkunft*, 116.

This commandment, therefore, is not directed first to the minor children but to the full Israelite citizen living in the extended family. He, too, remains under the authority of the heads of clan. Even where the adult son has taken over the responsibility for house and farm, especially the wisdom literature strongly suggests to him to serve his aging parents reverently: "Whoever mistreats his father, whoever drives away his mother is a disgraceful and shameless son" (Prov. 19:26).[46]

However, it appears that this commandment is rooted more deeply in the numinous foundations of our human existence. This is suggested by the peculiar legal provision in Deut. 21:18–21 that is often mentioned by Luther.[47] In it, the heads of the family are enjoined to drag a disobedient and recalcitrant son who lives as a glutton and drunk before the court of elders by the gate. The town community is to stone him, thereby executing God's ban on him. Over this process stands the commandment: "You shall burn out the evil from your midst; all Israel is to hear it and be afraid."

The formula "burn out the evil" appears frequently where offenses damage the web of human togetherness: in the context of seduction to idolatry (Deut. 13:1–6; 17:2–7), disrespecting the court (Deut. 17:8–13), false testimony (Deut. 19:15–21), adultery (Deut. 22:22), rape (Deut. 22:23f., 29), kidnapping of a full citizen (Deut. 24:7), and in the case of offenses that are primarily mentioned in the Decalogue. Behind these casuistic cases stands the age-old ban formula: "He shall surely be killed!"[48]

Here the foundations of human life together, as they are set forth and guaranteed by the Deity itself, stand in jeopardy. Whoever despises the parents attempts to destroy them no less than the person who rebels against the jointly worshiped deity or who raises his hand against his fellow man. In the entire Near East, as in all traditional cultures, the interpersonal ethos is not seen as something secular but is tied back to the gods. The clan's order is founded on reverence for the *elohim*.[49] "The *elohim* you are not to revile, and a *nāsī'* of your people—'a representative of the twelve tribes in matters concerning all of Israel'[50]—you are not to curse" (Exod. 22:28).[51]

46   Cf. Beer, *Exodus*, 102.

47   See especially the interpretation in "Dtn.-Vorl., 1523/24, zu Dtn. 21," WA 14:696.25–36 (see also AE 9:1–311); cf. *BSLK*, 606.6ff.

48   Cf. Alt, "Die Ursprünge des israelitischen Rechts," 311ff.; Noth, *Das zweite Buch Mose*, 145f. (on Exod. 21:12, 15–17).

49   Quell, πατήρ, *TWNT* 5:964.30ff., on the Decalogue: "The fact that man has a father is a divine order. Thus it is a good order, and to this corresponds in the Old Testament authors the certainty to encounter in the dignity of a father one source of genuine humanity borne out of God. The motifs of the father are acknowledged as the strongest safeguard against a depravation of the ethos, for there is something divine in the father because there is something fatherly in God."

50   According to Noth, *Das zweite Buch Mose*, 152.

51   Cf. 1 Kings 21:10.

In the Decalogue, this Fourth Commandment is put positively and, at the same time, formulated as comprehensively as possible. This is certainly the work of the Deuteronomist preachers who wanted to suggest it strongly to the pilgrims returning home.[52] The demand to honor the parents has been handed down to us in several variants. Perhaps it originally read: "You shall not curse your father and your mother!"[53] Alongside it, we read "not to dishonor them" (Deut. 27:16), "not to beat" (Exod. 21:15), not to mistreat them (Prov. 19:26).

The positive and comprehensive "honoring" shows the parenetic tendency and the social engagement of the preachers.[54] This is deepened by the promise connected to the commandment concerning parents, which is found only in the Decalogue.[55] In analogy to Ezekiel in his confessional manual,[56] the word of promise restates the old ban curse: "He shall surely die!" in a positive way: "He shall live!" Just as the ban executed under God's curse excluded a person from the life-community with Yahweh even to the extent of physical consequences, so the addressee gains life, earthly/physical life before God, by obeying the Commandments. Whosoever obeys Yahweh's statutes and decisions, and does them, will live by them (Lev. 18:5).[57] The addition in Deut. 5:16 of "so that it may be well with you" emphasizes the direct connection between man's obedience of the Commandments and the concrete blessing of God.

The promise itself—"so that your days may be long on the land that Yahweh, your God, wants to give you" (Exod. 20:12)—is frequently found in Deuteronomy,[58] which in its mediations on the covenantal bliss constantly circles around the blessing's gift of the land.[59] At the same time, it points back to the preamble as the self-introduction of the covenant God. Pointing to the Promised Land, the "you" addressed in the commandment is changed simultaneously. It is not only the Israelite full citizen in the network of his clan, but it is also the covenant people gathered at the sanctuary itself. By the reference back to Yahweh's covenant act on Israel, this commandment also is placed into a new horizon.

---

52 In the process of transformation into a positive formulation, the priestly Sabbath commandment might have played a role; thus von Reventlow, *Gebot und Predigt im Dekalog*, 63.

53 Thus Stamm, "Dreißig Jahre Dekalogforschung," 295, and *Der Dekalog im Lichte der neueren Forschung*, 52.

54 Lev. 19:3 has "to fear."

55 Cf. Kremers, "Die Stellung des Elterngebotes im Dekalog," 148f.

56 Ezek. 18:9, 17, 19, 21, (22,) 28.

57 Cf. von Rad, " 'Gerechtigkeit' and 'Leben' in der Kultsprache der Psalmen," esp. 234ff.

58 Cf. Deut. 4:40; 5:33; 6:2; 11:9; 17:20; 22:7; 25:15; and elsewhere.

59 Cf. von Rad, "Verheißenes Land und Jahwes Land im Hexateuch."

As already in the cultures of the Near East, the clan ethos was founded in the numinous, so Yahweh as the zealous holy Guarantor of the covenant with His people also enters into the commandments of the Second Table. The reverence toward the elders of the clans seeks to grow out of the fear and love of God. "We should fear and love God" so that we do not curse but honor the elders. In honoring the parents, Yahweh's *shalom* order is at stake. It is the question of whether or not His covenant people gain in it a share of all things pertinent to the salvific life before His face in the blessed land of the promise. This moves parents into the relation with God. Following Karl Barth,[60] Heinz Kremers has one-sidedly emphasized this "spiritual dignity" by pointing to the function of parents as "preachers and priests of their families and clans," formulating in summary: "To honor the parents means to let them be weighty for oneself as God's representatives, as preachers, teachers, and priests."[61]

In the New Testament, the commandment regarding the parents—which in Judaism was called the "heaviest among the heavy commandments"[62]—is mentioned in Jesus' conversation with the rich youth (Mark 10:19 and parallels) and in Jesus' criticism of the vow of sacrifices, whereby it was possible to withhold from the parents what was meant for them, thereby rendering God's commandment without effect by means of human statutes (Mark 7:10–13 and parallels).[63] The table of duties in Ephesians praises it as the first commandment with a promise (Eph. 6:2f.),[64] thereby taking this promise of God out of its Old Testament relation to the land of Canaan and broadening it to apply to the whole earth. Following Jerome, Thomas, by means of the *sensus spiritualis*, thinks of the promised eternal dwelling with God.[65] However, in the Large Catechism, as he paraphrases Exod. 20:12 freely as "in the land where you live," Luther emphasizes unabashedly this earthly walk of ours at the place assigned to us by God.[66]

For children, Paul derives from the commandment the demand for submissive obedience.[67] For their part, parents are not to take away the children's courage (Col. 3:21) or kindle evil anger in them (Eph. 6:4), but they

---

60 Barth, *Kirchliche Dogmatik* 3.4:273f.

61 Kremers, "Die Stellung des Elterngebotes im Dekalog," 159ff.

62 pPea 1:15ᵈ, 13 (*Bill.*, 1:705, where there are more parallels).

63 Cf. Karl Heinrich Rengstorf, κορβᾶν, *TWNT* 3:860–66.

64 On the interpretation, see Schlier, *Der Brief an die Epheser*, 281 n. 3, as well as Sirach 3:3ff. Luther applies this attack to the papacy, "Annotationes in aliquot capita Matthaei, 1538" (WA 38:584.34–586.11, esp. 585.27): "Yet Christ stands as stronger and more powerful: You all are cursed in God's commandment because you prefer your traditions to the authority and status of parents and civil powers."

65 According to Schlier, *Der Brief an die Epheser*, 281f.

66 *BSLK*, 594.10.

67 Eph. 6:1; Col. 3:20.

are to rear them in punishing discipline and encouraging admonition, in "an education that is founded in the Lord, that is inspired and moved by Him, that is focused on Him, and that is appropriate to Him."[68] In "Decem praecepta" ("Preaching of the Ten Commandments"), Luther takes up the phrase "Rear them in the discipline and correction of the Lord" in Eph. 6:4 and highlights the primarily spiritual charge to lead the young in Christ to God: "See . . . that you above all want to instruct children in spiritual matters, so that they are given over to God before they come to the trades of the world . . . . But it is the teaching of the Lord where they are taught to know the Lord Jesus Christ."[69]

CHARACTERISTICS OF LUTHER'S INTERPRETATION

1. ACCENTUATION AND BASIC THOUGHTS OF THE INTERPRETATION

Luther's understanding of the Fourth Commandment did not undergo the strong fluctuations seen in his interpretation of the first three commandments,[70] yet he does accentuate it quite differently. In "Preaching of the Ten Commandments," as well as in "Von den guten Werken" ("Sermon on Good Works"), Luther discusses especially the duties of parents and superiors. In "Preaching of the Ten Commandments," Luther had the Wittenberg congregation in view and focused more on the concrete vices of the simple people.[71] In the "Sermon on Good Works," however, he widens the view and discusses the high spiritual sins of the churchly authorities, calls on the secular lords to intervene, and thereby anticipates themes of his "An den christlichen Adel deutscher Nation" ("Call to the Christian Nobility of the German Nation").[72] In the catechism sermons, Luther returns to the simple wording of the commandment, and in doing so, he considers the insights on the two kingdoms gained previously to be so important that he dedicates section II to them. His basic theological insights can be summarized in the following theses.

1. The Fourth Commandment occupies a key position between the two Tables.[73] It already deals with our actions toward people,

---

68   Schlier, *Der Brief an die Epheser*, 283.

69   WA 1:450.3–451.7.

70   The development is presented in Hardeland, *Katechismusgedanken*, 103–30. On the wider context, see also Siirala, *Gottes Gebot bei M. Luther*, 178–266.

71   E.g., the training of children for professional prostitution; cf. WA 1:452.6–9.

72   WA 6:255–63 (see also AE 44:15–114).

73   Cf. *BSLK*, 586.49, 592.39ff., 605.37ff. Luther here develops an approach that is already hinted at in Augustine, *Sermon* 9:7: "For to his parents a person opens his eyes, and this life begins

which is why it belongs to the Second Table. However, from these people it lifts up the men who, by virtue of God's ordering, are placed before and over us and sets them between us and God. On them rests the majesty of God's ordering in creation and by the Word;[74] thereby they share in God's fatherly majesty itself.

2. This placing before and above is owed to all who share in the "authority" of the parents. The family becomes the original source of all secular and spiritual order.[75] Alongside the blood relatives, which include fathers and mothers, are the lords in the economic, political, and ecclesiastical realms.

3. All these "superior persons" have a dual charge that, according to Eph. 6:4, is implied in this commandment. They are not only to care for the earthly welfare of those entrusted to them, but first and foremost they also are to raise them for God's praise and honor, thereby the eternal salvation of their subjects is placed within their responsibility.[76] This dual charge is common to secular and spiritual "authorities."

4. Because by doing so the "superior persons" act in the name and by the command of God and stand in His stead, the subjects not only owe them neighborly love (as they do in the case of other people) but also fear, accompanied by love, is owed to them. We should fear and love the "authorities" because we fear and love God.

5. Tying the "authorities" back to God grants bondage and liberty at the same time to both superiors and inferiors. In all their sovereign liberty, the superiors remain bound to God's free sovereignty, which will hold them accountable with impartiality, regardless of whether they know and want this. In all their serviceable

---

with their friendship." Isidore of Seville (PL 83:302C) and Alcuin (PL 100:586D–587A) take this up verbatim. Bonaventure sees in the father the "person who begets, instructs, educates," to whom is owed, therefore, "the honor of reverence, obedience, and aid" (*Collationes de decem praeceptis* 5:4–9). And Thomas gives a reason for the commandment's position by pointing out that we are most obligated to the parents (*Summa theologiae* I/II, q. 100, a. 6).

74 "Kat.-Pred. zum 4. praeceptum vom 20.5.1528," WA 30.1:6.15: "In the parents an ordination of God is to be considered." Cf. *BSLK*, 590.31f., 591.22, 591.32, 592.41f., 613:15ff.

75 Cf. *BSLK*, 596.17ff., 613.10–32; "Pred. über Ex. 20 vom 5.11.1525," WA 16:505.26f.; "Kat.-Pred. zum 4. Gebot vom 17.9.1528," WA 30.1:35.3–24.

76 *BSLK*, 603.32–42, 604.21–30, 505.24f., 612.38–43; "Decem praecepta, 1518," WA 1:450.3–452.4; "Sermon von dem ehelichen Stand, 1519," WA 2:169.30–170.16 (see also AE 44:3–14); "Vom ehelichen Leben, 1522," WA 10.2:301.16–30 (see also AE 45:11–49); "Pred. zum 4.–6. Gebot vom 28.2.1523," WA 11:40.2ff.; "Pred. über Ex. 20 vom 5.11.1525," WA 16:503.28ff.; "Kat.-Pred. zum 4. Gebot vom 17.9.1528," WA 30.1:34.33ff.; "Gen.-Vorl., 1535–45," WA 43:487.21ff., 558.19ff. (see also AE 5:1–386); and elsewhere.

bondage, the subjects are genuinely free where they humbly obey solely for the sake of the common Lord who in Christ has set them free for service. Where under the Fourth Commandment a kind of obedience is demanded that contradicts the First Commandment, this free bondage to God will prove itself in the witness of suffering.[77]

6.   To every kind of autonomous and self-chosen service of men Luther harshly juxtaposes obeying those people to whom God has bound us in the concrete circumstances in which He has cast us. We can gain certainty before God only where we find ourselves within an already existing relationship of obedience, or also command, which is characterized by this genuine structure of being placed above and under, respectively.[78] Being open for whatever God sends us must not be blocked by self-chosen ties.

7.   In the catechism sermons as well as in the Large Catechism, one aspect is more heavily accentuated, an aspect that was present in a hidden way in "Preaching of the Ten Commandments" and which became crystallized, especially in the Fourth Commandment:[79] God keeps mankind in obedience to His Commandments by means of His creative commanding as well as His commanding creating. His fatherly hand of blessing and the striking fist of His judgment sustain mankind by the institutions of marriage and family, by the secular and spiritual authorities. They drive humanity toward final annihilation as well as eternal consummation.

2. COORDINATION OF THE FOURTH WITH THE FIRST COMMANDMENT[80]

Several times the reformer touches on the special position of the commandment regarding the parents in relation to the remaining commandments of the Second Table.[81] Obeying "superior persons" is still fully

---

77   "Von den guten Werken, 1520," WA 6:253.1 (see also AE 44:15–114): "Now, where the parents are so foolish that they raise their children in a worldly manner, there the children should not obey them in any way, for God in the first three commandments is to be regarded more highly than the parents."

78   "Pred. zum 4.–6. Gebot vom 28.2.1523," WA 11:41.3ff.; BSLK, 589.28, 590.2f., 591.22, 591.42, 597.24.

79   WA 1:448.34ff., 450.3–451.26.

80   BSLK, 586.35–587.50, 590.9–23, 592.32–593.6.

81   BSLK, 586.48f., 590.14–19, 592.34ff. Cf. the comments on the structure and outline of the Decalogue, pp. 99–101.

permeated by obeying God.[82] This is why all the works of this commandment rank higher than those of the following commandments of the Second Table. "Other than against God, I cannot commit a greater sin than to sin against a power instituted by Him, which indeed is God's honor."[83]

This preeminence of the Fourth Commandment in relation to the remainder of the Second Table is based on God's setting apart of parents. The Lord has placed their estate "at the top, even placed it in His stead on earth."[84] He has elevated them out of the equality of all humans and placed them "next to Himself."[85] This is why we have to regard them as "the highest" below God.[86] By virtue of God's ordering, parents have the "upper hand."[87] Accordingly, already in the 1518 "Instructio pro confessione peccatorum" ("Instruction for the Confession of Sin"), it says: "For parents and superiors God has placed in His stead and commanded to hold as His representatives."[88]

Thus the honor of the parents is tied back to God's honor, the Fourth Commandment to the First. In this we are not to look to the persons, "but to God's will that creates and orders it thus."[89] "Also in the Fourth Commandment, ultimately bowing before God's majesty is at stake."[90] Luther unfolds this in two directions.

We have not chosen our parents, they are given to us; this is why we can never escape from them. Behind this, Luther saw God's activity as Creator. The parents are the *officina* (workshop) in which God prepared [us].[91] They are not merely the hand by which He cast us into life, but they are at the same time the hand by which He keeps us alive. We do not only have "body and

---

82   Cf. "Decem praecepta, 1518," WA 1:461.10–16, 448.34ff.; "Eine kurze Form, 1520," WA 7:206.3–6; "Pred. über Ex. 20 vom 5.11.1525," WA 16:506.28–507.14; "Kat.-Pred. zum 5. Gebot vom 4.12.1528," WA 30.1:74.9 (see also AE 51:150–55).

83   "Pred. über Ex. 20 vom 5.11.1525," WA 16:506.4. "Von den guten Werken, 1520," WA 6:250.24 (see also AE 44:15–114): "This is why disobedience is a greater sin than murder, unchastity, stealing, deceiving, and whatever might be included in these." "Kat.-Pred. zum 4. Gebot vom 17.9.1528," WA 30.1:34.18: "The best service on earth after that to God and the best work is children obeying parents."

84   *BSLK*, 592.40.

85   *BSLK*, 587.15.

86   *BSLK*, 587.25.

87   *BSLK*, 587.43.

88   WA 1:258.21; cf. "Decem praecepta, 1518," WA 1:448.1ff.; "Eine kurze Form, 1520," WA 7:206.2.

89   *BSLK*, 587.36.

90   Brunner, *Lutherische Bekenntnis in der Union*, 69. "Kat.-Pred. zum 4. Gebot vom 3.12.1528," WA 30.1:68.2 (see also AE 51:145–50): "Since the First Commandment shines its light into the Fourth because of fear, God wants you to let the parents be your treasure."

91   "Decem praecepta, 1518," WA 1:448.27: "Therefore I will revere the workshop of my God, my Maker." Qid 30 b Bar: "Three come together to form a man: God, his father, and his mother. When a man honors his father and mother, God says: I credit it to them as if I lived in their midst and they honored Me" (*Bill.*, 1:706).

life" from our parents, but also at the same time we have been fed and raised by them. Without their daily care, each of us would have been "suffocated in his own excrements a hundred times"[92] or "rotted away in the dirt."[93] In this way, parents become a sign and symbol of God's fatherly care. "God is known and nicely copied in the image of the parents . . . . For God entrusts father and mother with the office of taking care of the children. There one can see as in a mirror how God is disposed toward us, namely, as a father's heart is to the children, so God's heart is disposed toward you."[94]

At the same time, however, it holds true that fatherly care is not rightly known and gratefully accepted by children without the Holy Spirit.[95] This is why God has fenced them in by the commandment of honoring parents: He not only promotes the commandment within His Old and New Testament revelation, but He has also engraved this commandment in the hearts of all heathen.[96] The commandment to honor the parents, however, does not merely grow out of drivelike instincts and rational insights. As something established by God, it holds true even where the natural circumstances seem to contradict it. Even where parents do not rightly administer their office, where they are contemptible and frail, where their manner of living is no example,[97] the commandment remains in force. Parents are set apart from all other people not only by the laws of procreation and socialization but also by God's word of command: "For one has to consider two things in the parents: first, that they are flesh and blood; second, the jewel God has placed on parents, namely, His Word, for He has comprehended them in His Word like a monstrance and clothed them in His will."[98] "Look at father and mother; there God's Word will teach you that you do not honor flesh and

92   BSLK, 593.27.

93   "Pred. über Ex. 20 vom 29.10.1525," WA 16:488.36; BSLK, 599.5, on secular authorities: "For by them, as by our parents, God gives us food, house and farm, protection and safety."

94   "Pred. über Ex. 20 vom 29.10.1525," WA 16:489.16–490.7. WA 16:490.5: "The father is the god, lord, judge, and teacher of the children. And, conversely, a good child trusts in no other creature as he does in his father. Such is God's relation to us and our relation to Him."

95   BSLK, 593.20f.

96   Cf. BSLK, 593.44f. Schrenk, πατήρ, TWNT 5:949, offers Epictetus, Dissertations 2:10.7, as a parallel to Luke 15:31: "Being a son means: to consider everything one has as possession of the father, to obey him in all things, never to criticize him before anyone, not to hurt him by word and deed, to give in to him in all things, and to support him with all one's strength." Popular Stoic philosophy called the parents second gods appeared on earth. Already Plato had called aged parents living at home living images of God (Laws XI, 931a, d), and Aristotle demands a godlike honoring of parents (Eth. Nic. 9.2, 1165a24). Ancestor worship is certainly in the background of statements such as these.

97   BSLK, 587.32–50.

98   "Pred. über Ex. 20 vom 29.10.1525," WA 16:491.20; "Pred. über Ex. 20 vom 29.10.1525," WA 16:491.3: "Let the son here open his eyes, seeing not the flesh of the father, which is nothing, but the Word of God. Oh, how great is the glory of the father because of this Word . . . . If the Word is there, God Himself is present. If God Himself or His will is there, then also the whole divinity is present."

blood when you honor father and mother, but God Himself, who has placed His Word on them."[99]

3. THE TWO KINGDOMS WITHIN THE FOURTH COMMANDMENT[100]

From the medieval practice of using the Decalogue as a confessional manual, Luther receives the custom to include spiritual and secular fathers and lords in the commandment regarding the parents. Already Thomas, in his *Duo praecepta*, added the apostles and prelates of the Church, as well as the kings and princes of the secular rule, and he placed them with the physical fathers under God's fatherhood: "Therefore all these are to be revered, because they all bear some resemblance to the Father who is in heaven."[101] In his *Collationes* on the Decalogue, Bonaventure mentions the political, ecclesiastical, and monastic authorities.[102] Following them, the later confessional manuals mention, first, the commandments of the holy mother Church and obedience to the spiritual fathers—from the prelates and bishops down to the pastors and father confessors. After this, some of the manuals mention the fathers of the house and the masters at work, as well as the secular authorities. Here and there, the heavenly parents are mentioned: the triune God, the Virgin Mary, and all saints.[103]

In his confessional manuals between 1518 and 1520, Luther, too, mentions after the parents, first the mother Church with the priestly estate, followed by the masters at work and the political authorities.[104] The emphasis is clearly on obeying the Church.[105] He also unfolds this in the "Sermon on Good Works,"[106] hinting at his program of reform as it is developed in the writings to the Christian nobility and on the Babylonian captivity of the

---

99 "Pred. über Ex. 20 vom 29.10.1525," WA 16:492.19; "Gen.-Vorl., 1535–45," WA 43:514.8 (see also AE 5:1–386): "Therefore who holds a governing office is like the incarnate God." Cf. *BSLK*, 694.43–695.8.

100 *BSLK*, 596.17–606.1.

101 Thomas Aquinas, *Duo praecepta* § 1257.

102 Bonaventure, *Collationes de decem praeceptis* 5:11–13: "auctoritas qui praeest rei politicae, sive ecclesiasticae sive monasticae." The broadening of the commandment is already hinted at in Philo; cf. Rentschka, *Dekalogkatechese*, 23. Such a solemn doctrine of the three estates or powers, however, first crystallizes in the high and late Middle Ages. This is illustrated by the important study by Maurer, *Lehre von den drei Hierarchien*, esp. 9–18.

103 Cf. Geffcken, *Bildercatechismus*, 69–72, and its appendix, col. 40, 60ff., 83, 95, 132, 143, 153, 170; as well as Weidenhiller, *Untersuchungen*, 42, 72f., 113, 150; Maurer, *Lehre von den drei Hierarchien*, 9ff.

104 "Eine kurze Erklärung, 1518," WA 1:252.35–253.2; "Instructio, 1518," WA 1:260.36–261.4; "Eine kurze Unterweisung, 1519," WA 2:62.15–20; "Eine kurze Form, 1520," WA 7:209.19–25.

105 Luther explicitly names heretics and schismatics, apostates, and the banned as transgressors of this commandment.

106 WA 6:255.18–258.31 (see also AE 44:15–114).

Church. First, Luther outlines the charge of the secular authority,[107] offering here, too, a reform program as well as a short list of duties for princes, thereby foreshadowing the 1523 writing on civil authority and his writings on education. The sermons on the Book of Exodus[108] are focused solely on civil authority, which also moves to first place in the 1528 catechism sermons, as well as in the Large Catechism.

In the Large Catechism, almost by necessity Luther lets the secular authority as *patres patriae* ("fathers of the country") grow out of the family by means of the house rule of the *patres et matres familias*.[109] In a subsidiary manner, the higher orders in society and state are added to the basic order of marriage and family. In fact, they are actually developed out of the original order of the house rule.[110] The "spiritual regiment," on the other hand, the reformer strangely adds as a separate entity: "Beyond these, there are also spiritual fathers."[111] The dogmatic weight of his sermonlike considerations is not easily assessed. We have to place it into the context of his teaching on the estates and kingdoms.[112]

The reformer takes as his starting point the irreversible structure of human life together, in which the historical nature of our existence manifests itself. By begetting, birth, and raising, we are all irreversibly chained to one another; "we all come from parents."[113] Parents remain the parents of their children, and children remain the children of their parents. Hereby a natural hierarchical order comes about, a structure of care and rule, of obedience and service. This "*kephalé* structure"[114] gains a binding force by God's

---

107 WA 6:258.32–263.4 (see also AE 44:15–114).

108 WA 16:505.25–506.17 (Nov. 5, 1525). "Pred. zum 4.–6. Gebot vom 28.2.1523" (WA 11:39ff.) only mentions the parents.

109 *BSLK*, 596.39; cf. *BSLK*, 596.17ff.

110 "In 15 ps. Grad. Comm., 1532/33," WA 40.3:221.1: "Out of the house grows the city; out of the city, the dukedom, the king. The city is an association of many economies or families. A kingdom is a union of many cities. The economy, therefore, is the source. When He was creating in paradise, He said: 'It is not good for man to be alone. Grow.' "

111 *BSLK*, 601.26. "Kat.-Pred. zum 4. Gebot vom 3.12.1528," WA 30.1:71.7 (see also AE 51:145–50): "The fourth are the bishops."

112 The literature on Luther's "doctrine of the two kingdoms or governments" has become impossible to compile. A helpful compilation is offered in the essays mentioned by Schrey, *Reich Gottes und Welt*, there also on p. 557ff. further literature. To be added are especially Duchrow, *Christenheit und Weltverantwortung*; Junghans, "Das mittelalterliche Vorbild für Luthers Lehre von den beiden Reichen." More pertinent for the catechisms, however, is Luther's doctrine of the estates or hierarchies, as well as their medieval forerunners. These connections have been largely overlooked during the past centuries, but now they have been worked out in an exemplary fashion by Maurer, *Lehre von den drei Hierarchien*. On this topic, see also: Althaus, *Ethik Luthers*, 43–48; Elert, *Morphologie*, 2:23–79; Hoffmann, *Die "Hausväterliteratur" und die "Predigten über den christlichen Hausstand."*

113 "Pred. über Ex. 20 vom 5.11.1525," WA 16:501.5. Cf. *BSLK*, 613.10–32; Brunner, *Das Gebot und die Ordnungen*, 324–55; Elert, *Das christliche Ethos*, 117–19.

114 Brunner, "Das Hirtenamt und die Frau," 328.

ordering and commandment. According to "Preaching of the Ten Commandments," it already begins in marriage, where God has placed man as woman's head.[115] From there, it reaches into the family and permeates our entire life together in society and economy, state and church.[116] "For out of that of the parents every other authority flows and spreads,"[117] since the house is the wellspring of all earthly authority and ordering structure.[118]

As in the case of the First Commandment,[119] Luther again connects observation from daily life and the wisdom of the nations with listening to Scripture.[120] "Out of the parents' authority everything else flows." This is first shown empirically. As so often in the Large Catechism, he starts with the father, who has the "upper hand";[121] in his office of raising his child other people enter in a subsidiary manner. This observation of daily life is deepened by the proverbial wisdom of antiquity.[122] It, too, understands the rule in house and state as being based on the office of father. For the Christians, the "spiritual mother," that is, the Church,[123] and the "spiritual fathers" step in as well as they "govern us and preside over us by God's Word."[124]

These far-reaching offices and services grow out of the family in such a way "that all those who are called lords stand in the parents' stead and have to take from them power and might to govern."[125] This strict deduction would contain two consequences, namely, the absolute precedence of the

---

115   WA 1:453.25–458.24, pointing to Gen. 3:16; 1 Cor. 14:34; 11:7; Col. 3:18; Eph. 5:22ff.; 1 Pet. 3:2, 7; 1 Thess. 4:4f.

116   WA 1:458.25–40.

117   *BSLK*, 596.20.

118   "Kat.-Pred. zum 4. praeceptum vom 20.5.1528," WA 30.1:6.36: "Out of the house comes the city, district, kingdom, etc. Fatherhood is the origin of all these." "Kat.-Pred. zum 4. Gebot vom 17.9.1528," WA 30.1:35.5: "Thus out of the fatherly power comes all obedience; secular authority altogether flows out of it, namely, out of the house, which is the origin and source of all the power of the world." This Aristotelian argumentation is also found in the late medieval books, e.g., in the confessional manual of Johannes Wolff. Cf. Maurer, *Lehre von den drei Hierarchien*, 15f.

119   See the commentary on pp. 123–24.

120   *BSLK*, 596.17–45; "Von den guten Werken, 1520," WA 6:251.32–252.2 (see also AE 44:15–114).

121   *BSLK*, 596.27.

122   On *pater familias*, cf. Schrenk, πατήρ, *TWNT* 5:950f. On *pater patriae*, cf. Schrenk, πατήρ, *TWNT* 5:951 n. 18. The saying "No one can show enough honor to God, parents, and teachers" that in *BSLK*, 593.30ff., is traced back to Aristotle (cf. Wander, *Sprichwörterlexikon*, 2:18, no. 371; "Kat.-Pred. vom 20.5.1528," WA 30.1:6.31f.; "Eine Pred. daß man Kinder, 1530," WA 30.2:579.29ff. [see also AE 46:207–58]) is already connected to the commandment in the annotated catechism tables, e.g., in the "Table of Christian Wisdom": "As already Aristotle testifies, God, father and mother, and our masters we can never honor enough" (Weidenhiller, *Untersuchungen*, 47).

123   "Von den guten Werken, 1520," WA 6:255.19 (see also AE 44:15–114).

124   *BSLK*, 601.30.

125   *BSLK*, 596.30. BSLK, 613.19: "For whatever spiritual and secular estates there are, they have to humble themselves and all be found in this estate (of marriage)."

natural order common to man and beast over the rather variable develop-ments of it, and the subsidiary assignment of the higher-order communities to the family.[126] The family would gain precedence not only over the state but also over the Church.

However, Luther's statements must not be pushed too far and forced into a system. He immediately puts them into their common spiritual focus on God. The wisdom and insight of the nations to call the masters of the house *patres familias* and the lords of the land *patres patriae* becomes, for Christians, the embarrassing hint at the charge of every "authority" that is fully disclosed only in God's Word. "According to Scripture," they "are all [called] fathers . . . as those who in their government exercise their fatherly office and should have a fatherly heart toward those who are theirs."[127] The decisive point is not a theological/rational deduction of the economic, po-litical, and churchly structure of order from the family, but the divine charge that includes all "authority."

Luther does not deduce secular and spiritual authority from the family. In fact, he does not even deduce it from the Fourth Commandment;[128] he merely places it into this commandment. Placing *oeconomia, politia,* and *ecclesia* (the orders of family, state, and church) into the family in this way accentuates the joint charge and, therefore, exhibits a significant tension in Luther's customary way of juxtaposing secular and spiritual governments.

In his doctrine of governments, Luther sees the secular government un-der the symbol of the sword.[129] In its form of exerting force, it is not founded in creation but in the fall. Luther still believes one finds the central word that institutes the government by sword in the age-old legal sentence: "Whoever sheds the blood of man, his blood shall be shed by men in return" (Gen. 9:6).[130] According to Luther, with these words God places His sovereign rights over life and death, which He had at first reserved for Himself, into man's hands. This is why out of them flows all law among men—the civil law

---

126 On the principle of subsidiarity, see the articles by Cord Cordes and Roman Herzog ("Subsid-iaritätsprinzip I," *ESL* 2264–66, and "Subisdiaritätsprinzip II," *ESL* 2266–72).

127 *BSLK*, 596.33.

128 Kinder, "Geistlichen und weltlichen 'Oberkeit,' " 282: "It is not at all the case that according to Luther the secular and spiritual governments as such are organically derived from the empiri-cal family, as if based on this, their common 'germ cell,' a fully harmonious relation existed between the two . . . . In fact, strictly speaking, there is not even a 'derivation' of this doctrine from the Fourth Commandment; rather, examined carefully, this view of the Fourth Com-mandment already presupposes the doctrine of the two governments."

129 "Sach.-Ausl., 1527," WA 23:514.1 (see also AE 20:153–347): "By 'sword,' I mean everything that belongs to secular government, e.g., secular privileges and laws, customs and habits, gestures, estates, different offices, persons, dresses, etc."

130 Cf. "Von weltl. Oberkeit, 1523," WA 11:247.31–248.14 (see also AE 45:75–129); "Pred. über Gen. 9, 1527," WA 24:203.13ff.; "Gen.-Vorl., 1535–45," WA 42:360.19–26, 361.28–32 (see also AE 2:1–399).

as well as the law of nations.[131] In this legal saying, then, God has instituted authority and given it the sword. Thus, for Luther, secular government did not simply originate in human contracts,[132] nor can it be considered to have grown organically out of the family structure. Behind secular government is God's word of institution; it is a *mandatum, ordinatio,* and *institutio* (mandate, ordaining, and institution) of God.[133] God instituted it so that government would protect our human life together as a watcher and defender against the breaking in of chaos. Secular authority's power of sword and force is not abrogated but confirmed by the New Testament.[134]

As the secular, so also the spiritual government is founded by God in an immediate institution, in the sending of His Son. The strongest words are found in the "Schulpredigt" ("School Sermon"). Here the reformer says that not only the spiritual government but also even the correlated spiritual estate is "instituted and established by God Himself . . . with His own blood and death."[135] Yet the proclamation of the salvific work of Christ and the pouring out of the Spirit did not first begin on Pentecost. In the hidden prophecy of the coming Messiah, the hope of the new life in God's gracious view is given already to the first human couple in the word concerning the Seed of the woman that would crush the head of the serpent.[136] Thus both governments do not simply flow out of the family; they are founded on an independent institution by God in word and deed.

Where Luther takes a look at these different institutions of God, he at the same time harshly distinguishes the character of the governments.[137]

---

131   Cf. "Gen.-Vorl., 1535–45," WA 42:360.30 (see also AE 2:1–399): "This, therefore, is source from whence flows all civil law and the laws of the nations" ["Hic igitur fons est, ex quo manat totum ius civile et ius Gentium"].

132   "Ps. 82 ausgelegt, 1530," WA 31.1:193.36 (see also AE 13:39–72): "Crazy, clever reason, together with all the worldly-wise know nothing about the fact that a community is a creation and order of God, yet they do not think it happens in any other way than that a people holds itself together." Cf. "Ob Kriegsleute auch in seligem Stande sein können, 1526," WA 19:633.20–31 (see also AE 46:87–137); "Gen.-Vorl., 1535–45," WA 42:361.33–41 (see also AE 2:1–399).

133   "Contra 32 articulos Lovaniensium theologistarum, 1545," WA 54:428, thesis 45 (see also AE 34:339–60): "Matrimony truly is a divine creation, gift, and ordination, just like the political estate and the magistrate." Cf. "Gen.-Vorl., 1535–45," WA 42:362.1–3 (see also AE 2:1–399); 44:218.12–18.

134   "Von weltl. Oberkeit, 1523," WA 11:248.20–31 (see also AE 45:75–129); "Wider die räuberischen u. mörderischen Rotten d. Bauern, 1525," WA 18:358.35–359.4 (see also AE 46:45–55); "Ob Kriegsleute, 1526," WA 19:627.15–628.17 (see also AE 46:87–137). In these places, Luther above all refers to Rom. 13:1ff.; 1 Pet. 2:13ff.; Matt. 26:52; Luke 3:14.

135   "Eine Predigt, daß man Kinder zur Schule halten solle, 1530," WA 30.2:530.20f., 583.22f., 526.33–527.25 (see also AE 46:207–58). Cf. Brunotte, *Das geistliche Amt bei Luther,* esp. 118–29; and Lieberg, *Amt und Ordination bei Luther und Melanchthon,* 104–32.

136   See on this the explanation on Gen. 3:15 in "Gen.-Vorl." (WA 42:141.1–143.7 [see also AE 1:1–359]).

137   E.g., "Von welt. Oberkeit, 1523," WA 11:251.1–11 (see also AE 45:75–129); "Ob Kriegsleute, 1526," WA 19:629.17–630.2 (see also AE 46:87–137).

Secular government is limited to this world and exists to defend against chaos. In it, the law is enforced by the sword. Here God established a hierarchical order that cannot be abrogated and gave the authority a share in His eschatological power as Judge. His divine wrath uses those "rod masters and executioners"[138] to punish evil and to preserve temporal peace. Judging eschatologically, everything that takes place in this realm, so long as it does not take place in brotherly love flowing out of trusting in Christ, remains under God's judgment.

The spiritual government, for its part, aims only at the eternal rescue of the human race. This is why the office of preaching the Gospel and administering the Sacraments has been established in the Church by the Lord. In the Church, the Risen One rules human souls, not by means of a law that coerces externally but by the Word and the Spirit, who changes the hearts from within and re-creates them. Because God desires the inward obedience of the heart, every power that only coerces externally falls short; at best, it results only in hypocrisy. At the same time, an externally coercive law would be meaningless among true Christians. "Where there is only suffering of injustice and doing justice, there is no need for arguments, dissensions, judgment, judge, punishment, law, or sword."[139] Among true Christians, there can be no hierarchical order, no rule and service in the worldly sense, since all are called to mutual subordination and service by the one Lord.[140]

The insights regarding the different institution and structure of both governments outlined here recede in the catechisms when it comes to the interpretation of the Fourth Commandment, even if they are present in a hidden way, and are brought to bear on the Fifth Commandment.[141] As already in his early interpretations of the commandment regarding the parents, Luther does not start out with the difference between the governments but with the joint charge of the three foundational institutions of God.

Where the reformer speaks about the four kinds of fathers—"of blood, in the house, in the land," as well as of the "spiritual fathers"[142]—there in the background is his doctrine of the three or four basic divine institutions: that

---

138   "Von welt. Oberkeit, 1523," WA 11:268.4 (see also AE 45:75–129): "For they are God's rod masters and executioners, and His divine wrath uses them to punish the evil and preserve outward peace." "Pred. über Ex. 20 vom 29.10.1525," WA 16:488.19: "For the authority of the princes and lords is not a lovely authority but a terrible one, for they are our Lord God's rod masters, judges, and executioners, with whom He punishes the evil knaves. But father and mother are not terrible in this way, but utterly kind."

139   "Von welt. Oberkeit, 1523," WA 11:250.4 (see also AE 45:75–129).

140   "Von dem Papsttum zu Rom wider den hochberühmten Romanisten zu Leipzig, 1520," WA 6:295.19–24 (see also AE 39:49–104); "Von welt. Oberkeit, 1523," WA 11:270.30–271.13 (see also AE 45:75–129).

141   See *BSLK*, 605ff., and *BSLK*, 629.25–34. Cf. the comments pp. 222–26.

142   *BSLK*, 601.25f., 601.30.

of marriage and family, which includes the house as a community of life and economy and which comprehends in it the mandate to work the earth and to wrest blessing from it, in other words, the institution of the *familia* and *oeconomia*; that of the secular sword government (*politia*); and that of the spiritual Word government (*ecclesia*). Luther can summarize the first double charge under the estate of marriage. Thus in the 1528 "Vom Abendmahl Christi, Bekenntnis" ("Confession of Christ's Supper"), he calls "the priestly office, the estate of marriage, the secular authority" the "three orders and true institutions" of God,[143] above all of which extends the "joint order of Christian love . . . wherein one not only serves within the three orders but also serves with all sorts of goodness everyone who is needy in general."[144]

These three (or four) members are prefigured in the three parts of the Platonic state, as well as in several medieval enumerations. Closest, perhaps, are the three parts of the *ecclesia militans* that are listed in a 1431 letter of the Hussites to the Council of Basel: the *presbyteri*, the "temporal lords," and the "the common people who are divided in many manual arts."[145] As we have seen, analogous compilations are found in the confessional manuals. Luther first mentions those three "estates" in the 1519 "Sermon über die Taufe" ("Sermon on Baptism"). God has "ordered many an estate that one is to practice and in which one is to learn to suffer. Some He has placed in the marital estate, others in the spiritual estate, others in the governing estate. He has commanded all to labor and work in order to kill the flesh and accustom it to dying."[146] In his later compilations, Luther places more emphasis on the global horizon of battle of these three orders and hierarchies; they are God's battle arrays in the fight against Satan: "For God ordained three hierarchies against the devil, namely, economy, state, and church."[147]

---

143   "Vom Abendmahl Christi, Bekenntnis, 1528," WA 26:504.30 (see also AE 37:151–372).

144   "Vom Abendmahl Christi, Bekenntnis, 1528," WA 26:505.11 (see also AE 37:151–372).

145   MCG sec. 15, pt. 1, p. 157 (quoted in Elert, *Morphologie*, 2:55). Cf. Elert, *Morphologie*, 2:52ff. Maurer, in his study on this doctrine, examines the highly variable and interesting history of this doctrine of the three hierarchies.

146   WA 2:734.24 (see also AE 35:23–43). Cf. "Weihnachtspost. über Joh. 21:19–24, 1522," WA 10.1.1:308.6–311–13; "Gen.-Vorl., 1535–45," WA 42:79.3–80.34 (see also AE 1:1–359).

147   "Zirkulardisp. über das Recht d. Widerstandes gegen den Kaiser, 1539," WA 39.2:42, thesis 52. "Von den Konziliis und Kirchen, 1539," WA 50.652.18 (see also AE 41:3–178): "These are three hierarchies (house, city, church), ordered by God; we need no more than these. We also have more than enough to do to live rightly in them against the devil." "Gen.-Vorl., 1535–45," WA 43:524.22 (see also AE 5:1–386): "These, therefore, are the three hierarchies that we drive home often, namely, economy, state, and the priesthood, or house, city, and church." Important parallels for this in "Sach.-Ausl., 1527," WA 23:511.33–515.11 (see also AE 20:153–347); "Ps. 117 ausgelegt, 1530," WA 31.1:240.21–36 (see also AE 14:1–39); "Ps. 111 ausgelegt, 1530," WA 31.1:399.24–400.6, 410.2–17 (see also AE 13:349–87); "Jes.-Vorl., 1527/30," WA 31.2:734.9–22, 735.11–22, 739.1–4 (see also AE 15:189–264); "Gen.-Vorl., 1535–45," WA 42:79.3–29, 354.23f. (see also AE 1:1–359; 2:1–399); "Gen.-Vorl., 1535–45," WA 43:74.37–75.8 (see also AE 3:1–365), 450.9–13, 524.22f., 535.18f. (see also AE 5:1–386); "Gen.-Vorl., 1535–45," WA 44:530.33 (see also AE 7:1–377); "Pred. von den Engeln vom 29.9.1539," WA 47:853.35–854.13, 857.37–

Where Luther takes the three archpowers as his point of departure, as in the catechisms, he has in view what is common to all these mandates of God: the dual charge as well as the corresponding exercise of the service required.

All estates—the house government, the secular as well as the spiritual authorities—have been commanded to do two things, as we demonstrated in the analysis of the prefaces.[148] Those to whom God entrusted the offices are, first, to feed and support physically those in their charge, but then they also are to rear them to praise and honor God.[149] Behind this is the twofold will of the triune God for us humans. On the one hand, God as the Creator and Sustainer of this world wants us, as bearers of God's authority, to care for the nonhuman creation. He also wants us to give to ourselves an order of law and peace and to help one another to a life in human dignity. On the other hand, God as our Redeemer and Consummator wants us to accept the message concerning our salvation in Christ in faith and to spread this message in and through the Word. Under these two charges, we go toward Him as the eternal Judge and Savior. This is why the two kingdoms interlock in such a confusing way. In the interpretation of the commandment, they turn their corresponding aspects toward each other.

Secular authority is not seen under the symbol of the sword—as is done in those writings where Luther reflects on the tension between Matthew 5 and Romans 13—but under that of bread.[150] The defensive office of the sword is, at its core, an office of protection and peace; it is based on law. "For the laws are really the true armor and weaponry that preserve and protect the empire and the secular kingdom."[151] This is the innermost meaning of the secular authority's order: it is to protect the human community and place it under the law. The most basic good of earthly well-being is at stake. In the Large Catechism, to demonstrate this in an emphatic way, Luther connected the Fourth Commandment and the Fourth Petition and placed both under the First Commandment and the First Article. By means of devout and law-

---

858.3; "Pred. über Ps. 72 vom 15.2.1540," WA 49:30.16–31.26; further texts in Maurer, *Lehre von den drei Hierarchien*, 3–9, 18–44, and Meyer, *Historischer Kommentar*, 482.

148 Cf. the comments on the prefaces, pp. 26–31.

149 *BSLK*, 603.32–42, 604.21–30, 612.38–43; "Decem praecepta, 1518," WA 1:450.3–452.6; "Sermon von dem ehelichen Stand, 1519," WA 2:169.33–170.16 (see also AE 44:3–14); "Von den guten Werken, 1520," WA 6:254.1–10 (see also AE 44:15–114); "Vom ehelichen Leben, 1522," WA 10.2:301.16–302.15 (see also AE 39:239–99); "Pred. zum 4.–6. Gebot vom 28.2.1523," WA 11:40.2ff.; "Pred. über Ex. 20 vom 29.10.1525," WA 16:490.11–25; "Kat.-Pred. zum 4. Gebot vom 17.9.1528," WA 30.1:34.34; "Gen.-Vorl., 1535–45," WA 42:159.30–36 (see also AE 1:1–359); passim.

150 *BSLK*, 680.20. Cf. the commentary on the Lord's Prayer, on the Fourth Petition.

151 "Eine Predigt, daß man Kinder zur Schule halten solle, 1530," WA 30.2:568.24 (see also AE 46:207–58). Cf. "Eine Predigt, daß man Kinder zur Schule halten solle, 1530," WA 30.2:557.18–562.21 (see also AE 46:207–58); "Ps. 101 ausgelegt, 1534," WA 51:242.1–245.12 (see also AE 13:143–224).

abiding authorities, we enjoy "protection and peace,"[152] so that we can eat
and keep the dear bread. By means of it, God gives to us "food, home and
farm, protection and safety,"[153] since it is "only the hand, pipes, and means
by which God gives everything."[154] Hereby, secular authority is included in
God's fight against the forces of chaos not only in a defensive way, as is done
in the symbol of the sword, but also at the same time, it is positively drawn
into God's blessed preservation and ongoing recreation of the world. Here
secular authority has the duty in particular to provide for the training of
the youth for service in both kingdoms.[155] In his "School Sermon," Luther
highlights the offices of jurist and theologian: "We theologians and jurists
must remain or else all will inevitably perish with us. Where the theologians
turn away, there God's Word turns away and only heathen, even only devils,
remain. Where the jurists turn away, there the laws, including peace, turn
away, and what remains is only robbery, murder, blasphemy, and violence,
even only wild beasts."[156]

In the Large Catechism, Luther adds the spiritual authority in a pecu-
liarly disconnected way.[157] In contradistinction from the secular authority,
Luther does not let it grow out of the family but goes back to 1 Cor. 4:14, to
the words of the apostle concerning his spiritual fatherhood in relation to
the congregation at Corinth. Luther is not afraid to talk about governing and
presiding over the Church by God's Word.[158] Thereby his statements come
into tension with the core thought that among true Christians there is no
ruling and being subservient, there is "no superior except for only Christ
Himself."[159] In the Large Catechism, Luther only hints at the *no* to the emancipation of the officeholders from the communion of service under God's
Word.[160] Now he struggles against the emancipation of the congregations
from their shepherds. Here he insists on the double honor that, according
to 1 Tim. 5:17, is owed to the ministers of the Word and pastors of the congregations.[161] To be sure, the New Testament—and with it the reformer—re-

---

152 *BSLK*, 680.24.

153 *BSLK*, 599.5.

154 *BSLK*, 566.21.

155 See the preface of the Small Catechism (*BSLK*, 505.19–47). Cf. "Kat.-Pred. zum 5. Gebot vom
     4.12.1528," WA 30.1:73.17–25 (see also AE 51:150–55).

156 "Eine Predigt, daß man Kinder zur Schule halten solle, 1530," WA 30.2:578.19 (see also AE
     46:207–58). On Luther's struggle against the jurists, cf. Köhler, *Luther und die Juristen*; Lier-
     mann, "Der unjuristische Luther"; Stein, "M. Luthers Meinung über die Juristen."

157 *BSLK*, 601.24–36.

158 Cf. *BSLK*, 601.30.

159 "Von weltl. Oberkeit, 1523," WA 11:271.3 (see also AE 45:75–129).

160 Cf. *BSLK*, 601.27ff.

161 Cf. *BSLK*, 601.36, 601.2f. In confession, the confessor addresses the pastor as "worthy,
     dear lord" (*BSLK*, 518.7). Luther defends this in his 1532 "Brief an die zu Frankfurt" (WA

ject for the spiritual realm a relationship characterized by ruling and being a subject, but they do enjoin reverence toward the spiritual fathers. In the spiritual realm there also remains the irreversible coordination of fathers and sons; it comes about in the historical process of carrying forward God's Word.

The "office of father"[162] connects the three arch-hierarchies and lets the *politia* and *ecclesia* come together harmoniously in the *familia*. With bright colors, Luther paints the picture of the office of the father of the house as house prince and house bishop.[163] He sees to it that we live under God in this smallest of cells of human communion. Luther seeks to give new life to the age-old function of the heads of clan. For him, too, God's *shalom* order is at stake in the honoring of the parents. The house becomes the decisive battleground in the global war between God and anti-god. The patriarchs serve as a point of reference for Luther; in fact, the family is still a reflection of the paradisiacal community, as Luther describes it emphatically in his great Genesis lecture.[164] Spiritual and secular authorities here still coincide, with the preeminence of the spiritual one.[165] According to Luther, the paradisiacal church is founded on God's Word to eat from all trees except the tree of knowledge (Gen. 2:16).[166] Before Eve was created and before the order of marriage and human society begins with her, God determined for man the place and form of worship. In the command to Adam, there is simultaneously given the duty to praise God's blessing and commandment. With the tree of life is given the place of worship and with the setting apart of the day of rest also its time. Luther demonstrates to his students this worship in concrete terms: If man had not fallen, Adam and his posterity would have gathered in the grove around the tree of life on the Sabbath day. He would have strengthened himself with them by eating its fruits, would have proclaimed God's gracious order, and would have praised Him for the dominion over creation. According to Luther, Psalms 148 and 149, with their call to all creation to

30.3:570.20–571.15).

162   *BSLK*, 596.35.

163   "Von den guten Werken, 1520," WA 6:254.9 (see also AE 44:15–114): "Oh, what a blessed marriage and house where there are such parents! Indeed, it would be a true church, a select monastery, even a paradise." "Pred. über Ex. 20 vom 5.11.1525," WA 16:504.11: "Father and mother in their houses are bishop, pope, doctors, emperor, princes, and lords." "Gen.-Vorl., 1535–45, zu Adam," WA 42:159.34 (see also AE 1:1–359): "He fed the family, governed it, and taught it in piety; he was father, king, and priest."

164   Cf. WA 42:80.19–81.14 (see also AE 1:1–359). On this Brunner, "Zur Lehre vom Gottesdienst," 119–25 (section "Der Gottesdienst des Ertsterschaffenen").

165   Here we still have the order Gospel—commandment. Cf. "Gen.-Vorl., 1535–45," WA 42:110.18 (see also AE 1:1–359): "For Adam this word was Gospel and Law, it was his worship, it was the servitude and obedience of which he was able in this state of innocence."

166   "Gen.-Vorl., 1535–45, zu Gen. 2:16," WA 42:79.3 (see also AE 1:1–359): "This is the institution of the Church before there is economy and the state, for Eve had not been created."

glorify God, hand down to us a kind of order of that paradisiacal praise of God. After this, man would have returned to his work, which represents the idea of the secular realm.[167] Man would have carried out his dominion over creation and his office of caretaker and guardian in God's garden without burden and violence. This was the order of both realms before the fall into sin, but as divine institutions, marriage and family still partake of this order. Here man stands totally under God's blessing hand, totally in the Gospel. For the time being, the Law and the threat of punishment connected with it delimit the abyss surrounding the realm of grace that human ken barely senses.[168] Even daily obedience in the secular realm is fully permeated by the spiritual joy in God.[169]

That paradisiacal idea is, at the same time, the eschatological goal that, however, has increased in brightness and depth because of God's curse cast over our sin, because of the servitude under the powers of doom, and because of Christ's sacrifice. The reformer opens the sinful reality of our daily family lives for that protological idea and this eschatological goal.[170] This is why a bright beam of divine blessing is cast over the interpretation of the Fourth Commandment. After all, this commandment is formulated positively and connected with a "lovely promise."[171] God Himself protects this foundational commandment of the Second Table, and thereby the foundations of our life together as human beings, by His gracious hand of blessing.

---

167 On the paradisiacal institution of the office of care without burden and violence and its change by the punishment for sin, see Törnvall, *Geistliches und weltliches Regiment bei Luther*, 23; Lau, "Leges charitatis," 78; Franz Lau, *Luthers Lehre bei den zweien Reichen* (Berlin: Lutherisches Verlagshaus, 1953) 49; Heckel, *Lex charitatis*, 68f.; Forck, *Die Königsherrschaft Jesu Christi bei Luther*, 62–65.

168 Cf. above p. 206 n. 165 and Brunner, "Zur Lehre vom Gottesdienst," 123 (section "Der Gottesdienst des Ertsterschaffenen").

169 "Gen.-Vorl., 1535–45," WA 42:71.30 (see also AE 1:1–359): "After Adam therefore had been created in such a way that he was, as it were, drunk of joy in God and rejoiced also in all other creatures, now is created a new tree for the distinction of good and evil so that Adam might have a certain sign of worship and reverence of God."

170 Kinder, "Geistlichen und weltlichen 'Oberkeit,' " 285f.: "The family . . . is by no means a relic of the original intact creation that has been preserved ontologically over the chasm of the fall into sin, in which preservation and creation and creation and salvation were still one. Rather, it is a sign of the 'paradisiacal order' that God has established in a creation corrupted and distorted by sin. As such, it can only be seen by faith and can only be realized in the believing anticipation of the uniform condition at the end of which God's secular and spiritual realm— each in their specific, distinct manner—aim and toward which they work. Both have especially teleological, goal-oriented coincidence."

171 *BSLK*, 594.6ff.

4. The Fourth Commandment as *Usus Practicus Evangelii*[172]

Luther harshly sets honoring parents against every kind of self-chosen obedience and in this way works out the Gospel-character of this commandment. Man inquires of the unknown and of uncertainty about the will of the invisible God. In doing so, he thinks to lay hold of the lofty God only by performing lofty works, far above the simple obedience of daily life. This is how he flies above the given orders and seeks a new, unheard-of form of worship.[173] In doing so, he falls deep into his own blinded reason and his self-referential pride of accomplishment. His works are marked by being inappropriate and self-chosen; they do not correspond to what is given but to what is self-chosen. This is why they are marked by travail and uncertainty. Because they have no real meaning in themselves, they are experienced as empty and meaningless. Because they receive their meaning first by means of our own instituting, we simultaneously sense their inner powerlessness. Luther does not separate following Jesus and prayer, on the one hand, and working in the world in the human community, on the other hand. Using the Decalogue as a confessional manual leads him to juxtapose honoring the parents and the monastic way.[174] As hermits, the Carthusians[175] become the negative foil for daily obedience in the vocation and estate ordered by God.

In this commandment to honor the parents, God Himself meets us. He Himself has commanded it and does not know a better one; thus we, too, will not do it any better.[176] Within the Second Table, this commandment occupies the first place; for our life together as humans, there can be no going beyond this commandment. By it God combats forward ideas that fly over His pointing us to our place in life while only looking to our own self; He wants to "keep us at home in obedience and service to our parents."[177]

In the commandment to honor the parents, our conscience gains a firm foothold against all doubts that quickly eat up our autonomous work. Here we find "a certain text and divine testimony"[178] by which we can make our

---

172   *BSLK*, 588.35–596.16.

173   The key texts are found in "De votis monasticis iudicium, 1521" (WA 8:573.30–574.10 [see also AE 48:329–36], 623.18–628.33). Cf. Esnault, "Le 'De votis monasticis' de M. Luther," 19ff., 58ff.; and Lohse, "Luthers Kritik am Mönchtum," 413ff., as well as Lohse, *Mönchtum und Reformation.*

174   "De votis monasticis iudicium, 1521," WA 8:626.26 (see also AE 44:243–400): "Yet it is impossible to prevent this worship of God, obeying the parents, and serving the neighbor; in fact, this very obedience and service of the neighbor is the genuine worship of God itself." Cf. "De votis monasticis iudicium, 1521," WA 8:623–29 (see also AE 44:243–400).

175   *BSLK*, 590.34, 591.19.

176   *BSLK*, 589.10–26, 601.13–23.

177   *BSLK*, 589.28. Cf. "Pred. über Ex. 20 vom 29.10.1525," WA 16:493.23–33.

178   *BSLK*, 591.22.

conscience firm before God. Tirelessly, Luther mentions the "joyous conscience," along with the divine blessing, as the treasure of this commandment.[179] To be sure, the joyous conscience does not refer primarily to the
foundational certainty: By faith in Christ's all-sufficient sacrifice I am God's
child. Rather, it refers to the added certainty of works:[180] We may "joyfully say and boast . . . Behold, this work is pleasing to my God in heaven;
this I know for certain."[181] On it rests God's earthly blessing and heavenly
reward.[182] By tying the deed back to faith, and by tying obedience to the
commandment back to the Gospel, this commandment becomes the *usus
practicus Evangelii*. To the free conscience of the child of God corresponds
the pleasure of the heavenly Father that includes not only the eschatological
salvation but also the earthly blessing.[183] As we walk in faith's obedience to
this commandment, we do so under the opened heaven.

Particularly in his interpretation of the Fourth Commandment, the reformer has made statements that seem to contradict his theology of divine
monergism: "This is why you should be glad in your heart and thank God
that He has chosen you and made you worthy to do such precious, pleasing
works for Him."[184] Already in his "Sermon on Good Works," he formulated
pointedly: God "wants us to work with Him and honors us by wanting to do
His work with us and through us."[185] Luther does not attempt to establish
in an abstract fashion, from the bird's-eye view of reflection, the relation
between a *causa prima* and its *causae secundae*.[186] He is concerned with the
personal certainty between us, who are born of dust and who never become
lords of life, and the eternal Giver of life. As we are in the midst of rushing toward death, we are permitted to achieve the insurmountable certainty
that the invisible Creator God Himself has put us on this place, has given

---

179 *BSLK*, 588.47, 590.2, 591.42, 597.24, 598.11; "In 15 Ps. grad. comm., 1532–33," WA 40.3:156.14:
     "Therefore this trust in the Lord requires you to be in that place, work, institution that is proper
     to your vocation." Cf. "Von den guten Werken, 1520," WA 6:255.9–17, 263.18–264.15 (see also
     AE 44:15–114); "Weihnachtspost. zu Joh. 21:19–24, 1522," WA 10.1.1:309.14ff.; "Das 7. Kap. S.
     Pauli zu den Korinthern, 1523," WA 12:132.23–31 (see also AE 28:1–56); and passim.

180 Cf. Peters, *Glaube und Werk*, 106–13; Modalsli, *Das Gericht nach den Werken*, 52–96.

181 *BSLK*, 590.2.

182 *BSLK*, 598.10ff., 599.20f., 601.13f., 602.37ff., 604.49f.

183 Cf. "Von Christus Brüdern und Schwestern ein anderer Sermon, Mt. 12:46–50, 1528," WA
     28:26.15–28.37; "Ausl. von Mt. 5–7, 1530/32," WA 32:409.17–410.33 (see also AE 21:1–294).

184 *BSLK*, 590.24. Particularly on the Fourth Commandment, Luther develops his insights on
     man's cooperation with God.

185 WA 6:227.30 (see also AE 44:15–114). In his study *Der Gedanke von Zusammenwirken Gottes
     und des Menschen in Luthers Theologie*, 9f., Seils takes this thought as his point of departure.

186 This is shown clearly in "Vorl. über Ps. 127, 1533," WA 40.3:214.19: ". . . for You (God) are the
     primary cause; I am a secondary cause. You are the Creator and do everything; I am only an
     instrument."

us "living parents,"[187] and has placed them near our heart by means of His commandment. His commandment thereby becomes our breathing space of the life of grace before His face.[188] As we bow before our parents, we directly and immediately bow before Him.[189] Our bodily man faces these bodily men; our inner man hides himself completely in the "treasure and sanctuary, namely, God's Word and commandment."[190] By doing so, the parents become a sacrament for us, a bodily sign of invisible grace.[191] As we face them, our trusting heart at the same time faces the eternal God in His word-like condescension itself. Concretely obeying the parents, however, only becomes a sacramental sign of saving grace and of the Creator's blessing where God's previous election of grace has met us and where His Holy Spirit has created our heart anew.[192] In this sense, Luther's pertinent remarks point again to the mysterious fact that the Creed and the Lord's Prayer are needed for the fulfillment of the Commandments. In fact, they show that the triune God Himself wants to fulfill the Commandments in and through us.[193] In this, God's monergism does not undo our cooperation; rather, it liberates it from egotistical selfishness and takes it up in a manner that breaks forth into the selfless freedom of God's Spirit.[194]

5. True Form and Divinely Established Limit of Obedience in the Fourth Commandment

In parents and lords, as the "superior persons" given us by God, we encounter God Himself. This insight shapes the form of our obedience. The presence of both fear and love, which permeated the First Commandment, is also hinted at in the Fourth by the key word "honor." This "honoring" adds to loving "a discipline, humility, and fear as toward a majesty hidden there."[195] In the "Sermon on Good Works," Luther describes this fear con-

---

187 *BSLK*, 592.29.

188 *BSLK*, 591.1f.

189 *BSLK*, 589.36.

190 *BSLK*, 590.31.

191 "Ausl. von Mt. 5–7, 1530/32," WA 32:424.20 (see also AE 21:1–294): "Yet Scripture teaches us not to look to ourselves but to God's Word and promise and to cling to it by faith, so that you, if you do the work out of the Word and the promise, have a sure sign that God is gracious to you. In this way, your own work, which God has now taken to Himself, is to be for you a sure sign of forgiveness."

192 *BSLK*, 598.7ff.

193 Cf. *BSLK*, 640.41ff., 661.37–42, 662.26ff.

194 Cf. Seils, *Der Gedanke vom Zusammenwirken*, 163ff., 191f.; Maurer, *Lehre von den drei Hierarchien*, 32ff., 40ff.; Schwarzwäller, *Theologia crucis*; Peters, "Reformatorische Rechtfertigungsbotschaft," 100ff.

195 *BSLK*, 587.18. Cf. *BSLK*, 588.14f.; "Decem praecepta, 1518," WA 1:447.30–449.2, 458.25–459.25; "Pred. über Ex. 20 vom 29.10.1525," WA 16:494.11–495.37, 487.35–488.18; Melanchthon, *Catechesis puerilis*, 1540 (Reu, *Quellen*, 1.2.2:32.13): "Honor, therefore, encompasses these three

nected with love strictly as *timor filialis* opposed to *timor servilis*.[196] The insight gained in the First Commandment is applied to the Fourth. The servile fear is indissolubly connected to secret hatred—the one who is caught in it flees the parents in his heart and fears their punishment more than angering them. The filial fear battles the hatred and comes near in love; it fears saddening the parents more than their punishment.

In all this, God watches over the structure of headship, that is, of people being ordered above and below each other, not only in the family but also in the vast realm of the social, political, and ecclesiastical life.[197] God does not want "that everybody wants to be his own master and be free of the emperor."[198] The reformer strikes out hard against violent emancipation. Whoever engages in insurrection rebels against God Himself, he is guilty of [high] treason: *crimen laesae maiestatis*.[199] As accuser and judge in one person, he anticipates the vengeance that God has reserved for Himself. Rebellion against tyrannical authorities is a sign of a lack of patience and confidence that God rules even where He does not seem to keep a tight rein. An insurrection against tyrannical authorities, which might also be violent, is mandated, first, where the authorities demolish the divine institutions and arch-hierarchies themselves—marriage and family, secular and spiritual authorities—in an open way, under the appearance of right. In that case, they take on the dimension of the antichrist for Luther.[200]

Thus the reformer, on the one hand, moves the "parents and lords" very close to the Lord of all lords. On the other hand, he clearly subjects them to

elements: first, acknowledgment of God's presence and of God's work and ordination; second, the kind of obedience by which we, from our heart, attribute the praise of wisdom and justice to parents and magistrates; third, clemency in covering their disadvantages and sins."

196 WA 6:251.5–15 (see also AE 44:15–114); cf. "Decem praecepta, 1518," WA 1:448.37–449.2.

197 *BSLK*, 703.37–704.12; "Eine treue Vermahnung, sich zu hüten vor Aufruhr und Empörung, 1522," WA 8:680.16–681.30 (see also AE 45:51–74); "Ermahnung zum Frieden auf die Rotten der Bauern, 1525," WA 18:303.27–307.36 (see also AE 46:3–43); "Wider die räuberischen u. mörderischen Rotten der Bauern, 1525," WA 18:358.3–32 (see also AE 46:45–55); "Ob Kriegsleute, 1526," WA 19:634.1–644.32 (see also AE 46:87–137); "Zirkulardisp. über das Recht d. Widerstandes, 1539," WA 39.2:42f., theses 61–70.

198 *BSLK*, 600.13.

199 "Ob Kriegsleute, 1526," WA 19.631.14 (see also AE 46:87–137): "Rebellion is worthy of death as *Crimen lese maiestatis* [sic]." Cf. "Ob Kriegsleute, 1526," WA 19:641.18–21 (see also AE 46:87–137). In the Large Catechism (*BSLK*, 628.5–21), Luther also places the slanderer into this class as a rebel against God's and the authority's office of judge.

200 On this question, see "Vom Kriege wider die Türken, 1529," WA 30.2:107–48 (see also AE 46:155–205); "Eine Heerpredigt wider die Türken, 1529," WA 30.2:160–97; "Zirkulardisp. über das Recht d. Widerstandes, 1539," WA 39.2:39–91. On it, see Hermann, "Luthers Zirkulardisputation über Matthäus 19:21"); "Gutachten zur Gegenwehr, 1536," (CR 3:128–31); "Gutachten zur Widerstandsfrage, 1539," WABr 8:515ff., no. 3369. Further texts are compiled and interpreted in Scheible, *Das Widerstandsrecht als Problem der deutschen Protestanten*. Luther's applicable thoughts are taken up in Thielicke, *Ethik*, 2.2:445–60 (§§ 2466–68).

the First Commandment. This is only hinted at in the Large Catechism.[201] It is unfolded more broadly in the "Sermon on Good Works": Where the parents rear the children only in a worldly manner, there "the children are not to obey them in any way."[202] Where the secular authority would "force a subject against God's commandment or hinder him in performing it, there obedience ends and duty is abrogated."[203] More harshly yet, Luther rejects the infringements of the spiritual authority.[204] It, too, has to bow under the first three commandments. The Large Catechism addresses these insights basically in the subordination of the Fourth Commandment under the First Table. Luther hints at it by warning the authorities that they, too, will have to give an account to God.[205] The accent, however, lies on drumming the commandment into the head of the "children" and the "common man," "so that they might be quiet, faithful, obedient, peaceful."[206]

Ultimately, it is not the preacher who teaches and drives this commandment home but the living God Himself: "The good that is sustained by the secular and spiritual orders is not a fruit of human efforts, but these orders are God's creatures, God's rule in the midst of man's evilness. And the good that comes out of these orders comes from God, though man abuses them. Both the *iustitia christiana* and the *iustitia civilis* are the *iustitia Dei*."[207] God Himself is "the Founder, Lord, Master, Fosterer, and Rewarder of both kinds of righteousness, of the spiritual and bodily one. There is no human order or power in them; they are an altogether divine matter."[208]

IMPORTANT TEXTS ON THE FOURTH COMMANDMENT

WA 1:447–60: from Decem praecepta Wittenbergensi praedicata populo, 1518

WA 2:166–71: Sermon von dem ehelichen Stand, 1519 (see also AE 44:3–14)

---

201 *BSLK*, 590.14ff.

202 WA 6:253.1 (see also AE 44:15–114). Similarly, Bonaventure, *Collationes des decem praeceptis* 5:10: "The Lord wants man not to quit doing what pertains to his salvation out of paternal affection." Judaism as well as Stoic philosophy established the principle that the affirmation of what is divine/good or of the Commandments of God, respectively, has to precede obeying one's parents (cf. Schrenk, πατήρ, *TWNT* 5:950.31ff., 975.28ff.).

203 WA 6:265.15 (see also AE 44:15–114). Cf. "Von weltl. Oberkeit, 1523," WA 11:261–71 (see also AE 45:75–129).

204 WA 6:256.37–257.6 (see also AE 44:15–114); "Pred. über Ex. 20 vom 29.10.1525," WA 16:496.10–16.

205 *BSLK*, 505.19–34, 590.14–19, 604.1–11.

206 *BSLK*, 505.1ff.

207 Siirala, *Gottes Gebot bei M. Luther*, 318f.; cf. Asheim, *Glaube und Erziehung bei Luther*, 252ff.

208 "Ob Kriegsleute, 1526," WA 19:629.30 (see also AE 46:87–137). Maurer, *Lehre von den drei Hierarchien*, 34: "Thus Luther neither wants to describe the social reality of his time nor offer a social theory with his doctrine of the three estates. Rather, he simply describes the creation of God that actively determines our life, whether we acknowledge it or not. The three orders are an expression of God's glory as Creator and simultaneously instruments in His hand to make every man His responsible servant and to exercise the Christian in sanctification."

WA 6:250–65: from Sermon von den guten Werken, 1520 (see also AE 44:15–114)

WA 10.2:292–304: from Vom ehelichen Leben, 1522 (see also AE 45:11–49)

WA 16:485–99: Predigt über Ex. 20 vom 29.10.1525

WA 16:500–506: from Predigt über Ex. 20 vom 5.11.1525

WA 30.2:517–88: Eine Predigt, daß man Kinder zur Schule halten solle, 1530 (see also AE 46:207–58)

Important Texts on the Doctrine of Estates (Fourth Commandment)

WA 11:245–81: Von weltlicher Oberkeit, 1523 (see also AE 45:75–129)

WA 19:623–62: Ob Kriegsleute auch in seligem Stande sein Können, 1526 (see also AE 46:87–137)

WA 43:558–63: from Genesisvorlesung zu Gen. 28:1f., 1535–45 (see also AE 5:1–386)

Literature on Luther's Doctrine of Estates

Maurer, Luthers Lehre von den drei Hierarchien und ihr mittelalterlicher Hintergrund

Kinder, "Luthers Ableitung der geistlichen und weltlichen 'Oberkeit' aus dem 4. Gebot"

Duchrow, Christenheit und Weltverantwortung

Junghans, "Das mittelalterliche Vorbild für Luthers Lehre von den beiden Reichen"

Hoffmann, Die "Hausväterliteratur" und die "Predigten über den christlichen Hausstand"

The Fifth Commandment[1]

Wording of the Commandment, Understanding and Arrangement of the Interpretation

Without wavering, Luther renders the commandment as "You shall not kill."[2] He probably uses the broader *killing* to avoid the "carnal" misunderstanding, as if only murder or intentional homicide were forbidden.[3]

In his interpretation of the prohibition against killing, Luther understands it consciously as a protective commandment. The Lord surrounds the bodily life of our neighbor with a shield wall,[4] lest we hurt him "in his body."[5] The word "body" circumscribes the neighbor's "own person"[6] in its earthbound physical existence. The phrase "in the body"[7] marks the place where we encounter the fellow man and where we can take his life. Thus "body" serves as a placeholder for the person as well as the life[8] and denotes the *homo huius vitae.*[9]

---

1   For texts on the Fifth Commandment, see p. 232.

2   *BSLK*, 508.29, 555.22, 605.36; "Eine kurze Erklärung, 1518," WA 1:251.6; "Von den guten Werken, 1520," WA 6:265.35 (see also AE 44:15–114); "Eine kurze Form, 1520," WA 7:206.12.

3   Only "Eine kurze Unterweisung, 1519" (WA 2:62.22): "You shall not commit homicide," as in several medieval texts. Cf. Meyer, *Historischer Kommentar*, 89.

4   *BSLK*, 607.6.

5   *BSLK*, 508.32.

6   *BSLK*, 611.3, according to "Kat.-Pred. zum 5. praeceptum vom 20.5.1528," WA 30.1:7.33.

7   *BSLK*, 607.8, 608.26; "Kat.-Pred. zum 5. Gebot vom 4.12.1528," WA 30.1:74.16 (see also AE 51:150–55).

8   *BSLK*, 608.48; "Kat.-Pred. zum 5. Gebot vom 18.9. bzw. 4.12.1528," WA 30.1:36.34, 74.12. Cf. furthermore *BSLK*, 648.14f., and the "Nürnberger Katechismuspredigten" (Reu, *Quellen*, 1.1:483.17, 483.25).

9   "Disp. de homine, 1536," WA 39.1:175.8 (see also AE 34:133–44).

The dual phrase "harm or hurt"[10] also appears in the Large Catechism,[11] the emphasis being on hurt.[12] "Love and doing good,"[13] as well as "all good and love,"[14] correspond to it positively. "Hurt" still describes for Luther the evil deed inflicted to the body,[15] while the pain caused to the neighbor is a connotation of this term.[16] Also "helping and promoting"[17] are exchangeable synonyms,[18] where the latter underlines the fostering that results from helping.[19]

While the reformer, in the explanation of the Small Catechism, only realizes the turn from the negative to the positive, from hurting to helping, in the Large Catechism he unfolds a dual progression. First, he drives the prohibition from what is outside to what is inside, and then he turns the negation into a positive formulation. By doing so, he follows Jesus' interpretation in the Sermon on the Mount (Matt. 5:21f.).[20] God is not satisfied when we merely withhold our hand from committing homicide; He demands "a patient, mild heart,"[21] not only when dealing with a friend but also when dealing with an enemy. God is not satisfied when we merely do not damage our neighbor in his bodily existence; rather, He wants us to "show him all good and love"[22] in every situation of need in his life. Luther bases the demanded active love of the heart toward all men on the fear and love of God that the First Commandment seeks in us. Thus in the Large Catechism he unfolds the inner structure of the relation between the commandments by means of the prohibition of killing, as it found its classic expression in the Small Catechism. We are not to harm our neighbor because we fear God's wrath; we

---

10   *BSLK*, 508.33.

11   *BSLK*, 607.8, 608.26; "Kat.-Pred. zum 5. Gebot vom 4.12.1528," WA 30.1:74.24 (see also AE 51:150–55).

12   *BSLK*, 607.8, 607.21, 608.6, 609.31; "Kat.-Pred. von 20.5. bzw. 4.12.1528," WA 30.1:7.16, 74.15.

13   *BSLK*, 608.38, 609.33.

14   *BSLK*, 609.32.

15   Here suicide is still paraphrased as "to hurt oneself."

16   Cf. *BSLK*, 608.6, 608.10f.; "Kat.-Pred. vom 4.12.1528," WA 30.1:74.15f. (see also AE 51:150–55), as well as the discussion in Meyer, *Historischer Kommentar*, 230.

17   *BSLK*, 508.33.

18   Cf. "Eine kurze Form, 1520," WA 7:206.11.

19   WA 30.1:75.15 (see also AE 51:150–55): "Promote the neighbor with hand, mouth, and heart."

20   In this, Luther follows the tradition shaped by Augustine. Cf. the commentary on the arrangement and structure, pp. 97f. and n. 59.

21   *BSLK*, 607.42. "Kat.-Pred. vom 20.5.1528," WA 30.1:7.26: "Therefore in this commandment He encourages mildness of heart toward the neighbor." Cf. "Von den guten Werken, 1520," WA 6:266.1 (see also AE 44:15–114); "Sermon über Mt. 5:20ff. vom 12.7.1523," WA 11:148.20; "Sermon über Mt. 5:20ff. vom 12.7.1523," WA 12:624.8f.; "Kat.-Pred. vom 4.12.1528," WA 30.1:74.26 (see also AE 51:150–55).

22   *BSLK*, 609.32.

are to help our neighbor because we love God in His gracious turn toward us. In this, Luther's understanding of this connection back to the First Commandment possessed by the Second through the Tenth Commandments shows that the phrase "so that we do not . . . but" is to be understood not only in a consecutive sense but also in a final one. That is, it not only means that we will act in this way because we are inwardly overcome by the fear and love of God but also that God wants this obedience and will enforce it in us. Anthropologically basing the bodily deed in the heart's relation to God is embraced and permeated by the theological reference of our walking in the commandments according to God's commanding and creating.

This inner structure of understanding shapes the external form and arrangement of the interpretation in the Large Catechism. In a first set of thoughts,[23] Luther establishes the position of the prohibition of killing in the Decalogue and determines the divinely established meaning thereof. (a) After the commandment to honor the parents, which proves the hierarchical ordering among us to be grounded in God's ordering, the Fifth Commandment concerns our relation to fellow human beings, our equals. This is why civil authority, standing in the parents' stead, is excepted from the prohibition of killing; civil authority has to exercise the office of punishment assigned to it by God.[24] (b) The spiritual meaning of the commandment is revealed by Christ in the Sermon on the Mount.[25] (c) In the prohibition of killing, God has erected a protective wall around the bodily life of our neighbor, shielding our neighbor against our anger.[26]

In the body of the interpretation,[27] Luther pushes from the outside in, from the negative to the positive. (a) First, he summarizes the movement from the outside in: God wants to remove the root of homicide, the angry heart. He seeks the heart that is patient toward enemies as well.[28] (b) Next, Luther demonstrates the steps of that movement from the outside in: it moves from the hand and its deed, touches on the tongue and its advice and on other means and ways, and reaches the stirrings of the heart.[29] (c) Finally, he develops the positive commandment: In all concrete situations of need, we are to show love, even toward those who give us reason to be angry. The six works of mercy demanded by Christ in the parable of the great judgment of the world (Matt. 25:42f.) underscore the commandment.[30]

---

23   *BSLK*, 605.37–607.19.
24   *BSLK*, 606.2–14, 606.22–30.
25   *BSLK*, 606.15–22.
26   *BSLK*, 606.31–607.19.
27   *BSLK*, 607.20–609.40.
28   *BSLK*, 607.20–608.2.
29   *BSLK*, 608.3–21.
30   *BSLK*, 608.22–609.40.

In conclusion, Luther connects positively the Fifth and the First Commandment.[31] (a) He bases the love of the neighbor on the love of God[32] and thereby, as in the case of the Fourth Commandment,[33] confronts (b) polemically the "true, noble, high works"[34] of the "common estate of the Christian"[35]—which are commanded of all men by God and which direct us to each other—with the sanctimonious, pious works of the so-called spiritual estates, where people isolate and affirm themselves.[36]

THE PROHIBITION OF KILLING
IN THE OLD AND NEW TESTAMENTS[37]

The prohibition of killing is the first commandment in the Decalogue whose apodictic form has been preserved unchanged. The preachers have passed this commandment along without interpreting it or enjoining it in a special way. In the prohibition of killing (Exod. 20:13; Deut. 5:17), a rare verb, raṣaḥ, is used,[38] which denotes a peculiar kind of killing, namely, the premeditated murder as well as the unintentional homicide committed by a person. Therefore it seems to circumscribe the "unlawful killing that negatively affects the community."[39] Perhaps the word can be delimited even more. It circumscribes "the premeditated deed as well as the unpremeditated one, the triggering deed as well as the revenge. Yet the term always denotes a deed that is part of the chain of strike and counterstrike, that is, in other words, part of a blood feud."[40]

Except for a few places where the deed of the killer is listed paradigmatically,[41] the texts focus on the laws for the cities of refuge[42] that are always mentioned next to the Levite cities.[43] By means of this law, Yahweh holds His protecting hand over the life of His covenant people and its

---

31   *BSLK*, 609.41–610.38.

32   *BSLK*, 609.41–610.8.

33   See p. 208f. Luther adds in *BSLK*, 610.8ff., as a new accent, the reluctance to suffer.

34   *BSLK*, 609.43.

35   *BSLK*, 610.11.

36   *BSLK*, 610.8–38.

37   Jepsen, "Du sollst nicht töten!"; von Reventlow, *Gebot und Predigt im Dekalog*, 71–77; Stamm, "Sprachliche Erwägungen zum Gebot: 'Du sollst nicht töten.' "

38   The verb is found 46 times, compared to *harag* (165 times) and *hemit* (Hiphil of *mut* (201 times).

39   Stamm, "Dreißig Jahre Dekalogforschung," 297; cf. Stamm, *Der Dekalog im Lichte der neueren Forschung*, 54.

40   Thus von Reventlow, *Gebot und Predigt im Dekalog*, 75.

41   E.g., Deut. 22:26; Job 24:14; 1 Kings 21:19.

42   Deut. 4:41–43; 19:1–13; Numbers 35; Joshua 20.

43   Numbers 35; Deuteronomy 18; Joshua 21.

members. By means of this sacred law of refuge, He wants to prevent, on the one hand, the shedding of innocent blood in His holy land.[44] On the other hand, He demands the life of the premeditating murderer that must not be redeemed by the payment of wergeld.[45] Only the blood of the murderer can atone for the blood of the murdered individual. In this way, Yahweh takes the blood feud out of the automatic chain of strike and counterstrike. At the same time, He makes the killing of a premeditating murderer the sacred duty of His covenant people, because man as His image also remains His property.[46]

Thus already by the related verb *raṣaḥ*, the commandment is related to the community of the covenant people. This is why it certainly allows for the execution of the death penalty that is laid on the community, as well as for the sacred ban to be executed in holy war.[47] After all, in the sacred order of refuge there is already laid the foundation for the bipolarity that is exacerbated in the New Testament, namely, between Jesus' radical prohibition of killing (Matt. 5:21f.) and the traditional statement of the apostle,[48] according to which the authorities, as God's servants and executors of God's judgment of wrath, do not bear the sword in vain (Rom. 13:1–7). In the Large Catechism, Luther mentions Deut. 21:18–21[49] and interprets the execution of God's judgment on an unruly member of the family by the court of elders in the gate as a hint at the fact that God has transferred His authority over life and death to "the civil authorities instead of the parents." This sets the stage for one of the knotty problems that Luther addresses following the tradition on the commandment, namely: How is civil authority related to this prohibition of killing?

The inner structure of Luther's interpretation emerges from the fact that the commandment has been made a part of the antitheses of the Sermon of the Mount (Matt. 5:21f.). By means of the pattern *not only—but already!*[50] a movement is carried out here that can also be observed as being analogously

---

44   Deut. 19:10; Num. 35:12.

45   Num. 35:31; see the Jewish practice described in *Bill.*, 1:257–75.

46   Cf. von Rad, *Das erste Buch Mose*, 109f. (on Gen. 9:6); *GnR* 34 (21c) (*Bill.*, 1:254): "Rabbi Aqiba has taught publicly: Who sheds blood, it is counted to him (by God) as if he had diminished the image of God."

47   Von Rad, *Der heilige Krieg im alten Israel*, 25ff.

48   Cf. Strobel, "Zum Verständnis von Rm 13," and Käsemann, "Römer 13,1–7 in unserer Generation," 316–76.

49   *BSLK*, 606.4–11. Cf. "Dtn.-Vorl., 1523/24," WA 14:696.25–36 (see also AE 9:1–311). Luther interprets also Deut. 19:1–13 analogously (WA 14:686.4–688.13 [see also AE 9:1–311]): The blood feud is taken out of the hands of the clan and handed over to the authorities by the order of refuge. Gerson/Geiler still mentions blood feud in his interpretation (see Geffcken, *Bildercatechismus*, app., col. 42).

50   Cf. Bornkamm, *Jesus von Nazreth*, 95.

strong in rabbinic exegesis.[51] Behind and above the commandment, God is revealed as the zealously holy judge who establishes the simple basic law: "With the measure you use, you will be measured" (Matt. 7:2).

God's zeal for undivided obedience limits the seemingly broad leeway on this side of breaking the commandment and drives the commandment deeper and deeper into our existence as human beings. Here, the prohibition extends beyond the mere intentional killing carried out against the community, as if everything else that does not go this far were allowed. In such an interpretation, the hardness of our heart (Matt. 10:5 and parallels) would triumph over God's call to conscience. No, the prohibition goes much deeper. Even the one who hurts his neighbor by words falls under God's judgment.[52] After all, on the Last Day we will have to give account of every useless word (Matt. 12:36). This advancement is made also in a saying attributed to Rabbi Eliezer: "Who hates his neighbor, behold, he belongs to those who shed blood."[53] As a murderer of men, he does not have any share in the life before God (1 John 3:15). This is how the prohibition of killing penetrates to the inner core of our existence. According to Jesus' words (Mark 7:21f. and parallels), every act of transgression comes from the heart. In this way, the steps are prepared: not killing by hand, by tongue, and by the thoughts of the heart.

However, the prohibition of killing not only wants to uproot all the bad shoots growing out of the root of the heart, but it also wants to change the heart itself in a fundamental way to actively love the neighbor. This is attested by the two places where the prohibition of killing is mentioned in the Epistles of the New Testament. In the Epistle to the Romans (13:9f.) as well as in the Epistle of James (2:11ff.), it is connected with the positive commandment to love the neighbor. The prohibition of killing is included and fulfilled also in loving dedication to fellow man as the royal law of freedom[54] and as the fulfillment of the Law.[55] Luther has thoroughly reflected on this change from the negative to the positive in the meaning of the prohibition under the influence of the holy will of God. Out of it grew the second and third thematic section of his interpretation: the spiritual understanding of the commandment that was first fully developed by Jesus, as well as the reference of the Fifth to the First Commandment.

---

51 Cf. *Bill.*, 1:276–82.

52 Texts *Bill.*, 1:280ff.

53 Dèrekh Ereç 10 (*Bill.*, 1:282); cf. bNᵉd 22ᵃ: "Who is angry is governed by all parts of the Gehenna" (*Bill.*, 1:277).

54 On James 1:25; 2:8, 12, cf. Walter Gutbrod, νόμος, *TWNT* 4:1073ff., and Lohse, "Glaube und Werke—Zur Theologie des Jakobusbriefes."

55 On Rom. 13:10, see Bultmann, *Christus des Gesetzes Ende*.

CHARACTERISTICS OF LUTHER'S INTERPRETATION

1. DIFFERENT ACCENTS IN WORKING OUT THE STRUCTURE OF THE COMMANDMENT

The inner structure of Luther's understanding of the prohibition of kill-ing is deeply anchored in his reformation insight regarding the killing Law and the recreating Gospel. Following the antitheses of the Sermon on the Mount (Matt. 5:21f.), he gained it already in "Decem praecepta Wittenber-gensi praedicata populo" ("Preaching of the Ten Commandments").[56] After that, Luther tirelessly elaborated on it in his interpretations of the command-ment, as well as in the sermons on Matt. 5:20–26, the historic Gospel read-ing for the Sixth Sunday after Trinity. There is a certain shift in accentuation, as Luther's earlier interpretations focus more on the inner change of heart, while especially after his 1525 sermons on Exodus, he accentuates more the protective character of the commandment.[57] Thus he first looks to the "meekness" that overcomes all anger and, along with the Epistle of James, battles in great detail against the sins of the tongue.[58] The form of the com-mandment itself at first takes a back seat in comparison to the struggle for a spiritual understanding of the Mosaic commandments in general that had first been fully developed by the antitheses of the Sermon on the Mount.

In the Large Catechism, where Luther summarizes the insights of the 1528 sermons in a rather free manner,[59] he strengthens with the sermon on December 4 the protective purpose of the commandment.[60] The command-ment is to cover the bodily life of the neighbor. Even as he strengthens the protective aspect, he does not neglect the insight of the earlier interpreta-tions: the commandment requires a patient and gentle heart.[61] There is a noteworthy change in one place: when Luther grounds the Fifth Command-ment on the First, the Christological accent is lost. There is an echo of the

---

56 WA 1:462.28–464.11. On the change in the interpretation of the commandment, see Harde-land, *Katechismusgedanken*, 131–49.

57 Cf. the commentary on arrangement and structure, p. 93f.

58 "Decem praecepta, zum Jakobusbrief," WA 1:473.12–479.16.

59 The sources cannot be indicated as precisely as in the previous commandments, since Luther in the Large Catechism expands on short references in the sermons.

60 In the first series, the accent still lies on the heart that is free of wrath ("20.5.1528," WA 30.1:7.26). In the second, the body of the neighbor receives more attention ("18.9.1528," WA 30.1:37.5, 37.14). In the third and in the Large Catechism ("4.12.1528," WA 30.1:74.12–16 [see also AE 51:150–55]; *BSLK*, 607.3–9), Luther explicitly calls the commandment a protective wall around the body of the neighbor, a wall erected by God against my anger. "4.12.1528," WA 30.1:75.8 (see also AE 51:150–55): "And the Fifth Commandment is to be seen as a wall that God has built against my anger." Cf. *BSLK*, 606.45ff., 607.41ff.

61 *BSLK*, 607.42.

Christological argument in the Large Catechism, but this augmentation has lost its evangelical character.[62]

2. PARTICIPATION OF THE CIVIL AUTHORITIES IN GOD'S WATCH OVER THE COMMANDMENT[63]

In the prohibition against killing, God shows Himself as the protective Lord of human life together. He places this commandment "between good and evil."[64] He guards us against perishing because of the instinct to seek revenge.[65] He lets the civil authorities participate in this protective office; for this purpose, He exempts them from the prohibition. They have the power, authority, and duty to execute the death penalty.[66] They are supposed to be angry, rebuke, and punish.[67] The government is supposed to break this commandment by serving it. In the Large Catechism, Luther merely poses this proposition without showing how it is possible for a Christian holding civil office to meet this demand also within his heart. He touches here on a question that Paul already alludes to by placing into the parenesis for the congregation in Romans 12f. statements concerning pagan authorities: How is it possible to reconcile the charge to exercise God's office of punishment and vengeance as His servant with the instructions to "Bless those who persecute you; bless and do not curse! . . . Do not avenge yourselves; give room for God's wrath!" (Rom. 12:14, 19) and with the prohibition of killing (Rom. 13:9)? How is the office of punishment connected in mutual love with the prohibition of killing as fulfillment of the Law, which overcomes evil with good (Rom. 12:21; 13:8–10)?

Already in "Preaching of the Ten Commandments," the reformer briefly mentions that Scripture identifies a divinely mandated office of wrath.[68] At the same time, he turns against the thesis offered on Matt. 5:22: "It is certainly commanded to leave wrath and anger in the heart, but not the signs of wrath, that is, as they say in German: forgiving but not forgetting."[69] Emphatically he rejects the distinction between a command and a counsel

---

62   Cf. pp. 230–32.

63   *BSLK*, 606.2–30.

64   *BSLK*, 606.34.

65   *BSLK*, 606.31–607.7.

66   *BSLK*, 606.2–14.

67   *BSLK*, 606.25.

68   WA 1:480.31ff., pointing to 1 Cor. 5:11; 2 Thess. 3:14f. Cf. Gustav Stählin, ὀργή, *TWNT* 5:419f.

69   "Ausl. von Mt. 5–7, 1530/32," WA 32:361.31 (see also AE 21:1–294). "Decem praecepta, 1518," WA 1:479.25: "Here some say that it is, to be sure, necessary to let go of anger but not of the signs of anger." Cf. "Sermon über Mt. 5:20ff. vom 12.7.1523," WA 11:148.36–149.6; "Sermon über Mt. 5:20ff. vom 12.7.1523," WA 12:625.5–20; "Pred. über Mt. 5:20ff. vom 20.7.1533," WA 37:112.17–25; "Hauspost. zu Mt. 5:20ff., 1533," WA 52:409.17–30.

that was based on the Sermon on the Mount. His polemics still echo in the Large Catechism,[70] where he juxtaposes the divinely commanded works and the self-chosen ones.[71] Yet the medieval theologians seek to bring out with these distinctions the same thing on which Luther reflects thoroughly. Already Thomas shows that God has taken the authorities out of this commandment,[72] and Bonaventure already points out that there is a fundamental difference between the punishing servant of the law and the lawbreaker. The former does not kill out of unbridled thirst for vengeance, but out of love of justice.[73]

Luther seeks to establish these different relations by the "two persons or twofold office" that come on a Christian.[74] By this formula, he does not want to seal off two areas against each other. Rather, for the time being, he wants to distinguish two chains of motivation in order to be able to connect them to each other all the more firmly. First, our relation to our fellow humans, our equals, is in view.[75] Then our protective office in the context of the given relations of rule and service is in view. Each view demands an externally contrary behavior—in the first case, one that is based on Matthew 5; in the second case, one that is based on Romans 13. Yet both are borne by one and the same basic inner attitude. The commandment of love applies to both views and behaviors: "Cursed and damned be all life that is lived and sought for its own use and advantage; cursed be all works that do not walk in love."[76]

This means for the Christian himself, in view of his person, he is taken out of that primordial law of every worldly order that is sanctioned by God. He is taken out of the necessity of adequate revenge: "eye for eye, tooth for tooth."[77] He has his eschatological home in God and, as a guest on this earth,

---

70   BSLK, 610.17f.

71   BSLK, 610.8–38. On the tension between commandment and counsel, see Lohse, "Mönchtum und Reformation," 106–75; and Kühn, Via caritatis, 113ff., 201f., 258f.

72   Thomas Aquinas, Duo praecepta § 1260: "For what is lawful for God is lawful for His servants, based on His mandate."

73   Bonaventure, Collationes de decem praeceptis 6:7 (5:527): "A man who is a servant of the law kills another man based on the law, not based on a desire for vengeance, but out of love of justice."

74   "Ausl. von Mt. 5–7, 1530/32," WA 32:390.10 (see also AE 21:1–294). Cf. "Ausl. von Mt. 5–7, 1530/32," WA 32:391.23 (see also AE 21:1–294): "Therefore learn well the distinction between the two persons whom a Christian must wear on earth, because he lives among other people and must use the emperor's goods as much as the heathen. For he has the very same blood and flesh that he must preserve, not from the spiritual realm but from the field and land that belongs to the emperor, etc., until he goes from this life to the next also in a bodily way."

75   BSLK, 605.41ff.

76   "Von weltl. Oberkeit, 1523," WA 11:272.1 (see also AE 45:75–129).

77   Cf. Alt, "Zur Talionsformel."

abides by the "common, strict law" of the Sermon on the Mount.[78] He suffers injustice and does not strike back; he also blesses his adversaries and prays for them. However, as he serves his neighbor and as he partakes in God's punitive office, he must exercise wrath.[79] Here he seemingly violates Jesus' prohibition of anger yet does justice to it within his heart. The wrath demanded in God's rule is a "Christian and fraternal, even fatherly wrath,"[80] which leaves behind all personal feelings of anger. This is why it can coexist quite well with a patient, meek heart.[81] After all, it is "love's wrath that wishes no evil on anyone, that is a friend of the person but an enemy of sin, as one can be taught by nature."[82] This "divine" and "necessary" wrath[83] that preserves God's civil and spiritual realm against the attacks of Satan is a high spiritual gift. Luther does not deny that we can make this *zelus iustitiae* into a cover for our evilness.[84] Yet even if we manage to deceive our fellow human beings and ourselves, before God our heart is not covered. He Himself will uncover it for us, as well as for the entire world, on the Day of Judgment.

For Luther, this office of wrath and punishment of the civil authorities in God's commandment and name encompasses both kingdoms. This is made apparent in an unsettling way by the inner monologue of a judge who awards a death sentence. Even if he has to make room for God's wrath over the evil deed, yet in the solidarity of sinners, he places himself right next to the perpetrator and says, "Oh, see how your soul might come under a harsh judgment of God. See how you might perish. I have to take off your body and see to it that your sin does no further damage. Although I cannot save your body, I have to see to it that I help the soul."[85] This is a view of the death penalty that cannot be applied directly to the modern secular

---

78   "Von weltl. Oberkeit, 1523," WA 11:259.18 (see also AE 45:75–129).

79   "Ausl. von Mt. 5–7, 1530/32," WA 32:368.24 (see also AE 21:1–294): "As far as your person is concerned, you are not to be angry at anyone, no matter how offended you are. But where your office calls for it, there you must be angry, even if you as a person have not been hurt."

80   "Ausl. von Mt. 5–7, 1530/32," WA 32:362.18 (see also AE 21:1–294).

81   *BSLK*, 607.42.

82   "Ausl. von Mt. 5–7, 1530/32," WA 32:262.25 (see also AE 21:1–294). Cf. "Decem praecepta, 1518," WA 1:464.12; "Sermon über Mt. 5:20ff. vom 27.7.1522," WA 10.3:255.3ff.; "Sermon über Mt. 5:20ff. vom 12.7.1523," WA 11:150.14–23 = WA 12:629.6ff.; "Pred. über Mt. 5:20ff. vom 16.7.1531," WA 34.2:8.7; "Hauspost. zu Mt. 5:20ff., 1533," WA 52:411.14–412.11.

83   "Ausl. von Mt. 5–7, 1530/32," WA 32:364.37f. (see also AE 21:1–294).

84   Cf. "Von weltl. Oberkeit, 1523," WA 11:261.9–24 (see also AE 45:75–129); "Pred. über Mt. 5:20ff. vom 8.7.1526," WA 20:455.37–456.36; "Ausl. von Mt. 5–7, 1530/32," WA 32:365.11–366.14 (see also AE 21:1–294); "Pred. über Mt. 5:20ff. vom 20.7.1533 bzw. 16.4.1534," WA 37:115.5–11, 382.27–384.23; "Pred. über Mt. 5:20ff. vom 20.7.1533 bzw. 16.4.1534," WA 41:578–90.

85   "Sermon über Mt. 5:20ff. vom 27.7.1522," WA 10.3:254.20. Cf. "Von den guten Werken, 1520," WA 6:267.18–26 (see also AE 44:15–114); "Ausl. von Mat. 5–7, 1530/32," WA 32:365.11–366.14, 392.8–11 (see also AE 21:1–294).

state.[86] The judge is moved by the same thoughts the apostle entertains in excommunication,[87] only the apostle carries them out in the manner of the spiritual rule "by the Word and without sword,"[88] while the judge carries them out in the power of the civil authority's office of the sword.[89] This

---

86 On the death penalty, see Alt, *Das Problem der Todesstrafe*; Althaus, *Die Todesstrafe als Problem der christlichen. Ethik*; Barth, *Kirchliche Dogmatik*, 3.4:499–515; Thielicke, *Ethik*, 3, §§ 1463–1518; Die Frage der Todesstrafe, *Zwölf Antworten*.

87 Cf. 1 Cor. 5:1–8; 1 Tim. 1:20.

88 "Ob Kriegsleute auch in seligem Stande sein können, 1526," WA 19:629.18 (see also AE 46:87–137).

89 Reinhold Schneider, *Das Richtschwert* (*The Sword of Judgment*):

Wenn ich dies Schwert tu' aufheben,
Wünsch' ich dem armen Sünder das ewige Leben.
(Inschrift eines alten Richtschwertes)

Ich richte nicht, ich muß das Schwert nur sein
und schlage nicht aus meiner Kraft. Das Recht
will mich zum Knecht an Gottes armen Knecht.
Er möge dir und möge mir verzeihn.

Und niemand herrsche denn der Herr allein.
Und seines Zeichens Siegel nur ist echt.
Aus deiner Fessel lös' ich dies Geschlecht,
Und doch ist keine Hand auf Erden rein.

Wir sind verbunden für die Ewigkeit
und müssen Hand in Hand vor Gott gelangen:
Da ich dich töte, bitt' ich um dein Leben.

Im heil'gem Ernste schattenhafter Zeit
hast du die Sünde dieser Welt begangen,
muß ich das Schwert, daß sie verzehrt, erheben.

When I lift up this sword,
I wish eternal life to the poor sinner.
(*Inscription on an old executioner's sword*)

I do not judge, I only must be the sword
And do not strike by my own power. The law
Wants me to serve God's poor servant,
May He forgive you, and may He forgive me.

And may no one reign but the Lord alone.
And only the sign of His seal is right.
Out of your bond I release this generation,
And yet there is no pure hand upon earth.

We are joined for eternity
And have to come before God hand in hand:
As I kill you, I plead for your life.

In the holy soberness of shadowy times
Since you committed the sin of this world,
Now I must raise the sword that consumes it.

ultimate identity of intention shows, however, that in Luther's view it is the triune God who wages war in both realms against the prince of this world.

3. The Commandment in Its Spiritual Meaning[90]

Despite all that has been said, it is apparent that in the Large Catechism Luther only hints at the participation of the civil authority in God's watching over this commandment and at the service of the Christian that grows out of this participation. Luther wants to interpret the commandment itself and, for this purpose, points to his annual sermons on Matt. 5:20–26,[91] to which we take recourse. By the thrust of the antitheses *not only—but already!* Luther points out the tension between the Old Testament wording and the new interpretation of Jesus. Here, the veil is removed, as it were, from the Law of Moses as well as from our hardened hearts (2 Cor. 3:12ff.), and the all-embracing totality and spiritual truth of the commandment is revealed. Luther seeks to uncover this in the wording of the commandment by accentuation of the little word "you." While his opponents focus on the verb "to kill" and thereby seek to reduce the commandment to its Old Testament/carnal meaning, the "you" presses onward to the subject "you" and shows how the person as a whole is under the commandment—this is how *you* will perceive the spiritual meaning of Jesus.[92] "For do you think that He speaks only of the fist when He says: 'You shall not kill'? What does 'you' mean? Not only your hand or foot, tongue, or another individual member, but everything that you are in body and soul, Just as when I say to someone: you shall not do this, then I don't speak to the fist but to the entire person."[93] " 'You' does not mean your hand, tongue, heart, body, or soul, but everything together with your entire being and nature, as you walk and stand, body and soul, reason and wit, whatever is on, from, and in you."[94] The human person is, in all its inner diversity, an indivisible whole that, however, cannot be accessed in a defining way.

Jesus' *not only—but already!* simultaneously reveals an irreversible direction of living out our existence. The origin and root of killing do not lie in our hand; they lie in the heart overcome by anger.[95] As Augustine, Thomas,

---

90   *BSLK*, 606.15–609.40.

91   *BSLK*, 606.15–30.

92   According to "Pred. über Mt. 5:20ff. vom 19.7.1528," WA 27:263.11ff.

93   "Ausl. von Mt. 5–7, 1530/32," WA 32:363.2 (see also AE 21:1–294). Cf. "Pred. über Mt. 5:20ff. vom 16.7.1525 bzw. 8.7.1526 bzw. 20.7.1533," WA 17.1:332.8f.; WA 20:455.8ff.; WA 37.113.15ff.

94   "Pred. über Ex. 20 vom 29.10.1525," WA 16.495.34. Luther's thoughts are taken up by Agricola, *Christl. Kinderzucht* (MGP 21:31f.), as well as in the "Nürnberger Katechismuspredigten" (Reu, *Quellen*, 1.1:484.1–7).

95   *BSLK*, 606.46ff.

and with them the entire late medieval interpretation of the commandment[96] already unfold an elaborate gradual progression following the basic outline *manu—ore—adiutorio—consensu—corde*, thus also Luther in the Large Catechism hints at this outline in the phrase "that one shall not kill by hand, heart, mouth, sign, gesture, help, and counsel."[97] In his interpretations of Matt. 5:21f., Luther develops a fourfold form of killing:[98] (1) killing intentionally, according to the carnal meaning of the commandment; (2) killing by words, to which he relates μωρέ (*fatue*): "You fool or idiot!"[99] (3) killing by signs and gestures, to which he relates the Aramaic (rendered as Greek) ῥακά (Matt. 5:22), which he interprets as an inarticulate guttural sound that expresses wrathful and angry contempt;[100] (4) killing by anger that flares up in the heart. These steps backtrack the path of our anger from the first flaring in the heart, passing through gestures and words, all the way to the deed. According to Luther, the Lord establishes already in this dark enigmatic word the death sentence over the first step of rushing to murder. Whoever is only angry at his brother in his heart is already under God's damnation,

---

96 Augustine, *De sermone Domini in monte; Contra Faustum*, M.l. XIX, c. 23; Thomas Aquinas, *Duo praecepta* § 1262 (*manu, ore, adiutorio, consensu*). An interpretation attributed to Bernard of Clairvaux (PL 184:1068ff.) offers *manu, praecepto, consilio, consensu, neglectu*. On the late Middle Ages, see Geffcken, *Bildercatechismus*, 73ff., app., col. 87, 93, 102, 125, 132, 144, 153, 171, 175, and passim; Weidenhiller, *Untersuchungen*, 73f.

97 *BSLK*, 606.19. "Kat.-Pred. zum 5.-7. Gebot vom 18.9.1528," WA 30.1:36.26 (see also AE 37:151–372): "You have heard often what this commandment wants: 'One is not to kill,' namely, by hand, mouth, heart, sign, help, counsel, and deed." This is passed on in Reformation catechisms, e.g., in the *Christl. Unterweisung* by Konrad Sam, quest. 110: "Christ Himself interprets the commandment in Matthew 5 and teaches that it means in summary: You are not to kill, that is, you are not to be angry or seek revenge; not to be greedy or hateful; not to despise or slander anyone; not to strangle anyone by counsel or advice, but are to behave in a peaceful and kind manner toward everyone. You are not to show anger or ill will, neither with gestures nor with signs, neither with words nor with works" (MGP 22:121.7). See, furthermore, among others, Schultz and Agricola, *Fragstücke* (MGP 22:213, 294); Althammer, quest. 29; Brenz, quest. 74 (MGP 22:25, 182); "Nürnberger Katechismuspredigten" (Reu, *Quellen*, 1.1:483ff.); Geneva Catechism, quest. 197; Heidelberg Catechism, quest. 105.

98 Carefully presented in "Decem praecepta, 1518," WA 1:462.39–463.37. A short summary is found in "Ausl. von Mt. 5–7, 1530/32," WA 32:363.39–364.36 (see also AE 21:1–294), also in "Sermon über Mt. 5:20ff. vom 12.7.1523," WA 11:149.22–31; "Sermon über Mt. 5:20ff. vom 12.7.1523," WA 12:627.1–15; "Pred. über Mt. 5:20ff. vom 12.7.1534 bzw. 8.7.1537 bzw. 20.7.1533," WA 37:482.6–10; WA 45:110.6–19; WA 52:407.34–408.7.

99 On μωρέ, cf. Georg Bertram, μωρός, *TWNT* 4:844–47.

100 "Decem praecepta, 1518," WA 1:463.22: "Certainly, if my judgment is permitted to think, *raka* seems to be used in all languages, for we, too, when we are indignant, sound forth some guttural noise such as *arch* or *rach*. . . . Therefore such sound, though it does not kill by word or work, nonetheless signifies that because of which he, moved by anger, wishes that he would not exist. Therefore he kills by sign." Cf. "Sermon über Mt. 5:20ff. vom 27.7.1522," WA 10.3:245.3–17; "Pred. über Mt. 5:20ff. vom 16.7.1525 bzw. 8.7.1526," WA 17.1:332.20–22; WA 20:455.24–26. On ῥακά, cf. Joachim Jeremias, ῥακά, *TWNT* 6:973–76.

even when the chain of judgment *court—high court—hell* seems to indicate different degrees of judgment.[101]

To the medieval tradition, Luther adds in his confessional manuals the so-called "alien sins" (1 Tim. 5:22),[102] which encompass indirect participation in somebody else's murder by giving order or consent. Thus there are the following degrees of the prohibition in the Large Catechism:[103] Harm no one (1) by hand or deed, (2) by tongue or speech, (3) by signs or gestures, (4) by offending him in any way, (5) by doing it yourself or by giving counsel or consent to others doing it. All this presses toward the heart; it shall not give room for anger or hatred.[104]

For Luther, a real movement takes place. God Himself drives the commandment deeper and deeper into our innermost being.[105] The individual believer is thereby included in Christ's entering into the commandment of Moses. The salvation-historical way from Moses to Christ is reflected in the anthropological movement of the prohibition from hand to heart. In the process, the person also gains anthropological knowledge concerning the inner structure of existence; the outward man in its bodily existence is correlated to the inner man in the heart. Here in the heart lie the "root and origin"[106] of all actual infractions against the commandment in thoughts, signs, words, and deeds; here the tinder of hatred smolders. God's commandment wants to burn out the original greed and hatred[107] in the heart. Jesus' radicalization with its pointed arrow of *not only—but already!* has made that clear.

---

101 "Decem praecepta, 1518," WA 1:465.2: "There is one punishment, namely, eternal damnation and the gehenna of fire, but it is to be imposed in different degrees, which is indicated by these orders of degrees." "Ausl. von Mt. 5–7, 1530/32," WA 32:364.19 (see also AE 21:1–294): "Thus everything is a punishment and damnation, yet the same is heavier and harder if the sin goes farther and erupts more powerfully." Cf. "Pred. über Mt. 5:20ff. vom 16.7.1525 bzw. 16.7.1531 bzw. 8.7.1537," WA 17.1:332.31ff.; WA 34.2:10.7ff.; WA 45:110.19ff. On the current interpretation, cf. Stählin, οργή, *TWNT* 5:421.3ff., and Jeremias, ρακά, *TWNT* 6:975f.

102 "Eine kurze Form, 1520," WA 7:212.1: "The alien sins happen in relation to all commandments, since one can sin against all commandments by commanding, advising, and helping." Cf. "Instructio, 1518," WA 1:261.6. Weidenhiller, *Untersuchungen*, 22: "The nine alien sins, that is, sins that (according to the *Confessionale*) take place by commanding, advising, permitting, praising, protecting, partaking, keeping secret, not resisting, not revealing. The oft-used mnemonic verse read: *Iussio, concilium, consensus, palpo, recursus / participans, mutus, non obstans, non manifestans*. Yet other sins are mentioned as well, e.g., not warning, not helping, not housing, not defending."

103 *BSLK*, 606.19ff., 608.5ff.

104 *BSLK*, 607.20–608.2.

105 *BSLK*, 608.6: "firstly, by hand or deed . . . finally . . . the heart." "Pred. über Mt. 5:20ff. vom 16.7.1525," WA 17.1:332.10: "Christ is drawn into the depth of the heart." Similarly, "Decem praecepta, 1518," WA 1:467.22–29; "Pred. über Ex. 20 vom 5.11.1525," WA 16:510.8–13; "Pred. über Mt. 5:20ff. vom 16.7.1531," WA 34.2:3.15ff.

106 *BSLK*, 607.31.

107 "Decem praecepta, 1518," WA 1:467.37: "One must, therefore, always think that not only anger but also anger's tinder itself and the entire Adam be killed, the tree with fruits and root."

The Lord shows this by simultaneously highlighting the commandment to love one's enemy (Matt. 5:46f.). In the Large Catechism, Luther takes up the view and very impressively describes the flaring of hatred and greed between neighbors.[108] First, in the situation of "temptation"[109] by the attacks of Satan, it becomes clear what really is in us. Luther here hints at three levels: To do evil to those who do good to us is not human; it is devilish.[110] To wish and do good to friends without grudge, that is still pagan,[111] even animal-like.[112] The Christian shows himself first in the love of the enemy. First, in the hour of conflict a person is revealed to himself, to the world, and also to God. This is why everything is to be related to the hour of temptation.[113] God does not want us to leave the sword of hatred of men in the sheath only to draw it out in these dark hours.[114] He wants us truly to lay it down and to exercise love. In "Sermon von den guten Werken" ("Sermon on Good Works"), Luther recommends as a spiritual "exercise" to imagine one's enemy and think about him in friendly terms, to wish him the best, to care for him, and to intercede for him.[115]

This already marks the transition from the prohibition of hatred to the commandment of active love of the neighbor. In the Large Catechism, Luther unfolds this by means of the eight works of mercy (Matt. 25:42f.) that Christ demands of us as Judge of the world.[116] At the same time, Luther takes up the traditional argument that is concentrated in the words attributed to Ambrose: "If you did not feed, you killed."[117] The heart's judgment is connected to a reasonable argument: the Judge of the world sticks to the

---

108 *BSLK*, 606.31–607.7. On loving one's enemy, cf. *BSLK*, 607.43f., 608.14ff., 609.33ff.; "Eine kurze Erklärung, 1518," WA 1:253.8f.; "Instructio, 1518," WA 1:261.16f.; "Eine kurze Form, 1520," WA 7:210.8f., 213.13; "Von den guten Werken, 1520," WA 6:266.14–22 (see also AE 44:15–114); "Pred. über Mt. 5:20ff. vom 3.7.1524," WA 15:646.30f.

109 *BSLK*, 606.36.

110 *BSLK*, 608.16ff.

111 *BSLK*, 609.35ff.

112 "Von den guten Werken, 1520," WA 6:266.4 (see also AE 44:15–114): "Even unreasonable animals, lions and snakes, heathen, Jews, Turks, knaves, murderers, evil women show such meekness."

113 "Decem praecepta, 1518," WA 1:469.18: ". . . everything refers to the hour of temptation and testing, that man there might know his spirit and his carnality when he will feel himself being violently dragged off to sinning and does not find in his flesh any good, so that he might groan for the grace of health."

114 "Decem praecepta, 1518," WA 1:472.12: "Thus man, even if he does not get angry in deeds, nonetheless has inside the sword of anger, though it is concealed in the sheath. But it does not please God unless he lays the sword down and throws it away."

115 WA 6:266.34–267.8 (see also AE 44:15–114). Cf. "Eine kurze Form, 1520," WA 7:213.10–14.

116 *BSLK*, 608.47–609.29. Cf. p. 98 n. 68 and Augustine, *Contra Faustum* M.l., XV, c. 7.

117 See p. 98 n. 67, additionally "Pred. über Phil. 2:5ff. vom 2.4.1531," WA 34.1:183.13; "Pred. über Mt. 5:20ff. vom 20.7.1533," WA 37:113.22; "An die Pfarrherrn, wider den Wucher zu predigen, 1540," WA 51.414.24. The argument indirectly takes recourse to 1 John 3:17 and James 2:15f.

Golden Rule written in the hearts of all.[118] Yet there remains a certain tension between the words of the universal Judge—that we have encountered Him in those who belong to Him[119]—and the commandment to love one's enemy. Are those who belong to Him only the Christians or all the needy?[120] For Luther, this remained a speculative question; apart from a few Jews, the hearers of his sermons and the readers of the Large Catechism would meet only baptized people.

This is how the reformer, according to Matt. 5:21f., by means of the commandment first follows hatred from its actual manifestations in deed, gesture, and word all the way to the thoughts of the heart in order fully to pull out its root, the *fomes irae*.[121] Then, from the patient heart of meekness, he lets break forth the "true, noble, and high works"[122] of loving one's enemy. The inner transformation in the core point of existence, however, is not unfolded. The real dialectic of Law and Gospel is not illuminated as in several parallel explanations.[123]

4. GROUNDING THE FIFTH COMMANDMENT IN THE FIRST[124]

A starting point for this offers the double-sided grounding of the prohibition of killing in the First Commandment. God's eternal sentence as a Judge, which Christ announces to us in the parable of the judgment of the world,[125] is meant to warn us against carelessly passing by our neighbor in his bodily needs and letting him perish heartlessly. God's promise that He wants to be our helper and advocate is meant to dampen our malice of taking revenge into our own hands and is meant to liberate our heart for meekness even toward enemies.[126] This reference remains in the schema Luther established for the word of threat and grace in Exod. 20:5f.:[127] God's threat of punishment deters us from transgressing; God's gracious promise liberates us for joyous obedience.

---

118   In "Pred. über Lk. 16:19–31 vom 6.6.1535," Luther spells out the thesis: one is punished by the sins one commits (WA 41:293–300).

119   *BSLK*, 609.11.

120   Luther interpreted the parable of the great judgment of the world only once, in "Pred. über Mt. 25:31ff. vom 25.11.1537" (WA 45:324–29). Here, too, he points to the Fifth Commandment and takes the preacher of the Gospel as a concrete example of the "least brother." Cf. Loewenich, *Luther als Ausleger der Synoptiker*, 198f.

121   "Decem praecepta, 1518," WA 1:467.37.

122   *BSLK*, 609.43.

123   Cf. Peters, *Glaube und Werk*, 207–24; Modalsli, *Das Gericht nach den Werken*, 138–78; Pesch, *Rechtfertigung bei Luther und Thomas*, 283–325.

124   *BSLK*, 609.41–610.5.

125   *BSLK*, 608.47–609.29.

126   *BSLK*, 609.41–610.5. "Ausl. von Mt. 5–7, 1530/32" (WA 32:403.1–404.33 [see also AE 21:1–294]) unfolds the goodness of the Creator according to Matt. 5:43–48.

127   Cf. pp. 134–41.

In the Large Catechism, however, God the Father and Christ take a remarkable position relative to the Law's threat of judgment and the Gospel's promise of grace. Christ appears merely on the side of the "terrible judgment."[128] By urging the radical love of enemies, the Lord makes the Fifth Commandment more difficult.[129] As Judge of the world, He condemns us: "Murderer."[130] On the other hand, God the Father appears not so much as the strict Lawgiver and Judge[131] but as the "kind Father."[132] He protects our human community against assaults of Satan and our hatred by the protective wall of the prohibition against killing.[133] He guarantees our protection by His presence,[134] as well as by the office to punish that has been placed into the hands of the authorities.[135] However, these statements remain strictly in the realm of earthly well-being, in the realm of the First Article. The dimension of salvation in Christ is not touched upon; thus Christ stands entirely on the side of the Law. This delimitation is strictly in keeping with the protective character of the commandment on earth. Again, the peculiarity of the interpretation of the Decalogue in the catechisms stands out. To be sure, Christ drives us under the Law, radically understood, but the obedience of the heart renewed in the Spirit seems to flow only from looking up to God's benevolent providence and kind care.[136]

A couple of observations can easily be connected to Luther's elaborations: (1) Christ not only interprets the commandment spiritually, but our transgressions also directly affect Him in His brethren. This view is hinted at in the reference to Matthew 25: in those suffering need we have met Him.[137] The early Luther says about the sword of our angry hatred of men: "This is the sword by which the Son of God is killed."[138]

(2) We are delivered from the law of "eye for an eye, tooth for a tooth" only by looking up to God. There we recognize not only that we are safe in God's protection and that our autonomous revenge interferes with God's authority, but we also recognize that our enemies, though their attacks can

---

128 *BSLK*, 609.2.

129 "Pred. über Mt. 5:20ff. vom 19.7.1528," WA 27:259.6: "In this (sermon) the Lord interprets the Law of Moses and makes it so hot that no one can abide before it. It is necessary that he come to the Gospel." Cf. "Pred. über Mt. 5:20ff. vom 3.7.1524," WA 15:648.1–5.

130 *BSLK*, 608.47–609.29. Cf. Modalsli, *Das Gericht nach den Werken*, 128–34 (*Christus iudex*).

131 Except for *BSLK*, 608.47, 609.30.

132 *BSLK*, 606.51.

133 *BSLK*, 607.6.

134 *BSLK*, 610.1.

135 *BSLK*, 606.2–30.

136 Ritschl's saying, "Faith in God's fatherly providence is the Christian *weltanschauung* in abbreviated form" (*Unterricht*, § 51), does not seem to be too far from this.

137 *BSLK*, 609.11f.

138 "Decem praecepta, 1518," WA 1:472.15.

affect our bodily life here on earth, deprive themselves of heaven. At the most they can kill our body, but by doing so they lose their soul. This should change our anger into compassion.[139]

(3) However, the central statement of the reformer on Law and Gospel, faith and work, from his sermon on Matt. 5:20–26 is here still held back regarding the Fifth Commandment: "Therefore the sentence is: no one fulfills the commandment of God unless he has love of God and the Holy Spirit, which comes out of love of Christ."[140] It is taken up at the conclusion of the interpretation of the Commandments[141] and is authoritatively unfolded, against the backdrop of the salvific work of God as retold in the Creed, in connection with the Lord's Prayer.[142] Thus Luther's interpretation in the catechisms of the prohibition against killing gives us insight into what this commandment really wants to tell us, as Christ has not only interpreted it spiritually but also has fulfilled it and gives us in the Holy Spirit the power to begin to fulfill it, only in such a way that is consciously tailored to suit the daily community here on this earth under the blessing and protection of the Creator and Sustainer.[143]

TEXTS ON THE FIFTH COMMANDMENT

WA 1:461–82: from Decem praecepta Wittenbergensi praedicata populo, 1518

WA 6:265–68: from Sermon von den guten Werken, 1520 (see also AE 44:15–114)

WA 16:506–10: from Predigt über Ex. 20 vom 5.11.1525

THE SERMONS ON MATTHEW 5:20–26 (GOSPEL FOR THE SIXTH SUNDAY AFTER TRINITY)

WA 103:242–56, on 27.7.1522

WA 11:147–50 = WA 12:621–29, on 12.7.1523

WA 15:644–49, on 3.7.1521

---

139 "Decem praecepta, 1518," WA 1:481.5: "For if you love God more than yourself, then you should get angry that he hurt God more than you, then equally have mercy that he hurt himself more inwardly than you outwardly."

140 "Pred. über Mt. 5:20ff. vom 3.7.1524," WA 15:649.8. Cf. "Pred. über Mt. 5:20ff. vom 3.7.1524," WA 15:648.13–21; "Pred. über Mt. 5:20ff. vom 27.7.1522 bzw. 12.7.1523," WA 10.3:244.19ff. and WA 11:148.1ff.; "Pred. über Mt. 5:20ff. vom 16.7.1525," WA 17.1:333.34–334.3.

141 *BSLK*, 640.39–45, 641.9–17.

142 Johann Brenz, in his *Fragstücke des christlichen Glaubens*, artfully works the Lord's Prayer and the Decalogue together; cf. MPG 22:176–85.

143 The conscious concentration on the horizon of the First Article is, on the one hand, distorted by the romanticizing German-Christian theology of blood and soil (see Fraas, *Katechismustradition*, 292ff.). On the other hand, it resists a premature identification of the Decalogue with the Christocentric paranesis of the New Testament. Here Luther's understanding also opposes Barth's schema *Gospel and Law* (cf. the exposition in Fraas, *Katechismustradition*, 39f., 228, 259, 290, 305ff.).

WA 17.1:331–34, on 16.7.1525

WA 20:454–57, on 8.7.1526

WA 27:263–73, on 19.7.1528

WA 32:359–69, Wochenpredigten über Matt. 5–7, 1530–32 (see also AE 21:1–294)

WA 34.2:1–15, on 16.7.1531

WA 37:111–15, 381–85, 480–83, on 20.7.1533, 16.4 und 12.7.1534

WA 41:637–41, on 23.7.1536

WA 45:109–13, on 8.7.1537

WA 52:404–12, Hauspostille 1544

A selection of texts is offered in Mülhaupt, *D. Martin Luthers Evangelien-Auslegung*, 2:84–97

LITERATURE

Hardeland, *Luthers Katechismusgedanken in ihrer Entwicklung bis zum Jahre 1529*, 131–49

Meyer, *Historischer Kommentar zu Luthers Kleinem Katechismus*, 223–31

THE SIXTH COMMANDMENT[1]

WORDING OF THE COMMANDMENT AND OUTLINE OF THE INTERPRETATION

In the commandment concerning adultery, Luther returns to Exod. 20:14 and consistently translates it as "You shall not commit adultery."[2] The late medieval confessional manuals, by and large, had moved unchastity to the center[3] or placed it next to adultery.[4] This also marks the two scopes that Luther discusses in his interpretation: God's *no* to every form of unchastity and God's protection of marriage. These two emphases shape Luther's interpretation in the Small and Large Catechisms.

The exposition in the Large Catechism can be divided into three sections. First, Luther broadens the commandment to include the struggle "against all unchastity."[5] The core is formed by a short instruction on the estate of marriage.[6] In conclusion, the reformer summarizes the commandment in positive terms in view of marriage.[7] The broadening of the commandment from what is Jewish to what is Christian follows the sermons on September 18 and May 22, 1528,[8] which interpret the commandment only briefly. The sermon on December 4 offers some basic remarks on the

---

1   For texts on Luther's understanding of marriage, see p. 261.

2   *BSLK*, 508.37, 555.23, 610.40; "Eine kurze Erklärung, 1518," WA 1:251.10; "Eine kurze Form, 1520," WA 7:206.17; "Eine kurze Unterweisung, 1519," WA 2:63.2: "You shall not commit adultery."

3   Gerson/Geiler (Geffcken, *Bildercatechismus*, app., col. 43): "You shall not commit unchaste works and live in unchastity." Similarly in *Der Seele Trost* (col. 103); *Spiegel des Christen-Glaubens* (col. 95) and in the *Traktat über die 10 Gebote* (col. 171). Cf. Weidenhiller, *Unter-suchungen*, 47, 67, 75f.

4   *Licht der Seele* (Geffcken, *Bildercatechismus*, app., col. 133): "You shall not be unchaste or an adulterer." Cf. *Spiegel des Christenmenschen* (col. 154).

5   *BSLK*, 611.28. Section 1: *BSLK*, 610.41–612.12.

6   Section 2: *BSLK*, 612.13–615.24.

7   Section 3: *BSLK*, 615.25–616.9.

8   Section 1 follows "Kat.-Pred. zum 5.–7. Gebot vom 18.9.1528," WA 30.1:37.14–27, and "Kat.-Pred. zum 6. Praeceptum vom 22.5.1528," WA 30.1:7.31–8.4.

married estate and at the end summarizes the commandment.[9] The design of the second and third sections of the Large Catechism, as well as the explanation in the Small Catechism, follows this sermon.

Interpreting the prohibition to include unchastity in section 1, Luther (a) first establishes the place of the prohibition of adultery in the Decalogue[10] and among the Jewish people.[11] (b) Then he expands it—following the schema worked out under the Fifth Commandment: from the outside in, from the negative to the positive[12]—to God's *no* to all unchastity,[13] and he offers (c) a positive version that aims at us and our neighbor: each should live "chastely for himself" and "also help the neighbor to do the same."[14]

The instruction on the married estate shows: (a) As the "most common and noblest estate"[15] in the world, marriage is "instituted before all others"[16] and blessed by God, confirmed in the Fourth Commandment and protected and guarded in the Sixth Commandment.[17] This is why both "spiritual and secular estates"[18] must be found in it.[19] (b) Marriage is a necessary estate, lest the charge to procreate implanted in us in creation go astray on godless paths.[20] (c) This commandment condemns monastic vows and liberates bound consciences.[21] (d) It combats the despising of the married estate and makes people willing to enter into marriage.[22]

The conclusion in section 3 once more summarizes the commandment of chastity in view of marital love and faithfulness and understands it from within as *usus practicus Evangelii.*

The Small Catechism, following the sermon on December 4[23] and running parallel to the summary in the Large Catechism,[24] formulates the issue only in a positive manner. In this, Luther differs from earlier confessional

---

9   WA 30.1:75.22–77.6 (see also AE 51:150–55).

10   *BSLK*, 610.41–611.12.

11   *BSLK*, 611.12–24. This expansion is already hinted at in Augustine, *Questiones in Heptateuchum* 2, quest. 71; and Thomas Aquinas, *Duo praecepta* § 1277; and it is taken up in the "Nürnberger Katechismuspredigten" (Reu, *Quellen*, 1.1:487.22ff.).

12   Cf. pp. 226–30.

13   *BSLK*, 611.25–612.3.

14   *BSLK*, 612.3–12 (quotation: *BSLK*, 611.43).

15   *BSLK*, 613.23.

16   *BSLK*, 612.25.

17   *BSLK*, 612.13–613.9.

18   *BSLK*, 613.19.

19   *BSLK*, 613.10–32.

20   *BSLK*, 613.33–614.12.

21   *BSLK*, 614.13–615.4.

22   *BSLK*, 615.5–24.

23   WA 30.1:77.2 (see also AE 51:150–55): "You shall keep yourself chaste in word and works and remain with your wife, love her, and you [wife] (are to) honor (your husband)."

24   Section 3: *BSLK*, 615.25–616.9.

manuals that apply the Old Testament series of prohibitions to the *corpus Christianum* and enumerate all sorts of persons, even nonhuman beings, with whom the person confessing his sins could have committed unchastity—a terrible indirect instruction in sinning.[25]

The first part of the explanation—"We should fear and love God so that we lead chaste and decent lives in words and deeds"[26]—runs parallel to the first summary in the Large Catechism.[27] The latter, however, follows more closely the schema handed down primarily in connection with the Fifth Commandment: *corde—ore—manu—adiutorio—consensu*, which dominates Luther's early confessional manuals.[28] In the concluding summary of the Large Catechism, Luther again returns to this in the phrase: the commandment demands "that everybody live chastely in works, words, and thoughts in his estate, and mostly in that of marriage."[29] In the Small Catechism, the "thoughts" are left out.[30] Also, the progress from outside in—from the works, through the words, to the thoughts—is not taken up, because it presupposes the elaborate unfolding only the Large Catechism can offer.[31] Thus the Small Catechism's phrase corresponds to the summarizing formulation of the sermon on December 4: "You shall keep yourself chaste in words and works."[32] The added word "decent"[33] lacks a parallel in the Large Catechism as well as in the 1528 sermons. Based on what is excluded thereby, it is prepared by the sermon on December 4.[34] These negations show that in "decent" Luther put the emphasis on self-control (*continentia*), while he does not want the "neat outward discipline" (*disciplina*)[35] to be excluded.[36] This is also suggested by his first positive summary of the commandment: "chastity, discipline, decency in works, words, gestures, and

---

25   See Geffcken, *Bildercatechismus*, 77–80. This danger was often recognized; fathers confessor are warned against incautious questions (cf. Gerson/Geiler, *Bildercatechismus*, suppl., col. 44; and *Spiegel des Sünders*, in *Bildercatechismus*, col. 72).

26   *BSLK*, 509.2.

27   *BSLK*, 611.25–612.12.

28   Cf. p. 227 nn. 96–100.

29   *BSLK*, 615.27.

30   The "Nürnberger Katechismuspredigten" add them, because they offer this unfolding (Reu, *Quellen*, 1.1:491.21, 491.30, 491.35, 491.41).

31   *BSLK*, 611.25–612.3. The "Nürnberger Katechismuspredigten" offer variations. Where they offer independently the movement from outside in, they have the triad *works—words—thoughts*. Where they recite the Small Catechism, they only add "thoughts" to the latter's pair of words and works.

32   WA 30.1:77.2 (see also AE 51:150–55).

33   *BSLK*, 509.3: "chaste and decent" (*keusch und züchtig; caste et pudice*).

34   WA 30.1:77.3ff., 76.9, 76.15 (see also AE 51:150–55).

35   *BSLK*, 521.4.

36   See the controversy between Theodosius Harnack and Meyer in Meyer, *Historischer Kommentar*, 238.

thoughts,"[37] which corroborates a solid nexus between the two words and shows how naturally Luther considers them to be a pair. This is underscored by the binary transgressions of the commandment in the confessional manuals where the incitement to evil lust stands next to active unchastity.[38]

The second scope of the explanation is connected by Luther somewhat roughly in the Small Catechism: ". . . and (that we) as husband and wife love and honor each other."[39] It summarizes the result of the marriage sermon in the Large Catechism[40] and seems to follow the sermon on December 4.[41] Here we notice an interesting tension. According to the sermon, the husband is to love his wife; the wife is to honor her husband. According to the Large Catechism, both spouses are to love and honor each other.[42] This tension is prefigured in the Epistle to the Ephesians, where the wife owes her husband honor and subordination as to her head, the husband is called to love his wife, while this irreversible coordination is embraced by the exhortation applying to all, which forms "a kind of headline"[43] for the entire household table: "Submit to one another in the fear of Christ" (Eph. 5:21–33). For Luther, love is commended to both spouses. Husband and wife ought to and may "live with each other in love and concord so that for each one this means regarding the other from the heart and in all faithfulness."[44] In his first sermon on marriage, the 1519 "Sermon vom ehelichen Stand" ("Sermon on the Estate of Marriage"), the reformer describes this love in pictures of bridal mysticism: "Love in marriage is a bridal love. It burns like fire and does not seek anything besides the spouse. It says, 'I do not want

---

37   "Eine kurze Erklärung, 1518," WA 1:255.6. Cf. "Eine kurze Form, 1520" (WA 7:213.16ff.) and "Instructio, 1518" (WA 1:263.24): "Chastity, modesty, shame, sobriety, temperance, fasting, vigils, occupation, and all things that promote chastity and subject the flesh." "Eine einfältige Weise zu beten, 1535," WA 38:370.1 (see also AE 43:187–211): "chaste and decent and modest." Cf. the stanza 7 of the hymn "Dies sind die heiligen zehn Gebot" (WA 35.427.16–20 [see also LSB 581; AE 53:277–79]).

38   "Eine kurze Erklärung, 1518," WA 1:253.13–17; "Instructio, 1518," WA 1:261.19–25; "Eine kurze Form, 1520," WA 7:210.18–30; "Eine einfältige Weise zu beten, 1535," WA 38:370.27f. (see also AE 43:187–211). The detailed exposition is found in "Decem praecepta, 1518" (WA 1:482–99).

39   BSLK, 509.3. Thus also according to Albrecht in WA 30.1:359 (Small Catechism) and Meyer, Historischer Kommentar, 238.

40   Section 3.

41   WA 30.1:77.3 (see also AE 51:150–55): "And remain with your wife, love her, and you [addressed is the wife] (are to) honor (your husband)." Cf. the summary of "Kat.-Pred. zum 7.–10. Gebot vom 7.12.1528" (WA 30.1:77.16 [see also AE 51:150–55]): ". . . fear God and live chastely, and do not commit adultery, but love your wife and honor your husband."

42   BSLK, 615.41: ". . . that one love and honor the other"; BSLK, 615.29: ". . . but also love and appreciate one's God-given spouse."

43   Schlier, Der Brief an die Epheser, 250. See also the detailed interpretation of the biblical exhortation to subordinate oneself by Kähler, Die Frau in den Paulinischen Briefen, esp. 138ff.

44   BSLK, 615.33. Meyer's commentary on the Small Catechism (Meyer, Historischer Kommentar, 238f.) is too one-sided; it contradicts what the Large Catechism says (BSLK, 615.41).

what is yours. I want neither gold nor silver, neither this nor that. I want you yourself. I want you totally or not at all.' All other kinds of love seek something else beside the loved one; this one alone wholly wants the loved one himself. And if Adam had not fallen, bride and bridegroom would have been the loveliest thing."[45]

Yet this love has a different form in the case of the husband than in that of the wife. Both love and honor in the spouse their God-given partner, but they do that within the headship structure that Luther unfolded according to the Scriptures first for the Fourth Commandment.[46] The wife owes to the husband *reverentia et oboedientia* in all things, because the husband is given her from God as her head.[47] The husband owes to the wife loving, caring sacrifice, because he is to reflect the sacrifice of his Lord for the Church and is to honor the weaker vessel in the wife.[48] Luther's marriage to Katharina von Bora shows here what a vast domain of care and responsibility opens up for the "helper" active in the house.[49]

THE PROHIBITION OF ADULTERY
IN THE OLD AND NEW TESTAMENTS[50]

The prohibition of adultery in the Decalogue (Exod. 20:14; Deut. 5:18) presupposes marriage; it "guards and protects" it.[51] The social and legal form of this institution is not reflected. It may change from polygamy to monogamy, from a marriage in which the husband replaces the father in a position of authority over the wife (*Munt-Ehe*) to more egalitarian designs of the marriage covenant. The patriarchal clan order, however, shows also in this commandment in that in this clan order the Israelite cult member is called on not to break into the marriage of his fellow member. The commandment protects

---

45 WA 2:167.29 (see also AE 44:3–14).

46 "Decem praecepta, 1518," WA 1:453.11–458.24.

47 "Decem praecepta, zu 1. Kor. 11:7," WA 1:456.27: "Great is the dignity of the male because he participates in the name and office of God. Therefore he is to be honored by his wife because God is the husband of the entire Church and of the soul, which is also the reason for a very great sacrament, which is why the wife ought to honor, fear, and hear the husband. Therefore turn the eye away from the flesh, and know and worship God in the man, and it will be easy to honor him." Cf. "Pred. über Eph. 5:22ff. vom 24.4.1536," WA 41:558.25–559.32.

48 On the husband's *amor castus* toward his wife according to 1 Pet. 3:7, see "Decem praecepta, 1518," WA 1:456.32–458.2.

49 On this topic, see Böhmer, "Luthers Ehe"; Kroker, *Katharina von Bora*; Ludolphy, "Katharina von Bora." For an English source, see Rudolph K. Markwald and Marilynn M. Markwald, *Katherina von Bora* (St. Louis: Concordia, 2002).

50 Cf. on this Friedrich Hauck, μοιχεύω, *TWNT* 4:737–43; Friedrich Hauck and Siegfried Schulz, πόρνη, *TWNT* 6:579–95; von Reventlow, *Gebot und Predigt im Dekalog*, 77–79.

51 *BSLK*, 612.22.

the full Israelite citizen in regard to the "closest good next to his body,"[52] his wife.[53] It addresses the man, since "the man could only break somebody else's marriage, while the wife could only break her own marriage."[54]

The prohibition of adultery does not mean, however, that extramarital sexual intercourse was seen as permitted and free. The oft-adduced examples of Judah and Tamar (Genesis 38), as well as Samson and Delilah (Judges 16), cannot prove this.[55] Genesis 38 states explicitly that Tamar tricked her father-in-law by dressing as a prostitute.[56] When her pregnancy became apparent, Judah wanted to have her burned (v. 24).[57] As a Philistine, Delilah was a foreigner, and Samson appears as an example of a waste of God's power that drags Israel's enemies into its own destruction (Judg. 16:30).[58] Seducing a young virgin who is not yet engaged is listed in Exod. 22:15f. as a crime against a man's property. The seducer has to pay the bride-price and take the seduced woman to be his wife; if the father does not want to give her to the man, he can redeem himself by paying the bride-price. Deuteronomy 22:13ff., however, shows that raping a virgin is considered a crime that deserves the death sentence, calling God's ban down on the perpetrator (v. 21). Only the marriage covenant, entered immediately and indissolubly (v. 29), can prevent the ordeal from happening. Apparently, the *prima nox* (the consummation on the first night) was viewed as the basic enactment of the marriage. Similar to homicide, and apart from a few late examples of the older right of the clan and the family (Gen. 38:24; Hosea 2:5), the "crime against the authority of the marriage law" has been removed from private avenging and handed over to public punishment in the Old Testament.[59] God's zealous holiness watches over this sphere.

At the same time, Israel had to struggle against sacred prostitution, through which the Canaanite fertility cults propagated their existence (1 Kings 14:23f.; Jer. 3:2). With passionate zeal, the prophets spoke against this evil and announced Yahweh's judgment.[60] The holy *no* of the covenant God to the sexual realm shaped the legal orders. A daughter dishonored by fornication profanes the land (Lev. 19:29); one born from fornication must not be a member of the congregation of Yahweh (Deut. 23:3). The curses in

---

52   *BSLK*, 611.4.

53   *BSLK*, 611.4–8, 611.45–612.2.

54   Procksch, *Theologie des Alten Testaments*, 88. Cf. Gen. 39:10ff.

55   With von Reventlow, *Gebot und Predigt im Dekalog*, 77, against Stade, *Biblische Theologie des Alten Testaments*, 1:199.

56   On this Hauck and Schulz, πόρνη, *TWNT* 6:586.

57   On the punishments for adultery, see Blinzler, "Die Strafe für Ehebruch in Bibel und Halacha."

58   Following von Rad, *Theologie des Alten Testaments*, 1:331f.

59   Following Friedrich Horst, "Ehe II," *RGG* 2:318.

60   E.g., Amos 2:7; Jer. 5:7.

Deut. 27:20ff., the Decalogue-like set of commandments in Lev. 18:6–25, as well as the list of crimes deserving death in Lev. 20:10–21,[61] corroborate: The prohibition of adultery is not to be seen in an isolated manner. In the Decalogue, it is given as a key example for the entire taboo realm of what is sexual. Everywhere the *no* to fornication is immediately connected to the *no* to idolatry and tied back to Yahweh's covenantal zeal, just as in the Canaanite fertility rites the sexual was amalgamated to the religious. By his proclamation and life, the prophet Hosea has made it absolutely clear that the prohibition of adultery is correlated to the prohibition of idols. Even, and especially, in this dark area, Yahweh wants to rule as the covenantal Lord of His people.[62]

The wisdom literature warns against seduction by the strange woman and describes Joseph as the example of the chaste man who overcame the sexual drive by praying and fasting (*Testament of Joseph* 4:8).[63] According to the Mishnah and the Talmud, only a case of adultery with an Israelite woman is punishable; the non-Israelite woman is not protected.[64] At the same time, readers are warned against the Gentiles as servants of sexual immorality.[65] While the religious courts abolish the death penalty and replace it with whipping,[66] the rabbis deepen the spiritual understanding of adultery: "We find that also he who commits adultery with the eyes is called an adulterer."[67]

Jesus presupposes monogamy (Mark 10:8 and parallels) and declares it to be indissoluble (Mark 10:9ff. and parallels). He rejects the legal possibility of the divorce letter, in existence since the late kingdom era,[68] as well as the rabbinical practice building upon it.[69] It is not God's commandment, not even a "permission" of Moses, but a regulation designed to expose man's hard-heartedness.[70] If the man marries after divorcing his wife, or if the divorced wife remarries, then this is adultery.[71] Even to desire another

---

61   Cf. Noth, *Das dritte Buch Mose*, 114–17, 126–31.

62   Literature on Hosea 1–3 in Wolff, *Hosea*, 6.

63   Cf. Hauck, μοιχεύω, *TWNT* 4:739.

64   See *Bill.*, 1:297.

65   See *Bill.*, 1:298; Hauck and Schulz, πόρνη, *TWNT* 6:589.

66   Cf. Hauck, μοιχεύω, *TWNT* 4:740 n. 8.

67   P^esiqR 24 (124^b) (*Bill.*, 1:299; cf. *Bill.*, 1:299–301).

68   Cf. Deut. 24:1; Jer. 3:8; Isa. 50:1.

69   See *Bill.*, 1:303–20; additionally, Baltensweiler, *Die Ehe im Neuen Testament*, 32–34, 37–39.

70   Matt. 10:2–12 (and parallels); Matt. 5:31f.; Luke 16:18. Greeven considers this to be the original meaning of the dominical word; cf. Greeven, "Zu den Aussagen des Neuen Testaments über die Ehe," 110–18, and "Ehe nach dem Neuen Testament," 57–73. On the New Testament view of marriage, see especially Baltensweiler, *Die Ehe im Neuen Testament* (literature!) and Schnackenburg, "Die Ehe nach dem Neuen Testament."

71   According to the early synagogue, the remarriage of a divorcee was prohibited (already Deut. 24:1ff.; Jer. 3:1), as well as the marriage of an adulteress with her lover. Cf. *Bill.*, 1:320f.

woman is, in God's sight, tantamount to doing the deed, and already the wish emerging in the heart is subject to the verdict (Matt. 5:28). At the same time, according to the apocryphally transmitted pericope of the adulteress (John 7:53ff.),[72] the Lord fights against any and all hypocritical self-righteousness. He calls the repentant to repent under God's holy commandment (John 8:11), forgives the guilt (Luke 7:47), and thereby opens again the access to the kingdom of God (Matt. 21:31f.).

According to the decree of the apostles, the primitive Church of Jerusalem demands that Gentile Christians not marry within the relations prohibited in Lev. 18:6–18.[73] At the same time, this commandment of the Decalogue is taken up and placed under the commandment of love (Rom. 13:9; James 2:11). Above all in the congregation in Corinth, the only city in the Greek world besides Athens where cultic prostitution was introduced successfully,[74] the apostle has to excommunicate the sexually immoral (1 Cor. 5:1–8). In the "household tables,"[75] there is the tireless call for marital faithfulness and love. As fellow heirs of eternal life, the women partake in the full honor (1 Pet. 3:7). Marriage is drawn into the mystery of Christ's sacrificial dedication to the congregation (Eph. 5:21–33). It is supposed to, and wants to, show and prove "its nature as imitation and repetition of the heavenly marriage of Christ to the Church also in the conscious and mindful behavior of the spouses."[76] Even where there is no human witness, it is important to keep the marriage bed pure before Him who sees what is hidden (Heb. 13:4). The Pastoral Epistles prohibit the remarriage of officeholders.[77]

---

72 See the interpretation by Baltensweiler, *Die Ehe im Neuen Testament*, 120–34.

73 Acts 15:20, 29; 21:25 are to be interpreted this way; cf. Haenchen, *Die Apostelgeschichte*, 390. Based on these texts, Baltensweiler, *Die Ehe im Neuen Testament*, 87–102, 141–43, would like to interpret Matt. 5:32; 19:9.

74 On the *haeterae*, cf. Hauck, πόρνη, *TWNT* 4:582ff.

75 Cf. Weidinger, *Die Haustafeln*, 50–79, and Baltensweiler, *Die Ehe im Neuen Testament*, 210–55.

76 Schlier, *Der Brief an die Epheser*, 277. On Eph. 5:21–33, see also Kähler, *Die Frau in den Paulinischen Briefen*, 88–140; Baltensweiler, *Die Ehe im Neuen Testament*, 218–35; Schnackenburg, *Die Ehe nach dem Neuen Testament*, 28–31; Greeven, "Ehe nach dem Neuen Testament," 77–79.

77 Cf. 1 Tim. 3:2; 5:9; Titus 1:6. On this, Baltensweiler, *Die Ehe im Neuen Testament*, 239ff., and Schulze, "Ein Bischof sei eines Weibes Mann." He also describes Luther's interpretation (291ff.). The Reformation interpretation forbidding simultaneous, not successive, bigamy was practically realized by Abraham Calov "by the doggedness by which he married again and again" ("Ein Bischof sei eines Weibes Mann," 297, wrongly identified by Schulze as a quotation from Barth, *Kirchliche Dogmatik* 3.4). "Finally, [Calov], at the age of 72 years, entered into his sixth marriage with the 18-year-old daughter of his colleague Quenstedt, which still lasted two years till his death. This unnatural relation rightly offended many contemporaries—not only enemies of Orthodoxy. As such, the remarriage of the lonesome man who, in addition to five wives, had also buried thirteen children was probably not the cause for this offense" ("Ein Bischof sei eines Weibes Mann," 297).

The apostle vigorously combats fornication. The body of the Christian is a member of the Body of the Lord and temple of the Spirit; he cannot and must not become one flesh with a prostitute (1 Cor. 6:15–20). Whoever commits adultery and fornication not only breaks an order among humans, but he also becomes liable to God's judgment (1 Thess. 4:3; 1 Cor. 6:18f.) and excludes himself from partaking in God's kingdom (1 Cor. 6:9; Eph. 5:5). He becomes liable of the second, eternal death (Rev. 21:8; 22:15). If he does not return in contrition and repentance, the congregation has to separate from him (1 Cor. 5:9ff.) and hand him over to Satan's dominion and God's judgment, lest the congregation become subject to God's ban as well.

The Old Testament connection between adultery and idolatry lives on in the phrase "evil and adulterous generation."[78] In the Revelation of John, Rome, the metropolis and world power, is placed under the symbol of godless Babylon and, as mother of all whores and abominations (Rev. 17:5), is juxtaposed to God's Church as the Bride of the Messiah (Rev. 21:9; 22:17). The latter is the heavenly Jerusalem to which no unclean person has access (Rev. 21:27).

CHARACTERISTICS OF LUTHER'S INTERPRETATION

In the Small and Large Catechisms, two aspects of the commandment are tied together: it commands all-inclusive chastity as well as marital love and faithfulness. The togetherness of both aspects has led to the hard transition in the Small Catechism and to the bipolarity of the exposition in the Large Catechism. Consciously, the reformer takes the prohibition of adultery out of its Old Testament narrowness. In this prohibition, not only is the marriage of the neighbor protected but also every form of unchastity is prohibited.[79]

1. THE COMMANDMENT OF CHASTITY

The broad interpretation of the commandment that includes chastity is the original one for Luther: "We are all baptized for chastity."[80] Herein he follows the tradition shaped by Augustine. In his catecheses, Augustine explained this commandment elaborately and carefully as that piece that "was needed the most among his people."[81] "For I see the entire human race lying in it (adultery)."[82] In his *Quaestiones in Heptateuchum*, Augustine therefore demands this broadening to include chastity in general and offers the

---

78 Matt. 12:39; 16:4; Mark 8:38; cf. James 4:4; Rev. 2:22; 14:1–5, and *Bill.*, 1:641f.

79 On the development of Luther in this matter, see also Hardeland, *Katechismusgedanken*, 150–61, and Meyer, *Historischer Kommentar*, 231ff.

80 "An den christl. Adel dt. Nation, 1520," WA 6:467.18 (see also AE 44:115–217).

81 *BSLK*, 504.44.

82 Augustine, Sermon 9:11 (*CCSL* 41:127f.); cf. Rentschka, *Dekalogkatechese*, 145f.

definition that Peter Lombard takes up verbatim and hands down to the confessional manuals: "And certainly, under the name of adultery should be understood as forbidden every illicit sexual intercourse and every illegitimate use of their members."[83]

In his confessional manuals, in "Decem praecepta" ("Preaching of the Ten Commandments"), as well as in "Sermon von den guten Werken" ("Sermon on Good Works"),[84] Luther interprets the commandment to cover "chastity" and "purity" without any special reference to marriage. He refers the transgression to his own person and to the neighbor and, with tradition,[85] works out an outline similar to the one regarding the previous commandment,[86] traces of which are contained in the Large Catechism.[87] (1) He mentions the sinful deeds.[88] (2) Then, showing covetousness and provoking to sin "with shameless words, songs, narratives, pictures," with looks, gestures, and jewelry,[89] (3) he adds secret desires and thoughts. (4) Luther hints at an additional group of sins when he says that the commandment is transgressed already when one "does not avoid the cause, such as gluttony, carousing, idleness, laziness, sleeping, and being around women or men."[90] (5) Then he underscores the relation to the neighbor: "Whoever does not help somebody else to preserve his chastity in word and deed."[91] Thus the reformer goes far beyond the wording of the commandment and juxtaposes "carnal impurity" and "spiritual purity."[92] Without question, here we see the continuing influence of the medieval practice prepared by Augustine, who

---

83   Augustine, *Quaestiones in Heptateuchum* 2, quest. 71.4 (*CCSL* 33:105; PL 34:622); Peter Lombard, *Sent.* III, dist. 37.3.

84   "Eine kurze Erklärung, 1518," WA 1:255.6; "Instructio, 1518," WA 1:263.24; "Eine kurze Form, 1520," WA 7:213.16; "Von den guten Werken, 1520," WA 6:268.11 (see also AE 44:15–114); "Decem praecepta, 1518," WA 1:498.30: "From all these it is clear that this commandment is not only negative, except only on the surface of words and letters, but also is highly affirmative because it commands chastity and the purest self-control within and without."

85   Likely immediately influenced through Gerson/Geiler; cf. Geffcken, *Bildercatechismus*, app., col. 44.

86   Cf. pp. 226–30.

87   *BSLK*, 611.25ff.

88   Cf. "Eine kurze Erklärung, 1518," WA 1:253.13ff.; "Instructio, 1518," WA 1:261.19ff.; "Eine kurze Form, 1520," WA 7:210.19ff.

89   Cf. "Eine kurze Erklärung, 1518," WA 1:253.15ff.; "Instructio, 1518," WA 1:261.21f.; "Eine kurze Form, 1520," WA 7:210.23ff., 210.28f.

90   Cf. "Eine kurze Erklärung, 1518," WA 1:253.17f.; "Instructio, 1518," WA 1:261.26f.; "Eine kurze Form, 1520," WA 7:210.26f.

91   Cf. "Eine kurze Erklärung, 1518," WA 1:253.19; "Eine kurze Form, 1520," WA 7:210.30; "Instructio, 1518," WA 1:261.28: "Who does not protect and guard the chastity of others, if he can, but produces (it) and ruins (them)."

92   WA 6:269.33(see also AE 44:15–114).

had summarized this whole area under the main sin of *luxuria*.[93] The Large Catechism draws these five levels of reference together in the phrase "that everybody may both live chastely for himself and help his neighbor to do the same."[94] While Luther hints at them only rather loosely in the Large Catechism, Agricola has offered a biblical proof for each in *Christliche Kinderzucht*, and the "Nürnberger Katechismuspredigten" ("Nürnberg Catechism Sermons") carefully structure them.[95]

Luther's detailed analysis in "Preaching of the Ten Commandments" shows the tension that we already have observed between the "external" and the "inner meaning" of the commandment.[96] On the one hand, following many medieval outlines,[97] Luther extensively classifies the individual sins and draws them together under eight headings.[98] On the other hand, this astonishing expansion of external transgressions is permeated by the analysis of the inner struggle of the heart between *castitas* and *luxuria*, where Luther points out God's workings under the antagonism and the hiddenness of the cross.[99] God hides the life of the saints from them. They barely feel the hidden groaning of the Spirit in view of the chaotic flood of temptation. Nonetheless, the Lord rules within and struggles against lust in the chastity of the spiritual man.[100] In "Sermon on Good Works," Luther emphasizes

---

93 According to Augustine, the commandment is directed against *libido* (Sermon 9:13). Additionally, Bonaventure juxtaposes *pudicitia* and *moechia* (*Collationes de decem praeceptis* 7:8). The later confessional manuals often expounded on the commandment only superficially and unfolded its contents in detail under the chief sin, *luxuria*. Cf. Geffcken, *Bildercatechismus*, app., col. 103, 133, and Weidenhiller, *Untersuchungen*, 48, 61f., 166.

94 *BSLK*, 611.43.

95 Agricola, in *Christl. Kinderzucht*, follows the schema *corde—oculo—verbo—facto* (MGP 21:32f.). Similarly, Althamer, *Katechismus*, quest. 31 (MGP 22:25); Sam, *Christl. Unterweisung*, quest. 114 (MGP 22:122); Brenz, *Fragstücke*, quest. 78 (MGP 22:183). On the "Nürnberger Katechismuspredigten," see Reu, *Quellen*, 1.1:489.35–45, 490.38–491.26. Furthermore, the Geneva Catechism, quest. 203, and the Heidelberg Catechism, quest. 108.

96 Luther distinguishes both sharply in "Pred. zum 4.–6. Gebot vom 28.2.1525," WA 11:41.23ff.

97 Cf. Bonaventure, *Collationes des decem praeceptis* 6:12 (5:527): "adultery, fornication, prostitution, torpor, sacrilege, incest, sin against nature." Cf. Peter Lombard, *Sent.* IV, dist. 41.4; Geffcken, *Bildercatechismus*, 78f.; and Weidenhiller, *Untersuchungen*, 75f.

98 "Decem praecepta, 1518," WA 1:483.12–23: "Simple fornication, prostitution, rape, abduction, adultery, incest, sacrilege, excess."

99 Already Gerson/Geiler understand this struggle as one of prayer; cf. Geffcken, *Bildercatechismus*, app., col. 44f. Similarly, *Spiegel des Sünders* says (*Bildercatechismus*, app., col. 73): "Flee to Mary, the mother of Christ, to all the saints, your guardian angel, and twelve messengers, etc."

100 "Decem praecepta, 1518," WA 1:486.16: "For God has so deeply hidden the entire life of the saints that they themselves cannot know it. . . . Thus as the living and true glory of the righteous consists in shame, their true wisdom in stupidity, their true rest in tribulation, their true joy in mourning, their true liberty in captivity, their true riches in poverty, so also their true chastity in luxuriousness; and the more shameful their luxuriousness, the more beautiful their chastity. . . . For that man is spiritual, that is, the affect of chastity remains and serves chastity, though he stirs up amazing piglets outside in his members and in the heart."

exclusively the spiritual meaning of the commandment. "For a precious chastity is not one at rest, but one that is at war with unchastity, constantly driving out all poison thrown in by flesh and mere spirit."[101] Here again the war of the new man against the old Adam is at stake; it is waged by means of God's Word and prayer, "by praying, fasting, watching, and working."[102] In this struggle, we are not to let ourselves be defined by covetousness, not give it any room in our hearts, but let our hearts be wholly permeated by the sight of the Crucified One,[103] since we all are to be conformed to His sacrificial death. Who thus rightly considers God's suffering in the Son is transformed by the Crucified One into His life of obedience. "Here the suffering of Christ works His true, natural, and most noble work, strangles the old Adam, drives out all lust, joy, and confidence one may derive from creatures, just as Christ was forsaken by all, even by God."[104]

This spiritual wrestling for chastity of the heart and purity of the body is laid on all Christians in all estates; all estates are estates of chastity. "This is why chastity is a virtue high above virginity. . . . Chastity hovers above all three estates, above marriage, above widowhood and virginity."[105]

2. THE DOCTRINE OF THE ESTATE OF MARRIAGE

Besides Luther's urging of chastity, there is the special task to teach people to understand marriage as God's protective wall against sin and to defend it against monastic devaluation and humanistic ridicule. Beginning in 1519, Luther's sermons on marriage develop this second thought, which he includes in the interpretation of the commandment and makes central in the Large Catechism.[106]

Luther did not want to establish new marriage laws. He only wished exclusively to counsel troubled consciences. Yet by declaring laws that had been in force up to that time as invalid before God, he created a situation of legal uncertainty. It could only be overcome if the new understanding of

---

101   WA 6:270.12 (see also AE 44:15–114); cf. "Decem praecepta, 1518," WA 1:487.15–22.

102   "Von den guten Werken, 1520," WA 6:269.4, 269.17, 270.10f. (see also AE 44:15–114); cf. "Decem praecepta, 1518," WA 1:498.27: "This is constantly to be put to death by groaning, vigils, labor, prayer, humiliation, and other parts of the cross, finally by death itself."

103   Cf. "Decem praecepta, nach Num. 21:9," WA 1:488.1–16.

104   "Sermon von der Betrachtung d. hl. Leidens Christi, 1519," WA 2:139.15 (see also AE 42:3–14); cf. "Sermon von der Betrachtung d. hl. Leidens Christi, 1519," WA 2:141.35f. (see also AE 42:3–14); "Sermon von der Bereitung zum Sterben, 1519," WA 2:689.3–23 (see also AE 42:95–115).

105   "Fastenpost. zu Lk. 8:4f., 1525," WA 17.2:159.2. "De votis monasticis iudicium, 1521," WA 8:612.4 (see also AE 44:243–400): "For everybody ought to serve God freely in his gift. All, however, ought to glory in the common virginity of faith in the one Christ where there is neither male nor female, thus neither virgin nor married, neither widow nor celibate, but all are one in Christ."

106   Section 2.

marriage also took on legal forms. Luther's writings on marriage laid the foundation for this. As institutions in the tension between secular and spiritual government, the consistories developed new laws as they wrestled with the traditional ecclesial and secular orders. In this struggle, the inner tension in Luther's understanding of marriage becomes apparent, though it is not fully recognized in research. In it is reflected the basic tension between natural law and the law of love, the *lex naturae* and the *lex charitatis*.[107]

As God's ordinance, marriage is an estate that, as a widely observed one, permeates not only Christendom but all of humanity.[108] It connects all who bear a human face; all people know it as a public estate and protect it in manifold forms and different shapes by means of custom and law. According to the "Traubüchlein" ("Marriage Booklet"), wedding and the estate of marriage are a "worldly business,"[109] not governed by the ministers of the Church. In "Sermon vom ehelichen Leben" ("Sermon on Married Life"), Luther calls it "an external, bodily matter like any other worldly business."[110] And in "Schrift von Ehesachen" ("Writing on Marriage Matters"), he calls it "an external worldly thing . . . like clothing and food, house and farm, subject to secular authority."[111] Emphatically, Luther resists attempts to assign marriage courts again to the Church and does not refrain from using the dominical word: "Let the dead bury their dead" (Matt. 8:22).[112]

At the same time, the reformer resists attempts to view the married estate with the eyes of the "blind world"; rather, he demands to look at it in light of God's Word,[113] because it is "confirmed" in the Fourth Commandment and "guarded and protected" in the Sixth.[114] Although marriage is a worldly business, it still rests on God's will. Looking up to Him, this secular business is transformed into a spiritual estate. Tirelessly, Luther showers

---

107 See pp. 73–86.

108 *BSLK*, 613.27–32.

109 *BSLK*, 528.6.

110 WA 10.2:283.8 (see also AE 45:11–49): "Know, therefore, that marriage is an external, bodily matter like other worldly business. As I now may eat, drink, sleep, walk, ride, buy, speak, and deal with a heathen, Jew, Turk, heretic, so may I also marry him and remain so." Cf. "Das 7. Kap. S. Pauli zu den Cor., 1523," WA 12:120.20f. (see also AE 28:1–56).

111 WA 30.3:205.12 (see also AE 46:259–320).

112 WA 30.3:205.2–206.34 (see also AE 46:259–320).

113 *BSLK*, 613.10–27.

114 *BSLK*, 612.13–26.

honorific titles on it: it is a divine and blessed,[115] honorable and necessary estate,[116] "pleasing and blessed" before God.[117]

According to the "Marriage Booklet" and the Large Catechism,[118] marriage combines three features, as it is God's "creature, order, and blessing."[119] (1) God has created man and woman differently and has implanted in them the intellectual powers, as well as the bodily urge, to marital union. This "bridal love"[120] and that "will to marriage"[121] permeate the sex drive, the στοργή φυσική,[122] with that profound love which means the loved one himself. Thus "married love is . . . to be sure, sexual love, but precisely as such it is the agape of love."[123] In sexual intercourse, the love of marriage goes beyond itself to the child and, therefore, to the family. In this, marriage is *opus* and *creatura* of God. (2) Yet God has not only implanted in man some dark urging toward marital communion, but He also has included both marriage and family and the serving lordship over the nonhuman creation in an explicit word and commandment (Gen. 1:28). He wants husband and wife to "beget children, feed, and raise" them to His honor.[124] As we saw on the Fourth Commandment,[125] also in this charge what is bodily is connected to what is intellectual/spiritual: the bodily raising is to serve the intellectual/spiritual introduction of the youth to the two kingdoms of God.[126] In this, marriage

---

115 "Das 7. Kap. S. Pauli zu den Cor., 1523," WA 12:107.34 (see also AE 28:1–56): "a truly heavenly, spiritual, and godly estate." Cf. "Das 7. Kap. S. Pauli zu den Cor., 1523," WA 12:105.22 (see also AE 28:1–56); "Pred. über Dtn. 1 vom 28.2.1529," WA 28:537.17ff.; "Luthers Vorrede zu J. Brenz' Wie in Ehesachen, 1531," WA 30.3:486.1ff.; BSLK, 529.30, 529.33, 529.37, 612.24, 615.8.

116 BSLK, 613.34f., 615.8, 339.18ff. (Ap XXIII).

117 BSLK, 533.35.

118 BSLK, 612.13–39.

119 BSLK, 534.13; Latin: *opus, ordinatio, benedictio.* "Vom ehel. Leben, 1522," WA 10.2:295.5 (see also AE 45:11–49): "Work, creature, and will"; cf. BSLK, 530.1, 530.12, 530.20; "Vorl. über Ps. 127, 1533," WA 40.3:256.21ff.; "Gen.-Vorl., 1535–45," WA 42:100.25f. (see also AE 1:1–359); "Contra 32 art. Lovaniensium theologistarum, 1545," WA 54:428, Thesis 45 (see also AE 34:339–60); "Contra 32 art. Lovaniensium theologistarum, 1545," WA 54:437, Thesis 46 (see also AE 34:339–60); BSLK, 87.19 (AC XXIII): "God's mandate and God's order"; BSLK, 336.12 (Ap XXIII): "order stamped by God on nature"; cf. Fagerberg, *Theologie der lutherischen Bekenntnisschriften*, 306f.

120 "Sermon von dem ehel. Stand, 1519," WA 2:167.30 (see also AE 44:3–14).

121 "Von Ehesachen, 1530," WA 30.3:236.11 (see also AE 46:259–320).

122 BSLK, 335.2ff., 336.22 (Ap XXIII).

123 Lähteenmäki, *Sexus und Ehe bei Luther*, 138.

124 BSLK, 612.29; "Vom Abendmahl Christi, 1528," WA 26:505.1 (see also AE 37:151–372): "Who is a father and a mother, governs the house well, and rightly raises children to God's service is truly also a sanctuary and holy work and holy order."

125 Cf. pp. 203f. and p. 26–31.

126 BSLK, 612.39–613.9.

and family are God's *ordinatio* and *mandatum*.[127] (3) Marriage cannot be preserved as God's battle order against chaos by the power and reason of man. In the last analysis, it lives out of the power to bless of the *Spiritus creator et vivificator*,[128] out of the pleasure of God the Creator who adorns and preserves this estate by His constant blessing.[129] Marriage is a *benedictio* of God. As God's work, commandment, and blessing, marriage is a divine estate, through which the reflection of God's good creation still shines.

Yet because of the original fall, sin and God's curse (Gen. 3:14ff.) now cling to the relationship of husband and wife. Genuine partnership became patriarchy,[130] giving birth to children became a torturous near-death experience for the wife, marital love was flooded by an unrestrained sex drive. Nonetheless, despite His curse, God holds on to marriage as His institution and hedges it in by His command.[131] In the struggle that now starts between chastity and unchastity, dedication and selfishness, virtue and vice—which is ultimately a struggle between God and the prince of this world[132]—marriage becomes a "necessary estate" in three ways.[133] (a) Although marriage was "God's will and work already before the fall into sin and without any regard for sin," now, after evil lust has broken in, marriage becomes a protective wall "against the unrestrained sexual drive and all dirt coming from it."[134] (b) After the fall, God has decreed marriage for us so that we would continue the human race even under His curse and help one another to bear the cross laid on all.[135] (c) For the Christian, marriage is, to be sure, not a sacrament, but the central exercising ground of faith that has been made worthy to serve as a sign and pointer to the mystery of the union between the Lord and His Bride, the Church. And marriage itself advances the procreation of the Church and, in this, is part of the work of redemption. In the Large Catechism, Luther highlights the first of these three necessities in the battle between God and anti-god.

---

127 "Gen.-Vorl., 1535–45," WA 42.100.25 (see also AE 1:1–359): "For a lawful union of a man and a woman is a divine ordination and institution."

128 "Vorl. über Ps. 127, 1533," WA 40.3:256.21: "This is why Scripture calls us back to itself and commands us to admire the matter and substance of marriage itself, which is the divine blessing." The relation between God's blessing and the Holy Spirit is unfolded by Luther in his interpretations of the account of creation. Cf. the commentary on the Creed.

129 *BSLK*, 612.31f.

130 Cf. "Pred. über Gen. 3 vom 17.5. bzw. 25.5.1523," WA 14:141.2ff., 151.12ff.; "Pred. über Gen. 27 vom 31.1.1524," WA 14:361.19ff.; "Gen.-Vorl., 1535–45," WA 42:103.8–104.40 (see also AE 1:1–359).

131 *BSLK*, 612.13–26.

132 *BSLK*, 612.39–613.9.

133 *BSLK*, 613.35.

134 Althaus, "Luthers Wort von der Ehe," 3.

135 *BSLK*, 610.8–38.

Here the marital estate gains the dignity of a commandment,[136] because Luther, even after the fall into sin, does not look at the husband's clinging to his wife and vice versa merely under the aspect of sin. It is the ongoing work of the Creator. Constantly Luther refers back to Gen. 1:27f. and 2:18.[137] In these words of Scripture, something implanted into all of us opens up for us; again, the testimony of Scripture and our daily experience complement and confirm each other in this point.

God decrees marriage for us so that we might guide the nature implanted in us by God along the course set by Him.[138] The demand to strive for true chastity, commonly imposed on all, turns specific in the duty to lay hold of the marital estate where we feel in us that God-implanted urging toward the other sex.[139] All those to whom God Himself has given the "high, supernatural gift" of celibacy do not fall under this commandment to accept the nature implanted in us by God and through marriage to hedge it in against abuse.[140] Whoever received this charisma may and shall live according to it.

By virtue of this basic insight, Luther feuds against the vows of celibacy[141] not only where they led to extramarital sexual intercourse, as was the case for many religious people in the late Middle Ages,[142] but also where they were outwardly observed. Normally, the urge toward the other sex is here turned inward and generates an "eternal burning and secret suffering"[143]

---

136 *BSLK*, 614.2f.

137 E.g., "Sermon von dem ehel. Stand, 1519," WA 2:166.15–167.21 (see also AE 44:3–14); "Vom ehel. Leben, 1522," WA 10.2:275.12–276.31 (see also AE 45:11–49); "Ermahnung an Herren dt. Ordens, 1523," WA 12:233.31–234.9 (see also AE 45:131–58); "Christl. Schrift an Reißenbusch, 1525," WA 18:275.12–276.19, taken up in "Nürnberger Katechismuspredigten" (Reu, *Quellen*, 1.1:487.36–488.42).

138 *BSLK*, 613.44ff.

139 *BSLK*, 613.48–614.12, 614.40–615.4. "Das 7. Kap. S. Pauli zu den Cor., 1523," WA 12:98.2: "Thus this is now the first conclusion (on 1 Cor. 7:2), that whoever does not feel this fine thing but feels fornication, he is commanded here to marry. And this commandment you should accept, not as one from a person, but from God." Cf. "Das 7. Kap. S. Pauli zu den Cor., Zusammenfassung der Ausl. v. 1. Kor. 7" (WA 12:141.23–27) and *BSLK*, 336.35–338.2 (Ap XXIII).

140 *BSLK*, 613.39ff. "Zusammenfassung der Ausl. v. 1. Kor. 7," WA 12:141.27: "If now somebody is not to be in this need, this has to be accomplished not by command nor vow nor proposition, but only by God's grace and miracle hand." Cf. furthermore "Vom ehel. Leben, 1523," WA 10.2:279.15–23 (see also AE 45:11–49); "Das 7. Kap. S. Pauli zu den Cor., 1523," WA 12:104.10–33 (see also AE 28:1–56); "Ausl. v. Mt. 5–7, 1530/32," WA 32:374.34–37 (see also AE 21:1–294); "Pred. über Mt. 19:10ff." WA 47:322.31–323.6, 324.36–326.26; "Nürnberger Katechismuspredigten" (Reu, *Quellen*, 1.1:489.6–11) and *BSLK*, 340.53 (Ap XXIII): ". . . virginity is a gift surpassing marriage."

141 *BSLK*, 614.13–615.4.

142 *BSLK*, 614.13–32.

143 *BSLK*, 614.29. Similarly, "Das 7. Kap. S. Pauli zu den Cor., 1523," WA 12:98.20–99.5, 115.22–31, 117.15–118.8 (see also AE 28:1–56); "Ausl. von Mt. 5–7, 1530/32," WA 32:371.10–15 (see also AE 21:1–294); "Gen.-Vorl., 1535–45," WA 43:651.19–40 (see also AE 5:1–386).

that permeate the entire person and absorb his mental powers. The religious person struggles against the nature implanted in him by God and gets tangled up within in increasingly subtle forms of unchastity. Whoever feels this need in himself is duty-bound to break his vow and to lay hold of marriage.[144] His vow strives against God's will in two ways.[145] He vows to do something that is not within his power; only God can give it but has withheld it from him. By doing so, he simultaneously strives against God's will and must pay for this by the inner growth of unchastity.[146] Therefore he is meant by God's strict commandment to accept the help of marriage offered to him by the Lord to overcome the inner unchastity of the heart that condemns him before God.

Luther supports this first thought by a second, where he gets into tension with the secondary thoughts of the apostle in 1 Corinthians 7.[147] Paul supports his guiding thought—whoever is unmarried is free for God and can more easily hurry to Him through the final tribulation—by the secondary hint: the married person is more firmly bound to the tribulations and joys of this world; the unmarried person is freed from these (1 Cor. 7:32ff.). Taken out of their reference to eschatological service, these last aspects played a rather problematic role in the pitch of the unmarried estate made by the Church of the early and medieval eras. Luther vehemently attacks the egotism manifesting itself in this. In his interpretation of 1 Corinthians 7, he juxtaposes the "good days of chastity" and the "evil days of the estate of marriage."[148] God does not want us to leave the human community behind; this is why He has implanted in us the "will to marriage" and ordered the estates, especially the married estate, so that we would jointly bow under the curse that He laid on the human race and bear it together. "For we are not created to run away from each other, but to live and suffer together. For

---

144 *BSLK*, 613.33ff.

145 On the question of monastic vows, see the literature on p. 208 n. 173.

146 According to "De votis monast., 1521," WA 8:658.33–36, 659.5–9 (see also AE 44:243–400); "Das 7. Kap. S. Pauli zu den Cor., 1523," WA 12:98.5–10 (see also AE 28:1–56); "Ermahnung an die Herren dt. Ordens, 1523," WA 12:242.8–18, 244.9ff. (see also AE 45:131–58); "Christl. Schrift an Reißenbusch, 1525," WA 18:275.12–17.

147 A certain *yes* to the greater liberty of the unmarried is found in "Vom ehel. Lebe, 1522" (WA 10.2:298.19–30 [see also AE 45:11–49]) and "Das 7. Kap. S. Pauli zu den Cor., 1523" (WA 12:137.26–29 [see also AE 28:1–56]). On 1 Corinthians 7, see the interpretations by Kähler, *Die Frau in den Paulinischen Briefen*, 14–43; Baltensweiler, *Die Ehe im Neuen Testament*, 150–209; Greeven, "Ehe nach dem Neuen Testament," 73–77; Schnackenburg, "Die Ehe nach dem Neuen Testament," 21–36. These most recent interpretations—in contradistinction from the older interpretation (especially Preisker, *Christentum und Ehe in den ersten drei Jahrhunderten*, and Delling, *Paulus' Stellung zu Frau und Ehe*)—seek to see the relationship of the apostle to marriage against the Jewish backdrop as positively as possible and focus his reluctance on the eschatological reservation. By doing so, they follow, certainly without being conscious of it, Luther's interpretation.

148 "Das 7. Kap. S. Pauli zu den Cor., 1523," WA 12:100.11 (see also AE 28:1–56).

because we are human, we must also help bear all sorts of human misfortune and the curse that affects us all."[149] The monks flee precisely the basic commandment of love of neighbor that, according to Paul (Rom. 13:8–10) and James (2:8–12), includes the prohibition of adultery. Precisely by their vows, they withdraw from the duty to bear the burden of their fellow man and fall into the original sin against the First Commandment as they seek themselves and what is theirs even before God.

In these two series of thoughts, what the Middle Ages viewed as almost spatially opposed becomes reflective and thereby ambivalent or unsure: the longing for God as the one highest good and the losing of oneself in the diversity of creatures. Amid the desert, I may be consumed by dark desires[150] and be chained to my old Adam; amid the world, I may be altogether with God in selfless service of the neighbor. God does not want us to run away from His creation. He wants us, precisely in the spiritual struggle against the prince of darkness, to remain in this world, "stand chivalrously, and struggle against many a temptation, and plough through with patience and win the victory."[151]

In the concluding admonition,[152] Luther seeks to place the married estate under the *usus practicus Evangelii*. By doing so, he opens up the Christ-dimension of a marriage consciously led in looking up to the Lord. As two young people risk binding themselves to each other without safeguards into the future, marriage becomes for them a practice ground for faith. Doubtlessly, the married estate is an "external, worldly thing," but precisely as such it "drives, chases, and forces" us human creatures "into the innermost, highest, spiritual nature, namely, into faith."[153] External uncertainty and need forces us to cast all cares on God in heartfelt trust.

Luther passionately combats the "filthy, depraved, disorderly character"[154] of premarital sexual intercourse, which was almost sanctioned

---

149   "Ausl. v. Mt. 5–7," WA 32:371.3 (see also AE 21:1–294). Cf. *BSLK*, 610.22–25; "Christl. Schrift an Reißenbusch, 1525," WA 18:276.12–14; "Vom ehel. Leben, 1522," WA 10.2:302.13 (see also AE 45:11–49): "God's Word and preaching make the chaste estate better than the married estate, as Christ and Paul have lived in it. By itself, however, it is much lower."

150   "Pred. über Mt. 19:3–12," WA 47:322.25: ". . . thus your heart is a veritable whorehouse that day and night thinks about whoring and does not lack the willingness, only the place and space to fornicate, and then attacks you like a mad dog." Luther offers by way of example what Jerome, Bernard, and Francis reported: "Pred. über Mt. 19:3–12," WA 47:326.16–26; "Das 7. Kap. S. Pauli zu den Cor., 1523," WA 12:98.30 (see also AE 28:1–56): "One has to have a heart for chastity; otherwise such a life is harder than hell and purgatory."

151   "Ausl. von Mt. 5–7, 1530/32," WA 32:371.15 (see also AE 21:1–294).

152   Section 3, but already starting at *BSLK*, 615.5.

153   "Das 7. Kap. S. Pauli zu den Cor., 1523," WA 12:107.22 (see also AE 28:1–56). "Winterpost. zu Joh. 2:1–11," WA 21:58.25: "Thus the estate of marriage is an estate of faith, because who accepts and undertakes this estate should do so in faith. All the works of God are ordered in such a way that one must grasp them by faith just like this one."

154   *BSLK*, 615.11.

by the civil and ecclesiastical order. The guild statutes that limited the number of craftsmen and the early placement in monasteries of daughters and sons who could not or were not supposed to marry excluded many people who otherwise were able and willing to marry. This necessarily produced brothels and quasimarital relationships.[155] The payments of penance by those priests who lived with their housekeepers as concubines represented an important source of income for bishops. In this situation, Luther propagates early marriage and encourages communities to offer to young couples an interest-free loan to help them get started.[156] For young men, he proposes getting married between ages twenty and twenty-four; for girls, he considers the ages fifteen through eighteen as especially suited for marriage.[157] He pushes for a large number of children, even if it affects the mother's health.[158] Keeping the family small by means of abortion is something that Luther brands as godlessness.[159] He views pure greed—decreasing the inheritance—as the driving force behind most cases of abortion.

As it serves children, marriage lived out under God's eyes partakes in His work as Redeemer. As we saw on the Fourth Commandment,[160] marriage moves from the secular to the spiritual realm and embraces both dimensions—that of earthly well-being and that of eternal salvation. Yet this is true not only for the family, but it also already applies to marriage. Where it is lived under the guidance of the triune God, it is a cell of His Church. In the "Marriage Booklet," Luther has Eph. 5:25–29 and 5:22–24 read as God's commandment pertaining to marriage[161] and thereby places marital love

---

155 Luther struggled mightily against brothels and apparently succeeded in closing the one in Wittenberg, but he did not manage to stop fornication. Cf. "Von den guten Werken, 1520," WA 6:262.19–28 (see also AE 44:15–114); "An den christl. Adel dt. Nation, 1520," WA 6:467.17–26 (see also AE 44:115–217); "An den Rat zu Erfurt, 1525," WA 18:537.16ff.; "Winterpost. zu Joh. 2:1–11," WA 21:61.38–62.14; "Pred. über Mt. 20:1ff. vom 24.1.1529," WA 29:44.25ff.; "Pred. über Mk. 8:1ff. vom 23.7.1531," WA 34.2:21.20–27; "Pred. über Lk. 7:11ff. vom 24.8.1531," WA 34.2:214.6ff.; cf. Werdermann, *Luthers Wittenberger Gemeinde*, 10; Eschenhagen, "Wittenberger Studien," 26.

156 In the "Leisniger Kastenordnung," this is hinted at in the "care for house-poor people" (see WA 12:26f. [see also AE 45:176–94]).

157 "Vom ehel. Leben, 1522," WA 10.2:299.29 (see also AE 45:11–49): "Rising and marrying early no one has to regret." Cf. "Vom ehel. Leben, 1522," WA 10.2:303.31f. (see also AE 45:11–49); "Pred. über Gen. 4 vom 26.5.1523," WA 14:157.8f.; Peter Lombard, *Sent.* IV, dist. 36.4, as well as Lähteenmäki, *Sexus und Ehe bei Luther*, 166.

158 "Vom ehel. Leben, 1522," WA 10.2:301.14 (see also AE 45:11–49): "Even if they bear themselves tired and finally dead (the mothers with children), that does no harm; just let them bear themselves to death. That is what they are there for. It is better to live healthily for a short time than to live sickly for a long time."

159 "Gen.-Vorl., 1535–45," WA 43:653.5 (see also AE 5:1–386): "It is inhuman and impious to feel aversion to one's offspring." Cf. "Gen.-Vorl., 1535–45," WA 42:89.22–30 (see also AE 1:1–359).

160 Cf. pp. 203–7.

161 *BSLK*, 532.27–533.11.

between husband and wife under the sacrifice of Christ for His congregation and the love of the congregation for Christ, its Head. In the concluding prayer of blessing over the newlyweds, the reference to the New Testament stands once again right next to the Old Testament reference. The Old Testament reference contains the creation of husband and wife and the estate of marriage that is commanded to them and blessed for them. In other words, this refers to the *opus, ordinatio,* and *benedictio* of marriage. With the juxtaposed New Testament reference, God has "signified" in marriage the "sacrament" of His dear Son, Jesus Christ, and the Church.[162] Thereby Christ as our Redeemer also enters into the marriage of believers.

However, the marriage of Christians certainly does not belong simply to the same category as proclaiming the Word and administering the Sacraments.[163] As two people give themselves to each other before God and His servant, they neither give each other the grace of salvation nor forgive each other's sin.[164] In this sense, their doing remains on earth in God's worldly realm. Yet where it takes place in faith, love, and hope under prayer, there it takes place before the triune God as our Creator and Redeemer, not only under the blessing of the Creator and Preserver but also under the saving grace of the Re-Creator and Consummator. The *usus crassus legis* is deepened into the *usus spiritualis.*[165] Via the accusation of the Law in conscience (*usus elenchticus*), God gives us, out of His saving grace, the desire and joy to walk together[166] in the *usus practicus Evangelii.* Christ enters into marriage, not only as commanding example but also as giving sacrament; this is also for Luther the abiding truth of the sacramental misunderstanding of marriage.

The Lord enters into marriage as sacrament in that He covers the "evil carnal lust," the abiding hard-heartedness, and the lovelessness of the old Adam with God's holy human nature.[167] Whatever arises from our sexual

---

162 *BSLK,* 534.9, 534.11. On the sources, cf. the commentary on the "Marriage Booklet."

163 In "De capt. Babylonica ecclesiae," Luther rejects the term "sacrament" for marriage; see WA 6:550.21–553.20 (see also AE 36:3–126).

164 Marriage as a vessel of grace is not yet found in Augustine (cf. Peters, *Die Ehe nach der Lehre des hl. Augustin*), it is still denied in Peter Lombard (*Sent.* IV, dist. 2.1), and is first defined magisterially at the Councils of Verona (1184) and Florence (1439) and Trent (1563) (H. J. Schroeder, ed. and trans., *Canons and Decrees of the Council of Trent* [St. Louis: Herder, 1941], 761, 1327, 1801). See the critique of Roman teaching on marriage in Barth, *Kirchliche Dogmatik* 3.4:134–38.

165 Cf. "Pred. zum 1. Gebot vom 24.2.1523," WA 11:31.8, 31.12, 31.21; "Pred. zum 4.–6. Gebot vom 28.2.1523," WA 11:41.23–30. This aspect is highlighted in the presentation by H. Leenhardt, *Le mariage chrétien* (Neuchatel: Delachaux & Niestle, 1946).

166 *BSLK,* 615.21f.

167 "Sermon von dem ehel. Stand, 1519," WA 2:168.30 (see also AE 44:3–14): "For the sake of marriage, since the commingling of husband and wife signifies such a great thing, the estate of marriage must enjoy such significance that the evil carnal lust, from which no one is free, is

desires that does not originate in God's good creation, but rather from human original sin, does not cast us into eternal damnation where we only allow Christ operative room in the marriage ordered by God and here place this matter also, by the entreaty of faith, into the all-sufficient sacrifice of Christ. In this sense, the sacrifice of Christ stands in the midst of every Christian marriage and covers the unchastity that is not overcome completely even in marriage, since marriage as a worldly thing is rightly grasped and lived only in faith. Additionally, the Lord promises by means of the miracle of the wine at the wedding at Cana that He wants to give joy and love by changing the water of marital sadness into the wine of marital joy.[168]

Thereby the Lord enters also as an example into the marriage of those who are His. Concluding his interpretation in the Large Catechism, Luther points to Eph. 5:22, 25 and Col. 3:18f.[169] The apostle exhorts to love sacrificially not by establishing some external law, but by magnifying the Christ-mystery also over marriage.[170] Marriage is lived rightly out of Christ's forgiveness.[171] In this looking up to Christ's selfless love of God and neighbor, marriage gains a share in the law of faith and love (*lex fidei et charitatis*) as the *lex Christi*. It is evident that this eschatological and Christological scope of Christian marriage can no longer be placed into the category of marriage as "worldly business" under God's ruling of the world.

By focusing precisely on the eschatological dimension of salvation in his counsels for the consciences of true Christians, Luther also transforms civil marriage law in view of Christ's loving obedience. At the same time, he is shaped by the Old Testament and out of it renews the correlation between marriage and family. In doing so, also in Luther the conflict between the two aspects appears, namely, between marriage as a worldly business and as a sacred Christian estate. Luther reflects on it thoroughly by having Matt. 19:7 supply the key word: Here it is not the holy will of God that governs. Here God's permission for the sake of man's hard-heartedness is at work.[172]

---

not damnable in the course of marital duty, though it is always deadly when it is done outside of marriage. Thus the holy humanity of God covers the shame of carnal, evil lust."

168   "Winterpost. zu Joh. 2:1–11," WA 21:59–61.

169   *BSLK*, 615.40ff.

170   "Hochzeitspred. für Cruciger über Eph. 5:22ff. vom 24.4.1536," WA 41:548.20–549.28, 557.25–559.24. Further testimonies in Jordahn, "Die Trauung bei Luther," esp. 20ff.

171   "Ausl. von Mt. 5–7, 1530/32," WA 32:381.16 (see also AE 21:1–294): "This is why our main article is nothing but plain forgiveness of sins, both in ourselves and toward others, so that, just as Christ unceasingly bears us in His kingdom and forgives all sorts of shortcomings, we, too, among us bear and forgive in all estates and matters."

172   "Antwort auf dial. Hul. Nebulonis, 1542," WA 53:196.30: ". . . the letter of divorce, which especially Christ condemns publicly in Matthew 19 and interprets the Law of Moses to mean that it was not a law but a dispensation, a doom, not for the weak and needy but for the hard, stubborn, malicious knaves. Now, there is a great difference between the Law and doom, patience and permission."

1. In the realm of God's worldly kingdom, marriage is in the *usus crassus legis*, a harsh emergency order against chaos. Human reason here draws on the *lex naturae corruptae*. As in the "permission" of the letter of divorce by Moses, here God must give in to the people who do not abide by His "spiritual commandments" so as to avert even bigger misfortune, such as, for example, mutual homicide. Yet even here God establishes a legal boundary. Present-day marriage legislation could follow this example. "Yet where there are no Christians or false Christians, it would be good even today to follow this law and to permit them, like the heathen, to divorce their wives and marry others, lest they, in their life of discord, have two hells, both here and there."[173]

2. The Christian congregation, however, must not simply give in here as well. To it apply the words of the Lord concerning the indissolubleness of marriage. Luther continues the quote above from his commentary on 1 Corinthians 7: "Yet they must know that by divorcing they are no longer Christians but heathen in the condemned estate."[174] The Church has the duty to apply church discipline even to those who have been legally divorced or, where the secular authorities do not punish divorce, exercise the ban.[175]

This is the place where, for Luther, the marriage law of the civil order and of the Church may, and if necessary must, break apart. This tension-filled duality of marriage as "worldly business" and as a "holy Christian estate of marriage" is embraced and held together by God's struggle against the forces of destruction in both kingdoms. The triune God has instituted

---

173 "Das 7. Kap. S. Pauli zu den Cor., 1523," WA 12:119.6 (see also AE 28:1–56). Cf. "Das 7. Kap. S. Pauli zu den Cor., 1523," WA 12:119.1–11 (see also AE 28:1–56); "Vom ehel. Leben, 1522," WA 10.2:288.10–22 (see also AE 45:11–49); "Dtn.-Vorl., 1523/24," WA 14:714.8–18 (see also AE 9:1–311); "Ausl. von Mt. 5–7, 1530/32," WA 32:376.38–378.3 (see also AE 21:1–294); "Pred. über Mt. 19:3–12," WA 47:317.24–318.19.

174 Cf. "Vom ehel. Leben, 1522," WA 10.2:288.20ff. (see also AE 45:11–49). Out of fear of falling into a shallow moralistic misunderstanding, that eschatological seriousness of the holy will of God has not been made clear by the current contributions of the Church on marriage matters, for example, in the *Denkschrift zur Reform des Ehescheidungsrechts in der Bundesrepublik Deutschland* and in the *Denkschrift zu Fragen zur Sexualethik*.

175 On divorce, see, above all, "De capt. Babyl. eccl., 1520," WA 6:558.8–560.18 (see also AE 36:3–126); "Vom ehel. Leben, 1522," WA 10.2:287.12–292.6 (see also AE 45:11–49); "Das 7. Kap. S. Pauli zu den Cor., 1523," WA 12:118.22–119.34 (see also AE 28:1–56); "Divortium vom 8.5.1524," WA 15:558, 562; "Von Ehesachen, 1530," WA 30.3:215.6–216.24, 232.24–233.23, 241.1–244.17 (see also AE 46:259–320); "Ausl. von Mt. 5–7, 1530/32," WA 32:376.14–381.22 (see also AE 21:1–294); "Brief an Barnes betr. Ehescheidung Heinrich VIII. vom 3.9.1531," WABr 6:175–88 (see also AE 50:27–40). Cf. Kinder, "Luthers Stellung zur Ehescheidung"; Gloege, "Vom Ethos der Ehescheidung"; *Ehe und Ehescheidung* (Studenbuch 30); Bornkamm, "Ehescheidung und Wiederverheiratung im Neuen Testament."

marriage and holds on to it through all foolishness and wisdom of man. It is an emergency order of the Creator against chaos; by it God preserves the human race all the way to the Last Day, whether man knows and acknowledges it or not. Yet where marriage is entered into and lived in the name of the triune God as our Creator and Redeemer, there it reaches over into the spiritual kingdom. Thus marriage primarily remains a part of God's worldly kingdom. Yet God wants marriage to be lived consciously before His face and as a means to help build both kingdoms and not to seek to destroy them. The Christian congregation cannot keep silent about this dual will of God without denying its Lord. By joining couples in wedlock in the stead of civil authorities, the Church does so in the name of the triune God, the Creator and Preserver, the Redeemer and Re-Creator of the human race. This dual aspect in its manifold references is comprehensively described in a definition of marriage in the great "Genesisvorlesung" ("Genesis Lecture"): "Yet the true definition is this: marriage is the divine and lawful union of a male and female in hope of children, or at least to avoid the cause of fornication and sin, to God's glory. Its ultimate end is to obey God; to remedy sin; to call upon God; to seek, love, and educate children to God's glory; to live with one's spouse in the fear of the Lord; and to bear the cross."[176]

3. Critical Remarks on the Tension Between the Commandments of Chastity and Marriage

The key demand of the Sixth Commandment is bodily and spiritual chastity. This struggle for an inner and outer discipline goes right through all estates; in it, only God's grace can help.[177] Luther connects this basic demand with the call to marriage. In this form, this call is controversially dependent on the "unbiblically overdrawn ideal of virginity"[178] of the Middle Ages. The reformer takes up from this tradition the tension between the

---

176 WA 43:310.24 (see also AE 4:1–409). WA 43:558.19 (see also AE 5:1–386): "Marriage is the lawful and divine union of one male and one female ordained for the purpose of calling on God and sustaining and educating offspring for the administration of church and state." WA 43:559.1 (see also AE 5:1–386): ". . . marriage has a double goal: First, to be a remedy against lust. The second is actually the principal one, to be fountain and origin of the human race so that children might be born and the human race be enlarged. . . . Yet from the holy letters one ought to add this goal, to educate children in the discipline and fear of the Lord so that they might be fit to govern the church and the state." Cf. "Sermon von dem ehel. Stand, 1519," WA 2:169.30–37 (see also AE 44:3–14); "Vom ehel. Leben, 1522," WA 10.2:294.27ff. (see also AE 45:11–49); "Ermahnung an die Herren dt. Ordens, 1523," WA 12:241.3ff. (see also AE 45:131–58), as well as the definition by Melanchthon (Studienausgabe 2.2:801.13–24) and Peter Lombard (Sent. IV, dist. 30.4, 31.1). On the current understanding of marriage, see the literature listed in the Denkschrift zu Fragen der Sexualethik, 65–68.

177 BSLK, 614.5f., 615.21f.

178 Kinder, "Luthers Stellung zur Ehescheidung," 30. On the evidence in the New Testament, see von Campenhausen, "Die Askese im Urchristentum."

bodily/sexual and psychic/spiritual dimensions of marriage.[179] While the tradition places the accent on what is "spiritual," Luther emphasizes what is bodily/creaturely.[180] However, hereby what is bodily gains an almost deterministic power. Dealing with the Old Testament might have coalesced here with the heritage of German peasantry.

Luther's *no* to the monastic devaluation of marriage certainly ought to be retained. Celibacy must not divorce itself from serving in God's kingdoms. Where this takes place, it is ultimately motivated by egotistic reasons that have lost their legitimacy in view of Jesus' self-sacrifice. Above all, however, the estate of the religious person must not be supported by the promise of greater merit and special closeness to Christ.[181] Doing so would be sinning against God's free grace and despising the special charismas that God gives to individual Christians. Celibacy and the married estate both must be placed into the general call to fight along in God's fight in both His kingdoms against the forces of chaos and to help bear the curse that lies on all of us.

Once this is accepted, we may reduce Luther's overemphasis of marriage to the measure commanded by the New Testament. He himself points here and there in the direction chosen by us. In the Old Testament, preference is given to marriage in view of the blessing of children, because the earthly blessing of God manifested itself in offspring and moved the people in the chain of generations toward the promised Messiah.[182] After the coming of Christ and His strictly transcended preaching of salvation, the two kingdoms separate more clearly; the begetting in the Holy Spirit is distinguished from the physical birth. Marriage cannot find its meaning as exclusively in children, a meaning that Luther almost always emphasizes. Marriage remains limited to this age that is perishing (Mark 12:25 and parallels). At the same time, the celibate way has been opened and inwardly fulfilled by Jesus

---

179   "Das 7. Kap. S. Pauli zu den Cor., 1523," WA 12:114.6 (see also AE 28:1–56): "Additionally, a Christian is spirit and flesh. Because of the spirit, he does not need any marriage. But because his flesh is of the common flesh, corrupted in Adam and Eve and filled with evil lust, he needs marriage because of the very same disease, and it is not within his power to abstain from it. For his flesh rages, burns, and copulates like the animals (*samet*) just as much as anyone else's where he does not help it with marriage as with a necessary remedy."

180   "Das 7. Kap. S. Pauli zu den Cor., 1523," WA 12:113.24 (see also AE 28:1–56): "For though we are Christians and have the Spirit in faith, this does not abrogate God's creature, the fact that you are a woman and I am a man. And the Spirit lets the body go on with his manner and natural work, that it eats, drinks, sleeps, digests, excretes as somebody else's body."

181   In "Das 7. Kap. S. Pauli zu den Cor., 1523" (WA 12:134.11–22 [see also AE 28:1–56]), Luther rejects the "crowns of virginity." On the teaching on merits, see Pesch, "Die Lehre vom 'Verdienst' als Problem für Theologie und Verkündigung."

182   "Pred. über Gen. 4, 1527," WA 24:122.3: "Before Christ, virginity was condemned and no one was allowed to remain a virgin because of the coming Seed, of whom it was not known out of which woman He would come." Cf. "Pred. über Gen. 4 vom 26.5.1523," WA 14:156.21ff.; "Antwort auf dial. Hul. Nebulonis, 1542," WA 53:198.30–201.26.

Himself. There now exists the possibility of becoming a eunuch for the sake of the kingdom of heaven (Matt. 19:12), even of leaving behind one's family members (Luke 18:29f. and parallels). Marriage must not interfere with the Christian and his service in the kingdom of God.[183] The fact that Jesus participated in the wedding at Cana cannot be more important than the basic fact that He remained a eunuch for the sake of the kingdom of heaven.[184] In this sense, there exists a real decision for the celibate estate besides marriage.[185] Both estates are about joint service in God's kingdoms.

Next to this theological/exegetical line of thinking a theological/anthropological one has to be placed. This, too, is present in rudimentary form in Luther when he says: God's grace is necessary "for the heart also to be chaste."[186] The inner suffering of hidden unchastity is not overcome automatically by entering into marriage. In most cases, the will to marry implanted in us will assist us in our struggle for inner purity. Yet it, too, is perverted by sin. This is why, as Luther constantly enjoins, the spouse is not to be looked at according to flesh and blood but according to God's Word.[187] Could not the vow of celibacy be understood analogously? Luther, too, does not reject it completely. Under the all-sufficient and only saving sacrifice of Christ, he wanted to let the monastic life remain as an estate of bodily discipline, of concrete service to the community, and of prayerfully studying Scripture.[188] He did not want to retain lifelong vows. In his view, here something would be promised that is not in our hand. Yet could the same argument not also be advanced against lifelong marriage? Is not also by it praised the charisma of chastity that only God can give? Yet the difference mentioned by Luther remains. Whoever cannot keep the vow of the celibate estate without inner deformations may and ought to get married. The Church cannot discipline him in the same way as the person committing adultery or even, as happened during the time of the Reformation, have the

---

183 Luther's interpretations of Matt. 19:21ff. are compiled in Mülhaupt, *Evangelien-Auslegung*, 2:665–72. On the interpretation of Matt. 19:10–12, see Mülhaupt, *Evangelien-Auslegung*, 2:650–54, and Baltensweiler, *Die Ehe im Neuen Testament*, 102–12. On the "eschatological reservation," cf. Wendland, "Zur Theologie der Sexualität und der Ehe," 121–23.

184 Luther often builds his sermons on the marital estate on John 2:1–11; cf. Mülhaupt, *Evangelien-Auslegung*, 4:96–111.

185 "Das 7. Kap. S. Pauli zu den Cor., 1523," WA 12:105.5 (see also AE 28:1–56): "Now, since both are a gift from God, and marriage is given to everybody as a common gift, but chastity is a special peculiar gift given to very few people, it is shown here that each must examine himself whether he finds himself having the common or the special gift." Cf. Barth, *Kirchliche Dogmatik* 3.4:205; von Campenhausen, "Die Askese im Urchristentum," 138–53.

186 *BSLK*, 614.5f.

187 E.g., "Ausl. vom Mt. 5–7, 1530/32," WA 32:372.11–27 (see also AE 21:1–294).

188 E.g., "De votis monast., 1521," WA 8:604.9–39 (see also AE 44:243–400); cf. *Die Regel von Taizé*, 42: "If the celibate life brings with it a greater availability to occupy oneself with the things of God, it cannot be accepted unless as a means to give oneself for the neighbor with the very love of Christ."

civil authorities bring him back to the monastery. Despite this difference, which is diminished even more by the fact that Luther, according to 1 Cor. 7:10f., did not permit divorce in the case of a deep conflict between spouses or of one spouse's incurable disease,[189] it should be emphasized more what both marriage and celibacy have in common. In both cases, we are to receive trustingly the indistinguishable blend of fate and charisma out of the hand of the Creator and Redeemer. In the vow of marriage, as well as in consciously making oneself a eunuch for the sake of the kingdom of heaven, the point is this acceptance of fate and charisma as God's call, as *vocatio* into a *status*.[190] Where the legitimate objections of Luther are accepted, there should be no valid biblical argument left that would forbid those who desire to serve God in the celibate estate from doing what is demanded of those who desire to live their marriage before God.

In both estates, God calls us into His service in the secular as well as the spiritual kingdom. In both we lay hold of this call as being bound to concrete human beings and let ourselves be pointed and bound to them. In both it is important to struggle against unchastity and lack of discipline for the purity of heart and body. In both we take refuge in prayerful trust in God's command and promise. Both can ultimately only be lived successfully in looking up to the Lord.[191] Christ is not only *sacramentum* and *exemplum* of marriage but also, and no less, *sacramentum* and *exemplum* of celibately serving in the kingdom of God.

Luther's understanding of marriage shows the problem of his entire ethics. The spiritual interior of the heart is correlated strictly to the double commandment of love of God and neighbor. Here the *usus practicus Evangelii* rules; here the call sounds forth to obey spontaneously out of a liberated conscience. Yet this inner impulse does not fully penetrate the bodily man turned to the world. The New Testament attitude of the heart does not translate fully into a corresponding social order. The outward bodily man is, as it were, still under the patriarchal clan ethos of the Old Testament, which becomes concrete in the *usus crassus* of this commandment. The inner man renewed in the Holy Spirit and the superficial old Adam of the earthbound body are joined together in a somewhat forced manner. The superficial man surrounds the inner man with his hard and securely joined carapace, and

---

189   "Vom ehel. Leben, 1522," WA 10.2:291.15–292.6 (see also AE 45:11–49); "Von Ehesachen, 1530," WA 30.3:216.3–13 (see also AE 46:259–320).

190   Cf. *Denkschrift zu Fragen der Sexualethik*, 25 (no. 34): "There are single men and women who consciously do not enter into matrimony in order to be free for a special service or some other form of communal life. Such a decision can be founded on the certainty to follow thereby a call of God." Cf. Präger, *Frei für Gott und die Menschen*.

191   *Geistl. Weisungen zur Regel von Taizé*, 79: "Without this desire to see Christ, we cannot hope to remain firm in the purity of heart and flesh."

thus prevents through such means the growth into a living being that is part and parcel of spiritual Christian obedience.

TEXTS ON LUTHER'S UNDERSTANDING OF MARRIAGE

WA 2:166–71: Sermon von dem ehelichen Stand, 1519 (see also AE 44:3–14)

WA 6:550–60: from De captivitate Baylonica, 1520 (see also AE 36:3–126)

WA 8:573–669: De votis monasticis iudicium, 1521 (see also AE 48:329–36)

WA 10.2:275–304: Vom ehelichen Leben, 1522 (see also AE 45:11–49)

WA 12:92–142: Das siebente Kapitel S. Pauli zu den Corinthern, 1523 (see also AE 28:1–56)

WA 12:232–44: An die Herren deutschs Ordens, daß sie falsche Keuschheit meiden und zur rechten ehelichen Keuschheit greifen, Ermahnung, 1523 (see also AE 45:131–58)

WA 15:163–69: Daß Eltern die Kinder zur Ehe nicht zwingen noch hindern, und die Kinder ohne der Eltern Willen sich nicht verloben sollen, 1524 (see also AE 45:379–93)

WA 18:275–78: Christliche Schrift an W. Reißenbusch, sich in den ehelichen Stand zu begeben, 1525

WA 26:517–27: De Digamia Episcoporum Propositiones, 1528

WA 30.3:205–48: Von Ehesachen, 1530 (see also AE 46:259–320)

WA 32:369–81: from der Auslegung von Mt. 5–7 in den Wochenpredigten zur Bergpredigt zu Mt. 5:27–32, 1532 (see also AE 21:1–294)

WA 47:312–26: Predigten über Mt. 19:3–12 aus Mt. 18–24 in Predigten ausgelegt, 1537–40

From Genesis-Vorlesung, 1535–45: on Gen. 2:18ff., WA 42:87–105 (see also AE 1:1–359); on Gen. 3:16, WA 42:148–51 (see also AE 1:1–359); on Genesis 24, WA 43:292–351 (see also AE 4:1–409); on Gen. 28:1ff., WA 43:558–66 (see also AE 5:1–386); on Gen. 29:9ff., WA 43:622–24 (see also AE 5:1–386); on Genesis 28f. WA 44:304–78 (see also AE 7:1–377)

WA 53:190–201: Antwort auf den Dialogum Hulrichi Nebulonis, 1542 (writing against bigamy)

Wedding sermons on John 2:1–11 in Mülhaupt, D. Martin Luthers Evangelien-Auslegung, 4:96–111

Interpretation on Psalm 127f. in Mülhaupt, D. Martin Luthers Psalmen-Auslegung, 3:503–38

LITERATURE

Althaus, "Luthers Wort von der Ehe"; Die Ethik Martin Luthers, 88–104

Elert, Morphologie des Luthertums, 2:80–109

Kawerau, Die Reformation und die Ehe

Kinder, "Luthers Auffassung von der Ehe"; "Luthers Stellung zur Ehescheidung"

Lähteenmäki, Sexus und Ehe bei Luther (with further literature)

Lohff, "Die Ehe nach evenglischer Auffassung"

Piltz, *Luthers lära om äktenskapet*

Seeberg, "Luthers Anschauung von dem Geschlechtsleben und der Ehe und ihre geschichtliche Stellung"

Zarcke, "Der Begriff der Liebe in Luthers Äußerungen über die Ehe"; "Der geistliche Sinn der Ehe bei Luther"

THE SEVENTH COMMANDMENT[1]

WORDING AND STRUCTURE
OF THE INTERPRETATION

Following tradition, Martin Luther translates the Seventh Commandment as follows: "You shall not steal."[2] By this commandment, God protects the "temporal goods"[3] of our neighbor, the *res corporales*[4] that Luther moves to the center of his interpretation already in his early confessional manuals.[5] In the Small Catechism, this is paraphrased as "money or goods," as well as "goods and sustenance" (*Gut und Nahrung*).[6] While the negative portion, which prohibits forcible and cunning appropriation, places the easily understood term "money" next to the basic term "goods," the positive portion enhances the core term with the use of "sustenance" (*Nahrung*), which is difficult to grasp in its meaning. In the usage of the time, it not only denotes food and drink but also more broadly "livelihood," as this is hinted at already in the phrase of the Small Catechism, "need and sustenance" (*Notdurft und Nahrung*),[7] and becomes apparent in the conjunction "work and seek sustenance" (*erbeiten und Nahrung suchen*).[8] If the "goods" of the neighbor

---

1   For Luther's texts on property, labor, economy, see p. 285.
2   *BSLK*, 509.7, 555.24, 616.11; "Eine kurze Erklärung, 1518," WA 1:251.14; "Von den guten Werken, 1520," WA 6:270.26 (see also AE 44:15–114); "Eine kurze Form, 1520," WA 7:206.20. On the tradition, see Meyer, *Historischer Kommentar*, 90.
3   *BSLK*, 616.13. "Temporal goods" already in "Von den guten Werken, 1520" (WA 6:270.31 [see also AE 44:15–114]); "Eine kurze Form, 1520" (WA 7:206.21f.). "Eine kurze Erklärung, 1518," WA 1:251.15: "alien goods." "Kat.-Pred. zum 7. praeceptum vom 22.5.1528," WA 30.1:8.6: "temporale bonum in terris." "Heidelberger Bilderhandschrift" (Geffcken, *Bildercatechismus*, app., col. 7): "You shall not steal anybody's goods / then you shall be safe from the gallows and hell."
4   "Decem praecepta, 1518," WA 1:506.12.
5   "Eine kurze Erklärung, 1518," WA 1:251.15ff.; "Instructio, 1518," WA 1:259.2ff.
6   *BSLK*, 509.10, 509.12.
7   *BSLK*, 510.39, 514.3; cf. *BSLK*, 619.21 (LC): "money, wages, and sustenance."
8   "Von den guten Werken, 1520," WA 6:271.33 (see also AE 44:15–114).

include everything he owns, then "sustenance" (*Nahrung*) includes everything on which he sustains himself.[9]

In the Large Catechism, the reformer paraphrases the word "stealing" as
"taking somebody else's goods unjustly."[10] By doing so, he follows Augustine,
who coined the classic definition: "Under the name of theft he wanted the
meaning to be well-understood as every illegal taking of somebody else's
goods,"[11] which was handed down verbatim by Peter Lombard. It was slightly modified by Thomas and Bonaventure.[12] This general definition is unfolded in two directions: next to direct theft as "taking" and stealing "out of
sheer violence and blasphemy,"[13] Luther places the typical form of cunningly
taking advantage of a person in the transactions of economic life, gaining
possession "with false merchandise or dealings."[14] This, too, is broadly unfolded in the late medieval confessional manuals[15] and taken up by Luther
already in 1518.[16] Here, he places next to thievery, robbery, and usury the
employment of false weights and measures, as well as deception regarding
merchandise. Pointing to 1 Thess. 4:6, Agricola makes this aspect central;[17]
the catechisms prior to Luther's Small Catechism follow Agricola in this.[18]
In "Sermon von den guten Werken" ("Sermon on Good Works") and in the
catechism sermons, Luther adds taking advantage of the economic cycle and
overpricing by merchants and craftsmen.[19]

---

9   The word thus has the four meanings listed by Meyer, *Historischer Kommentar*, 244: (1) food;
     (2) livelihood; (3) fortune, income for meeting one's livelihood; (4) vocation, profession, activ-
     ity to earn one's livelihood. Here, perhaps with an accent on the fourth nuance.

10   *BSLK*, 616.17.

11   Augustine, *Quaestiones in Heptateuchum* 2, q. 71; cf. Serm. 178.

12   Peter Lombard, *Sent*. III, dist. 37.3 (PL 192:832); Thomas Aquinas, *Duo praecepta* § 1290: "In
     this commandment, every evil taking away is prohibited"; Bonaventure, *Collationes de decem
     praeceptis* 6:18 (5:528): "Theft is the handling of somebody else's goods against the will of the
     owner."

13   "Ausl. von Mt. 5–7, 1530/32," WA 32:394.25 (see also AE 21:1–294).

14   *BSLK*, 509.11; cf. *BSLK*, 617.37–45; "Kat.-Pred. zum 7.–10. Gebot vom 7.12.1528," WA
     30.1:77.30–78.5 (see also AE 51:155–61).

15   See the overview in Geffcken, *Bildercatechismus*, 80–87; the texts in Weidenhiller,
     Untersuchungen, 47, 67, 74f., 113, 151, 185, 193, 229ff.; and the compilation in Meyer, *Histo-
     rischer Kommentar*, 242f.

16   "Eine kurze Erklärung, 1518," WA 1:253.22: "Who uses false weight or measure or sells bad
     merchandise as good." Cf. "Instructio, 1518," WA 1:261.32f.; "Eine kurze Form, 1520," WA
     7:211.3; "Eine kurze Unterweisung, 1519," WA 2:63.21; "Decem praecepta, 1518," WA 1:502.12;
     "Pred. über Ex. 20 vom 5.11.1525," WA 16:515.19.

17   Agricola, *Christl. Kinderzucht* (MGP 21:33); cf. *130 Fragen*, quest. 123 (MGP 21:294); "Decem
     praecepta, 1518," WA 1:502.12–15.

18   E.g., Schultz, *Kat.*, quest. 47f. (MGP 21:214); Gräter, *Kat.*, quest. 15 (MGP 21:330); Althamer,
     Kat., quest. 33 (MGP 22:25); Sam, *Christl. Unterweisung*, quest. 116 (MGP 22:121f.).

19   WA 6:270.33–36 (see also AE 44:15–114); "Pred. über Ex. 20 vom 5.11.1525," WA 16:516.18–
     36; cf. *BSLK*, 617.43ff.

Additionally, there is in the Large Catechism another way in which a person breaks off and shortens what belongs to the neighbor,[20] which, in the Small Catechism, can only be indirectly derived from the positive terminology, namely, that we "neglect and waste out of laziness, lack of diligence, or malice" what belongs to our neighbor.[21] This is the sin of the servants, of hired hands, and craftsmen. In the early confessional manuals, Luther mentions only the corresponding guilt of the employer: the withholding of deserved wages.[22]

The positive phrase in the Small Catechism—"but help him improve and keep his goods and sustenance"[23]—is remarkable in two ways. First, while Luther in the Large Catechism mentions first "protecting" and then "promoting,"[24] here "improving" stands before "protecting." Luther certainly moved the three-syllable word at the end for rhythmic and mnemonic reasons. At the same time, he apparently wanted to accentuate what is positive: we are not to "break off or shorten"[25] what belongs to our neighbor but promote and improve it. Perhaps the reformer wanted to hint, at least indirectly, at the central sin of servants, with which he opens the list of sins in the Large Catechism[26] and which he always mentions as confessional formula for servants:[27] treating entrusted property carelessly and thoughtlessly. What is even more remarkable about this phrase is how strongly Luther urges us to understand our doing and leaving undone as an active contribution to increasing, not decreasing, the livelihood of our neighbor. This view emerged from the protective character of the Commandments. Perhaps there is still something of what Johannes Meyer pointed out: Our help is not to confirm and leave our fellow man in beggary and laziness but to get him out of there and place him on his own two feet.[28] In his writings on usury, Luther hints

20   *BSLK*, 616.15.

21   *BSLK*, 616.40. Cf. "Kat.-Pred. zum 7. praeceptum vom 22.5.1528," WA 30.1:8.11f.; "Kat.-Pred. zum 5.–7. Gebot vom 18.9.1528," WA 30.1:38.7–30; "Kat.-Pred. zum 7.–10. Gebot vom 7.12.1528," WA 30.1:79.10–15 (see also AE 51:155–61).

22   "Eine kurze Erklärung, 1518," WA 1:253.24; "Eine kurze Form, 1520," WA 7:211.5; cf. Thomas Aquinas, *Duo praecepta* § 1292.

23   *BSLK*, 509.12.

24   *BSLK*, 619.19ff. Cf. "Kat.-Pred. zum 7. praeceptum vom 22.5.1518," WA 30.1:8.16: "You shall not diminish or obstruct anybody's goods, but promote them"; "Kat.-Pred. zum 7.–10. Gebot vom 7.12.1528," WA 30.1:81.2 (see also AE 51:155–61): "You shall not do any damage to anybody's goods, but be fostering and helping wherever and however you can."

25   *BSLK*, 616.15.

26   *BSLK*, 616.36–617.14.

27   *BSLK*, 518.15–19, 519.3; cf. also *BSLK*, 504.45–505.1. On the current situation, see von Nell-Breuning, "Wo Diebstahl salonfähig wird."

28   Meyer, *Historischer Kommentar*, 243; cf. "An die Pfarrherrn, wider den Wucher zu predigen, 1540," WA 51:383.17–384.3. "An die Pfarrherrn, wider den Wucher zu predigen, 1540," WA 51:385.18: "No, this our Lord Christ does not want, that I with my goods become a beggar and make the beggar into a lord."

at yet another dimension in our relation to fellow man: we are not to subject our neighbor to us by our help, or force him under the yoke of Mammon, but help him to reach the freedom of the children of God in relation to earthly possessions.[29]

In the Large Catechism, the reformer places the prohibition of stealing under this scope: the holy zealous God watches over our human community and protects the possessions of our neighbor against infringements of our greed. In an artful arrangement, he unfolds this zealous watching of God over all sectors of our economic life together.

In a first set of thoughts,[30] Luther outlines this realm, uncovers everywhere infringements of our avarice, and places God's wrath before our eyes. (a) To do so, he sets out by locating the commandment in the whole of the Decalogue[31] and by a first definition: "Stealing means . . . to get somebody else's goods unjustly."[32] (b) Transgressing the prohibition of stealing, this "widespread, common vice,"[33] is pursued into all areas of life:[34] (1) The servants neglect and waste the goods of their masters.[35] (2) Craftsmen, workers, and day laborers get paid well for bad work and rob their employers in this way.[36] (3) In the trade and business life, one seeks to take advantage of another by all sorts of tricks and cunning.[37] (4) With the Roman *Curia* as their protectors, all banks and trade associations, which plunder all of Germany, are at the top of the guild of thieves.[38] (c) Luther summarizes transgression as well as fulfillment and places both under God's zealous holiness.[39] (1) This is life among humans: the little thieves are hanged; the big ones are honored.[40] (2) Nonetheless, the preachers have the duty to announce

---

29 "An die Pfarrherrn, wider den Wucher zu predigen, 1540," WA 51:398.23: "So very sweet is the juice of the apple in Paradise that they wanted Mammon to be their god and by his power become gods over poor, miserable, wretched people, not to help or rescue them but only to have them perish deeper and more." Cf. "An die Pfarrherrn, wider den Wucher zu predigen, 1540," WA 51:390.21–27; "Ausl. von Mt. 5–7, 1530/32," WA 32:410.6–411.37 (see also AE 21:1–294).

30 Section 1: *BSLK*, 616.12–619.40.

31 *BSLK*, 616.12–26. Already similarly in Thomas Aquinas, *Duo praecepta* § 1289.

32 *BSLK*, 616.16–20.

33 *BSLK*, 616.21. "Kat.-Pred. zum 7. praeceptum vom 22.5.1528," WA 30.1:8.7: "That is a widespread trade"; "Kat.-Pred. zum 5.–7. Gebot vom 18.9.1528," WA 30.1.38.3: "It is the most common vice."

34 A similar unfolding is already done by Thomas Aquinas, *Duo praecepta* §§ 1290–96. Cf. furthermore Geffcken, *Bildercatechismus*, app., col. 7, 42f., 64ff., 97, 103f., 134f., 154, 172, 216. The "Nürnberger Katechismuspredigten" additionally unfold the sins of the secular and spiritual authorities in great detail before the ears of the youth (Reu, *Quellen*, 1.1:492.15–493.7).

35 *BSLK*, 616.36–617.14.

36 *BSLK*, 617.15–36.

37 *BSLK*, 617.37–618.17.

38 *BSLK*, 618.18–35.

39 *BSLK*, 618.35–619.40.

40 *BSLK*, 618.35–619.17.

fearlessly to them God's judgment.[41] (3) God's commandment not only demands of us not to steal or decrease our neighbor's goods but also to protect and improve them.[42]

In a second set of thoughts,[43] which corresponds to the first one,[44] Luther describes God's zeal for a genuine community of labor and commerce among us. (a) God's judgment affects those at the bottom and those at the top. His curse afflicts (1) the faithless servants;[45] (2) the malicious craftsmen and day laborers;[46] (3) the merchants who "make out of the open, free market nothing but a flayed corpse and den of thieves."[47] (b) God's zeal for His Law among us (1) is taught by daily experience;[48] (2) thereby the cry for help of those oppressed gains power,[49] and (3) the spiritual and secular authorities are to assist God in this zeal.[50]

In conclusion, Luther[51] offers a summary of the interpretation of the commandment in which he (a) emphasizes helping our neighbor in an active way[52] and (b) turns our attention to the blessing Creator's promise of reward.[53]

THE PROHIBITION OF STEALING IN THE OLD AND NEW TESTAMENTS[54]

The prohibition of stealing (Exod. 20:15; Deut. 5:19) seems to go beyond the realm of sacred law into the realm of property law. However, as Albrecht Alt has demonstrated as probable,[55] this commandment, too, originally referred

41   BSLK, 619.17–29.
42   BSLK, 619.29–40.
43   Section 2: BSLK, 619.41–623.32.
44   This artful structure is foreshadowed in "Kat.-Predigt vom 18.9.1528" (WA 30.1:37.31–39.33). "Kat.-Predigt vom 7.12.1528" concentrates God's zealous watching (WA 30.1:79.15 [see also AE 51:155–61]: "I am the zealous God"), on hearing the cry for help of the oppressed (WA 30.1:78.13ff., 79.6ff. [see also AE 51:155–61]), and demands of the craftsmen to write the commandment on their tools (WA 30.1:80.8f., 81.6f. [see also AE 51:155–61]).
45   BSLK, 619.48–620.23.
46   BSLK, 620.23–621.2.
47   BSLK, 621.3–32 (quotation: BSLK, 621.4f.).
48   BSLK, 621.33–622.20.
49   BSLK, 622.21–623.10.
50   BSLK, 623.11–32.
51   Section 3: BSLK, 623.33–624.23.
52   BSLK, 623.33–48.
53   BSLK, 623.48–624.23.
54   Literature on this topic: Alt, "Das Verbot des Diebstahls im Dekalog"; Horst, "Der Diebstahl im Alten Testament"; Herbert Preisker, κλέπτω, TWNT 3:753–56; Gerhard Delling, πλεονέκτης, TWNT 6:266–74.
55   See n. 54 above. His view is taken up, among others, by von Reventlow, Gebot und Predigt im Dekalog, 79ff., and Stamm, Der Dekalog im Lichte der neueren Forschung, 58f.

to the person of the fellow man and prohibited taking a free, full Israel-ite citizen and fellow shareholder in the inheritance of the Promised Land and "enslaving him forcibly, be it for one's own use or for sale to others."[56] The statutes prohibiting this—Exod. 21:16 and Deut. 24:7, as well as ancient Near Eastern parallels[57]—suggest such an understanding, echoes of which can still be heard in the Talmud.[58]

By leaving out the object of the verb, the prohibition gained an all-en-compassing meaning and, at the same time, a breadth that is difficult to limit. Out of the core area of the sacred law that threatened the ban of God, it moves into the realm of casuistic law that had its place in life in the elders' court at the gate. While the sacred atonement, harsher than in the other legal codes of the Near East, often calls for the death penalty,[59] the substitutionary penalties for theft laid down in the covenant code (Exod. 21:37; 22:1ff.) are comparatively mild.[60]

The prophets Hosea (4:2) and Jeremiah (7:9) take recourse to the Deca-logue to show Israel her sins and to announce the judgment over its apostasy. In these contexts, stealing stands right next to the sins under God's ban—next to murder and adultery, next to false swearing and idolatry.[61] Yahweh's covenant zeal penetrates all areas of human community and covers the pos-sessions of the neighbor in a protective manner. Yet also in the widening and deepening, to which not only the prophets but also the Deuteronomistic preachers contributed, the Decalogue prohibition is limited to active infrac-tions. It prohibits the concrete actions by which we "take something away" and "bring it to the side."[62]

In the New Testament, the apostle lets also this defensive prohibition be surrounded and fulfilled in the loving dedication to the neighbor (Rom. 13:8ff.). Whoever joined the congregation as a thief, or perhaps even relapsed

---

56   Noth, *Das zweite Buch Mose*, 133.

57   *Die Gesetze Hammurabis*, § 14.

58   Cf. Gottstein, "Du sollst nicht stehlen." In Luther's arrangement of theft, judicially colored as it is, this crime is called *plagiatus* ("Decem praecepta, 1518," WA 1:500.37). In the short 1519 instruction on how to confess one's sins (WA 2:63.25), it is called *ablatio hominis*—there, how-ever, referring to a dependent human being.

59   See the list of the crimes deserving death and curse compiled by Alt, "Die Ursprünge des isra-elitischen Rechts," 320.

60   Proof-texts in Horst, "Der Diebstahl im Alten Testament," 19ff., and Hempel, *Das Ethos des Alten Testaments*, 126ff. Already Luther has pointed out this difference between adultery and theft in "Decem praecepta, 1518" (WA 1:500.37–501.37) and "Instructio, 1518" (WA 1:259.3ff.).

61   The prophetic preaching of judgment aims especially at the upper class in the capital cities Jerusalem and Samaria, which distances itself from the community and pushes the masses into the proletariat. Pertinent texts given by Friedrich Hauck and Wilhelm Kasch, πλοῦτος, *TWNT* 6:322.

62   On the etymology, see Kopf, "Arabische Etymologien," 169.

into thievery, is to purchase goods with the work of his own hands in order to be able to share with the needy (Eph. 4:28).

Out of Hellenistic and Jewish traditions,[63] the New Testament takes up the struggle against the "desire to have more." The thief and the greedy are handed over to God's judgment; they are denied a share in God's kingdom.[64] The congregation is to separate from them (1 Cor. 5:10f.; 6:10), since they reveal the evil in their hearts (Mark 7:21ff. and parallels), their state of being handed over to sin via God's wrath.

In this harsh *no* to theft and avarice, the habit of clinging to this perishing world itself becomes a target. The strictly futuristic/eschatological message of Jesus opens the Old Testament's faith in creation to this creation's rush to appear before God's face. The fact that we are being woven into this earthly world is not denied in this message in an ascetic manner; property and possessions, labor and commerce are not condemned in a rigorist fashion. Rather, they are accepted in unreflective casualness.[65] The merciless battle begins where man has lost himself to the world to such a degree that he is owned and ruled by it.[66] In the mouth of Jesus, Mammon appears as the adversary and opponent of God.[67] In addition to avarice[68] and striving for filthy lucre, which threatens also the servants of the Gospel,[69] there is, on the other hand, paralyzing worry.[70]

Both avarice and worry are fought while looking up to God as the Creator and the Vanquisher of the world. Paul formulates the core thought: "Possessing as if one did not possess; using the world as if one did not use it; for the form of this world perishes" (1 Cor. 7:29ff.).[71] This assault on the will to have as the "root of all evil" (1 Tim. 6:10) not only wants to strike the attitude of the heart,[72] but it also seeks the limitless willingness to help and have mercy that is lived out following Jesus. The call to follow Jesus is directed to the entire congregation and wants to imprint in a Christ-formed shape of

63 On this, see Delling, πλεονέκτης, *TWNT* 6:266–70.
64 1 Cor. 6:9f.; Eph. 5:3ff.; Col. 3:5; cf. 1 Pet. 4:15.
65 See the texts compiled by Weber, "Das Eigentum nach dem Neuen Testament," 492 (taken up by Thielicke, *Ethik*, 3, § 772). Cf. furthermore Bienert, *Die Arbeit nach der Lehre der Bibel.*
66 A certain parallel is found in Seneca, *De vita beata* 22.5: "At last, I own riches; you are owned by riches."
67 Matt. 6:24; Luke 16:13; cf. Friedrich Hauck, μαμωνᾶς, *TWNT* 4:390–92.
68 E.g., Luke 16:14; 1 Tim. 6:10; 2 Tim. 3:2.
69 E.g., 1 Tim. 3:3, 8; Titus 1:7, 11; 1 Pet. 5:2; 2 Pet. 2:3; cf. also already 1 Thess. 2:5; 2 Cor. 7:2.
70 E.g., Matt. 6:25–34; Luke 12:22–31; 21:34.
71 On this Bultmann, *Theologie des Neuen Testaments*, 353.
72 Already Clement of Alexandria in *Quis dives salvetur*: "Which rich person will be saved?" following Stoic philosophy and Philo of Alexandria, placed the decision that Jesus required of the rich young man in the inner life. Contrariwise, external wealth is seen as something neutral and harmless. Cf. Hauck and Kasch, πλοῦτος, *TWNT* 6:320f., 324, 330, and von Campenhausen, "Die Askese im Urchristentum," 128.

obedience.[73] Inner childlike freedom and joy in God show in stepping outside of the old human bonds;[74] in serving dedication to the new community of Christ;[75] and in imaginative, self-giving sacrifice,[76] because the believers know themselves to be covered by God's presence of grace and salvation.[77]

CHARACTERISTICS OF LUTHER'S INTERPRETATION

1. TENSION BETWEEN THE COMMANDMENT'S LITERAL MEANING IN THE OLD TESTAMENT AND ITS SPIRITUAL MEANING IN THE NEW TESTAMENT

In Luther's interpretation of the prohibition to steal,[78] there again appears the tension between the external carnal understanding and the inner spiritual view of the commandment. In "Decem praecepta" ("Preaching of the Ten Commandments"), Luther outlines, on the one hand, the five legally defined forms of theft,[79] delimits the area permitted for the charging of interest, and speaks out strongly against gambling. On the other hand, he focuses the positive meaning of the commandment on poverty of spirit.[80] Accordingly, its fulfillment reads in the confessional manuals: "Poverty of spirit, mildness, willingness to loan and give one's goods, living without all greed and avarice."[81] In "Sermon on Good Works," he impressively works out the inner attitude of the heart: poverty of spirit and mildness of heart grounded in trust in God are to overcome avaricious greed that ultimately is rooted in doubting God's help.[82] In the catechisms, Luther again underlines

---

73 Cf. on this Dinkler, "Jesu Wort vom Kreuztragen"; Schweizer, *Erniedrigung und Erhöhung bei Jesus und seinen Nachfolgern.*

74 E.g., Mark 10:21, 28ff.; Luke 14:33; Matt. 8:20.

75 E.g., Acts 2:42; 2 Corinthians 8f.; Phil. 4:14ff.

76 E.g., Mark 12:44; Luke 19:1ff.; 1 Cor. 4:1–13; 2 Cor. 6:3–10; 11:16–33.

77 1 John 3:1–4:21; John 13:35; 14:15ff.; 15:9ff.

78 An overview can be found in Hardeland, *Katechismusgedanken,* 161–70.

79 WA 1:500.34ff.: "Therefore theft is the taking of somebody else's goods against the will and without the knowledge of the owner. This means that if it takes place in the private sphere it is simple theft; if in the sacred sphere, it is sacrilege; if in the public sphere, it is embezzlement; if in the leading away of beasts of burden and animals, it is plundering; if in the leading away of men, it is kidnapping." Cf. "Eine kurze Unterweisung, 1519," WA 2:63.21–28.

80 WA 1:500.9: "The spirit of this letter is poverty of spirit, which is why it is manifest that without God's grace no one fulfills this law, because man, because of the vice of the first sin, is greedy by nature."

81 "Eine kurze Erklärung, 1518," WA 1:255.10; "Instructio, 1518," WA 1:263.29; "Eine kurze Form, 1520," WA 7:213.22; "Von den guten Werken, 1520," WA 6:270.28 (see also AE 44:15–114).

82 WA 6:272.20 (see also AE 44:15–114): "The cause of greed is distrust, but the cause of mildness is faith."

the protective character of the commandment: it watches over the possessions of the neighbor.

This tension between looking to the goods to be protected, on the one
hand, and, on the other hand, to the right attitude of the heart is connected—as already in the case of the Fifth Commandment[83]—with two different
words from Scripture. By means of the Old Testament prohibition "You shall
not steal," Luther already in the sermon on March 2, 1523,[84] unfolds the *usus
crassus et externus*, which is also going to be the emphasis in the 1528 sermons and in the catechisms. By means of Jesus' word in the Sermon on the
Mount (Matt. 5:40ff.), Luther paraphrases in the early confessional manuals
and in his writings on usury the *usus spiritualis et internus* of the commandment in three dimensions: "Giving for free, lending without interest, and
letting go in peace what is taken by force."[85] These different accentuations in
Luther's interpretations raise again the problem of rightly understanding the
Old Testament prohibition in light of the revelation of Christ.

The Lord, by taking up also this commandment—albeit indirectly—in
the Sermon on the Mount, reveals its spiritual meaning and unlocks its positive form. Luther emphasizes strongly the breaking in of the eschatological
dimension into creation. With the first of the Beatitudes, this commandment also seeks the poor in spirit.[86] It wants to disconnect us from depending on this world and its god, the powerless yet omnipotent Mammon. It
wants to strike at the root of our earthbound existence—that worrying/
greedy clinging to what is visible and at hand—and to focus our trust only
on the otherworldly and invisible God. Christ again erects over us the First
Commandment: what we first sought from dead Mammon, this we are now
to seek from the living God.[87] The Lord wants to establish in us "a peaceful,
pure, and heavenly life."[88] This is why He gives that threefold commandment, which He does not devalue as a counsel for the perfect but wants all
to observe strictly.[89]

---

83   Cf. pp. 226–30.

84   "Kat.-Pred. zum 7. Gebot," WA 11:45f.

85   "Gr. Sermon von dem Wucher, 1520," WA 6:51.11; cf. "Ausl. von Mt. 5–7, 1530/32," WA
     32:395.13f. (see also AE 21:1–294); "An die Pfarrherrn, wider den Wucher zu predigen, 1540,"
     WA 51:380.23.

86   According to "Decem praecepta, 1518," WA 1:500.3–11.

87   *BSLK*, 561.7ff. (LC, First Commandment), 563.11ff.

88   "Gr. Sermon von dem Wucher, 1520," WA 6:40.9.

89   Texts on this threefold commandment: "Kl. Sermon von dem Wucher, 1519," WA 6:3.5–19;
     "Gr. Sermon von dem Wucher, 1520," WA 6:36.16–31; "Pred. über Lk. 6:36ff. vom 13.7.1522,"
     WA 10.3:227.1–16; "Von Kaufshandlung u. Wucher, 1524," WA 15:300.26–301.27 (see also
     AE 45:231–310); "Pred. über Ex. 22, 1526," WA 16:554.18–26; "Pred. über Ps. 112, 1526," WA
     19:321.1–9, 321.13–32 (see also AE 13:389–420); "Ausl. von Mt. 5–7, 1530/32," WA 32:395.13–
     396.35 (see also AE 21:1–294); "An die Pfarrherrn, wider den Wucher zu predigen, 1540," WA
     51:337.30–378.26. Texts on the polemics against the understanding as a counsel: "Kl. Sermon

1. We are to lend to everyone who comes to us for help in his need without taking interest or insisting on the return. The command is not limited, as it was in Israel, to members of one's own ethnicity and religion.[90] It also includes our enemies and opponents.[91]

2. We are to give freely to everyone who needs and desires it.[92] This commandment also is hinted at in the Old Testament but is extended by Christ also to include enemies.[93]

3. Both instructions come to a head in the third one: "to let go in peace what is taken by force"[94] and to be ready, if the assailant "wishes to take more, to give that too."[95] Thereby Christians are forbidden to argue and sue for their possessions before secular courts. This is the unequivocal meaning of the Sermon on the Mount and is confirmed by 1 Cor. 6:6.[96]

These instructions are so radical and inclusive that they must raise the question of right purchase and property in general. When Luther looks to God's merciless *no* to man's clinging to this perishing world, then he accentuates this threefold commandment. However, when he looks to the neighbor and his "temporal goods," then this demand does not emerge in its harshness. In the few positive phrases of the Large Catechism, we find only hints at Christ's first two mandates: "Where he (the neighbor) suffers need, help, share, lend both friend and foe."[97] In the early interpretations, this was the goal of fulfilling the commandment: "willingness to lend and give one's goods."[98] Next to it stood as spiritual foundation the attitude in the heart: "poverty of spirit, mildness . . . living without any greed and avarice."[99] This

---

von dem Wucher, 1519," WA 6:4.12–5.22; "Gr. Sermon von dem Wucher, 1520," WA 6:38.1–39.5, 48.19–23; "An die Pfarrherrn," WA 51:393.23–33.

90 Thus Deut. 23:19f.; Lev. 25:36f.; see *Bill.*, 1:346–53.
91 "Von Kaufshandlung u. Wucher, 1524," WA 15:301.15–27 (see also AE 45:231–310).
92 "Kl. Sermon von dem Wucher, 1519," WA 6:3.15.
93 "Von Kaufshandlung u. Wucher, 1524," WA 15:301.5–14 (see also AE 45:231–310); "Gr. Sermon von dem Wucher, 1520," WA 6:42.36–43.27.
94 "Gr. Sermon von dem Wucher, 1520," WA 6:51.12. "Decem praecepta, 1518," WA 1:503.15: ". . . indeed, it is also not enough that you do not lust in your heart, unless you bear it in the greatest equanimity when what is yours is taken from you."
95 "Kl. Sermon von dem Wucher, 1519," WA 6:3.10.
96 "Gr. Sermon von dem Wucher, 1520," WA 6:39.26–40.7.
97 *BSLK*, 623.45.
98 "Eine kurze Erklärung, 1518," WA 1:255.10; "Instructio, 1518," WA 1:263.29; "Eine kurze Form, 1520," WA 7:213.22. Cf. "Von den guten Werken, 1520," WA 6:272.27–273.14 (see also AE 44:15–114).
99 WA 1:255. Cf. "Decem praecepta, 1518," WA 1:502.40: ". . . namely, poverty of spirit is his true intention in order to put to death that insatiable beast, the accursed hunger for gold, avarice, love of money, and greed, the root of all evil" (1 Tim. 6:10).

freedom from property, from clinging to this world while longingly waiting for the revelation of God's glory, is only hinted at in the Large Catechism's discussion of the First Commandment,[100] but it is unfolded in the Lord's Prayer. The willing, yet confident suffering of the cross with Christ,[101] as it is expressed, for example, in the fourth stanza of "Ein Feste Burg" ("A Mighty Fortress"), sounds forth only starting with the Third Petition.

The interpretation of the prohibition against stealing in light of the Sermon on the Mount—which Luther practices in an impressive way in his early confessional manuals, in the writings on trade and usury, and even in his interpretation of Matthew 5–7—recedes in the catechisms. Here the reformer remains, even in hinting at God's reward, fully within the earthbound horizon of the Old Testament.[102]

2. LUTHER'S JUDGMENTS ON PROPERTY, LABOR, AND MONEY

Luther's lively and drastic description of thievery—the "most common craft and greatest guild on earth"[103]—contains more indirectly than directly a judgment above all on the use of money, a judgment that offers the theological reason for tirelessly "holding up and driving home God's wrath."[104] This is why we must at least outline it.

The reformer offers a conditional *yes* to property and possessions; this is already given by his understanding of the Commandments as protective. Church doctrine had read out of the words of Jesus to the rich young man (Matt. 19:21) a counsel for those "perfect" ones who desired to be obedient to God beyond the commandments of the Decalogue.[105] Luther interprets those dominical words as a strict commandment but, at the same time, limits them to the *status confessionis*. In the realm of the Second Table, God grants us property and commands us to protect and increase it in order to be able to provide for the people whom God puts into our charge and to provide for the needy.[106] However, where the First Commandment and God's Word are at stake, there one is joyfully to leave everything and follow the

---

100 *BSLK*, 571.40–572.14. "Gr. Sermon von dem Wucher, 1520," WA 6:41.6: "Such commandments want to disconnect us from the world and make us long for heaven." Cf. "Ausl. von Mt. 5–7, 1530/32," WA 32:455.17–29, 457.17–33.

101 *BSLK*, 677.19–26.

102 Cf. *BSLK*, 619.9ff.

103 *BSLK*, 617.47.

104 *BSLK*, 619.8.

105 Cf. on this issue von Campenhausen, "Die Askese im Urchristentum," 121ff.; Lohse, *Mönchtum und Reformation*.

106 "Zirkulardisp. über das Recht d. Widerstandes gegen den Kaiser zu Mt. 19:21, 1539," Thesis 4, WA 39.2:39: "It is apparent that the Second Table commands to seek and possess everything, as he says: Do not steal." Cf. "Ausl. von Mt. 5–7, 1530/32," WA 32:307.4–309.20 (see also AE 21:1–294); "Pred. über Mt. 19:23ff.," WA 47:349.1–354.40; "An die Pfarrherrn, wider den Wucher zu predigen, 1540," WA 51:384.19–385.26.

Lord to the cross.[107] Yet as long as "God's cause" is not at risk,[108] God directs us to serve men. At the same time, He demands of us the poverty of spirit that is quite compatible with external possessions. Apparently, Luther addressed primitive Christianity's common possession of goods only once.[109] He considered it to be an exceptional situation that soon turned into poverty so that Gentile Christian congregations had to help out, all of which came to an end with the conquest of Jerusalem. "This is no example to be followed, but a miracle."[110] Today, the demand to purchase goods is in force.

However, as demonstrated already, Luther connects this with the spiritual asceticism of the heart. The Christian is free from the goods of this world; he lives among them only like a guest in a foreign inn.[111] He seeks no more than "fodder and a blanket," food and clothing. He does not forget that he has entered this world naked and bare and will leave it likewise. He clings to the Word applying to all, for him also "all men's rhyme remains: filling and wrapping, around and on, that's enough."[112]

The reformer develops a similar view of labor (*Arbeit*).[113] For him, the term still has the Old German and Middle High German passive overtones. Labor is not our free and spontaneous activity; it is the suffering imposed on us, our toil and need.[114] After the fall into sin, labor is connected with burdensome sweat and futile effort. Indeed, the characteristic of the world is: "It is futile to rise early."[115] By no means does Luther proclaim the maxim "work for work's sake."[116] He would have rejected such a thought as idolatry. The Christian labors not out of love of work, but out of love of God and neighbor. The Christian does not lose his heart to work, but in his labor, he raises his

---

107 "Zirkulardisp. über das Recht d. Widerstandes gegen den Kaiser zu Mt. 19:21, 1539," Theses 21–29, WA 39.2:40. Theses 23f.: "Because, then, what you rightly have and own in the Second Table for this life is joyfully to be given up for the First Table, that is, for eternal life. If the First Table or confession is not at stake, all things are to be bought, served, defended, administered."

108 "Pred. über Mt. 19:23ff.," WA 47:354.13.

109 "Pred. über Apg. 2:42ff. vom 12.6.1538," WA 46:428–33.

110 "Pred. über Apg. 2:42ff. vom 12.6.1538," WA 46:432.6. Similarly, for example, Bultmann, *Theologie des Neuen Testaments*, 577; von Campenhausen, "Die Askese im Urchristentum," 125ff.; Haenchen, *Die Apostelgeschichte*, 189ff.

111 Cf. pp. 130–31.

112 "An die Pfarrherrn, zu 1. Tim. 6:7f.," WA 51:375.28–376.30.

113 On Ps. 90:10, see Althaus, "Und wenn es köstlich gewesen ist."

114 In the glosses, the Old High German word *arbeit* translates the Latin terms: *labor, tribulatio, pressura, persecutio, afflictio*, etc. Synonyms are *angist, nôt, leit, sêr, müeje, müejesal, ungemach*. See the compilation in Geist, "Arbeit," 83ff.

115 "Vorl. über Ps. 127, 1533," WA 40.3:245.20.

116 Contra Elert, *Morphologie*, 2:468, and Holl, "Der Neubau der Sittlichkeit," 261f.; "Die Kulturbedeutung der Reformation," 474f.

heart up to God.[117] Next to watching, praying, and fasting, laboring is for the Christian a work to discipline the flesh.[118]

As he lets his labor be permeated by the prayerful look up to God, the Christian walks on the regal *via media*, right between the Scylla of self-reliance and the Charybdis of despair.[119] When he succeeds in his work, he does not inflate himself to the "I have done it."[120] If it does not succeed, he does not immediately cast everything down. Above all, he does not allow himself to be eaten up by torturous cares. He is to be diligent and provide in a wise manner for those people entrusted to him. Here the Franciscan "doing what is in us"[121] has its God-intended meaning and legitimacy. Yet our heart is to be free from clinging to labor, from hanging on to cares. Our doing and our leaving undone we may and ought to let go and place it prayerfully into God's hand of blessing.[122] In view of property and labor, Luther's thoughts circle one and the same mystery: to be sure, we live with our property and in our labor, but never do we live "out of" them, only out of God. Whoever wants to live "out of" his property and "out of" his labor sins against the First Commandment.[123] God gives him over to Mammon and allows him to enslave himself to the work of his own hands.

In these elaborations on labor and property, Luther combines three things: a serving dedication to one's neighbor, looking up to the returning Judge and Savior, and rejoicing in creation. (1) We have our possessions not as loot, but for service. This is confirmed by these words: "Your goods are not yours; you are only a steward, set over them to distribute them to those who need them."[124] (2) The burning yearning that rushes toward God through the world speaks in the following sentences: "Indeed, there has to

117 "Vorl. über Ps. 127, 1533," WA 40.3:237.28: " 'I believe in one God,' that is, God wants to remain God, the Creator and Maker of all things; but He wants to have us as cooperators, or rather instruments, not as originators."

118 "Ein Sermon von dem hl. hochwürdigen Sakrament der Taufe, 1519," WA 2:734.27. "Ausl. von Ps. 127, 1524," WA 15:367.17: "that labor be an exercise in this life to discipline the flesh."

119 "Vorl. über Ps. 127, 1533," WA 40.3:212.30: "Let us learn to march in the middle of the road."

120 "Vorl. über Ps. 127, 1533," WA 40.3:225.35: "When they sang: I have done it, this was soon followed by: I am lost." "Vorl. über Ps. 127, 1533," WA 40.3:226.29: "We condemn what . . . they paint on their forehead: EGO. God does not want to bear this addition, in fact, He cannot. Nor even should He bear it."

121 Cf. "Vorl. über Ps. 127, 1533," WA 40.3:234.20–36.

122 "Vorl. über Ps. 127, 1533," WA 40.3:253.35: "One must work physically and sweat, but in joyful conscience and trusting in God's blessing. . . . All our things depend on divine blessing, not our care." Further texts in Reymann, *Glaube und Wirtschaft*, 66–68.

123 "Ausl. von Ps. 147, 1532," WA 31.1:436.7 (see also AE 14:107–35): "Yet is not all our labor in the field, in the garden, in the town, in the house, in battle, in governing nothing in comparison to God, but is children's work by means of which God wants to give His gifts in the field, in the house, and everywhere? It is our God's *larvae*, underneath which He wants to be hidden and do everything." Cf. also "Vorl. über Ps. 127, 1533," WA 40.3:210.26–211.23, 255.13–256.24.

124 "Pred. über Ex. 20 vom 5.11.1525," WA 16:514.15.

be a great burning and fire of love that burns in such a way that the person can let go of everything—house and farm, wife, child, honor and goods, body and life—even despise and tread them underfoot, only to retain the treasure that he does not see and that is despised in the world but is offered only in the bare Word and believed with the heart."[125] (3) The childlike joy over the gifts of the Creator is heard in the following words: "Indeed, this would be a great life, eat and drink what God gives, be joyful with your wife and child—only let not that be all, as if it were your entire comfort."[126]

In light of this overview, we also have to understand Luther's attitude toward trade and the monetary economy. Again, he places this entire realm under the Golden Rule that wants to govern especially the Seventh Commandment.[127] With Matt. 7:12, Luther lets the *regula aurea* thrust toward us in a one-sided fashion and reformulates it negatively: "Where you see an advantage of the neighbor that you are not willing to grant to him, there love ends and the natural law is torn in pieces."[128] The law of supply and demand—"I may sell my merchandise at as high a price as I can"[129]—is not Christian; whoever acts according to it is subject to eternal damnation. The Christian says, "I may sell my merchandise for as much as I am supposed to or as is lawful and equitable."[130] The price of the merchandise should not be established according to the leeway of the free market, but according to one's expenditures.[131] Each should take as much as he has invested into the merchandise in terms of money, energy, and risk, so that he, "properly sustained,"[132] could serve his fellow men in the future. Luther suggests that the authorities have trustees and arbitrators establish standard prices.

---

125 "Ausl. von Mt. 5–7, 1530/32," WA 32:457.28 (see also AE 21:1–294).

126 "Pred. über Mt. 19:23ff. vom 7.11.1537," WA 47:361.23.

127 Cf. "Decem praecepta, 1518," WA 1:502.16–26; "Kl. Sermon von dem Wucher, 1519," WA 6:8.15ff.; "Gr. Sermon von dem Wucher, 1520," WA 6:46.9ff., 49.5ff., 49.20–28, 52.9f.; "Ausl. von Mt. 5–7, 1530/32," WA 32:494.28ff. (see also AE 21:1–294); "An die Pfarrherrn, wider den Wucher zu predigen, 1540," WA 51:393.18–29.

128 "Kl. Sermon von dem Wucher, 1519," WA 6:8.15.

129 "Von Kaufshandlung u. Wucher, 1524," WA 15:295.19 (see also AE 45:231–310); cf. *BSLK*, 621.9ff., 636.40ff. Konrad Peutinger, the legal advisor to the Augsburg merchants, wrote in a 1530 legal opinion (Strieder, *Studien zur Geschichte kapitalistischer Organisationsformen*, 62): "Every merchant legally sells his merchandise for as much as he can and is able to, and in this he does not commit anything against the law or enter into illegal agreements." Max Weber (*Wirtschaftsgeschichte*, 7) defines the price as "a compromise of chances of purchase that is only arrived at in the struggle of man against man on the market."

130 "Von Kaufshandlung u. Wucher, 1524," WA 15:295.21 (see also AE 45:231–310).

131 On calculating the price, see "Von Kaufshandlung u. Wucher, 1524," WA 15:295.31–298.4 (see also AE 45:231–310).

132 Fabiunke, *Martin Luther als Nationalökonom*, 148: "The goal of society's production . . . the safeguarding of adequate consumption that appeared 'natural' to him."

A difficult problem arose with the emergence of early capitalism. In the Large Catechism, Luther speaks of the "great, powerful archthieves"[133] under the protection of the *Curia*.[134] The reformer strictly prohibits sureties; in it, mortal man pawns his future, which is in God's hand alone.[135] At the same time, he considers every act of lending on interest, as well as gaining interest on capital, as egotistic exploitation of others and self-enrichment without any labor. He strictly insists on the commandment of the Sermon on the Mount: "Give freely; lend without interest."[136] "Whoever lends something and takes more or something better in return is a usurer and condemned as a thief, robber, and murderer."[137] He is to be excommunicated as a public servant of the idol Mammon.[138] Luther only wants to permit a "little emergency usury"[139] for the old and sick who otherwise would have to be fed by the congregation.

However, next to this strict commandment of the Sermon on the Mount as the basic order of Christian love, which Luther does not want to evaporate to some eschatological sign, stands the natural law of reason that has to rule in God's worldly realm. Here the Golden Rule does not apply only to the Christian in strict exclusivity and one-sidedness; here it enjoins both partners to act appropriately, which includes a justified interest. As the father of the house, because he has to take care of those who are his, cannot carelessly and thoughtlessly help every needy person; as the authorities have to punish injustice and contain violence with violence;[140] as the merchant cannot give for free but must demand an appropriate price, so it also seems sensible and necessary that the lender receives an appropriate compensation and share for the opportunities he opens up for the borrower of the money. Luther could not ignore these insights. Yet he demanded a strict distinction between legitimate interest (*usura*) and illegitimate usury (*foenus*). The secular legal codes should fix the standard interest rate at 4 to 6 percent, and the authorities should ensure that this be kept.[141] At the same time, Luther urged

---

133 *BSLK*, 618.20.

134 *BSLK*, 618.9–35.

135 "Von Kaufshandlung u. Wucher, 1524," WA 15:299.1 (see also AE 45:231–310): "Standing surety is a work too high for man and improper. With hubris it reaches into God's work." Cf. "Von Kaufshandlung u. Wucher, 1524," WA 15:298.5–300.25 (see also AE 45:231–310).

136 "Gr. Sermon von dem Wucher, 1520," WA 6:51.11.

137 "An die Pfarrherrn, wider den Wucher zu predigen, 1540," WA 51:367.30.

138 "An die Pfarrherrn, wider den Wucher zu predigen, 1540," WA 51:367.30–371.24, 421.29–422.30.

139 "An die Pfarrherrn, wider den Wucher zu predigen, 1540," WA 51:372.20.

140 "Gr. Sermon von dem Wucher, 1520," WA 6:37.32: "The laws permit to combat force by force."

141 On the standard interest rate, cf. "Gr. Sermon von dem Wucher, 1520" (WA 6:58.12–16, 59.14–18); "An die Pfarrherrn" (WA 51:332.32–333.21, 373.25–33); as well as the texts in Reymann,

Christians not to take advantage of the emergency situation of the neighbor and to distribute the risk between borrower and lender adequately.

These abiding insights and demands of Luther, however, are connected with his judgment on the economic situation in which an economic thought is intertwined with a theological one.

The reformer resists man's attempt to disconnect himself from the primary bonds to the soil and the small human community. In this, Luther saw the arrogant attempt to wiggle oneself out of the hand of the Creator God. Luther's *no* to modern development has three specific applications. We have already hinted at two of them and can briefly summarize them; to the third one we have to turn in greater detail. (1) Because Luther views labor as partaking in the burden of God's curse over the soil and because he warns against enjoying the world, he wants to stop far-flung trade. "This I know for certain, that it would be much godlier to increase agriculture and to decrease trade."[142] When we have "fodder and blanket,"[143] it is enough; luxury spoils man, which is why trade in luxury goods should be stopped.[144] (2) The trade companies reach beyond the immediate area of mutual obligation, beyond the community in city, land, and people.[145] No longer does man carry out his activities in reaction to the demands brought to him by the nonhuman creature and the immediate community. By means of sureties and interest contracts, he develops his activity in a planned fashion, autonomously reaching into the future. He begins to count on what he does not yet have. What monks did in the spiritual realm with their vows reappears among merchants in the secular realm in their contracts. They avail themselves of their future; they commit themselves and bind others. (3) The advance of the merchants was coupled to disconnecting money from landed property. Coined money became credit money as the credit for consumption was transformed into one for production.[146] Luther passionately resisted this step;[147] by doing so, he held on to the tradition of antiquity that the

Glaube und Wirtschaft, 50f. n. 2; Barge, *Luther und der Frühkapitalismus*, 15f.; and Fabiunke, *Martin Luther als Nationalökonom*, 124ff., 132ff.

142   "An den christl. Adel dt. Nation, 1520," WA 6:466.40 (see also AE 44:115–217).

143   "An die Pfarrherrn," WA 51:375.28–376.30.

144   "Von Kaufshandlung u. Wucher, 1524," WA 15:293.29–294.10 (see also AE 45:231–310).

145   Elert (*Morphologie*, 2:484f.) emphasizes this aspect and connects it with the nationalistic position of self-sufficiency.

146   Cf. Fabiunke, *Martin Luther als Nationalökonom*, 124f.

147   Therefore Marxist economic science characterizes Luther—whom Karl Marx "quoted most often in a positive sense among the bourgeois economists of Germany" (Fabiunke, *Martin Luther als Nationalökonom*, 157)—as "a petit feudal, petit peasant, and petit bourgeois economist during the period of incipient transition from feudalism to capitalism, as a conservative, even reactionary, economic romantic who did not want to leave behind feudalism and the simple economy based on goods in favor of capitalism and who, therefore, rejected the goals proclaimed by monetarism" (Fabiunke, *Martin Luther als Nationalökonom*, 148).

Church had taken up, but which since the fourteenth and fifteenth centuries had been softened.[148] Luther juxtaposed the sterile money and the fertile soil: "By nature, money is infertile and does not multiply. This is why, where it multiplies, as in usury, there it is against the nature of money. For it does not live nor bear anything as a tree or soil does, which gives more every year, because it neither is nor lies idly or without fruit as does the *gulden* by nature."[149] This argumentation limps, as Luther himself has to admit. As coined money, it remains sterile, but as means of credit, it can work. Thus the later theologians go beyond Luther by taking recourse to the Golden Rule. Aegidius Hunnius and Johann Gerhard[150] pointed to it, not to prohibit the taking of interest, but to give a reason for giving interest. The person who has been enabled by a creditor to improve his possessions will, out of human equity and Christian love, return an appropriate share to his creditor. Thus credit business opens up working and planning in the future.

Yet here again we run into what Luther actually fought against, namely, early capitalism's incipient emancipation of the secondary world of human planning from the primary world of our being directed to the soil. The reformer sensed something sinister in this process. He saw at work the primal human drive to power and increase of might. The quick multiplication of capital appeared to him uncanny and impossible to understand.[151] As one who had to live off of fixed income from landed property, he was painfully struck by the flip side of this multiplication, namely, inflation. As little as his contemporaries did he understand the individual factors working together in the process: the growing production of precious metals as well as

---

148   In 1139, the Second Lateran Synod decreed a general prohibition of charging interest; however, it was circumvented and softened. In a July 1515 disputation in Bologna, John Eck—in agreement with and likely also on orders of Jacob Fugger—sought to justify a credit given for trade by basing it on reliable contracts. By using the difficult construction of a threefold agreement (*contractus trinus*), he managed to show that an interest rate of 5 percent was permissible: "A gives B 1000 gulden in the reasonable hope that the deal will yield an earning of 10 percent (society contract). A leaves to B 2 percent of the hoped-for earnings under the condition that B is liable for the entire sum loaned by A (security contract). A—in order to secure a certain albeit modest gain—leaves to B 3 percent of the remaining 8 percent gains, if B pays him every year an assured 5 percent (purchase contract)" (Barge, *Luther und der Frühkapitalismus*, 11). This complicated thought brings about the Church's blessing for early capitalism. Yet the standard interest rate and the rate of gains in reality were as high as 20 to 30 percent. Between 1511 and 1527, the Fuggers of Augsburg would even make earnings of 55 percent each year (Strieder, *Jakob Fugger der Reiche*, 88).

149   "An die Pfarrherrn," WA 51:360.25. Luther explicitly quotes Aristotle and Cato, as well as the ancient tradition defined by them ("An die Pfarrherrn," WA 51:357.19–365.29; "Decem praecepta, 1518," WA 1:501.38–502.11). Cf. Barge, *Luther und der Frühkapitalismus*, 7–13.

150   Gerhard, *Loci* 24:118: "One has to distinguish between money itself and money used in business and trade. Money by itself, immediately and without regard of being used in business dealings, does not yield any fruit. But by means of use in civil society, it can yield fruit very abundantly." Cf. Elert, *Morphologie*, 2:488f.

151   "An die Pfarrherrn," WA 51:364.21–25.

the decreasing quality of coins, the importation of luxury goods, the accumulation of capital, and the emergence of monopolies, as well as poor harvests and population growth.[152] He felt he had to speak a harsh *no* in God's name to this development. Whoever in his lust for power would promote this emancipation, and thereby places the actual burden and risk on other people, would bring much suffering on the earth. Finally, God will give him over to the hands of men and ultimately throw him into eternal death. Thus the reformer seems radically to condemn modernity as it breaks forth into dominance.

However, in the separation as well as coordination of the two approaches of the Sermon of the Mount and of the natural law, there is a trace—albeit a rather indirect one—of a positive evaluation of the emancipation. These are no more than hints that would have to be articulated in a totally new way. Also the secondary world of planning designs can be, and wants to be, shaped as a human one by means of the Golden Rule. For fellow man and for the entire community, the space to enjoy life, freedom, and peace is to be gained in imaginative caring and providing. Yet this care of ours remains on this earth. Time and again, we experience that we cannot make or manufacture by ourselves what is essential. Where we attempt this, we overburden ourselves and become enslaved by our own plans. This is why also this struggle drives us into faith that prayerfully places into God's hand knowing and doing the right and the good, but also failure and lack of success. In all our efforts, we are free from ourselves, safe in God. These basic insights in Luther's evaluation of property and labor, money and economy remain. Their premature and one-sided identification with the precapitalist structure of society and economy is behind us and is to be broken up critically.

3. THE RESPONSIBLE PARTICIPATION OF MAN IN THE CIVIL AND SPIRITUAL KINGDOM IN GOD'S WATCHING OVER THE SEVENTH COMMANDMENT

Luther does not unfold the confusing web of trade and economy in the Large Catechism. Here, he consciously—"for the common people, a bit coarsely"[153]—works out only those things that are considered, or at least ought to be considered, theft in the common sense of good and evil, even already according to civil laws.[154] The vast realm of daily transgressions he places under God's holy zealous watching. God watches even where the human arm fails. He is, first and foremost, the advocate of those whom human

---

152 On this, see Eschenhagen, "Wittenberger Studien," 72ff., 83f.; Reymann, *Glaube und Wirtschaft*, 23f.; Barge, *Luther und der Frühkapitalismus*, 35ff.

153 *BSLK*, 616.34.

154 *BSLK*, 620.40–621.2.

society will not or cannot offer legal protection. He hears the cries of the oppressed and counts their tears.[155]

Luther describes both the wrath and blessing of God in bright colors and limits both, with the Old Testament, to this earth. Only in the enjoyment "with a joyous conscience,"[156] as was the case in the Fourth Commandment,[157] is his view of justification hinted at.[158] Stronger than at the end of the interpretation in the Large Catechism,[159] Luther presses the issue of God's promises of reward in his sermons on the Sermon on the Mount and in "Vermahnung an die Pfarrherrn, wider den Wucher zu predigen" ("Admonition to the Pastors, to Preach Against Usury"): Do not seek usury with the poor, helpless idol Mammon, or with men disappearing in their tomb, but with the living God. He alone is your Guarantor for time and eternity. "From here comes abundant life and everything aplenty both here and there eternally, without any harm to the neighbor."[160] Again, Luther takes recourse to the exuberant promise of blessing in Exod. 20:6.

Next to it, however, he places the threat of punishment. Both are concentrated strictly on this earth in the Large Catechism, because at stake is the protection of the temporal goods. Here, too, the age-old experiences of humanity and God's word of curse go hand-in-hand. God shows Himself as highly powerful in history. The blessing opens up an infinite horizon; it spans the generations. The curse, however, eats itself so deeply into the chain of generations that it breaks, or it lets the illegitimately gained goods disappear so that they cannot be passed on. The wisdom of the nations confirms the basic law of Exod. 20:5f.: "The preservation of God's grace for a thousand devout generations and the visitation of sins in the third and fourth

---

155 *BSLK*, 622.34–623.10. "Kat.-Pred. zum 7.–10. Gebot vom 7.12.1528," WA 30.1:79.7 (see also AE 51:155–61): "They will carry a complaint against you into heaven that will be too heavy for you, your house, and your children." "Gen.-Vorl., 1535–45," WA 44:82.24 (see also AE 6:1–607): ". . . it reeks all the way up to heaven and fills our God's nose so that He says: Stop it—I will hear no more of it."

156 *BSLK*, 624.10.

157 *BSLK*, 588.48, 590.2, 591.42, 597.24, 598.11. Cf. pp. 208–11.

158 "Kat.-Pred. zum 5.–7. Gebot vom 18.9.1528," WA 30.1:39.19: "If you truly worked diligently and faithfully and took what is just, you would have a propitious God who would bless also your wages and make you rich, and you would not have an evil conscience. Yet on the reverse side, if you do not do and have all this, then you would lose both the eternal and temporal good."

159 *BSLK*, 624.4–23.

160 "An die Pfarrherrn," WA 51:420.25. Cf. "An die Pfarrherrn," WA 51:418.32–420.33. Proverbs 19:17 is quoted here, as well as in the Large Catechism (*BSLK*, 624.4). "Ausl. von Mt. 5–7, 1530/32," WA 32:410.16 (see also AE 21:1–294): "But what devil tells you to do such works—thinking thereby to earn the world's honor and favor, which are uncertain and soon perish and can change—instead of investing them in a better way, namely, with God, where they cannot be lost to you, since He wants to reward you richly both here and there?"

generation thus pertain to the nature of blessing and curse."[161] The reformer here lists "sayings in all languages" and points to "examples that can be seen, grasped, tasted, smelled, heard, and perceived with all senses" that unjustly gained goods neither prosper nor are passed on to the next generations.[162]

To this experience accessible to all men, which manifests itself in the proverbs of the nations, is added the testimony of Scripture "with lots of thunder and hellfire that God wants to extirpate them (the usurers) in the third and fourth generation (as it says in the First Commandment)."[163]

God enforces His commandment in human community by very different means. He has engraved it into the hearts and consciences of man and has it proclaimed by the preachers of God's Word.[164] He has established civil authorities so that they, as His servants, would enforce the laws by means of the sword and rein in the all-embracing striving for profits using the fence of a just order. Lastly, it is not below Him to rein in the egotism of the one by that of the other; He even lets the unreasonable creature rise against the avarice of men. In the Large Catechism, Luther impressively describes these three dimensions in God's watch over the prohibition of stealing.

1. God keeps the greed of men at bay by pronouncing His curse[165] on what they stole together and exposing it to the forces of non-human and human creation. Luther mentions as a typical example the perishing of heaped-up treasure[166] and arson.[167] "This art God has mastered . . . to punish one thief by another one."[168]

2. God has charged civil authorities with the office of order.[169] By means of laws and orders, civil authority is to end at least public

---

161   Scharbert, "Formgeschichte und Exegese von Ex. 34,6f.," 144; cf. Scharbert, *Solidarität in Segen und Fluch im Alten Testament und in seiner Umwelt*; Koch, "Gibt es ein Vergeltungsdogma im Alten Testament?"

162   "An die Pfarrherrn," WA 51:397.26–398.19, 420.29ff.; *BSLK*, 621.40f.

163   "An die Pfarrherrn," WA 51:398.18. Cf. "An die Pfarrherrn," WA 51:398.19ff.; "Pred. über Ex. 20 vom 5.11.1525," WA 16:517.15ff.; "Eine einfältige Weise zu beten, 1535," WA 38:371.23 (see also AE 43:187–211); "Ein christl. schöner Trost, aus Röm. 8, 1535," WA 41:330.8; "Gen.-Vorl., 1535–45," WA 43:474.5–18 (see also AE 5:1–386). Luther adduces the late medieval proverb: "The third heir does not rejoice in the things ill sought" (Hempel, *Lateinischer Sentenzen- und Sprichwörterschatz*, no. 3853). On the tense relation between the general sapiential insight into a "fate-working sphere of action" and the Israelite trust in God's sovereign intervention, see Knierim, *Die Hauptbegriffe für Sünde im Alten Testament*, 73–112, as well as von Rad, *Weisheit in Israel*, 106–11, 127–30, 170–78, 245–55, 272–74, 283–85.

164   "An die Pfarrherrn," WA 51:397.26–400.20, 421.29–423.27.

165   *BSLK*, 621.20–32.

166   *BSLK*, 621.20–32.

167   *BSLK*, 621.44–622.20.

168   *BSLK*, 622.7. Cf. "Von Kaufshandlung u. Wucher, 1524," WA 15:311.8–32 (see also AE 45:231–310).

169   *BSLK*, 620.40–621.2, 623.21–32.

abuses, because it does not bear the sword in vain. According to Luther, civil authority has the task of watching over prices[170] and establishing the standard interest rates.[171] For this purpose, it is to set up an office of oversight and arbitration. It should harshly punish manifest usury[172] and is to stop monopolies by means of some kind of antitrust law.[173] Luther additionally ponders mandatory sales in emergency situations and demands establishing public supplies[174] and care for the poor and sick of the community.[175] These and other measures certainly point in the direction of the welfare state.

Yet to our ear they sound foreign, having an Old Testament foundation. Primarily, the authorities are thereby to protect themselves and their subjects against God's threatened wrath. It is not to "burden itself with other people's sins."[176]

3.   This is even more true for the spiritual government. It must shake up the consciences by means of the powerless word.[177] By doing so, it mortgages its own existence with God's Word, as it were.[178] In the background, Luther sees the word concerning the bloodguilt of the watchman (Ezek. 3:16–21), which is taken up in Acts (18:6; 20:26) and to which Luther returns tirelessly: "I want to do my duty. Everybody will have to answer for himself in his death and on the Last Day, and then certainly remember my faithful warning."[179] It is the office of the preacher, as well as that of the schoolteacher supporting him,[180] to hold up all of God's

---

170   "Kat.-Pred. zum 5.–7. Gebot vom 18.9.1528," WA 30.1:39.28f.; "Von Kaufshandlung u. Wucher, 1524," WA 15:296.11–16 (see also AE 45:231–310).

171   "An die Pfarrherrn," WA 51:372.27–373.24.

172   "An die Pfarrherrn," WA 51:365.30–366.25, 421.25–28.

173   "Von Kaufshandlung u. Wucher, 1524," WA 15:312.1–313.27 (see also AE 45:231–310).

174   "Von Kaufshandlung u. Wucher, 1524," WA 15:306.10–23 (see also AE 45:231–310); "Ausl. von Mt. 5–7, 1530/32," WA 32:439.20–441.35 (see also AE 21:1–294).

175   E.g., "Leisniger Kastenordnung, 1523," WA 12:23, 25f. (see also AE 45:176–94)

176   *BSLK*, 632.27. "An die Pfarrherrn," WA 51:422.26: "And even if they remained unpunished on account of their own sin, God shall nonetheless punish them on account of other people's sins so that they might become impoverished, perish, leave country and people behind, or at least totally dry up with their generation and family, as has happened to many."

177   *BSLK*, 619.17–40, 623.11–21.

178   *BSLK*, 622.49ff.

179   "Wider die Bulle des Endchrists, 1520," WA 6:617.5. From the writings on usury: "Gr. Sermon von dem Wucher, 1520," WA 6:36.5–15; "Von Kaufshandlung u. Wucher, 1524," WA 15:293.20–28, 313.22–33 (see also AE 45:231–310); "An die Pfarrherrn," WA 51:331.26–332.31, 421.29–422.30, 418.23–31. Further texts in Peters, *Glaube und Werk*, 188 n. 28.

180   *BSLK*, 623.11–21.

commands, regardless of the complaints, even of the baptized, and to save at least the youth from general decay. In his "Admonition to the Pastors, to Preach Against Usury," Luther accentuates this even more harshly. The servant of Word and Sacrament has to condemn usury publicly. He must excommunicate the person who lends on interest or overprices his merchandise. He shall deny him Absolution, the Lord's Supper, and a church funeral and say to him: "Why should I give my soul for you and to you and condemn myself with your sin? . . . Therefore repent and do what is right. If not, you might as well simply go to the devil without me and my absolution instead of going there doubly with my absolution and taking me along, without any guilt of my own, by virtue of your guilt. No, my friend. Here is how it works: You go ahead. I will stay here. I am not a pastor in order to go to the devil with everybody, but to bring everybody with me to God."[181] In this, the preachers themselves in their uncertain situation are in danger of seeking the favor of the members of their congregations on whom they, with their wife and children, are dependent and, by doing so, to neglect their office of watchman.[182]

We again see how Luther places civil authorities and the servants of God's Word under the one charge of God. Both have to watch over the keeping of the commandment: the authorities by means of law and ordinances; the servants of the Word, by means of instruction and warning. The authorities receive into their hands the sword; the servants of the Word are entrusted with the anathema of excommunication. Both are there to protect the people entrusted to them from the earthly and eternal effects of God's wrath. Both are not to bring themselves into condemnation by burdening themselves with somebody else's guilt. The difference is limited to the tension between the outside and the inside. The civil government ought not and cannot enforce the inner obedience of the heart by external means. It merely demands the external legality of the external action. The proclamation urges the joyous obedience of the child of God.

This is how the triune God fights man's egotism in this threefold manner and shows zeal for His sovereignty against the worshipers of Mammon: in the spiritual realm, by the proclamation of His commandment, by the enticing and luring of the *usus practicus Evangelii*, but also by the threat of excommunication; in the secular realm, by the laws and punishments of the authorities, but also by the violence of avarice unfettered by ourselves,

---

181   "An die Pfarrherrn," WA 51:370.31. Cf. WA 51:367.31–368.32, 421.29–422.18.
182   "An die Pfarrherrn," WA 51:412.23–34; "Ausl. von Mt. 5–7, 1530/32," WA 32:466.10–24 (see also AE 21:1–294).

which He directs back at us like a boomerang. In Luther's eyes, the greed that breaks out under the proclamation of the Gospel in all estates is a sign of the aging world coming close to its end.[183] His preaching against every form of clinging to the earth is especially harsh and implacable "because these are almost the most harmful plagues that are always around where the Gospel is taught and a person wants to live accordingly: first, the false preachers who corrupt the doctrine; second, the greed of the *Junker* that prevents a person from living well."[184]

LUTHER TEXTS ON PROPERTY, LABOR, AND THE ECONOMY

WA 6:3–8: (Kleiner) Sermon von dem Wucher, 1519

WA 6:36–60: (Großer) Sermon von dem Wucher, 1520

WA 10.3:222–27: Predigt über Lk. 6:36ff. vom 13.7.1522

WA 15:293–313: Von Kaufshandlung und Wucher, 1524

WA 32:368–97, 436–72: from Wochenpredigten über Mt. 5–7 (Ausl. von Mt. 5–7), 1530/32 (see also AE 21:1–294)

WA 39.2:39–51: Thesen d. Zirkulardisp. über das Recht d. Widerstandes gegen den Kaiser zu Mt. 19:21, 1539

WA 40.3:202–69: Vorl. über Ps. 127, 1533

WA 40.3:269–309: Ausl. von Ps. 128, 1533

WA 51:200–264: Ausl. von Ps. 101, 1534/35 (see also AE 13:143–264)

WA 51:331–424: An die Pfarrherrn, wider den Wucher zu predigen, 1540

LITERATURE

Eschenhagen, "Wittenberger Studien"

Geist, "Arbeit: Die Entscheidung eines Wortwertes durch Luther"

Reymann, *Glaube und Wirtschaft bei Luther*

Barge, *Luther und der Frühkapitalismus*

Elert, *Morphologie des Luthertums*, 2:440–520

Kahlert, "Luthers und Melanchthons Stellung zu den Wirtschaftsfragen ihrer Zeit"

Fabiunke, *Martin Luther als Nationalökonom*

Althaus, *Die Ethik Martin Luthers*, 105–15

---

183 "Ausl. von Mt. 5–7, 1530/32," WA 32:451.29 (see also AE 21:1–294): "What is this world, other than a great, vast, wild sea of all malice and rascality, decorated with good appearance and paint, which can never be fathomed? This is true especially now during these last days, which is a sign that it will stand not much longer and has come close to the tomb. For it is as one says: The older, the stingier, the longer, the worse; and everything becomes so greedy that no one can have food or drink before the other anymore, though everything is given in sufficient amounts by God. Yet this is the reward for the ingratitude and disrespect shown to the Gospel."

184 "Ausl. von Mt. 5–7, 1530/32," WA 32:437.13 (see also AE 21:1–294).

THE EIGHTH COMMANDMENT[1]

WORDING OF THE COMMANDMENT
AND ITS INTERPRETATION AND ARRANGEMENT
IN THE LARGE CATECHISM

The translations of the Eighth Commandment vary slightly: "You shall not speak false testimony against your neighbor."[2] Following tradition, Luther wavers between *Zeugnis* and *Gezeugnis* for *testimonium*. *Loqueris* he typically translates verbatim as "speak"—here and there also with "give,"[3] as is done in most of the late medieval texts.[4] More conscious than Augustine and the tradition,[5] Luther consistently adds "against your neighbor"[6] and thereby underlines the specific direction of the commandment toward the neighbor, which characterizes his interpretation.

The interpretation of the Small Catechism, following Augustine, goes beyond the original limitation of the commandment to the witness in court and is directed against lying in general. The commandment seeks a "peaceful, helpful tongue that does not hurt anyone but helps everyone."[7] It not only prohibits lying assertions about the neighbor, but it even prohibits us from dragging the secret sins of the neighbor into the light and discussing

---

1   For texts on the Eighth Commandment, see pp. 302.

2   *BSLK*, 509.16 (SC). Cf. "Eine kurze Erklärung d. 10 Gebote, 1518," WA 1:251.19. *BSLK*, 555.25 (LC) reads "no" instead of "not." *BSLK*, 624.25 (LC), and "Eine kurze Form d. 10 Gebote, 1520" (WA 7:206.24) read "Gezeugnis" instead of "Zeugnis."

3   "Eine kurze Unterweisung, wie man beichten soll, 1519," WA 2:63.55; "Von den guten Werken, 1520," WA 6:273.15 (see also AE 44:15–114).

4   See Meyer, *Historischer Kommentar*, 90.

5   On Augustine, see Rentschka, *Dekalogkatechese*, 128. On the medieval confessional manuals, see Meyer, *Historischer Kommentar*, 90.

6   It is missing only at *BSLK*, 624.40 (LC), and "Eine kurze Unterweisung," WA 2:63.35.

7   "Eine kurze Form, 1520," WA 7:213.27. Cf. "Eine kurze Erklärung, 1518," WA 1:255.13; "Instructio pro confessione peccatorum, 1518," WA 1:263.32; "Decem praecepta, 1518," WA 1:514.25: "This commandment requires a tongue that is faithful, just, helpful, harmless, and totally given to the services of the brother, and this out of the most intimate favor of the heart."

them with others.[8] The interpretation is strictly bound to a concrete situation: We are in a conversation with a third party about a neighbor without
this neighbor's knowledge or even his presence. In this concrete situation,
one is not to infringe on the honor of the absent but is to defend it.

The defensive prohibition is paraphrased by the four verbs: "lie, betray,
slander, or hurt one's reputation."[9] The first verb, *belügen*, presupposes a
different situation from our modern understanding, namely, the personal,
face-to-face interaction with one's neighbor, for indeed only in this manner
could we lie to him. For Luther, however, *belügen* means to attach lies to or
to heap lies on another.[10] *Betraying* paraphrases a loveless disclosure of secret shortcomings or sins that is done "not on orders or for improvement."[11]
Here Luther holds: "I may well see and hear that my neighbor sins, but I
am not ordered to pass this on to others."[12] *Afterreden* ("calumny") is a Low
German word that appears in this or a similar way quite frequently[13] in confessional manuals. It describes the act of the slanderer:[14] He neither directly
and secretly admonishes the person slandered nor brings the matter before
the responsible bearers of God's governments. Rather, he slanders the other
behind his back before a third party[15] who need not be concerned about the
matter.[16] The last expression, "hurt one's reputation," looks to the result of the
whole activity: the neighbor's "reputation," his honor, his right, and his good
name[17] are taken away from him. Thus the four verbs highlight individual

---

8   *BSLK*, 626.38–49, 633.24–30.

9   *BSLK*, 509.20.

10   According to Ebeling, *Der Kleine Katechismus Luthers*, 25.

11   *BSLK*, 632.12.

12   *BSLK*, 627.25. A compilation quite similar is found in Nicolas of Lyra (see Geffcken, *Bildercat-echismus*, 88).

13   *Achtersprake* (Geffcken, *Bildercatechismus*, app., col. 136f.); *achter* ("after") *kotzen* (Geffcken, *Bildercatechismus*, 93, and app., col. 8, 126); *achterklappen* (Geffcken, *Bildercatechismus*, app., col. 155, 173).

14   *BSLK*, 627.1: "*afterreden oder verleumbden*" calumny or slander. Cf. "Pred. zum 8.–10. Gebot vom 3.3.1523," WA 11:47.331ff.; "Pred. über Ex. 20:16 vom 12.11.1525," WA 16:523.19ff.; "Nürnberger Katechismuspredigten" (Reu, *Quellen*, 1.1:498.32ff.).

15   See Laurent/Jan van Rode in Geffcken, *Bildercatechismus*, app., col. 85. Cf. Geffcken, *Bildercat-echismus*, app., col. 97, 155.

16   In the Large Catechism (*BSLK*, 627.40–628.21), Luther describes the sin of the "*Afterreder*" in a dual direction. Our neighbor is ashamed of his misstep and wants to keep it concealed. As a slanderer, we drag it into broad daylight and wallow in the sin like sows in manure ("Pred. über Ex. 20:16 vom 12.11.1525," WA 16:524.1): "Qui autem ex aliorum peccatis detrahendo delectantur, sunt ut sues, Dreckfresser." At the same time, we reach into God's office of judge and commit the crime of treason, *crimen laesae maiestatis*.

17   *BSLK*, 624.30: "Honor and good reputation"; *BSLK*, 624.34: "reputation, name [*Glimpf*], and justice"; *BSLK*, 629.9: "honor and name [*Glimpf*]"; "Pred. über Ex. 20:16 vom 12.11.1525," WA 16:519.25: "honor and name [*Name*]"; "Nürnberger Katechismuspredigten," Reu, *Quellen*, 1.1:496.12: "name [*Name*], reputation, repute"; cf. "Nürnberger Katechismuspredigten," Reu, *Quellen*, 1.1:496.26ff.

aspects of one and the same sin of the tongue. "Made-up sins are heaped on the neighbor; real sins are mercilessly exposed. With all this one stays behind the neighbor's back, and thus his good reputation is destroyed."[18]

The adverb "falsely" recalls "false testimony" and is therefore probably attached to all four verbs. For his part, Luther first, with tradition,[19] liked to use "harmfully,"[20] whereby attention is drawn more to the resulting damage. The adverb "falsely" looks more to the way the slanderer acts: he is unable to corroborate publicly the accusations brought against the neighbor, nor does he want to do so, but he secretly speaks to third parties behind the back of the affected because all this is not done to better the neighbor or out of love for the truth.[21] As Luther shows in the Large Catechism,[22] there is an uncovering of our neighbor's sins that is commanded by God. The little word "falsely" keeps the door open for this as it points to what is positive out of the negation.

The three positive terms—"excuse him and speak well of him and explain everything in the best way"[23]—want to help shore up the neighbor's honor. In them, too, there is a visible analogous movement. By the "excusing," we cover the shortcomings and sins of the neighbor; by "speaking well of him," we adorn his honor. The third term, then, shows us the all-embracing basic striving as well as the actual goal of our action: we turn the bad into good by "interpreting all things well and explaining them in the best way or making allowances."[24]

Here, then, the Old Testament prohibition also shows its New Testament interior, its "true and spiritual understanding."[25] We are no longer a lying witness against the good reputation of our neighbor; we are henceforth a true advocate and defender of our neighbor, even where he has exposed his faults. Thus we show ourselves to be sons of the Paraclete who holds up for us the good word of adoption in Christ against the accusation of Satan and of our own conscience.[26]

---

18   Meyer, *Historischer Kommentar*, 250.

19   Cf. Geffcken, *Bildercatechismus*, app., col. 104, 136, 185; and Weidenhiller, *Untersuchungen*, 76.

20   "Eine kurze Erklärung, 1518," WA 1:253.29; "Eine kurze Form, 1520," WA 7:211.15: "Who lies and deceives harmfully."

21   *BSLK*, 631.34–38.

22   *BSLK*, 630.8–632.6.

23   *BSLK*, 509.22 (SC).

24   *BSLK*, 632.50. The positive summary in the Large Catechism (*BSLK*, 632.7–21) structures somewhat differently. Here, what summarizes is mentioned first: "say ... the best of everyone." Then follows the unfolding in the two directions, namely, covering of shortcomings and the adorning of honor.

25   "Decem praecepta, 1518," WA 1:514.35.

26   According to "Decem praecepta, 1518," WA 1:514.20–25.

If, in the Small Catechism, the reformer has broadened the commandment to apply to all sins of the tongue against the "neighbor's temporal
honor and good reputation,"[27] then it appears to have vacated its original
Sitz im Leben. After all, the prohibition originally was about the function of
the public witness or accuser before the legal community assembled "in the
gate" and not about the secret slandering of the neighbor behind his back.
In the Large Catechism, Luther aims at this original situation, but he does so
in the depth mandated by the New Testament. He raises the positive question: What has to be done for the betterment of the neighbor and the good
of the community? Because of this question, the interpretation in the Large
Catechism gains a dual scope and the following structure.[28]

The commandment protects the neighbor's honor.[29] (a) In the Old Testament, it referred to the witness (and the judge) in the public trial.[30] (b) In
its spiritual sense, it includes also the good battle for the truth of the Gospel.[31] (c) At the same time, it must be broadened to apply to "every sin of the
tongue by which one may harm the neighbor or step on his toes."[32]

At this point, attention must be paid to the dual service demanded by
this commandment: on the one hand, in the specific office and government
of God; on the other hand, in the general service entailing love of neighbor.[33]
(a) Whoever does not hold God's punishing office is not to reveal secret sins
in a slanderous manner. By doing so, he would infringe on God's government and commit the *crimen laesae maiestatis*, [high] treason.[34] (b) Whoever serves in office has to uncover and punish what is hidden.[35]

Christ has established the true order of punishing secret sin to better,
not to harm, the brother in Matt. 18:15–18.[36] (a) As the "daily government

---

27 "Eine kurze Form, 1520," WA 7:206.21.

28 Sections 1–3 follow quite closely "Katechismuspredigt zum 8.–10. Gebot vom 19.9.1528" (WA
    30.1:39.35–42.8). The summary is designed based on the schematic worked out on the Fifth
    Commandment (*BSLK*, 632.7–633.30) and picks up the reference to 1 Cor. 12:22f. in "Katechis-
    muspredigt zum 7.–10. Gebot vom 7.12.1528" (WA 30.1:82.3–6 [see also AE 51:155–61]).

29 Section 1: *BSLK*, 624.28–627.16, according to "Kat.-Pred. zum 8.–10. Gebot vom 19.9.1528,"
    WA 30.1:39.35–40.33.

30 *BSLK*, 625.6–626.16.

31 *BSLK*, 626.17–37.

32 *BSLK*, 626.38–627.16 (quote: *BSLK*, 626.39). "Kat.-Pred. zum 8.–10. Gebot vom 19.9.1528,"
    WA 30.1:40.26: "Every sin of the tongue is forbidden, which we can commit by the tongue, by
    which we can harm the neighbor."

33 Section 2: *BSLK*, 627.17–630.7, according to "Kat.-Pred. zum 8.–10. Gebot vom 19.9.1528,"
    WA 30.1:40.33–41.16.

34 *BSLK*, 627.40–629.24. On *crimen laesae maiestatis*, see the commentary on the Fourth Com-
    mandment, pp. 210–12 and n. 199.

35 *BSLK*, 629.25–630.7.

36 Section 3: *BSLK*, 630.8–632.6, according to "Kat.-Pred. zum 8.–10. Gebot vom 19.9.1528," WA
    30.1:41.16–42.8.

of the house" shows, it begins with the secret rebuke in private.[37] (b) If this does not work, witnesses are to be drawn in. If necessary, the matter has to be brought "publicly before the congregation."[38] (c) Public sin, on the other hand, must be punished publicly.[39] In conclusion, Luther offers a positively phrased summary of the commandment.[40] He (a) underlines it by referencing the Golden Rule (Matt. 7:12),[41] as well as natural behavior toward one's own body (1 Cor. 12:22f.),[42] and (b) calls for the fulfillment of the commandment by looking up to God's hand of blessing.[43]

THE PROHIBITION AGAINST FALSE WITNESS AS WELL AS LYING IN GENERAL IN THE OLD AND NEW TESTAMENT[44]

The wording of the prohibition varies in the Decalogue: in Exod. 20:16 the established term is 'ēd šeqer, "lying witness,"[45] which Deut. 5:20 paraphrases and broadens in a sermon-like way as ēd šāw'. In both cases, 'ēd is to be translated as referring to a witnessing person, not (as Luther does when he follows the tradition) as referring to his testimony. The word šeqer means, first, the lie, and then, based on this, also what is deceitful and useless. In the case of šāw', the meaning of "empty, unreal" is primary, which secondarily moves into what is "unreal" and lying.[46] The unique Deuteronomistic phrase 'ēd šāw' wants to stop even those statements that no longer can be qualified as manifest lies.

The verb 'anah often means "to answer," but it can, as in this case, also become the technical term for the parties answering questions before a court, as God's accusation in Mic. 6:1–5, which has been integrated into the improperia of Good Friday, shows. Or it denotes the statements of the witness (Num. 35:30).

Thus the prohibition reads: "You shall not (in court) make statements against your neighbor as a lying witness!" As Luther shows in the Large

---

37 BSLK, 630.8–631.2.

38 BSLK, 631.3–38.

39 BSLK, 631.39–632.6.

40 Section 4: BSLK, 632.7–633.30.

41 BSLK, 632.21–28.

42 BSLK, 632.29–46.

43 BSLK, 632.46–633.30.

44 Literature: Fichtner, "Der Begriff des 'Nächsten' im Alten Testament mit einem Ausblick auf Spätjudentum und Neuem Testament"; Stoebe, "Das achte Gebot"; Johannes Fichtner and Heinrich Greeven, πλησίον, TWNT 6:309–14, 314–16.

45 Thus also Ps. 27:12; Prov. 6:19; 12:17; 14:5; 19:5, 9; 25:18.

46 According to Stamm, Der Dekalog im Lichte der neueren Forschung, 59f.

Catechism,[47] the place of this prohibition in the life of the Old Testament is the legal community gathered "in the gate." It prohibits the "lying statement of a witness in the trial."[48] Thereby it protects the Israelite citizen's honor and access to justice as a fellow member of the Yahweh covenant, as well as of the legal community,[49] and addresses adult men. The prohibition is not directed against lying in general but protects the concrete fellow covenant members with whom one interacts in this specific situation.

The prohibition is unfolded in the manuals for judges (Exod. 23:1–9; Lev. 19:15–18; Deut. 16:19) that, however, do not—as Luther's hint[50] suggests and as his interpretations enunciate[51]—mean professional judges, but exhort "all free Israelites who participated and decided in the local legal community."[52] They are not to show any partiality, neither twisting the rights of the poor and oppressed out of fear of the rich and powerful nor favoring the poor out of pity (Lev. 19:15). They are also to grant legal protection to the stranger who does not have direct access to the court. They are neither to take bribes nor to decide matters out of anger or personal vengeance. They are neither to help the evildoer nor twist the laws in general or consent in such twisting of the laws.

Originally, the prohibition might have been correlated even more directly to the Yahweh congregation and its sacred laws. Hans Joachim Stoebe points to Deut. 19:16–18, which, in a reworked and diluted statute, speaks of an "accuser concerning an act of violence."[53] In light of Lev. 5:1; Jer. 29:23; Deut. 13:6ff., he wants to assume that it is actually about an Israelite who became witness to an act of violence or to an act of blasphemy punishable by Yahweh's ban. He then would have the duty to stand up as a public accuser in order to prevent the bloodshed or the blasphemy from affecting the whole congregation.[54] Accordingly, the Eighth Commandment would then be set against an abuse of such a public accusation of an act of violence;

---

47   BSLK, 624.42–625.5.

48   Noth, Das zweite Buch Mose, 133.

49   The word rea' means, "especially in the Deuteronomy but also in the holiness code, the fellow member of the covenant, the member of the congregation of God"—in general, "the person of personal choice, friend and lover, additionally, the fellow man, in the most general sense the other" (Fichtner, "Der Begriff des 'Nächsten' im Alten Testament mit einem Ausblick auf Spätjudentum und Neuem Testament," 41).

50   BSLK, 625.26–43.

51   "Dtn.-Vorl., 1523/24 zu Dtn. 16:19," WA 14:664–67 (see also AE 9:1–311); "Predigten über Ex. 23:1–9, 1526," WA 16:564–73.

52   Noth, Das zweite Buch Mose, 152; cf. Noth, Das dritte Buch Mose, 122.

53   Stoebe, "Das achte Gebot," 120–26. Von Reventlow, Gebot und Predigt im Dekalog, 82f., follows Stoebe. Stamm, "Dreißig Jahre Dekalogforschung," 300f., has a different view.

54   Stoebe, "Das achte Gebot," 125: "For the community in which it takes place, an unjust accusation apparently represents the same burden that would exist if the deed in question had actually been carried out. Consequently, it has to be punished in the same way."

here, the one shown to lie also would fall under the ban (Deut. 19:19).[55] This connection to sacred law is supported by parallel prescriptions in the Code of Hammurabi,[56] as well as by the observation that in some enumerations of the commandments of the Decalogue the Eighth Commandment comes close to, and becomes similar to, the desecration of the name of Yahweh,[57] because perjury was committed by calling on the name of God.[58]

Whether this prohibition was originally at home in the primeval sphere of taboo of the sacred curse of the ban or perhaps more in the legal community "in the gate," its integration into the Decalogue confirms this: it is not only about the private honor and public access to justice of the Israelite man but also about the divine Lord of the covenant watching over the holiness of His covenant people. In the prophetic woes over the upper class in the capital cities,[59] in the psalms of lament, in the songs of confidence of those wrongly accused,[60] and in the warning of the wisdom literature against lying testimony,[61] this prohibition begins to break up the narrow realm of formal legal acts and to permeate human life together.

In the New Testament, the congregation of God is distanced from what is political and national. In view of the secular courts, the apostle admonishes the "saints" who will judge the world not to take their legal arguments before those outside (1 Cor. 6:1–8). According to the narrative of Ananias and Sapphira (Acts 5:1–11), God's Spirit Himself executes the ban on the liars, no longer by the physical sword or the fists of the congregation of Yahweh[62] but by the spiritual sword of the uncovering and convicting word. According to the "paranesis of neophytes"[63] in Eph. 4:25 and Col. 3:8f., the baptized cast off lying along with their old pagan perversions and live henceforth in communion as members of Christ's Body in the truth of the Spirit of God.

According to the lists of vices in Rom. 1:29ff. and 1 Tim. 1:9f., lying belongs to the perishing age. Whoever loves it and does it remains outside the gates of the city of God, according to the Revelation of John (21:27; 22:15). He is not written in the book of life and falls into the second, eternal death

---

55 In his interpretation, Luther combines Deut. 19:16ff. with Matt. 18:15ff.; see "Dtn.-Vorl., 1523/24," WA 14:688.19–33 (see also AE 9:1–311).
56 *Die Gesetze Hammurabis* §§ 11, 126f. Cf. Stoebe, "Das achte Gebot," 125.
57 Cf. Lev. 19:11f.; Hosea 4:1f.; Jer. 7:9f.
58 See the commentary on the Second Commandment, pp. 159–62.
59 Amos 2:6f.; 5:10f.; Mic. 3:9ff.; Isa. 5:23; 10:1f.; Jer. 5:28; and passim.
60 See Kraus, *Psalmen*, 15.1:40ff. (excursus on Ps. 5:7: "The enemies of the individual"); Westermann, *Das Loben Gottes in den Psalmen*, 48ff.
61 Cf. p. 291 n. 45; von Rad, *Weisheit in Israel*, 112–22.
62 Haenchen, *Die Apostelgeschichte*, 195f., points to Joshua 7 as the Old Testament counterimage, the ban of Achan.
63 According to Schlier, *Der Brief an die Epheser*, 223; the parallels, Schlier, *Der Brief an die Epheser*, 224.

(Rev. 21:8). No lie is found in the mouth of those purchased and marked by blood of the Lamb (Rev. 14:5). The Gospel of John and the First Epistle of John uncover—stronger yet than Romans (1:15; 3:4)—the connection of lying to what is inimical to God. Lying is more than a transgression of our tongue; in the final analysis, "the lie" is our *no* to the self-disclosure of God in the Son and as such the core act of unbelief. In view of the breaking in of the light of God, we want to remain in darkness. In this, we show ourselves to be sons of Satan, the liar and murderer from the beginning (John 8:44).[64] We step out of our darkness in a paradoxical double step: first, by bowing our sinful nature in the confession of guilt under the sacrifice of Christ, thereby not making God a liar in His saving act (1 John 1:5–10); second, by again and again overcoming selfishness in active love to the visible brother, thus proving our love to the invisible God (1 John 2:3–6, 21–25; 4:19ff.).[65] In both movements, we reject the lie and do the truth.

This translation of the prohibition from the Old to the New Testament changes it from something negative to something positive and broadens it very much. Next to the court, there are now all other locales and situations of human communication.[66] All of them demand the *no* to the lie and the *yes* to the truth. Yet even this vast area remains under God's zeal in wrath and salvation.

Characteristics of Luther's Interpretation

1. Shifts in Accentuation within the Dual Scope of the Commandment

In the following phrase, Luther summarizes the dual scope of the commandment, its Old Testament starting point as well as its New Testament broadening: "In summary, you shall confess the truth in court, speak no evil or falsehood about your neighbor, but only the best."[67] In the Small Catechism especially, Luther departs from the Old Testament reference, and the commandment is broadened to "all sins of the tongue by which one may harm one's neighbor or step on his toes."[68] In general, this broadening to

---

64   See Bultmann, *Das Evangelium des Johannes*, 243f. Cf. also 1 John 3:15ff.; 2 Thess. 2:9ff.

65   See Augustine, *Contra mendacium* 20.40.

66   Cf. "Nürnberger Katechismuspredigten," Reu, *Quellen*, 1.1:499.24: ". . . be it in court or elsewhere." This dual aspect was already summarized by Thomas Aquinas, cf. *Duo praecepta* § 1300: ". . . either in court or in common speech." This is taken up in the catechisms of the Reformation, e.g., Althamer, *Kat.*, quest. 35 (MGP 22:25); Sam, *Christl. Unterweisung*, quest. 118 (MGP 22:123); Geneva Catechism, quest. 209f.; Heidelberg Catechism, quest. 112.

67   "Kat.-Pred. zum 7.–10. Gebot vom 7.12.1528," WA 30.1:83.8 (see also AE 51:155–61).

68   *BSLK*, 626.39.

our "mouth"[69] is carried out by Augustine in his writing *De mendacio*.[70] Augustine does not see the lie in relation to the commandment to love as a sin against the neighbor; he sees it, in analogy to unchastity, as a staining of our own soul that should be turned toward the eternal God as the primordial Truth. This understanding of the commandment, which puts less emphasis on the protection of the neighbor than on the purity of one's own soul, shapes, in part, also the medieval confessional manuals,[71] which repeatedly mention lying in the auricular confession itself.

Luther also first[72] gathers rather abstractly in "Decem praecepta" ("Preaching of the Ten Commandments") the different violations of the commandment of truth and summarizes the commandment in "Sermon von den guten Werken" ("Sermon on Good Works") quite generally: "This commandment . . . means in German to tell the truth and contradict lies."[73] Yet from the beginning—and unlike Augustine and the medieval tradition[74]— Luther had students memorize the "against your neighbor" as well, so already in "Preaching of the Ten Commandments," he aims the general prohibition of lying at the protection of our neighbor's honor.[75] The confessional manuals accentuate this: the commandment wants to teach us "how to behave in relation to the neighbor's honor and good reputation, not to weaken but to increase it, protect it, and defend it."[76] God does not want an abstract battle for truthfulness that ultimately turns loveless, but a truthfulness that protects concretely "the neighbor's honor, right, cause, and blessedness."[77]

In the early interpretations of the commandment, however, this "honor" of the neighbor goes beyond "the recognition of the membership of a person in the societal context."[78] Luther adds the dimension of the spiritual government to the realm of the secular government. God is not only concerned about the temporal honor of our neighbor as His creature; He also protects

---

69 *BSLK*, 626.43.

70 Augustine, *De mend.* 5:6 (PL 40:491): "It includes every lie, for whoever says anything bears witness to his soul."

71 See Geffcken, *Bildercatechismus*, 88–95, and app., col. 7, 45, 74ff., 97, 104, 136, 155, 173, 185, 211, 216.

72 See the overview in Hardeland, *Katechismusgedanken*, 170–76.

73 WA 6:273.18 (see also AE 44:15–114). "Kat.-Pred. zum 7.–10. Gebot vom 7.12.1528," WA 30.1:81.15 (see also AE 51:155–61): "The sum of this commandment is: you are to bear witness rightly and say the truth"; "Eine kurze Erklärung," WA 1:255.15; "Instructio," WA 1:263:32.

74 Cf. p. 287 n. 5.

75 WA 1:506.11: "Therefore as it is prohibited to harm the person himself, those who belong to the person, physical property, so now it is prohibited to harm the good that consists of the reputation, praise, honor, and name."

76 "Eine kurze Form," WA 7:206.21. (thus first in 1520). In "Eine kurze Erklärung, 1518," and "Instructio, 1518," there is merely a hint (WA 1:253.13f., 262.5).

77 "Eine kurze Form," WA 7:213.30.

78 Trillhaas, *Ethik*, 289.

our neighbor's "blessedness," his salvation, as a being called into fellowship with God.[79]

In his writings on lying, Augustine already had dealt extensively with the "lie in religious doctrine," and Thomas had qualified it as mortal sin.[80] In "Preaching of the Ten Commandments," Luther enumerates four main forms of the lie: false doctrine, lying when dealing with men, double-tongued flattering, and false testimony in court. Among these, false doctrine therefore takes first place. Luther here begins with the doubly grave violation of the spiritual murderers of the soul and torturers of consciences[81] and places the Aristotelian philosophers and the preachers of miracles next to the jurists, heretics, and scholastics.[82] As jurists do not seek peace and truth in a legal battle but their own honor in the victory over their opponent, thus heretics rely on their own good opinion in their soul-destroying work without any genuine fear of God. And the scholastics torture consciences by preaching works-righteousness, at the same time giving Scripture a wax nose by their allegories. The Aristotelians honor their master as a messenger of divine truth and are in disagreement over the correct interpretation of his teachings.[83] The miracle preachers testify against God and His saints by attaching their fairy tales to the latter.[84] In "Sermon on Good Works," Luther still leaves the accent on the good fight "for the Gospel and the truth of the faith,"[85] but, according to the wording of the commandment, Luther takes the secular courts as his point of departure.[86] The March 3, 1523, "Dekalog-predigt" ("Decalogue Sermon")[87] unfolds in great detail the Old Testament *usus externus* of the commandment. Then it moves on from the testimony in court to the inner struggle for the betterment of the neighbor out of the on-going forgiveness of sins. The 1525 sermons on Exodus[88] show an analogous movement. They, too, first describe the right behavior of judge and witness "in public court," and then broaden the commandment to "all lies . . . that

---

79   According to Barth, *Kirchliche Dogmatik* 3.4:753; cf. Bonhoeffer, *Ethik*, 283–90.

80   Augustine, *De mend.* 8:11; 10:16f.; *Contra mend.* 16:33; Thomas Aquinas, *Duo praecepta* § 1313; *Summa Theologiae* II/II, quest. 110, a. 4.

81   WA 1:508.6–36.

82   WA 1:506.15–508.5, the monks, heretics, and scholastics; WA 1:508.6–36, the jurists; WA 1:508.37–509.17, the Aristotelians; WA 1:509.18–510.8, the miracle preachers.

83   "Decem praecepta, 1518," WA 1:509.13: "There are the Thomists, Scotists, Albertists, Modernists, and so you have a four-headed Aristotle and a kingdom divided in itself."

84   "Decem praecepta, 1518," WA 1:509.31: "They give false testimony not against men but against God and the saints already ruling in heaven."

85   WA 6:274.15 (see also AE 44:15–114).

86   WA 6:273.21ff. (see also AE 44:15–114).

87   WA 11:47f.

88   WA 16:519–25.

can harm the neighbor"[89] before underlining the protective character of the commandment. God gave it because He knows that every one of us, "insofar as he is human, is a false witness, betrayer, liar, and that no true word goes out of our mouth when we are in danger."[90]

Thus we have reached the dual scope of the 1528 sermons and the Large Catechism. The reformer begins with the Old Testament at the public trial,[91] first applies this to the secular realm, while the "the spiritual court or government"[92] is glanced at only briefly.[93] Luther already touched on the struggle for God's Word in the Second Commandment[94] and will unfold it in the First Petition of the Lord's Prayer.[95] After broadening the commandment to apply to all sins of the tongue, Luther returns on a higher level to the public trial. At the core of the positive interpretation of the Eighth Commandment is God's holy and gracious trial in which He wants to defeat sin and lift up the sinner in all of His kingdoms through our cooperation. For this purpose, Christ gave the community rule in Matthew 18. And for it, God has the house of the burgher and town hall, church and school work together.

2. LUTHER'S EVALUATION OF THE NECESSARY LIE

The reformer does not tie the duty of truthfulness primarily to the salvation of one's own soul but subsumes it under the basic duty of loving one's neighbor. Although the Eighth Commandment is not explicitly mentioned in Romans (13:9), it is nonetheless included and contained in the basic commandment: "You shall love your neighbor as yourself." Luther develops this in his statements on necessary lies, which brings him into a certain tension with Augustine, Thomas, and Kant. In *De mendacio*, Augustine had originally enumerated eight kinds of lies; medieval scholasticism reduced it to three: the malicious lie, the humorous lie, and the useful or necessary lie.[96] Luther

---

89 WA 16:523.12.

90 WA 16:521.24.

91 *BSLK*, 625.6–626.16.

92 *BSLK*, 626.18.

93 *BSLK*, 626.17–37. Cf. "Kat.-Pred. zum 8. Gebot vom 22.5. bzw. 19.9 bzw. 7.12.1528," WA 30.1:8.20ff., 40.21–26, 81.14f. (see also AE 51:155–61).

94 Cf. pp. 154–59.

95 Cf. the commentary on the First Petition of the Lord's Prayer.

96 The eight kinds are found in Augustine, *De mend.* 14:25 (PL 40:505): "(1) One is to avoid the capital lie and is to run far away from it, which takes place in the doctrine of religion; (2) that he should hurt someone unjustly, which is such that it helps no one and harms someone; (3) that he helps one in such a way that he harms another, though he does not harm him by bodily defilement; (4) that which takes place only out of a desire to lie and deceive; (5) what takes place to satisfy a desire concerning smooth talking; (6) that which harms no one and helps someone, as if somebody, to take somebody's money unjustly, lies that he does not know where it is when asked, though he does know where it is; (7) that which harms no one and helps someone, except when the judge asks . . . ; (8) that which harms no one and helps to

takes up this division as originating from Augustine.[97] While Origen, Hilary, Chrysostom, and Cassian considered the lie to be permitted under certain circumstances,[98] Augustine, who had still wavered in *De mendacio*, arrived at a more rigorous position in *Contra mendacium*. Based on the words of Scripture, especially on the Johannine juxtaposition of lie and truth;[99] on the cleansing upward movement of the soul to the one and true God; on the difficulty that, if lying is permitted once, one could no longer draw any clear boundaries,[100] he wants to call every lie a sin, even if it is excusable in desperate emergencies. Thomas takes up this stricter judgment of Augustine.[101] Kant likewise considers the lie *eo ipso* immoral. Since this abstract position is impossible to maintain in cases of conflict,[102] Catholic moral teaching takes recourse to mental restriction, qualifying what was said, and to amphiboly, that is, intentional equivocation. In these cases, however, the "intended and true meaning of the saying" has to be recognizable "based on the way it was said or based on the personal or objective circumstances."[103] However, these tricks do not eliminate the intention to deceive; rather, they embody it on a higher level. Therefore Luther rejects them as deception, not only of the neighbor but also of our own conscience before God.

Luther's opinion is also conditioned by the fact that he interprets the biblical examples collected already by Augustine,[104] especially those of the

---

protect someone from physical defilement." Following Augustine, the glosses of Peter Lombard on Ps. 5:6 (PL 191:96BD; cf. also the *Glossa ordinaria* on Ps. 5:6, PL 113:851A) and *Sent.* III., dist. 38.1, reduce it to the threefold genus of lies: (1) "for the use and advantage of someone"; (2) "what happens in jest"; (3) "what happens out of malice." Thomas Aquinas, *Summa Theologiae* II/II, quest. 110, a. 2; and Bonaventure, *Collationes des decem praeceptis* 7:3–5, discuss in great detail the relation between the eight and the three parts of the lie. This discussion is passed on in the confessional manuals (*Summa angelica*; Nicholas of Lyra; Lanzkranna, and others; see the appendix to Geffcken, *Bildercatechismus*). On this topic, see Maćkowiak, "Die ethische Bedeutung der Notlüge"; Müller, *Die Wahrhaftigkeitspflicht*.

97   "Decem praecepta, 1518," WA 1:510.9–38; "Gen.-Vorl., 1535–45," WA 42:470.23–471.6 (see also AE 2:1–399); WA 43:456.9–40 (see also AE 5:1–386); additional texts in Köhler, *Luther und die Lüge*, 165ff.

98   See the summary by Gregor Müller, *Lüge*, LTK 6:1198–1200.

99   Augustine pulls together three things in *De mend.* 19:40 (PL 40:514): "Yet these need to be observed for the sake of sanctity: the purity of the body, the chastity of the soul, and the truth of doctrine."

100 Augustine, *Contra mend.* 18:36f.; *Enchiridion* 7:22. On Augustine, see also Golinski, *La doctrine de St. Augustin sur le mensonge*.

101 Thomas Aquinas, *Summa Theologiae* II/II, quest. 110, a. 3.

102 The cases of conflict are discussed in detail by Thielicke, *Ethik*, 2.1:122–89 (§§ 372–641).

103 Mausbach, *Die katholische Moral und ihre Gegner*, 112ff.; on this Köhler, *Luther und die Lüge*, 172ff.

104 E.g., Augustine, *De mend.* 5:5ff.; *Contra mend.* 9:20–11:25, 15:31–17:34; Peter Lombard, *Sent.* III, dist. 38; Thomas Aquinas, *Summa Theologiae* II/II, quest. 110, a. 3, ad 3. Cf. the compilation in Köhler, *Luther und die Lüge*, 167f.

patriarchs, according to the Eighth Commandment. He speaks well of them and explains everything in the best way.

In "Preaching of the Ten Commandments," Luther still defines the necessary lie as a lie "for the good and use of oneself or another without hurting anybody."[105] Yet in his later interpretation, one's own advantage or salvation clearly recedes. This is why the account of the endangerment of the matriarch, told three times in Genesis (chs. 12, 20, 26), poses for him the greatest difficulty, as it did for Augustine.[106] Later, Luther is not afraid to talk of a *peccatum infirmitatis*[107] of the patriarchs, but he lets it be surrounded by their trust in God's faithfulness to His promise. To this Luther directs our attention; in this believing trust, as well as in that caring circumspection, the patriarch remains our example.[108] In one place, Luther considers the necessary lie not only to be permitted but also to be commanded, namely, where it protects the neighbor from unlawful infringement, where it prevents harm and shame, sin and murder. Here he is not afraid of calling it a felicitous deception and lie of love,[109] an honorable and pious lie, even a duty of love.[110] This is how he clearly subordinates the duty of truthfulness to the basic commandment to love one's neighbor.

3. The Protection of the Neighbor's Honor and the Struggle to Get Him to Stop Sinning in God's Threefold Government

The core commandment to love one's neighbor becomes concrete in the struggle for the outward honor and inward betterment of the neighbor. Luther unfolds this in the two central sections of the Large Catechism.[111] For this purpose, he moves the ecclesiastical and secular authorities under the congregational rule in Matthew 18[112] and takes the "daily house

---

105 WA 1:510.20.

106 According to Augustine, the patriarchs did not deny the truth concerning their wives; they merely kept silent about it. Cf. *Contra mend.* 10:23 (PL 40:533): "Thus he kept silent about something that is true; he did not say anything that was false. When he kept silent about the wife, he spoke about the sister. . . . It is therefore not a lie when the truth is hidden under silence, but when by speaking the falsehood is brought out." Cf. *De civ. Dei* 16:19.

107 "Gen.-Vorl., 1535–45," WA 42:472.5 (see also AE 2:1–399); "Gen.-Vorl., 1535–45," WA 43:114.7 (see also AE 4:1–409): "Here he fell out of infirmity."

108 "Gen.-Vorl., 1535–45," WA 42:472.25–473.42 (see also AE 2:1–399).

109 "Pred. über Mt. 2:13ff. vom 5.1.1528," WA 27:12.16–36.

110 "Gen.-Vorl.," WA 43:456.16–34 (see also AE 5:1–386): ". . . it is therefore an official lie by which one looks out after the well-being, the reputation of body or soul . . . . It is therefore an honest and pious lie and is rather to be called a service of love. Although Augustine calls it a lie, he nonetheless extenuates it by the epithet 'official.' " The adjective is found in Augustine, *De mend.* 1:1.

111 *BSLK*, 627.17–632.6.

112 *BSLK*, 631.3–22.

government"[113] as their example. As in his annotations to Deuteronomy, Luther connects Deut. 19:16ff. with Matt. 18:15ff.:[114] God's ban is on the sin that destroys the communion, yet God's visiting grace and forgiveness is open to the sinner. At the same time, Luther distinguishes between secret and public sin.

Public sin is to be punished publicly so that everybody might be careful to avoid it.[115] In the Large Catechism, Luther here points to the false doctrine of the papacy as it was published and defended in writings and bulls.[116] In his September 19 sermon, he mentions public transgressions of the Second Table.[117] Where we encounter this, we must not be silent, because it is our duty to convict the evil ones and better them.[118]

This public fight against evil, however, is entrusted to those who participate in God's office of watchman in the three overarching hierarchies (*Erzhierarchien*). Luther takes recourse to the distinction, unfolded in the Fifth Commandment, between "two persons or two offices"[119] that a Christian must discharge.[120] "Without an office, on his own,"[121] no one is to judge and condemn another person;[122] however, whoever participates in God's punishing office is to uncover and condemn evil. In this public office of punishment, the bearers of the secular and spiritual government stand side by side. Both again seem to be directed to the house government as the most primitive order. The list "secular authorities, preachers, father and mother"[123] is reminiscent of what has been said on the Fourth Commandment.[124] The one *Corpus Christianum* is under God's spiritual and secular government; the Christian congregation and the civil community still appear as one.[125]

God's will permeating both becomes concrete in the struggle for the brother who has fallen into secret sin. The community rule in Matthew 18, as well as the daily example of the house father, instructs us to get him out

---

113 *BSLK*, 630.29–42.

114 "Dtn.-Vorl., 1523/24," WA 14:688.19–33 (see also AE 9:1–311). First Corinthians 3:13 also hearkens back to the old ban formula, Deut. 19:19.

115 *BSLK*, 631.39–632.6.

116 *BSLK*, 631.47ff.

117 WA 30.1:42.18–22.

118 *BSLK*, 631.10–22.

119 "Ausl. von Mt. 5–7, 1530/32," WA 32:390.10 (see also AE 21:1–294).

120 *BSLK*, 629.25–49. Cf. pp. 223f.

121 *BSLK*, 629.43.

122 "Kat.-Pred. zum 8.–10. Gebot vom 19.9.1528," WA 30.1:40.32: "No one is there to be somebody else's judge unless he has the order to judge."

123 *BSLK*, 629.27. See *BSLK*, 629.50ff.; "Pred. über Ex. 20 vom 12.11.1525," WA 16:523.6, 523.34f.; "Kat.-Pred. zum 8. Gebot vom 22.5. bzw. 19.9. bzw. 7.12.1528," WA 30.1:8.30f., 42.28, 82.12f. (see also AE 51:155–61).

124 Cf. pp. 197–208.

125 *BSLK*, 631.10–22.

of there.[126] If somebody has fallen into disorder and become entangled in guilt, it is not our task to accuse him behind his back in the presence of un-involved third parties, thereby depriving him of his good name. First, we are to admonish him in private, and then to get witnesses and helpers involved. Thus Christ teaches us, and thus every understanding master deals with his servant. The duty to intervene and to admonish here grows out of the given coordination among people that is, as such, willed by God. The hierarchical headship structure is broadened to the general love structure among equals; siblings and friends are added to the authorities and parents.[127] They all are duty-bound "to punish evil where it is necessary and useful."[128] However, with Matt. 18:16, Luther's point in this coordination that grows out of God's work in the world is to win the brother back from the dominion of sin[129]—in Old Testament terms, the "fellow covenant member" and the "member of the congregation of God"[130] is in view. If we do not win the brother back by our secret admonition, then we are to draw in one or two witnesses (Matt. 18:16; Deut. 19:15), again without making the still-secret sin public beyond this limited group. First, where this second call to repentance is not heeded, the whole congregation in its civil or ecclesiastical organs is to be approached.[131] Here, Luther outlines a "certain form and manner" of using the Office of the Keys that Christ Himself has instituted. The reformer has laid it out in great detail in his 1530 writing "Von den Schlüsseln" ("On the Keys").[132]

The early Christian community order combines both the outward pro-tection of the honor of the neighbor and the active urging of his "better-ment," which shows it not to be an arbitrary rule but deeply anchored in our joint existence under the gracious will of God our Creator.[133] Luther again adduces the Golden Rule.[134] In it, the Creator discloses the basic law of all true living that we, despite all sinful perversion, still bear within us. We know both of its sides addressed by this commandment from our daily lives in the body: the shameful covering as well as the healing intervention

126 BSLK, 630.8–631.2.

127 BSLK, 629.50ff.

128 BSLK, 630.1. Cf. "Kat.-Pred. zum 7.–10. Gebot vom 7.12.1528," WA 30.1:82.21–24 (see also AE 51:155–61).

129 BSLK, 630.42–631.2.

130 Fichtner, "Der Begriff des 'Nächsten' im Alten Testament," 41.

131 BSLK, 631.3–22.

132 WA 30.2:462ff., 501ff. (see also AE 40:321–77).

133 Elert, Das christliche Ethos, 187: "Honor is public order whose breaking reveals the force of evil."

134 BSLK, 632.21–28. That Luther again mentions the Golden Rule might be because of the fact that with it Luther concluded the interpretation of the Commandments. Since he did not inter-pret the last two commandments, he attached the regula aurea to the Eighth Commandment, as done in "Eine Kurze Form, 1520" (WA 7:206.25ff.) and in "Ex.-Predigt vom 12.11.1525" (WA 16:525.16ff.). See furthermore, p. 276 n. 127.

in what is hidden. Regarding the former, Luther recalls the example of the apostle (1 Cor. 12:22f.), taken from our body for the right living together of the weak and the strong in the congregation: out of shame, we cover the dishonest and fragile members.[135] For the latter, he adduces the example of a physician who, in order to heal, "sometimes . . . has to see and operate in secret places."[136] In the Large Catechism, the reformer thus shows how also the twofold fulfilling of this commandment stands under the one basic law of loving the neighbor, which the Creator engraved deeply into His creatures, "for nature teaches what love does, that I should do what I want done to me."[137] In the "Sermon on Good Works," where Luther had accentuated the witness for the faith, he closes by pointing to Christ as sacrament and example, and to faith as the doer also of this commandment.[138]

Texts on the Eighth Commandment

WA 1:504–10: from Decem praecepta Wittenbergensi praedicata populo, 1518

WA 6:273–76: from Sermon von den guten Werken, 1520 (see also AE 44:15–114)

WA 14:664–67: from Dtn.-Vorlesung, 1523/24 zu Dtn. 16:19 (see also AE 9:1–311)

WA 16:519–25: from Predigt über Ex. 20:16f. vom 12.11.1525 zu Ex. 20:16 (Eighth Commandment)

WA 16:564–73: from 3 Predigten über Ex. 23 vom 29.5–1.7.1526 zu Ex. 23:1–9

WA 32:381–86: from Wochenpredigten über Mt. 5–7 (Ausl. von Mt. 5–7), zu Mt. 5:33f., 1530/32 (see also AE 21:1–294)

WA 42:470–78: from Genesis-Vorlesung, 1535–45, zu Gen. 12:11ff. (see also AE 2:1–399)

WA 43:455–57: from Genesis-Vorlesung, 1535–45, zu Gen. 20:9 (see also AE 5:1–386)

Literature

Köhler, *Luther und die Lüge*, 154–205

Maćkowiak, "Die ethische Bedeutung der Notlüge in der altheidnischen, patristischen, scholastischen und neueren Zeit"

Müller, *Die Wahrhaftigkeitspflicht und die Problematik der Lüge*

---

135 *BSLK*, 632.29–46. Cf. "Kat.-Pred. zum 7.–10. Gebot vom 7.12.1528," WA 30.1:82.1–6 (see also AE 51:155–61).

136 *BSLK*, 629.49–630.7.

137 "Von weltl. Oberkeit, 1523," WA 11:279.19 (see also AE 45:75–129).

138 WA 6:275.22–37 (see also AE 44:15–114).

The Ninth and Tenth
Commandments[1]

Wording of the Commandment and Its
Interpretation in the Small Catechism,
and the Structure of the Interpretation
in the Large Catechism

In his interpretations, Martin Luther always treated this double commandment as one;[2] only in the Small Catechism does he seek to arrive at two commandments. In "Eine kurze Form" ("Short Form") and in the catechisms, he follows Exod. 20:17: "You shall not covet your neighbor's house. You shall not covet your neighbor's wife, manservant, maidservant, animals, or what is his."[3] Although he translates it in his Bible as "You shall not lust," he sticks to the familiar translation of the Vulgate's *non concupisces* for the catechism texts: "You shall not covet."

Regarding the demarcation of these commandments, there is "a veritable Babylonian confusion of languages"[4] in the tradition. Augustine, who was the first to split up the prohibition of coveting, did not do so in a uniform way.[5] He primarily followed Deut. 5:21, beginning with the "neighbor's wife" and following with the "goods of the neighbor." The majority of late medieval confessional manuals take up this structuring. This structure is supported by pointing back to the prohibitions of adultery and theft. Accordingly, the Ninth Commandment prohibits imagining what is prohibited in the command against adultery; and by means of the catechetical

---

1   For texts on the double commandment, see pp. 315–16.
2   "Pred. über Ex. 20 vom 12.11.1525," WA 16:525.32: "Several interpreters divide the two commandments; not much depends on the division. St. Paul takes it as one in Romans 7, where he says: 'You shall not crave.' Thus there now lustful craving is prohibited."
3   *BSLK*, 509.26 (SC); WA 7:207.7. *BSLK*, 555.30, 633.34 (LC) read "his wife." Cf. also "Decem praecepta, 1518," WA 1:515.1–4.
4   Geffcken, *Bildercatechismus*, 96. In Geffcken, *Bildercatechismus*, 96, and in Meyer, *Historischer Kommentar*, 90, a detailed overview is offered.
5   Cf. Rentschka, *Dekalogkatechese*, 128.

abbreviation "anything that belongs to your neighbor,"[6] the Tenth Commandment intensifies God's *no* to theft.[7]

In "Eine kurze Erklärung, 1518," ("Short Explanation"), Luther still follows this Augustinian tradition. He first mentions the neighbor's "wife, daughter, and maidservant,"[8] then his "house or goods."[9] This sequence still resounds in the Large Catechism when it combines "wife and goods."[10] Luther also receives the pointing back to the prohibition of adultery and theft,[11] and this is why he, according to the scope of the Sixth and Seventh Commandments, places next to the housewife only the other female members belonging to the family, at once expanding the house to the *res proximi*.

Yet beginning in 1520, Luther follows Exod. 20:17 and begins with the neighbor's house, while at the same time seeking to maintain a distinction between the things owned by the neighbor and the people belonging to his house. After all, the attempt to take away cunningly from the neighbor what is his takes a different form, depending on whether dead things, irrational animals, or reasonable humans are concerned.

The demarcation of these two commandments must remain somewhat artificial. In the Small Catechism, where Luther carries it out, he takes the *res proximi*, "the goods of the neighbor,"[12] out of the Tenth Commandment and places it into the Ninth by situating the "inheritance"[13] next to the house. Thus in the interpretation of the Ninth Commandment, he now focuses on the cunning practices that seek to take from the neighbor his physical possessions under the appearance of right. As the Large Catechism shows,[14]

---

6 "Non concupisces ullam rem prosimi tui."

7 Cf. Augustine, *Quaestiones in Heptateuchum* 2, quest. 71:3; Sermon 9:13; 8:10f. Similarly, for example, Hollen and Schobser (Geffcken, *Bildercatechismus*, 97ff.); Gerson/Geiler (Geffcken, *Bildercatechismus*, app., col. 45f.); Laurent (Geffcken, *Bildercatechismus*, app., col. 85); *Spiegel des Christenmenschen* (Geffcken, *Bildercatechismus*, app., col. 155f.); probably following Peter Lombard, *Sent.* III, dist. 40.1.

8 WA 1:251.21. "Instructio pro confessione peccatorum, 1518," WA 1:259.8: "uxor proximi tui." "Eine kurze Unterweisung, wie man beichten soll, 1519," WA 2:64.11: "your neighbor's housewife."

9 WA 1:251.23. "Instructio, 1518," WA 1:259.10: "domum proximi tui, non servum nec omnia quae illius sunt &c. [your neighbor's house, neither any servant, nor anything at all that is his]." "Eine kurze Unterweisung, 1519," WA 2:64.12: "Your neighbor's goods."

10 *BSLK*, 634.1. "Decem praecepta, 1518," WA 1:515.6: "concupiscentia uxoris et rei proximi. [coveting of the neighbor's wife and goods]." Stanza 10 of "Dies sind die heilgen zehn Gebot," WA 35:428.6 (see also AE 53:280–81): "wife and house." "Wider die Sabbather, 1538," WA 50:335.18 (see also AE 47:57–98): "wife and house." *BSLK*, 634.30 (LC): "what is his, such as wife, servants, house and farm, field, meadows, animals."

11 "Decem praecepta, 1518," WA 1:515.5–9; "Pred. über Ex. 20 vom 12.11.1525," WA 16:525.4–526.7; "Kat.-Pred. zum 8.–10. Gebot vom 19.9.1528," WA 30.1:42.33; *BSLK*, 633.40ff. (LC).

12 "Decem praecepta, 1518," WA 1:515.6f. In tradition, the phrase "goods of the neighbor" translates the Augustinian *res proximi*.

13 *BSLK*, 509.31.

14 *BSLK*, 634.27–637.20.

they tie in with the Seventh Commandment. The Tenth Commandment, for its part, is now grouped with the Sixth Commandment,[15] but Luther expands it in the direction of the Seventh. The luring away of servants, which is only briefly touched on in the Large Catechism,[16] and the stealing of animals, which the Large Catechism mentions only in the summaries,[17] are added to the infringement on somebody else's marriage, which is at the center in the Large Catechism. Thus the Tenth Commandment is concentrated on the behavior toward those intelligent beings that belong to the neighbor. The cunning legal tricks in the Ninth and the luring away of persons and animals in the Tenth Commandment are by no means secret desires and longings of the heart, but practical ruses and actions. Since by and large they rely on the Seventh Commandment, we can limit ourselves to interpreting some typical phrases and analyzing the structure of the interpretation in the Large Catechism.[18]

In the Ninth Commandment, Luther underlines the crafty act of remaining on the lookout for an opportune moment and the care to preserve formal legality. While the Seventh Commandment applied to simple thieves, this commandment is meant for the pious and distinguished Israelites, the upper class in the capital cities, as Luther likely gleans from the prophetic preaching of judgment.[19] To them he adds the legal controversies concerning inheritance matters[20] and the contemporary tricks of merchants.[21] He likes to paraphrase the practices employed here with the word "finance" or "financery."[22] Looking out for one's own advantage is enunciated in proverbial sayings[23] in which the naïve selfishness and greed of the old Adam unabashedly articulates itself. Again, the reformer bends this vast area of inheritance and process law, of trade and economy, under equity flowing out of the Golden Rule.[24]

---

15   *BSLK*, 637.21–50.

16   *BSLK*, 634.3–11, 634.19–26, 637.46–50.

17   *BSLK*, 634.10, 32.

18   Cf. the comments on the Seventh Commandment, pp. 273–80.

19   *BSLK*, 635.33–636.4.

20   *BSLK*, 636.5–29.

21   *BSLK*, 636.30–637.20.

22   *BSLK*, 636.19. "Kat.-Pred. zum 8.–10. Gebot vom 19.9.1528," WA 30.1:42.36: "They have used finance to steal each other's houses." Cf. "Kat.-Pred. vom 7.12.1528," WA 30.1:83.14, 83.29 (see also AE 51:155–61); WADB 7:32 (gloss on Rom. 1:30): "Financers who bring up many new findings, as seen among merchants, jurists, and courtiers." Cf. "Vier tröstl. Psalmen, 1526, zu Ps. 62:2," WA 19:572.10–20 (see also AE 14:207–77).

23   *BSLK*, 636.40ff. Cf. Wander, *Sprichwörterlexikon*, "Erste," no. 19, "Schanze" (= chance), nos. 2, 10, 33. *BSLK*, 635.19. Cf. Wander, *Sprichwörterlexikon*, "Recht," no. 45f. See also the comments on the Seventh Commandment, pp. 275–76.

24   *BSLK*, 635.14, 637.5. "Enarrationes epistolarum, 1521, Postille zu Phil. 4:4," WA 7:515.25: "You see, therefore, that modesty or equity in this place means, first, our fairness, appropriateness,

In explaining the Tenth Commandment, Luther uses verbs that express influence on the will and responsibility of those people who are given to the neighbor. The frequently used term *abspannen*[25] is etymologically related to *span*, [mother's] breast or teat, which in modern German is still contained in *Spanferkel* ("suckling piglet"). Therefore it should be spelled with a single *n*, *abspanen* ("wean off"). Luther spells the word always with a double *n*, but he uses it primarily in relation to persons.[26] The basic sense of *ablocken* ("luring away")[27] thus seems to have been stronger than the secondary meaning of *ausspannen* ("unyoke"). The second verb in the Small Catechism, *abdringen* ("urge away"),[28] underlines more strongly the personal input of the subject. The third verb, *abwendig machen* ("turn away"),[29] describes the result of that luring and urging coaxing. The Christian, however, will use his zeal and persuasiveness to sustain and strengthen not only the wife but also the servants in their faithfulness to the master of the house. Even in the Small Catechism, this positive influence on the responsible will cannot relate to animals. The behavior toward animals is not specially articulated in the Small or in the Large Catechism.

In the Large Catechism, Luther expands on the short 1528 sermons.[30] First, he outlines in a historical overview the original and the constant basic meaning of the double commandment.[31] (a) The commandments not to seek to gain the neighbor's wife and goods, as intensifying supplementation

---

and temperateness when it comes to the weakness or stupidity or iniquity of others and, second, the remission of our harshness and of the law." Cf. "Enarrationes epistolarum, 1521, Postille zu Phil. 4:4," WA 7:513.24–516.24. Further texts in Holl, "Der Neubau der Sittlichkeit," 263–72.

25 *BSLK*, 634.40, 637.43. "Kat.-Predigten 1528," WA 30.1:9.8, 42.35, 84.9, 84.11, 85.1, 85.5f. (see also AE 51:155–61); "Eine einfältige Weise zu beten, 1535," WA 38:372.19 (see also AE 43:187–211); "Wider die Sabbather, 1538," WA 50:335.18 (see also AE 47:57–98). Cf. the literature in p. 303 n. 1.

26 Only "Kat.-Pred. vom 7.12.1528" (WA 30.1:85.5f. [see also AE 51:155–61]) on horse and garden; "Eine einfältige Weise zu beten, 1535" (WA 38:372.19 [see also AE 43:187–211]) on goods.

27 "Kat.-Pred. vom 7.12.1528," WA 30.1:84.23, 84.28 (see also AE 51:155–61): *abspennig machen* ("entice away").

28 *BSLK*, 634.21. Cf. *BSLK*, 637.41ff.; "Eine einfältige Weise zu beten, 1535," WA 38.372.19 (see also AE 43:187–211).

29 *BSLK*, 638.15: "desired it and turned away from him." Cf. *BSLK*, 634.16, 637.44: *entfrömbden* ("alienate").

30 Echoes of "Kat.-Predigt vom 7.12" can be heard: the opening is the same (WA 30.1:83.12ff. [see also AE 51:155–61]), as well as the reference to the court battles of the princes (*BSLK*, 636.5–29; WA 30.1:84.1–3 [see also AE 51:155–61]), the example of Herod (*BSLK*, 637.21–39; WA 30.1:84.10ff. [see also AE 51:155–61]). Additionally, the sermon mentions David (WA 30.1:84.12 [see also AE 51:155–61]) and remembers Naboth's vineyard from 1 Kings 21 (WA 30.1:85.4 [see also AE 51:155–61]). The "Nürnberger Katechismuspredigten" unfold this collection of examples (Reu, *Quellen*, 1.1:503.30–37).

31 Section 1: *BSLK*, 633.38–634.46.

to the Sixth and Seventh Commandments, are first given only to the Jews.[32] (b) However, even among Christians, they retain their concrete meaning: we should not try to take away what belongs to our neighbor, not even under the appearance of right.[33] In a second set of thoughts, Luther stakes out the vast realm of the double prohibition.[34] (a) He describes the rather subtle infringements on the physical possessions of the neighbor above all in inheritance proceedings and in business and distinguishes them from the grosser infraction against the prohibition of theft.[35] (b) He mentions intrusions into the *familia* of the neighbor and distinguishes them from the prohibition of adultery.[36] (c) He points to God's zealous holiness that punishes even the things that are beyond the reach of secular laws.[37] At the end, Luther turns also this double commandment into a positive formulation and hints at its New Testament meaning:[38] it fights greed as the root of all evil (1 Tim. 6:10) and seeks the pure heart that is free from all covetousness.

THE PROHIBITION OF "COVETING" IN THE OLD AND NEW TESTAMENTS[39]

The double commandment concluding the Decalogue—"You shall not covet . . ." (Exod. 20:17; Deut. 5:21)—protects the property of the full Israelite citizen and partaker in the inheritance of the people, everything that is in his hand and power. As Luther notes,[40] his wife and household slaves are also part of his "possession"; his children are not mentioned in the commandment.

It is peculiar that the verb is repeated, which encouraged Augustine to count two commandments. Equally peculiar is that the listing of the objects that one is forbidden to covet varies, which led to the confusion in the demarcation of the two commandments. In Exod. 20:17, the "house" is mentioned first, and then, in a second approach, the neighbor's entire property and space of existence is covered.[41] Deuteronomy 5:21 lets the wife be followed by the possession of goods, people, and animals.

---

32   *BSLK*, 633.38–634.26.

33   *BSLK*, 634.27–46.

34   Section 2: *BSLK*, 634.46–638.28.

35   *BSLK*, 634.46–637.20.

36   *BSLK*, 637.21–50.

37   *BSLK*, 638.1–28.

38   Section 3: *BSLK*, 638.29–639.10.

39   Literature on this topic: Herrmann, "Das zehnte Gebot"; Friedrich Büchsel, ἐπιθυμεία, *TWNT* 3:168–72; Otto Michel, οἶκος, *TWNT* 5:122–36.

40   *BSLK*, 634.3–26.

41   Noth, *Das zweite Buch Mose*, 134: ". . . beginning with the wife, who, according to OT property law, was part of the man's property, and ending with a general formulation that makes the further listing of details unnecessary."

It is usually assumed that the commandment read originally: "You shall not covet your neighbor's house."[42] One maintains that it was then explained by a list that both interprets and complements, seeking to cover both nuances of the term *bayīt*, namely, *domus* and *familia*. Johannes Herrmann[43] supports this view by the following observation: "house" (*bayīt*) has four meanings in the Old Testament: (1) the established house or building as opposed to the tent; (2) the "home" as a protective sphere, the inside as opposed to the foreign and hostile outside; (3) the family and offspring whereby, next to the wife and the servants, especially the children are in view; and, finally, (4) beyond the extended family, the clan and nation. The actual perspective of the prohibition—everything the neighbor has, what makes up his "house" as his property and fortune—is therefore not unequivocally described by the term "house." It first needs to be unfolded.

Perhaps this double commandment was formed out of the remainders of an apodictic series of prohibitions that featured the verb *āmad* as the key word. Taken out of priestly tradition, it was meant to complement the Seventh Commandment, which originally was about the theft of the full citizen.[44]

Whatever the origin of this double commandment and however it came about, it is clear that it rounds off the Decalogue and simultaneously complements the prohibitions of theft and adultery.

In the Septuagint, the verb *āmad*—like *hit'awweh*, the one paralleled to it in Deut. 5:21—is translated as ἐπιθυμεῖν and, therefore, has traditionally been interpreted to denote the desires of the heart. However, Johannes Herrmann has shown that by *āmad*, the Hebrew denotes an affect that pushes beyond itself to action.[45] There is "still the naïve marveling" in this word that reaches out to what grabs its interest[46] and exclaims: "Oh, if I could only have it!"[47] Thus the prohibition aims not at "a mere attitude." Rather, it wants to

42   For the LCMS position, see the publisher's introduction, pp. 10–11.

43   Herrmann, "Das zehnte Gebot," 75–79, taken up by von Reventlow, *Gebot und Predigt im Dekalog*, 87f.

44   Thus von Reventlow, *Gebot und Predigt im Dekalog*, 90f., who mentions as a reason the old age of apodictic forms, who additionally points to the independence of the two pillars of the set—the house and the wife—and who also remembers the firmly established chain of the elements between the two pillars and similar sets in Lev. 18:16ff.; 20:11–13, (15,) 18, 20; Deut. 27:20–23.

45   Herrmann, "Das zehnte Gebot," 71–75, referencing Deut. 7:25; Josh. 7:21; Mic. 2:2; Ps. 68:17; Exod. 34:24. His interpretation was taken up by, among others, Alt, "Das Verbot des Diebstahls im Dekalog," 333ff.; Stamm, *Der Dekalog im Lichte der neueren Forschung*, 56ff.; von Reventlow, *Gebot und Predigt im Dekalog*, 85ff.; and Köhler, "Der Dekalog," 183.

46   Kaiser, *Der königliche Knecht*, 99.

47   "Kat.-Pred. zum 8.–10. Gebot vom 19.9.1528," WA 30.1:43.9.

stop "the preparatory activities that lead to actually taking possession, that precede the latter but are already actions."[48]

The prophetic preaching actualizes this prohibition in a changed situation. Especially in the area of the capital cities Jerusalem and Samaria, the economy of large royal landed estates and a certain accumulation of capital had pushed the small landowners into a crisis. They were pushed out of their inherited property by the princes and large landowners. The gentry thus acquire house after house and connect field to field (Isa. 5:8) until they alone are left as heirs of the Promised Land. The prophets condemn this early capitalist speculation as infringement on the sacred order of soil by equating it with the age-old blasphemy of moving the boundary stones (Hosea 5:10), which was punishable by God's ban (Deut. 17:17; 19:14). Not only was being a citizen in Israel tied to the possession of land, as was the case in all agrarian forms of society, but having a share in land and soil was also a concrete expression of a person's participation in God's covenant. After all, the following word of God applied to owning land: "The land is Mine; you are only strangers and aliens with Me" (Lev. 25:23).[49] The property of those who do not have full legal standing—such as widows, orphans, and strangers—is explicitly placed under God's ban (Exod. 22:23f.). To rob them was considered an especially serious blasphemy,[50] all the way to Jesus' announcement of God's judgment on the scribes who "devour the houses of the widows" (Mark 12:40; Luke 20:47).[51]

Already the Deuteronomic preachers drive this double commandment forward against the heart of the addressees. In Deut. 5:21, lō' tit'awweh is added to lō' taḥmōd. The accent in the former lies on the longing of the inner man, since it is also applied to an ultimately personal event that we cannot bring about by ourselves, such as the breaking in of Yahweh in judgment and grace.[52] This verb thus "spiritualizes" the commandment. "This observation is not surprising when one considers the general tendency of the sermon . . . to address the heart of man and to summon its thoughts before its tribunal."[53] The Septuagint's οὐκ ἐπιθυμήσεις intensifies the turn inward and transmits it to Judaism.

In Philo and probably also in 4 Maccabees, the Old Testament impulse is connected to Stoic-Hellenistic ideas. According to the Stoa, reason is to

48   Von Reventlow, *Gebot und Predigt im Dekalog*, 86; cf. Noth, *Das zweite Buch Mose*, 133.

49   Von Rad, *Theologie des Alten Testaments*, 1:298, calls this sentence "the theological foundation for the entire ancient Israelite land law."

50   Job 24:2ff. and Prov. 23:10, with the Egyptian parallel. Cf. Ringgren, *Sprüche*, 93f.

51   Cf. Michel, οἰκία, *TWNT* 5:134 n. 3.

52   Amos 5:18; Jer. 17:16; Isa. 26:9.

53   Von Reventlow, *Gebot und Predigt im Dekalog*, 87; cf. Stamm, "Dreißig Jahre Dekalogforschung," 302; *Der Dekalog im Lichte der neueren Forschung*, 59.

order and overcome all passions that especially as ἐπιθυμεία emerge from the sphere of the sensual/sexual.[54] Judaism teaches to wrestle with the "evil inclination" of the heart that seeks to live itself out in coveting as the root of every transgression. Thus God's will is concentrated in the commandment not to covet. "Based on the fact that it is the (reliable) law that said we should not lust, I think it possible to show you in a much more convincing fashion (than by the individual example of Joseph) that reason is able to rule over the desires" (4 Maccabees 2:6).[55]

According to James, the evil desire is the motivation behind all individual sinful acts and brings about death (James 1:14f.). According to John, in its different forms the evil desire bears the stigma of this world of death (1 John 2:15–17). Paul summarizes these individual statements.[56] The evil desire cannot be limited to what is sensual/sexual; it reveals itself in the Jewish quest for boasting in the law, as well as in Hellenistic pride in knowledge of wisdom and intellectual power (1 Cor. 1:1f.). In all this, there is still the old man at work who trusts in his flesh, who wants to assert himself in an autonomous reach for life, and who, by doing so, is condemned to death. Against the original will of man to self-assertion and self-aggrandizement, God establishes His prohibition of coveting. The instruction "Do not covet" not only summarizes, according to Rom. 13:9, the last two commandments, but according to Rom. 7:7,[57] it also summarizes the entire Decalogue, even the entire Law.[58]

In a centuries-long process of reflection, this double commandment that concludes the Decalogue also is driven forward against the innermost parts of man. God alone wants to rule in the core of man's heart, as the basic commandment of selfless love of God commands. As the prohibition "You shall not covet" leaves behind its objects, it steps right next to the prohibition of idols and returns to the opening of the Decalogue. As our Creator and Redeemer, God does not want us to get bogged down in this perishing world of death and idolize what is perishable. This is why He prohibits coveting as the root of all idolatry. He takes our eyes off the earth and turns them upward to Himself. Yet in this process, the double commandment loses its concrete form. The protection of the neighbor and his earthly possessions

---

54   According to Büchsel, ἐπιθυμεία, *TWNT* 3:168–72. The commandment begins to focus on sexuality and is interpreted as a call to self-discipline that also requires the mastery over one's eyes, following 2 Sam. 11:2; Job 31:1.

55   According to the rendition by Deissmann in Kautzsch, *Die Apokryphen*, on the verse. Cf. also *Bill.*, 3:234–37 (on Rom. 7:7).

56   On this Bultmann, *Theologie des Neuen Testaments*, 224, 227f., 241–48; *Christus des Gesetzes Ende*; Bornkamm, "Sünde, Gesetz und Tod (Röm 7)."

57   The active dimension of *amad*, on the other hand, is preserved in the translation as μὴ ἀποστερήσῃς in Mark 10:19. Cf. *Shepherd of Hermas, Mandates* 8:5; *Similitudes* 6:5.5.

58   Cf. 1 Cor. 10:6.

is no longer part of the reflection; the protective character of the commandment is lost.

LUTHER'S INTERPRETATION IN THE TENSION BETWEEN THE OLD TESTAMENT AND NEW TESTAMENT SCOPES OF THE DOUBLE COMMANDMENT[59]

Luther was aware of the Old Testament meaning of the word *āmad*.[60] Already in "Decem praecepta" ("Preaching of the Ten Commandments"), he mentions that the Jewish interpretation of the double commandment refers to the "external effort" and the "manifest judgment of a deed."[61] In the catechisms, Luther limits himself almost entirely to the "basic meaning"[62] of those instructions given "to the Jews in particular."[63] Different than the Seventh and Sixth Commandments, this double commandment is there not only to stop "acts of aggression." It also prohibits the "indirect ways"[64] to possess somebody else's goods or lure away persons from one's neighbor, even those ways that are not directly against the laws and that therefore cannot be punished by an earthly judge. God's zeal also watches over these dark practices.[65]

Although Luther knew all this from the very beginning, he nonetheless did not interpret the double commandment in his early confessional manuals. After all, he did not intend to lecture the Christians entrusted to him on the probable basic meaning of an Old Testament text, but he wanted to introduce them to the will of the God who disclosed Himself in a final way in Jesus Christ. Christ, however, intensified the prohibition of adultery and theft in the Sermon on the Mount, and His apostle also concentrated this double commandment on the dark coveting of the heart.[66] Since Christ already in Matt. 5:28 had condemned as adultery the covetous look at somebody else's woman, it made sense to render a part of the double commandment as: "You

---

59 On this, Hardeland, *Katechismusgedanken*, 176ff.; Meyer, *Historischer Kommentar*, 252f.

60 This was noted by Herrmann, "Das zehnte Gebot," 75, while it was missed by Stamm, *Der Dekalog im Lichte der neueren Forschung*, 56, and von Reventlow, *Gebot und Predigt im Dekalog*, 85.

61 WA 1:516.13.

62 *BSLK*, 638.30.

63 *BSLK*, 633.38.

64 Von Reventlow, *Gebot und Predigt im Dekalog*, 86.

65 *BSLK*, 638.1–28.

66 "Decem praecepta, 1518," WA 1:515.5–14, 516.3–9; "Von den guten Werken, 1520," WA 6:276.14 (see also AE 44:15–114).

shall not covet your neighbor's wife, daughter, or maidservant,"[67] and to interpret it under the Sixth Commandment. Since Christ had taken up the prohibition of theft, albeit only indirectly, and intensified it in the Sermon on the Mount's threefold demand: "Giving for free, lending without interest, and letting go in peace what is taken by force,"[68] it made sense to reformulate the other part of the double commandment as: "You shall not covet your neighbor's house or goods,"[69] and to interpret it under the Seventh Commandment. Yet what is left of the meaning of the double commandment, since it had to cede its concrete objects to the radicalized Sixth and Seventh Commandments? All that remained was to take it with the apostle (Rom. 13:9) as one commandment that reads: "You shall not covet."

By doing so, Luther merely draws the conclusion out of the occidental tradition of Decalogue catechesis. Already Augustine had taught that this double commandment—first split by him—aims at the double-faced coveting of the heart, at "adulterous thinking" and at "lust."[70] Thomas adds that the divine Law goes beyond all orders of the earthly world precisely in that it judges not only the deeds and words but also the thoughts of the heart.[71] And Bonaventure formulates already quite similarly to Luther that this double commandment strikes at the desires of the flesh as the tinder of all sins, even as the fever that has affected all children of Adam and hatches all evil.[72]

The German-language confessional manuals take up this view and thereby connect this double commandment with the prohibitions of adultery and theft. While these prohibit the practical coveting and stealing, this one prohibits already the "concupiscence of the flesh and of temporal goods"[73] and demands the total turning away from the perishing creature

---

67   "Eine kurze Erklärung, 1518," WA 1:251.21.

68   "Gr. Sermon von dem Wucher, 1520," WA 6:51.11 (see also AE 45:231–310). Cf. p. 271.

69   "Eine kurze Erklärung, 1518," WA 1:251.23.

70   Augustine, Sermon 9:13.

71   Thomas Aquinas, *Duo praecepta* § 1315: "Haec est differentia inter legem divinam et mundanam: quia lex mundana iudicat facta et dicta; divina autem non haec tantum, sed etiam cogitata. [There is a difference between divine Law and that of the world; for the worldly law judges facts and words, while the divine does not judge so much those things as it rather judges thoughts]." Melanchthon, *Catechesis puerilis*, 1540 (Reu, *Quellen*, 1.2.2:48.25): "The remaining two commandments are added in order to interpret the Law and to set God's Law apart from human laws and philosophy." Cf. Melanchthon, *Loci*, in *Studienausgabe* 2.1:311.26–312.23.

72   Bonaventure, *Collationes des decem praeceptis* 6:6 (5:530): "The unlawful inner act is prohibited, and here is prohibited the concupiscence of the eyes or lust, which is the root of all evils. Here is prohibited the concupiscence of the flesh, which is the fountain of all sins. . . . This is the fever in which sons of Adam lie and which generates all evils."

73   Bonaventure, *Collationes des decem praeceptis* 6:8; similarly Herp, Hollen, Schobser (Geffcken, *Bildercatechismus*, 97ff.), Gerson/Geiler, *Spiegel des Sünders*, Laurent, et al. (Geffcken, *Bildercatechismus*, app., col. 45f., 76ff., 85, 88, 137f., 155f.).

and the radical turning to the God who alone gives life.[74] Despite these insights, one primarily interprets also this double commandment in great detail and repeats what was said before.

Luther draws the conclusion out of these insights and interprets Rom. 13:9. As God prohibits carnal coveting in general, He turns our eyes back to Himself and, as Rom. 7:7f.[75] shows, uncovers by the Law the original source of all actual sins, the rebellious heart itself: "Whoever resolves to watch, to pray, to help the neighbor will always find a rebellious flesh that has totally different things in mind."[76] This original sin of our flesh that rebels against God's will is the "essential or causal impurity"[77] at the bottom of all our violations of the commandments of the entire Decalogue in thoughts, words, and deeds. This egotistic thirst for life, this greedy clinging to the earth, this natural referring everything to oneself—we all are born into it, we have inherited it without our will and collaboration, but we have accepted it in the core of our existence. Luther summarizes this original guilt, which is simultaneously and collectively the inherited basic enslavement of the entire human race and the willful self-enslavement of my own ego, in the fitting saying: "the inherited sin or natural sin or personal sin, the real main sin."[78]

As the "You shall not covet" of the double commandment, according to the early Luther, penetrates into this abyss, it summarizes, according to Rom. 7:7f., the entire Law and reveals its ultimate intention, which the Lord fixed in the *not only—but already* of the antitheses of the Sermon on the Mount. This prohibition thereby becomes the anthropological counterpart to the First Commandment. It demands "perfect chastity and radical contempt of temporal lust and goods."[79] If the double commandment is understood in this way, then it can no longer be part of the confession before men[80] when God wills to uproot precisely and above all this root of every actual transgression. This is why Luther only mentions this commandment in the confessional manual but does not interpret it. It is to point to the goal,

---

74 This underlines Markus von Lindau (Geffcken, *Bildercatechismus*, 99; cf. Geffcken, *Bildercatechismus*, app., col. 137f.).

75 On the relationship between Paul and Luther, see Althaus, *Paulus und Luther über den Menschen*; Ellwein, "Das Rätsel von Römer 7"; Joest, "Paulus und das Lutherische Simul Iustus et Peccator"; Peters, *Glaube und Werk*, 137–83.

76 "Röm.-Vorl., 1515/16," WA 56:342.4: "Qui vigilare, orare, operari proximi proponit, semper invenit rebellam carnem et alia machinantem atque cupientem."

77 "Decem praecepta, 1518," WA 1:516.6: "Therefore, here the tinder's evil and, as I might say, the essential and causal impurity in us is prohibited."

78 "Weihnachtspost. zu Lk. 2:21, 1522," WA 10.1.1:508.20.

79 "Eine kurze Erklärung, 1518," WA 1:255.17; "Eine kurze Form, 1520," WA 7:214.2.

80 Cf. "Eine kurze Erklärung," WA 1:253.35–254.2; "Instructio, 1518," WA 1:262.9–13; "Eine kurze Form," WA 7:211.24–27; "Pred. zum 8.–10. Gebot vom 3.3.1523," WA 11:48.11–15; "Eine kurze Unterweisung, 1519," WA 2:64.10–17.

to the "purest chastity and poverty of spirit,"[81] which begins in our life on earth but is fully achieved first through the fire of judgment. Luther accentuates the apostle's cry for deliverance (Rom. 7:24) and teaches those "spiritual children" to whom he is a Father Confessor to long for physical death and for the fire of the Last Day,[82] because only the eschatological breaking forth of the divine zeal of wrath and salvation finally burns out that original sin that has eaten itself so deeply into our being as humans.

Many reformation catechisms take over this understanding of the double commandment. It shines into "the abyss and depth of human nature."[83] The "Nürnberger Katechismuspredigten" ("Nürnberg Catechism Sermons") develop before the youth a psychologically oriented doctrine of original sin and by it defend infant baptism.[84] Melanchthon, Calvin, and the Heidelberg Catechism also underline the spiritual meaning of the double commandment.[85] As the anthropological counterpart to the First Commandment, it completes the circle of the Decalogue by turning our eyes back to the basic movement of faith.

In the November 12, 1525, sermon,[86] in the 1528 catechism sermon, and in the catechisms, Luther returns to the Old Testament understanding of the last two commandments that he had rejected in "Preaching of the Ten Commandments" as "understanding of the Jews or rather pigs."[87] However, again the basic difference can be observed. In "Preaching of the Ten Commandments," Luther had harshly turned against limiting the interpretation of *āmad* to active deeds as an expression of the desire to absolve thereby the inner desires of the heart and the covetous thoughts from sin. In the Large Catechism, to be sure, he moves primarily on the level of the "savvy findings and quick manipulations,"[88] but he consciously concludes with the reference to the Pauline view.[89] God has given the double commandment "in particular against envy and tiresome greed."[90] Luther wants to pull out the root (1 Tim. 6:10) of all attacks on the neighbor and seeks as the

---

81   "Instructio," WA 1:264.2.

82   "Decem praecepta," WA 1:515.21ff.; "Von den guten Werken, 1520," WA 6:276.17ff. (see also AE 44:15–114). Cf. the comments on the Last Petition of the Lord's Prayer.

83   Agricola, *Christl. Kinderzucht* (MGP 21:34f.); cf. *130 Fragen,* quest. 126 (MGP 21:295); Gräter, *Catechesis,* quest. 18 (MGP 21:330f.); Brenz, *Fragstücke,* quest. 77–83 (MGP 22:183f.).

84   "Nürnberger Katechismuspredigten" (Reu, *Quellen,* 1.1:500.23–501.4).

85   On Melanchthon, see p. 312 n. 71; Calvin, Geneva Catechism, quest. 213–16; Calvin, *Inst.* 2:8.49f.; Heidelberg Catechism, quest. 113f.

86   WA 16:525–28.

87   WA 1:516:10–18; cf. "Pred. über Ex. 20 vom 12.11.1525," WA 16:526f.

88   *BSLK,* 635.4.

89   *BSLK,* 638.29–639.10.

90   *BSLK,* 638.37.

eschatological goal of our existence before God the heart that is free from the inherited sin of worldly coveting.[91]

At the end of the Decalogue interpretation, we again encounter its characteristic. Especially on this double commandment, Luther preserves, in the Small Catechism more than in the Large,[92] the Old Testament colors of a patriarchal way of living that gave the master of the house legal authority also over wife and servants. Yet in this one-sided correlation, which lies behind us and is not to be repristinated, Luther urges obedience toward God in relation to our fellow man according to the standard of the Golden Rule. Along with the entire Second Table, Luther sees in this rule also a summary of this last commandment.[93] It prohibits the external practices as well as the inner envy and tiresome greed in all areas of human life together. "The fulfillment consists in love of the other and not of ourselves, for man already does, leaves undone, and seeks enough for himself, so that this need not be taught but resisted. This is why that person lives best who does not live for himself. And that person lives worst who lives for himself."[94]

Greed, however, is a sign of unbelief, of lacking trust in God: "The cause of greed is mistrust, but the cause of mildness is faith."[95] Thus the double commandment turns our eyes back to God and to our heart. In his interpretation, Luther primarily moves about the "basic meaning"[96] of the *usus crassus et puerilis decalogi*, but in conclusion he cautiously and, as it were, from afar points to the *usus spiritualis* fully disclosed by Christ, which he, however, here describes as *usus elenchticus legis*.[97] This double commandment, above all, accuses us and by doing so points us beyond itself to the Creed and the Lord's Prayer as the power sources for the fulfillment of the Commandments.[98]

TEXTS ON THE DOUBLE COMMANDMENT

WA 1:515f.: from Decem praecepta Wittenbergensi praedicata populo, 1518

WA 16:525–28: from Predigt über Ex. 20 (9. u. 10. Gebot) vom 12.11.1525

---

91 *BSLK*, 638.43ff. "Kat.-Pred. zum 9. u. 10. Praeceptum vom 22./23.5.1528," WA 30.1:9.11: "We ought to have a heart free from greed and unchastity." "Pred. über Ex. 20 vom 12.11.1525," WA 16:527.2: "Concupiscence or the lust and will is here condemned."

92 *BSLK*, 634.3–26.

93 *BSLK*, 637.5f., 635.14f. Cf. p. 276 n. 127.

94 "Eine kurze Form, 1520," WA 7:214.15.

95 "Von den guten Werken, 1520," WA 6:272.20 (see also AE 44:15–114).

96 *BSLK*, 638.30.

97 *BSLK*, 639.2ff.

98 See the comments on the relationship between the first three chief parts, esp. pp. 45–51.

LITERATURE

Ahrens, "Was heißt 'abspannen' in Luthers Erklärung zum 10. Gebot?"

Malo, "Abspannen, abdringen, abwendig machen"

Sprenger, "Abspannen"

Conrad, "Das 9. und 10. Gebot"

Gareis, "Zum 9. und 10. Gebot"

Hardeland, *Luthers Katechismusgedanken in ihrer Entwicklung bis zum Jahre 1529*, 176–78

Meyer, *Historischer Kommentar zu Luthers Kleinem Katechismus*, 252–56

Bibliography

Achelis, Ernst Christian. *Der Dekalog als katechetisches Lehrstück.* Gießen: Töpelmann, 1905.

Ahrens, R. "Was heißt 'abspannen' in Luthers Erklärung zum 10. Gebot?" *Zeistchrift für den evangelischen Religionsunterricht* 4 (1893): 149f.

Albrecht, Otto. "Besondere Einleitung in den Kleinen Katechismus." Pages 537–665 in vol. 30.1 of *D. Martin Luthers Werke: Kritische Gesamtausgabe.* Weimar: Herman Böhlau, 1910.

———. "Bibliographie zum Großen Katechismus." Pages 499–521 in vol. 30.1 of *D. Martin Luthers Werke: Kritische Gesamtausgabe.* Weimar: Herman Böhlau, 1910.

———. *Luthers Katechismen.* Schriften des Vereins für Reformationsgeschichte 33, no. 121/122. Leipzig: Verein für Reformationsgeschichte, 1915.

———. "Streiflichter auf Luthers Erklärung des ersten Gebots im Kleinen Katechismus." *Theologische Studien und Kritiken* 90 (1917): 421–95.

———. "Vorbemerkungen zu beiden Katechismen." Pages 426–74 in vol. 30.1 of *D. Martin Luthers Werke: Kritische Gesamtausgabe.* Weimar: Herman Böhlau, 1910.

Alt, Albrecht. "Die Ursprünge des israelitischen Rechts (1934)." Pages 278–332 in vol. 1 of *Kleine Schriften zur Geschichte des Volkes Israel.* Munich: Beck, 1953.

———. "Das Verbot des Diebstahls im Dekalog (1949)." Pages 333–40 in vol. 1 of *Kleine Schriften zur Geschichte des Volkes Israel.* Munich: Beck, 1953.

———. "Zur Talionsformel." *Zeitschrift für die Alttestamentliche Wissenschaft* 52 (1934): 303–5. Reprinted as pages 341–44 in vol. 1 of *Kleine Schriften zur Geschichte des Volkes Israel.* Munich: Beck, 1953.

Alt, Hans-Peter. *Das Problem der Todesstrafe.* Munich: Kaiser, 1960.

Althaus, Paul. *Die Ethik Martin Luthers.* Gütersloh: Gütersloher, 1965.

———. "Luthers Wort von der Ehe." *Luther* (1953): 1–10.

———. *Paulus und Luther über den Menschen.* 2d ed. Gütersloh: Bertelsmann, 1951.

———. *Die Theologie Martin Luthers.* Gütersloh: Gütersloher, 1962.

———. *Die Todesstrafe als Problem der christlichen Ethik.* Sitzungsberichte der Bayerischen Akademie der Wissenschaften, Philosophisch-historische Klasse 2. Munich: Bayerischen Akademie der Wissenschaften, 1955.

———. "Und wenn es köstlich gewesen ist (1934)." Pages 151–61 in vol. 2 of *Theologische Aufsätze.* Gütersloh: Bertelsmann, 1935.

Ambrose. *De mysteriis.* In Corpus scriptorum ecclesiasticorum latinorum 73.

Asheim, Ivar. *Glaube und Erziehung bei Luther.* Heidelberg: Quelle & Meyer, 1961.

Athanasius. *Die Fest-Briefe des Heiligen Athanasius Bischofs von Alexandria.* Translated and edited by F. Larsow. Leipzig-Göttingen, 1852.

Auerbach, Elias. "Das Zehngebot: Allgemeine Gesetzes-Form in der Bibel." *Vetus Testamentum* 16 (1966): 255–76.

Augustine. *De sermone Domini in monte libros duos.* In Corpus Christianorum: Series latina 35.

———. *Enchiridion.* In Corpus Christianorum: Series latina 46:49–114.

———. *Quaestiones in Heptateuchum.* In Corpus Christianorum: Series latina 33:1–377.

———. *Sermones.* In Corpus Christianorum: Series latina 41. Especially sermon 8: *De decem plagis Aegyptiorum et decem praeceptis legis* (Corpus Christianorum: Series latina 41:79–99) and sermon 9: *De decem chordis* (Corpus Christianorum: Series latina 41:105–51).

Bachmann, Philipp. *Luthers Kleiner Katechismus als Aufgabe für die Gegenwart.* Leipzig: Deichert, 1929.

———. *Luthers Kleiner Katechismus als Urkunde evangelischer Frömmigkeit.* Leipzig, Deichert, 1929.

———. "Die Reihenfolge der drei ersten Hauptstücke." *Neue Kirchliche Zeitschrift* 26 (1915): 367–82.

Baltensweiler, Heinrich. *Die Ehe im Neuen Testament.* Zurich: Zwingli, 1967.

Baltzer, Klaus. *Das Bundesformular.* Wissenschaftliche Monographien zum Alten und Neuen Testament 4. Neukirchen: Neukirchener, 1960.

Bandt, Hellmut. *Luthers Lehre vom verborgenen Gott: Eine Untersuchung zu dem offenbarungsgeschichtlichen Ansatz seiner Theologie.* Berlin: Evangelische Verlagsanstalt, 1958.

Barge, Hermann. *Luther und der Frühkapitalismus.* Schriften des Vereins für Reformationsgeschichte 58, no. 168. Gütersloh: Bertelsmann, 1951.

Barth, Hans-Martin. "Glaube als Projektion: Zur Auseinandersetzung mit Ludwig Feuerbach." *Neue Zeistchrfit für Systematische Theologie und Religionsphilosophie* 12 (1970): 363–82.

———. *Der Teufel und Jesus Christus in der Theologie Martin Luthers.* Göttingen: Vandenhoeck & Ruprecht, 1967.

Barth, Karl. *Die Kirchliche Dogmatik.* Zurich: Evangelischer, 1932ff.

———. *Die protestantische Theologie im 19. Jahrhundert.* Zurich: Evangelischer, 1947.

Bauernfeind, Otto. *Eid und Frieden: Fragen zur Anwendung und zum Wesen des Eides.* Stuttgart: Kohlhammer, 1956.

Baynes, Norman H. "Idolatry and the Early Church." Pages 116–43 in *Byzantine Studies and Other Essays.* London: Athlone Press, 1960.

Beer, Georg. *Exodus.* Handbuch zum Alten Testament 1.3. Tübingen: Mohr, 1939.

Die Bekenntnisschriften der evangelisch-lutherischen Kirche. Edited by Deutscher Evangangelischer Kirchenausschuß. 9th ed. Göttingen: Vandenhoeck & Ruprecht, 1982.

Bernhardt, Karl Heinz. *Gott und Bild: Ein Beitrag zur Begründung und Deutung des Bilderverbotes im Alten Testamentum.* Berlin: Evangelische Verlagsanstalt, 1956.

Beyerlin, Walter. *Herkunft und Geschichte der ältesten Sinaitraditionen.* Tübingen, 1961.

Bienert, Walther. *Die Arbeit nach der Lehre der Bibel.* Stuttgart: Evangelisches Verlagswerk, 1954.

Billerbeck, Paul, and Hermann Leberecht Strack. *Kommentar zum Neuen Testament aus Talmud und Midrasch.* (*Bill.*) 2d ed. Munich: Beck, 1956.

Blinzler, Joseph. "Die Strafe für Ehebruch in Bibel und Halacha." *New Testament Studies* 4 (1957/58): 32–47.

Böhmer, Heinrich. "Luthers Ehe." *Luther Jahrbuch* 7 (1925): 40–76.

Bonaventure. *Collationes de decem praeceptis.* Pages 507–32 in vol. 5 of *S. Bonaventurae Opera Omnia,* edited by Studio et Cura PP. Collegii a S. Bonaventura. Florence, 1891.

———. *Libri sententiarum.* In *Opera theologica selecta.* 4 vols. Edited by Leonardi M. Bello et al. Florence, 1934–49.

Bonhoeffer, Dietrich. *Ethik.* Munich: Kaiser, 1949.

Bornkamm, Günther. "Ehescheidung und Wiederverheiratung im Neuen Testament." Pages 50–53 in *Die Mischehe.* Edited by W. Sucker et al. Göttingen, 1959. Reprinted as pages 56–59 in vol. 1 of *Geschichte und Glaube.* Munich: Kaiser, 1968.

———. "Die Häresie des Kolosserbriefes." Pages 139–56 in *Das Ende des Gesetzes: Paulusstudien.* Munich: Kaiser, 1952.

———. *Jesus von Nazareth.* Stuttgart: Kohlhammer, 1956.

———. "Sünde, Gesetz und Tod (Röm 7)." Pages 51–69 in *Das Ende des Gesetzes: Paulusstudien.* Munich: Kaiser, 1952.

Bornkamm, Heinrich. *Luther und das Alte Testament.* Tubingen: Mohr 1948.

Botterweck, Gerhard Johannes. "Form- und überlieferungs geschichtliche Studie zum Dekalog." *Concilium* 1 (1965): 392–401.

———. "Der Sabbat im Alten Testament." *Theologisch-praktische Quartalschrift* 134 (1954): 134–36, 448–57.

Breit, Herbert. *Die Predigt des Deuteronomisten.* Munich: Kaiser, 1933.

Bring, Ragnar. *Das Verhältnis von Glauben und Werken in der lutherischen Theologie.* Munich: Kaiser, 1955.

Brunner, Emil. *Das Gebot und die Ordnungen.* 4th ed. Zurich: Zwingli, 1939.

Brunner, Peter. "Das Hirtenamt und die Frau (1959)." Pages 310–38 in vol. 1 of *Pro ecclesia.* Berlin: Lutherisches Verlagshaus, 1962.

———. *Das Lutherische Bekenntnis in der Union.* Gütersloh: Bertelsmann, 1952.

———. "Zur Lehre vom Gottesdienst der im Namen Jesu versammelten Gemeinde." Pages 83–364 in vol. 1 of *Leiturgia.* Edited by F. Müller and W. Blankenburg. Kassel: Staude, 1954.

Brunotte, Wilhelm. *Das geistliche Amt bei Luther.* Berlin: Lutherisches Verlagshaus, 1959.

Buber, Martin. *Moses.* 2d ed. Heidelberg, 1952.

Buchberger, Michael and Eugen Seiterich, eds. *Lexicon für Theologie und Kirche.* (*LTK*) 2d rev. ed. 11 vols. Freiburg, 1957–65.

Bultmann, Rudolf. *Christus des Gesetzes Ende.* Pages 3–27 of Beiträge zur evangelischen Theologie 1. Munich: Lempp, 1940. Reprinted as pages 32–58 in vol. 2 of *Glauben und Verstehen.* 2d ed. Tübingen: Mohr, 1958.

———. *Das Evangelium des Johannes.* Kritisch-exegetischer Kommentar über das Neue Testament 2. 10th ed. Göttingen: Vandenhoeck & Ruprecht, 1941.

———. *Jesus.* 2d ed. Berlin: Dt. Bibliotek, 1929.

———. *Theologie des Neuen Testaments.* Tübingen: Mohr, 1958.

Calvin, John. *Opera selecta.* Edited by P. Barth and W. Niesel. Munich: Kaiser, 1926–36.

———. *Unterricht in der christlichen Religion.* Translated and edited according to the last edition by O. Weber. 4th ed. Neukirchen: Neukirchener, 1986.

Campenhausen, Hans Freiherr von. "Die Askese im Urchristentum." Pages 114–56 in *Tradition und Leben, Kräfte der Kirchengeschichte, Aufsätze und Vorträge.* Tübingen: Mohr, 1960.

———. "Die Bilderfrage als theologisches Problem der alten Kirche." Pages 216–52 in *Tradition und Leben, Kräfte der Kirchengeschichte, Aufsätze und Vorträge.* Tübingen: Mohr, 1960.

———. "Die Bilderfrage in der Reformation." Pages 361–407 in *Tradition und Leben, Kräfte der Kirchengeschichte, Aufsätze und Vorträge.* Tübingen: Mohr, 1960.

Carrington, Philip. *The Primitive Christian Catechism.* Cambridge: Cambridge University Press, 1940.

Cicero. *De legibus.* Edited by Konrat Ziegler. 2d ed. Heidelberg: Kerle, 1963.

Cohrs, Ferdinand, ed. *Die evangelischen Katechismusversuche vor Luthers Enchiridion.* 3 vols. Berlin: Hofmann, 1900f. (= *Monumenta Germaniae Paedagogica* [*MGP*]. Edited by K. Kehrbach. Vols. 20–22).

Conrad, Paul (?). "Das 9. und 10. Gebot." Pages 361–64 in *Pastoralblatt* (1892/93).

Delling, Gerhard. *Paulus' Stellung zu Frau und Ehe.* Stuttgart: Kohlhammer, 1931.

Denkschrift zu Fragen der Sexualethik. Edited by Kirchenkanzlei der EKD. Gütersloh, 1971.

Denkschrift zur Reform des Ehescheidungsrechts in der Bundesrepublik Deutschland. 3d ed. Edited by Kirchenkanzlei der EKD. Gütersloh, 1970.

Denzinger, Heinrich, and Adolfus Schönmetzer, eds. *Enchiridion Symbolorum.* 36th ed. Freiburg: Herder, 1976.

Dinkler, Erich. "Jesu Wort vom Kreuztragen." Pages 110–29 in *Neutestamentliche Studien für Rudolf Bultmann.* Edited by Walther Eltester. Berlin: Töpelmann, 1954.

Dittrich, Ottmar. *Luthers Ethik in ihrem Grundzügen dargestellt.* Leipzig: Meiner, 1930.

Dodd, Charles Harold. *Gospel and Law.* Cambridge: Cambridge University Press, 1950.

Dress, Walter. "Die zehn Gebote in Luthers theologischem Denken." *Wissenschaftliche Zeitschrift der Humboldt-Universität zu Berlin, gesellschafts- und sprachwissenschaftliche Reihe* 3, no. 3 (1953/54): 213–18.

Duchrow, Ulrich. *Christenheit und Weltverantwortung: Traditionsgeschichte und systematische Struktur der Zwei-Reiche-Lehre.* Stuttgart: Klett, 1970.

Dürr, Lorenz. "Die Wertung des Lebens im Alten Testament und im alten Orient." *Verzeichnis der Vorlesungen an der Staatlichen Akademie zu Braunsberg* (1926/27): 1–43.

Ebeling, Adolf. *Der Kleine Katechismus Luthers*. 2d ed. 1902.

———. "Das zweite Gebot in Luthers Kleinem Katechismus." *Theologische Studien und Kritiken* 74 (1901): 229–41.

Ebeling, Gerhard. *Gott und Wort*. Tübingen: Mohr, 1966.

———. *Luther: Einführung in sein Denken*. Tübingen: Mohr, 1964.

Eggersdorfer, Franz Xaver. *Der Heilige Augustinus als Pädagoge und seine Bedeutung für die Geschichte der Bildung*. Freiburg: Herder, 1907.

Ehe und Ehescheidung. Stundenbuch 30. Hamburg, 1963.

Elert, Werner. *Das christliche Ethos*. Hamburg: Furche, 1949.

———. "Gesetz und Evangelium." Pages 132–69 in *Zwischen Gnade und Ungnade*. Munich: Evangelischer Presseverband für Bayern, 1948.

———. *Morphologie des Luthertums*. 2 vols. Reprint Munich: Beck, 1958.

———. "Zur Frage des Soldateneides." *Deutsches Pfarrblatt* 52 (1952): 385–87, 418–20, 453–55.

Ellwein, Eduard. "Das Rätsel von Römer 7." *Kerygma und Dogma* 1 (1955): 247–68.

Eschenhagen, Edith. "Wittenberger Studien: Beiträge zur Sozial- und Wirtschaftsgeschichte der Stadt Wittenberg in der Reformationszeit." *Luther Jahrbuch* 9 (1927): 9–118.

Esnault, Réné. "Le 'De votis monasticis' de M. Luther." *Etudes théologiques et religieuses* 31 (1956).

Evangelisches Kirchenlexikon. (*EKL*) 4 vols. Göttingen, 1956–61.

Fabiunke, Günter. *Martin Luther als Nationalökonom*. Berlin: Akademie, 1963.

Fagerberg, Holsten. *Die Theologie der lutherischen Bekenntnisschriften von 1529 bis 1537*. Göttingen: Vandenhoeck & Ruprecht, 1965.

Feuerbach, Ludwig. *Sämtliche Werke*. Newly edited by Wilhelm Bolin and Friedrich Jodl. Stuttgart: Frommann, 1959–64.

Fichtner, Johannes. "Der Begriff des 'Nächsten' im Alten Testament mit einem Ausblick auf Spätjudentum und Neuem Testament." *Wort und Dienst* NS 4 (1955): 23–52.

Fohrer, Georg. "Das sog. apodiktisch formulierte Recht und der Dekalog." *Kerygma und Dogma* 11 (1965): 49–74.

Forck, Gottfried. *Die Königsherrschaft Jesu Christi bei Luther*. Berlin: Evangelische Verlagsanstalt, 1959.

Fraas, Hans-Jürgen. *Katechismustradition: Luthers Kleiner Katechismus in Kirche und Schule*. Göttingen: Vandenhoeck & Ruprecht, 1971.

Die Frage der Todesstrafe: Zwölf Antworten. Munich, 1962.

Frör, Kurt. "Theologische Grundfragen zur Interpretation des Kleinen Katechismus D. Martin Luthers." *Monatsschrift für Pastoraltheologie* 52 (1963): 478–87.

Galling, Kurt. "Die Beichtspiegel." *Zeitschrift für die Alttestamentliche Wissenschaft* 47 (1929): 125–30.

————, ed. *Religion in Geschichte und Gegenwart.* (*RGG*) 7 vols. 3d ed. Tübingen, 1957–1965.

Gareis, Reinhold (?). "Zum 9. und 10. Gebot." *Katechetische Zeitschrift* (1902): 112–17.

Geffcken, Johannes. *Der Bildercatechismus des fünfzehnten Jahrhunderts und die catechetischen Hauptstücke in dieser Zeit bis auf Luther.* Vol. 1. Leipzig: Weigel, 1855.

————. "Der Bilderstreit des heidnischen Altertums." *Archiv für Religionswissenschaft* 19 (1916–19): 286–315.

Geist, Hildburg. "Arbeit: Die Entscheidung eines Wortwertes durch Luther." *Luther Jahrbuch* 13 (1931): 83–113.

Gemser, B. "The Importance of the Motive Clause in Old Testament Law." Pages 50–66 in Supplements to Vetus Testamentum 1. Leiden: Brill, 1953.

Gerdes, Hayo. *Luthers Streit mit den Schwärmern um das rechte Verständnis des Gesetzes Mose.* Göttingen: Göttinger, 1955.

Gerrish, B. A. *Grace and Reason: A Study in the Theology of Luther.* Oxford: Clarendon, 1962.

Gerstenberger, Erhard. *Wesen und Herkunft des "apodiktischen Rechts."* Neukirchen: Neukirchener, 1965.

Gese, Hartmut. "Der Dekalog als Ganzheit betrachtet." *Zeitschrift für Theologie und Kirche* 64 (1967): 121–38.

Die Gesetze Hammurabis. Edited by Hugo Winckler. Leipzig, 1904.

Girgensohn, Herbert. *Katechismus-Auslegung.* Vol. 1. Witten, 1956.

Gloege, Gerhard. "Vom Ethos der Ehescheidung." Pages 335–58 in *Gedenkschrift für D. Werner Elert: Beiträge zur historischen und systematischen Theologie.* Edited by Friedrich Hübner et al. Berlin: Lutherisches Verlagshaus, 1955. Reprinted as pages 152–83 in vol. 2 of *Verkündigung und Verantwortung.* Göttingen, 1967.

Golinski, Z. *La doctrine de St. Augustin sur le mensonge.* Lublin, 1948.

Gottschick, Johannes. "Katechetische Lutherstudien I: Die Seligkeit und der Dekalog." *Zeitschrift für Theologie und Kirche* 2 (1892): 171–88.

————. *Luther als Katechet.* Gießen, 1883.

Gottstein, M. H. "Du sollst nicht stehlen." *Theologische Zeistschrift* 9 (1953): 394f.

Grabmann, Martin. *Die Werke des hl. Thomas von Aquin.* 3d ed. Münster: Aschendorffsche, 1949.

Gräf, Erwin. *Das Rechtswesen der heutigen Beduinen.* Walldorf: Verlag für Orientkunde, 1952.

Greeven, Heinrich. "Ehe nach dem Neuen Testament." Pages 37–79 in *Theologie der Ehe.* Edited by Gerhard Krems and Reinhard Mumm. Regensburg-Göttingen: Pustet, 1969.

————. "Zu den Aussagen des Neuen Testaments über die Ehe." *Zeitschrift für evangelische Ethik* 1 (1957): 109–25.

Grether, Oskar. *Name und Wort Gottes im Alten Testament.* Gießen: Töpelmann, 1934.

Grüneisen, Ernst. "Grundlegendes für die Bilder in Luthers Katechismus." *Luther Jahrbuch* 20 (1938): 1–44.

Gühloff, Otto. *Gebieten und Schaffen Gottes in Luthers Auslegung des ersten Gebotes.* Göttingen, 1939.

Hägglund, Bengt. *Theologie und Philosophie bei Luther und in der occamistischen Tradition.* Lund: Gleerup, 1955.

Haenchen, Ernst. *Die Apostelgeschichte.* Kritisch-exegetischer Kommentar über das Neue Testament 3. 10th ed. Göttingen: Vandenhoeck & Ruprecht, 1956.

Hahn, Friedrich. *Die evangelische Unterweisung in den Schulen des 16. Jahrhunderts.* Heidelberg: Quelle & Meyer, 1957.

Hardeland, August. *Der Begriff der Gottesfurcht in Luthers Katechismen.* Gütersloh: Bertelsmann, 1914.

———. *Das erste Gebot in den Katechismen Luthers: Ein Beitrag zur Geschichte der Rechtfertigungslehre.* Leipzig: Dörffling & Franke, 1916.

———. "Luthers Erklärung des ersten Gebotes im Lichte seiner Rechtfertigungslehre." *Theologische Studien und Kritiken* 92 (1919): 201–61.

———. *Luthers Katechismusgedanken in ihrer Entwicklung bis zum Jahre 1529.* Gütersloh: Bertelsmann, 1913.

Harnack, Theodosius. *Katechetik und Erklärung des Kleinen Katechismus Dr. Martin Luthers.* Erlangen: Diechert, 1882.

Heckel, Johannes. *Lex charitatis: Eine juristische Untersuchung über das Recht in der Theologie Martin Luthers.* Munich: Verlag der Bayerischen Akademie der Wissenschaften, 1953.

———. "Naturrecht und christliche Verantwortung im öffentlichen Leben nach der Lehre M. Luthers." Pages 242–65 in *Das blinde undeutliche Wort "Kirche": Gesammelte Aufsätze.* Edited by Siegfried Grundmann. Köln: Böhlau, 1964.

Heidegger, Martin. *Sein und Zeit.* 8th ed. Tübingen: Niemeyer, 1957.

Heintze, Gerhard. *Luthers Predigt von Gesetz und Evangelium.* Munich: Kaiser, 1958.

Hempel, Hermann, ed. *Lateinischer Sentenzen- und Sprichwörterschatz.* Bremen, 1890.

Hempel, Johannes. *Das Bild in Bibel und Gottesdienst.* Sammlung gemeinverständlicher Vorträge und Schriften aus dem Gebiet der Theologie und Religionsgeschichte 212. Tübingen: Mohr, 1957.

———. *Das Ethos des Alten Testaments.* Berlin: Töpelmann, 1938.

Hermann, Rudolf. "Luthers Zirkulardisputation über Matthäus 19,21." *Luther Jahrbuch* 23 (1941): 36–93. Reprinted as pages 206–50 in *Gesammelte Studien zur Theologie Luthers und der Reformation.* Göttingen: Vandenhoeck & Ruprecht, 1960.

Herrmann, Johannes. "Das zehnte Gebot." Pages 69–82 in *Sellin-Festschrift.* Edited by A. Jirku. Leipzig, 1927.

Hirsch, Emanuel. *Geschichte der neuern evangelischen Theologie.* Gütersloh: Bertelsmann, 1949ff.

Hoffmann, Georg. "Der Kleine Katechismus als Abriß der Theologie Martin Luthers." *Luther* 30 (1959): 49–63.

Hoffmann, Julius. *Die "Hausväterliteratur" und die "Predigten über den christlichen Hausstand."* Weinheim: Beltz, 1959.

Holl, Karl. "Die Kulturbedeutung der Reformation." Pages 468–543 in vol. 1 of *Gesammelte Aufsätze zur Kirchengeschichte*. 2d/3d eds. Tübingen: Mohr, 1923.

———. "Der Neubau der Sittlichkeit." Pages 155–287 in vol. 1 of *Gesammelte Aufsätze zur Kirchengeschichte*. 2d/3d eds. Tübingen: Mohr, 1923.

Holsten, Walter. *Christentum und nichtchristliche Religion nach der Auffassung Luthers*. Gütersloh: Bertelsmann, 1932.

Horst, Friedrich. "Der Diebstahl im Alten Testament." Pages 19–28 in *Studien zur Geschichte und Kultur des nahen und fernen Ostens: Festschrift für Paul Kahle*. Edited by W. Heffening and W. Kirfel. Leiden: Brill, 1935.

Huber, Hans. *Geist und Buchstabe der Sonntagsruhe*. Salzburg: Otto Müller, 1958.

Irenaeus. *Adversus haereses libri quinque*. In Patrologia graeca 7:433–1224.

Ivarsson, Henrik. *Predikans uppgift*. Lund: Gleerup, 1956.

Jenni, Ernst. *Die theologische Begründung des Sabbatgebotes im Alten Testament*. Theologische Studiën 46. Zurich, 1956.

Jepsen, Alfred. "Du sollst nicht töten! Was ist das?" *Evangelisch-Lutherische Kirchenzeitung* 13 (1959): 384–85.

Joest, Wilfried. *Gesetz und Freiheit: Das Problem des Tertius usus legis bei Luther und die neutestamentliche Parainese*. Göttingen: Vandenhoeck & Ruprecht, 1951.

———. *Ontologie der Person bei Luther*. Göttingen: Vandenhoeck & Ruprecht, 1967.

———. "Paulus und das Lutherische Simul Iustus et Peccator." *Kerygma und Dogma* 1 (1955): 269–320.

Jordahn, Bruno. "Katechismus-Gottesdienst im Reformationsjahrhundert." *Luther* 30 (1959): 64–77.

———. "Die Trauung bei Luther." *Luther* 25 (1953): 11–26.

Junghans, Helmar. "Das mittelalterliche Vorbild für Luthers Lehre von den beiden Reichen." Pages 135–53 in *Vierhundertfünfzig Jahre lutherische Reformation, 1517–1967: Festschrift für Franz Lau*. Göttingen: Vandenhoeck & Ruprecht, 1967.

Kähler, Else. *Die Frau in den Paulinischen Briefen*. Zurich: Gotthelf, 1960.

Käsemann, Ernst. "Römer 13,1–7 in unserer Generation." *Zeitschrift für Theologie und Kirche* 56 (1959): 316–76.

Kahlert, Helmut. "Luthers und Melanchthons Stellung zu den Wirtschaftsfragen ihrer Zeit." *Luther* 27 (1956): 122–33.

Kaiser, Otto. *Der königliche Knecht*. Göttingen: Vandenhoeck & Ruprecht, 1959.

Karrenberg, Friedrich, ed. *Evangelisches Soziallexikon*. (*ESL*) Stuttgart: Kreuz, 1954.

———, and K. v. Bismark, eds. *Verlorener Sonntag?* Stuttgart: Kreuz, 1959.

Kautzsch, Emil, ed. *Die Apokryphen und Pseudepigraphen des Alten Testaments*. Hildesheim: Georg Olms, 1962.

Kawerau, Waldemar. *Die Reformation und die Ehe*. Halle: Verein für Reformationsgeschichte, 1892.

Kehrbach, K., ed. *Monumenta Germaniae Paedagogica*. (*MGP*) Vols. 20–22.

Keller, C. A. "Das Wort OTH als 'Offenbarungszeichen Gottes.' " Diss., Basel, 1946.

Kierkegaard, Søren. *Leben und Walten der Liebe*. Translated by Chr. Schrempf. In *Gesammelte Werke*. Jena: Diederich, 1909–22.

Kinder, Ernst. *Gottes Gebote und Gottes Gnade im Wort vom Kreuz*. Munich: Verlag des Evangelischen Presseverbandes für Bayern, 1949.

————. "Luthers Ableitung der geistlichen und weltlichen 'Oberkeit' aus dem 4. Gebot." Pages 270–84 in *Für Kirche und Recht: Festschrift für J. Heckel*. Edited by S. Grundmann. Köln, 1959. Reprinted as pages 221–41 in *Reich Gottes und Welt*. Edited by Heinz-Horst Schrey. Darmstadt: Wissenschaftliche Buchgesellschaft, 1969.

————. "Luthers Auffassung von der Ehe." Pages 325–34 in *Bekenntnis zur Kirche: Festgabe für Ernst Sommerlath*. Berlin: Evangelische Verlagsanstalt, 1961.

————. "Luthers Stellung zur Ehescheidung." *Luther* 25 (1953): 27–38.

Kittel, G., and G. Friedrich, eds. *Theologische Wörterbuch zum Neuen Testament*. (*TWNT*). Stuttgart, 1932–79.

Kittel, Rudolf. *Geschichte des Volkes Israel*. 2d ed. Gotha, 1912ff.

Knierim, Rolf. "Das erste Gebot." *Zeitschrift für die Alttestamentliche Wissenschaft* 77 (1965): 20–39.

————. *Die Hauptbegriffe für Sünde im Alten Testament*. Gütersloh: Gütersloher, 1965.

Koch, Klaus. "Gibt es ein Vergeltungsdogma im Alten Testament?" *Zeitschrift für Theologie und Kirche* 52 (1955): 1–42.

Köhler, Karl. *Luther und die Juristen*. Gotha, 1873.

Köhler, Ludwig. "Der Dekalog." *Theologische Rundschau* NS 1 (1929): 161–84.

Köhler, Walther. *Luther und die Lüge*. Schriften des Vereins für Reformationsgeschichte 30, no. 109/110. Leipzig: Haupt, 1912.

Kopf, L. "Arabische Etymologien und Parallelen zum Bibelwörterbuch." *Vetus Testamentum* 8 (1958): 161–215.

Kraus, Hans Joachim. *Gottesdienst in Israel*. 2d ed. Munich: Kaiser, 1962.

————. *Psalmen*. Biblischer Kommentar, Altes Testament 15. Neukirchen: Neukirchener, 1960.

Kremers, Heinz. "Die Stellung des Elterngebotes im Dekalog." *Evangelische Theologie* 21 (1961): 145–61.

Kroker, Ernst. *Katharina von Bora: Martin Luthers Frau*. 5th ed. Berlin: Evangelische Verlagsanstalt, 1959.

Krüger, Paul, ed. *Corpus Iuris Civilis*. Vol. 2 (Codex Iustinianus). 11th ed. Dublin-Zurich, 1954.

Krumwiede, Hans Walter. *Glaube und Geschichte in der Theologie Luthers*. Göttingen: Vandenhoeck & Ruprecht, 1952.

Krusche, Werner. "Zur Struktur des Kleinen Katechismus." *Lutherische Monatsheft* 4 (1965): 316–31.

Kühn, Ulrich. *Via caritatis: Theologie des Gesetzes bei Thomas von Aquin*. Göttingen: Vandenhoeck & Ruprecht, 1965.

Kutsch, Ernst. "Erwägungen zur Geschichte der Passafeier und des Massotfestes." *Zeitschrift für Theologie und Kirche* 55 (1958): 1–35.

Lackmann, Max. "Thesaurus sanctorum: Ein vergessener Beitrag Luthers zur Hagiologie." Pages 135–71 in vol. 1 of *Festgabe für Joseph Lortz*. Edited by Erwin Iserloh and Peter Manns. Baden-Baden: Grimm, 1958.

Lähteenmäki, Olavi. *Sexus und Ehe bei Luther*. Helsinki, 1955.

Lau, Franz. "Erstes Gebot und Ehre Gottes als Mitte von Luthers Theologie." *Theologische Literaturzeitung* 73 (1948): 719–30.

———. "Leges charitatis." *Kerygma und Dogma* 2 (1956): 76–89. Reprinted as pages 528–47 in *Reich Gottes und Welt*. Edited by Heinz-Horst Schrey. Darmstadt: Wissenschaftliche Buchgesellschaft, 1969.

———. *Luthers Lehre von den beiden Reichen*. Berlin: Lutherisches Verlagshaus, 1952.

Leeuw, Gerardus van der. *Phänomenologie der Religion*. Tübingen: Mohr, 1933.

Lieberg, Hellmut. *Amt und Ordination bei Luther und Melanchthon*. Göttingen: Vandenhoeck & Ruprecht, 1962.

Liermann, Hans. "Der unjuristische Luther." *Luther Jahrbuch* 24 (1957): 69–85.

Loewenich, Walther von. *Luther als Ausleger der Synoptiker*. Munich: Kaiser, 1954.

Lohff, Wenzel. "Die Ehe nach evangelischer Auffassung." Pages 42–69 in *Ehe und Ehescheidung*. Stundenbuch 30. Hamburg, 1963.

Lohfink, Norbert. *Das Hauptgebot: Eine Untersuchung literarischer Einleitungsfragen zu Dtn 5–11*. Rome: E. Pontificio Instituto Biblico, 1963.

Lohse, Bernhard. "Luthers Kritik am Mönchtum." *Evangelische Theologie* 20 (1960): 413–32.

———. *Mönchtum und Reformation*. Göttingen: Vandenhoeck & Ruprecht, 1963.

———. *Ratio und Fides: Eine Untersuchung über die ratio in der Theologie Luthers*. Göttingen: Vandenhoeck & Ruprecht, 1958.

Lohse, Eduard. "Glaube und Werke—Zur Theologie des Jakobusbriefes." *Zeitschrift für die Neutestamentliche Wissenschaft und die Kunde der älteren Kirche* 48 (1957): 1–22.

———. "Jesu Worte über den Sabbat." Pages 79–89 in *Judentum, Urchristentum, Kirche*. Edited by Walther Eltester. Berlin: Töpelmann, 1960.

Ludolphy, Ingetraut. "Katharina von Bora die 'Gehilfin' M. Luthers." *Luther* (1961): 69–83.

Luther, Martin. *D. Martin Luthers Werke: Kritische Gesamtausgabe*. Weimar: Herman Böhlau, 1883–.

———. *D. Martin Luthers Werke: Kritische Gesamtausgabe. Deutsche Bibel*. Weimar: Herman Böhlau, 1906–61.

———. *D. Martin Luthers Werke: Kritische Gesamtausgabe. Briefwechsel*. Weimar: Herman Böhlau, 1930ff.

———. *D. Martin Luthers Werke: Kritische Gesamtausgabe. Tischreden*. Weimar: Herman Böhlau, 1912ff.

Maćkowiak, Wenzeslaus Sadok. "Die ethische Bedeutung der Notlüge in der altheidnischen, patristischen, scholastischen und neueren Zeit." Diss., Fribourg, 1933.

Malo, H. "Abspannen, abdringen, abwendig machen." *Zeistchrift für den evangelischen Religionsunterricht* 4 (1893): 228f.

Maurer, Wilhelm. "Die geschichtliche Wurzel von Melanchthons Traditionsverständnis." Pages 166–80 in *Zur Auferbauung des Leibes Christi: Festgabe für Peter Brunner.* Edited by Edmund Schlink and Albrecht Peters. Kassel: Stauda, 1965.

———. *Luthers Lehre von den drei Hierarchien und ihr mittelalterlicher Hintergrund.* Munich: Verlag der Bayerischen Akademie der Wissenschaften, 1970.

Mausbach, Joseph. *Die katholische Moral und ihre Gegner.* 2d ed. Köln, 1911.

McCarthy, Dennis J. *Treaty and Covenant.* Rome: Pontifical Biblical Institute, 1963.

McDonough, Thomas M. *The Law and the Gospel in Luther.* Oxford: Oxford University Press, 1963.

Melanchthon, Philipp. *Loci communes* (1521) and *Loci praecipui theologici* (1559). In vol. 1 of *Melanchthons Werk: Studienausgabe.* Edited by H. Engelland. Gütersloh: Bertelsmann, 1952f.

———. "Spruchbüchlein (1527)." Pages 61–73 of vol. 1 of *Supplementa Melanchthoniana.* Edited by F. Cohrs. Leipzig: Haupt, 1915.

Mendenhall, George E. *Law and Covenant in Israel and the Near Ancient East.* Pittsburgh: Biblical Colloquium, 1955. German: *Recht und Bund in Israel und dem Alten Vorderen Orient.* Theologische Studiën B, 64. Zurich, 1960.

Merz, Georg. "Gesetz Gottes und Volksnomos bei M. Luther." *Luther Jahrbuch* 16 (1935): 51ff.

Meyer, Hans. *Thomas von Aquin.* 2d ed. Paderborn, 1961.

Meyer, Johannes. "Fürchten, lieben und vertrauen: Eine geschichtliche Erörterung zu Luthers Katechismen." *Neue Kirchliche Zeitschrift* 24 (1913): 793–811.

———. *Historischer Kommentar zu Luthers Kleinem Katechismus.* Gütersloh: Bertelsmann, 1929.

———. "Luthers Dekalogerklärung 1528 unter dem Einfluß der sächsischen Kirchenvisitation." *Neue Kirchliche Zeitschrift* 26 (1915): 546–70.

———. *Luthers Großer Katechismus.* Leipzig: Deichert, 1914.

Modalsli, Ole. *Das Gericht nach den Werken.* Göttingen: Vandenhoeck & Ruprecht, 1963.

Mowinckel, Sigmund. *Le Décalogue.* Paris: Felix Alcan, 1927.

———. *Psalmstudien.* Vol. 1. Oslo, 1921.

———. "Zur Geschichte der Dekaloge." *Zeitschrift für die Alttestamentliche Wissenschaft* 55 (1937): 218–35.

Mülhaupt, Erwin, ed. *D. Martin Luthers Evangelien-Auslegung.* 2d ed. Göttingen: Vandenhoeck & Ruprecht, 1954.

———. *D. Martin Luthers Psalmen-Auslegung.* Göttingen: Vandenhoeck & Ruprecht, 1965.

Müller, E. F. Karl, ed. *Die Bekenntnisschriften der reformierten Kirche.* Leipzig: Deichert, 1903.

Müller, Gregor. *Die Wahrhaftigkeitspflicht und die Problematik der Lüge.* Freiburg: Herder, 1962.

Müller, Hans Michael. "Der christliche Glaube und das erste Gebot." *Theologische Blätter* 16 (1927): 269–81.

Nell-Breuning, Oswald von. "Wo Diebstahl salonfähig wird." Pages 59–65 in *Die zehn Gebote*. Edited by G. Bauer. Stuttgart, n.d.

Niesel, Wilhelm, ed. *Bekenntnisschriften und Kirchenordnungen der nach Gottes Wort reformierten Kirche*. 3d ed. Zurich: Evangelischer Verlag, 1938.

Noth, Martin. *Das dritte Buch Mose*. Das Alte Testament Deutsch 6. Göttingen: Vandenhoeck & Ruprecht, 1962.

———. *Das zweite Buch Mose*. Das Alte Testament Deutsch 5. Göttingen: Vandenhoeck & Ruprecht, 1959.

Origen. *Homilien zum Hexateuch in Rufins Übersetzung*. In vol. 2 *Die Homilien zu Numeri, Josua und Judices*. Edited by W. A. Baehrens. Leipzig, 1921.

Otto, Rudolf. *Das Heilige: Über des Irrationale in der Idee des Göttlichen und sein Verhältnis zum Rationalen* (1917). 31st–35th eds. Munich, 1963.

Peichl, H., ed. *Der Tag des Herrn: Die Heiligung des Sonntags im Wandel der Zeit*. Wien, 1958.

Perlitt, Lothar. *Bundestheologie im Alten Testament*. Neukirchen: Neukirchener, 1969.

Pesch, Otto Hermann. "Die Lehre vom 'Verdienst' als Problem für Theologie und Verkündigung." Pages 1865–907 in vol. 2 of *Wahrheit und Verkündigung: Festschrift für Michael Schmaus*. Edited by Leo Scheffczyk, Werner Dettloff, and Richard Heinzmann. Munich: Paderborn, 1967.

———. *Die Theologie der Rechtfertigung bei M. Luther und Thomas von Aquin*. Mainz: Matthias-Grünewald, 1967.

Peter Lombard. *Sententiarum libri quatuor*. In Patrologia latina 192:521–962.

Peters, Albrecht. "Gegenwart Gottes—Wort Gottes." Pages 201–22 in *Zur Auferbauung des Leibes Christi: Festgabe für Peter Brunner*. Edited by Edmund Schlink and Albrecht Peters. Kassel: Stauda, 1965.

———. *Glaube und Werk: Luthers Rechtfertigungslehre im Lichte der Heiligen Schrift*. Berlin: Lutherisches Verlagshaus, 1962.

———. "Reformatorische Rechtfertigungsbotschaft zwischen tridentinischer Rechtfertigungslehre und gegenwärtigem evangelischen Verständnis der Rechtfertigung." *Luther Jahrbuch* 31 (1964): 77–128.

Peters, J. *Die Ehe nach der Lehre des hl. Augustin*. Görres-Gesellschaft 32. Freiburg, (?) 1918.

Pettirsch, F. "Das Verbot der opera servilia in der Hl. Schrift und in der altkirchlichen Exegese." *Zeitschrift für Katholische Theologie* 69 (1947): 257–327, 417–44.

Philo. *Opera quae reperiri potuerunt omnia*. 2 vols. Edited by Thomas Mangey. London, 1742.

Piltz, Signe. *Luthers lära om äktenskapet*. Lund: Gleerup, 1952.

Pinomaa, Lennart. "Die Heiligen in Luthers Frühtheologie." *Studia theologica* 13 (1959): 1–50.

———. "Luthers Weg zur Verwerfung des Heiligendienstes." *Luther Jahrbuch* 29 (1962): 35–43.

Pöhlmann, Horst Georg. *Rechtfertigung*. Gütersloh: Gerd Mohn, 1971.

Präger, Lydia, ed. *Frei für Gott und die Menschen: Evangelische Bruder- und Schwesternschaften der Gegenwart in Selbstdarstellung*. Stuttgart: Quell, 1959.

Preisker, Herbert. *Christentum und Ehe in den ersten drei Jahrhunderten*. Berlin: Trowitzsch & Sohn, 1926.

Prenter, Regin. *Schöpfung und Erlösung: Dogmatik*. Göttingen: Vandenhoeck & Ruprecht, 1958ff.

Preuss, Hans. *Martin Luther: Der Künstler*. Gütersloh: Bertelsmann, 1931.

Procksch, Otto. *Theologie des Alten Testaments*. Gütersloh: Bertelsmann, 1950.

Quervain, Alfred de. *Die Heiligung*. Vol. 1 of *Ethik*. 2d ed. Zürich: Evangelischer Verlag, 1946.

Rabast, Karlheinz. *Das apodiktische Recht im Deuteronomium und im Heiligkeitsgesetz*. Berlin: Heimatdienst, 1948.

Rad, Gerhard von. "Der Anfang der Geschichtsschreibung im alten Israel (1944)." Pages 148–88 in vol. 1 of *Gesammelte Studien zum Alten Testament*. Munich: Kaiser, 1958.

———. "Die deuteronomistische Geschichtstheologie in den Königsbüchern." Pages 189–204 in vol. 1 of *Gesammelte Studien zum Alten Testament*. Munich: Kaiser, 1958.

———. *Deuteronomium-Studien*. 2d ed. Göttingen: Vandenhoeck & Ruprecht, 1948.

———. *Das erste Buch Mose*. Das Alte Testament Deutsch 2. 5th ed. Göttingen: Vandenhoeck & Ruprecht, 1958.

———. "Es ist noch eine Ruhe vorhanden dem Volke Gottes (1933)." Pages 101–8 in vol. 1 of *Gesammelte Studien zum Alten Testament*. Munich: Kaiser, 1958.

———. "Das formgeschichtliche Problem des Hexateuch (1938)." Pages 9–86 in vol. 1 of *Gesammelte Studien zum Alten Testament*. Munich: Kaiser, 1958.

———. " 'Gerechtigkeit' und 'Leben' in der Kultsprache der Psalmen (1950)." Pages 225–47 in vol. 1 of *Gesammelte Studien zum Alten Testament*. Munich: Kaiser, 1958.

———. *Der heilige Krieg im alten Israel*. Zurich: Zwingli, 1951.

———. *Theologie des Alten Testaments*. 2d ed. Munich: Kaiser, 1958.

———. "Verheißenes Land und Jahwes Land im Hexateuch (1943)." Pages 87–100 in vol. 1 of *Gesammelte Studien zum Alten Testament*. Munich: Kaiser, 1958.

———. *Weisheit in Israel*. Neukirchen: Neukirchener, 1970.

———. "Zelt und Lade (1931)." Pages 109–29 in vol. 1 of *Gesammelte Studien zum Alten Testament*. Munich: Kaiser, 1958.

Die Regel von Taizé. 5th ed. Gütersloh, 1969.

Rentschka, Paul. *Die Dekalogkatechese des Hl. Augustinus*. Kempten, 1905.

Reu, Johann Michael, ed. *Quellen zur Geschichte des kirchlichen Unterrichts in der evangelischen Kirche Deutschlands zwischen 1530 und 1600*. Gütersloh: Bertelsmann, 1904ff.

Reventlow, Henning Graf von. *Gebot und Predigt im Dekalog*. Gütersloh: Gütersloher, 1962.

————. *Wächter über Israel: Ezechiel und seine Tradition.* Berlin: Töpelman, 1962.

Reymann, Heinz. *Glaube und Wirtschaft bei Luther.* Gütersloh: Bertelsmann, 1934.

Ringgren, Helmer. *Sprüche.* Das Alte Testament Deutsch 16.1. Göttingen: Vandenhoeck & Ruprecht, 1962.

Ritschl, Albrecht. *Die christliche Lehre von der Rechtfertigung und Versöhnung.* 3d ed. Bonn: Marcus, 1889.

————. *Unterricht in der christlichen Religion.* 6th ed. Bonn: Marcus, 1903.

Röthlisberger, Hugo. *Kirche am Sinai: Die Zehn Gebote in der christlichen Unterweisung.* Zurich: Zwingli, 1965.

Rordorf, Willy. *Der Sonntag: Geschichte des Ruhe- und Gottesdiensttages im ältesten Christentum.* Zurich: Zwingli, 1962.

Rost, Leonhard. "Die Schuld der Väter." Pages 229–33 in *Solange es "heute" heißt: Festgabe für Rudolf Hermann.* Berlin: Evangelische Verlagsanstalt, 1957. Reprinted as pages 66–71 in *Studien zum Alten Testament.* Beiträge zur Wissenschaft vom Alten und Neuen Testament 101. Stuttgart: Kohlhammer, 1974.

Scharbert, Josef. "Formgeschichte und Exegese von Ex 34,6 f und seiner Parallelen." *Biblica* 38 (1957): 130–50.

————. *Solidarität in Segen und Fluch im Alten Testament und in seiner Umwelt.* Bonner Biblische Beiträge 14. Bonn: Hanstein, 1958.

Scheible, Heinz, ed. *Das Widerstandsrecht als Problem der deutschen Protestanten 1523– 1546.* Gütersloh: Gütersloher, 1969.

Schilling, Otto. *Die Staats- und Soziallehre des Heiligen Thomas von Aquin.* 2d ed. Munich: Hueber, 1930.

Schleiermacher, Friedrich. *Der christliche Glaube.* 7th ed. Berlin: de Gruyter, 1960.

Schlier, Heinrich. *Der Brief an die Epheser.* 2d ed. Düsseldorf: Patmos, 1958.

Schloemann, Martin. *Natürliches und gepredigtes Gesetz bei Luther.* Berlin: Töpelmann, 1961.

Schloenbach, Manfred. *Heiligung als Fortschreiten und Wachstum des Glaubens.* Helsinki, 1963.

Schnackenburg, Rudolf. "Die Ehe nach dem Neuen Testament." Pages 9–36 in *Theologie der Ehe.* Edited by Gerhard Krems and Reinhard Mumm. Regensburg-Göttingen: Pustet, 1969.

Schott, Erdmann. "Der Dekalog in der Theologie Luthers." In *Gottes ist der Orient: Festschrift für Otto Eißfeldt.* Berlin: Evangelische Verlagsanstalt, 1959.

————. "Luthers Verständnis des ersten Gebots." *Theologische Literaturzeitung* 73 (1948): 199–204.

Schrade, Hubert. *Der verborgene Gott: Gottesbild und Gottesvorstellung in Israel und im alten Orient.* Stuttgart: Kohlhammer, 1949.

Schrage, Wolfgang. *Die konkreten Einzelgebote in der paulinischen Paränese.* Gütersloh: Gerd Mohn, 1961.

Schrenk, Gottlob. "Sabbat oder Sonntag." *Judaica* 2 (1946): 169–89.

Schrey, Heinz-Horst, ed. *Reich Gottes und Welt: Die Lehre Luthers von den zwei Reichen.* Darmstadt: Wissenschaftliche Buchgesellschaft, 1969.

Schubert, Alois. *Augustins Lex-aeterna Lehre nach Inhalt und Quellen.* Münster: Aschendorff, 1924.

Schulze, Wilhelm A. "Ein Bischof sei eines Weibes Mann." *Kerygma und Dogma* 4 (1958): 287–300.

Schwarzwäller, Klaus. *Theologia crucis: Luthers Lehre von der Prädestination nach De servo arbitrio 1525.* Munich: Kaiser, 1970.

Schweizer, Eduard. *Erniedrigung und Erhöhung bei Jesus und seinen Nachfolgern.* Zurich: Zwingli, 1955.

Seeberg, Alfred. *Die Didache des Judentums und der Urchristenheit.* Leipzig: Deichert, 1908.

———. *Der Katechismus der Urchristenheit.* Leipzig: Deichert, 1903.

Seeberg, Reinhold. "Luthers Anschauung von dem Geschlechtsleben und der Ehe und ihre geschichtliche Stellung." *Luther Jahrbuch* 7 (1925): 77–122.

Sehling, Emil, ed. *Die evangelischen Kirchenordnungen des 16. Jahrhunderts.* Leipzig: Reisland, 1902ff.

Seils, Martin. *Der Gedanke vom Zusammenwirken Gottes und des Menschen in Luthers Theologie.* Gütersloh: Gütersloher, 1962.

Siirala, Aarne. *Gottes Gebot bei M. Luther.* Helsinki, 1956.

Smend, Rudolf. *Die Bundesformel.* Zurich: EVZ, 1963.

———. *Die Mitte des Alten Testaments.* Zurich: EVZ, 1970.

Sormunen, Eino. *Die Eigenart der lutherischen Ethik.* Helsinki: Tiedeakatemia, 1934.

Sprenger, R. "Abspannen." *Zeistchrift für den evangelischen Religionsunterricht* 4 (1893): 220.

Stade, Bernhard. *Biblische Theologie des Alten Testaments.* Vol. 1. Tübingen: Mohr, 1905.

Stamm, Johann Jakob. *Der Dekalog im Lichte der neueren Forschung.* 2d ed. Bern: Haupt, 1962.

———. "Dreißig Jahre Dekalogforschung." *Theologische Rundschau* NS 27 (1961): 189–239, 281–305.

———. "Sprachliche Erwägungen zum Gebot: 'Du sollst nicht töten.' " *Theologische Zeistchrift* 1 (1945): 81–90.

Stein, Albert. "M. Luthers Meinung über die Juristen." *Zeitschrift für Religions- und Geistesgeschichte* 85 (1968): 362–75.

Steinmeyer, Franz-Ludwig. *Der Dekalog als katechetischer Lehrstoff.* Beiträge zur Praktischen Theologie 2. Berlin, 1875.

Stoebe, Hans Joachim. "Das achte Gebot." *Wort und Dienst* NS 3 (1952): 108–26.

Strieder, Jakob. *Jakob Fugger der Reiche.* Leipzig: Quelle & Meyer, 1925.

———. *Studien zur Geschichte kapitalistischer Organisationsformen.* Munich-Leipzig: Duncker & Humblot, 1914.

Strobel, August. "Zum Verständnis von Rm 13." *Zeitschrift für die Neutestamentliche Wissenschaft und die Kunde der älteren Kirche* 47 (1956): 67–93.

Szabó, Andor. "Sabbat und Sonntag." *Judaica* 9 (1959): 129–42.

Thielicke, Helmut. *Theologische Ethik.* Tübingen: Mohr, 1951ff.

Thieme, Karl. *Die sittliche Triebkraft des Glaubens: Eine Untersuchung zu Luthers Theologie.* Leipzig: Dörffling & Franke, 1895.

Thomas Aquinas. *In duo praecepta caritatis et in decem legis praecepta expositio.* Pages 245–71 in vol. 2 (= §§ 1128–332) of *S. Thomae Aquinatis Doctoris Angelici opuscula theologica.* Edited by Raymundi M. Spiazzi. Turin: Marietti, 1954.

———. *Sancti Thomae Aquinatis doctoris angelici ordinis praedicatorum opera omnia.* Vol. 13: *Expositio in omnes S. Pauli epistolas.* Parma: Petri Fiaccadori, 1862.

———. *Summa Theologiae.* Edited by Petri Caramello. Turin: Marietti, 1952–56.

Thomas, Wilhelm. "Erneuerung des Sonntags als Auferstehungstag." *Monatsschrift für Pastoraltheologie* 48 (1959): 259–69.

———. "Der Sonntag im frühen Mittelalter." Diss., Göttingen, 1929.

Törnvall, Gustaf. *Geistliches und weltliches Regiment bei Luther.* Munich: Kaiser, 1947.

Trillhaas, Wolfgang. *Ethik.* Berlin: Töpelmann, 1959.

Vaccari, Albert. "De praeceptorum Decalogi distinctione et ordine." *Verbum domini* 17 (1937).

Vögtle, Anton. *Die Tugend- und Lasterkataloge im Neuen Testament.* Münster, 1936.

Volz, Paul. *Mose und sein Werk.* 2d ed. Tübingen: Mohr, 1932.

Vossberg, Herbert. *Luthers Kritik aller Religion.* Leipzig: Deichert, 1922.

Vriezen, Theodorus Christiaan. " 'Ehje 'aser 'ehje." Pages 498–512 in *Festschrift für Alfred Bertholet.* Edited by Walter Baumgartner, O. Eißfeldt, K. Elliger, L. Rost. Tübingen: Mohr, 1950.

Wander, Karl Friedrich Wilhelm, ed. *Deutsches Sprichwörterlexikon.* Leipzig: Brockhaus, 1870. Reprint, Aalen, 1963.

Weber, H. E. "Das Eigentum nach dem Neuen Testament." Pages 491–98 in *Christliche Daseinsgestaltung.* 3d ed. Edited by Heinz-Horst Schrey. Bremen: Schünemann, 1962.

Weber, Max. *Wirtschaftsgeschichte.* Edited by S. Hellmann and M. Palyi. Munich: Duncker & Humblot, 1923.

Weidenhiller, Egino. *Untersuchungen zur deutschsprachigen katechetischen Literatur des späten Mittelalters.* Munich: Beck, 1965.

Weidinger, Karl. *Die Haustafeln.* Leipzig: Hinrichs, 1928.

Wendland, Heinz-Dietrich. "Zur sozial-ethischen Bedeutung der neutestamentlichen Haustafeln." Pages 34–46 in *Die Leibhaftigkeit des Wortes: Festgabe für Adolf Köberle.* Edited by Otto Michel and Ulrich Mann. Hamburg: Furche, 1958.

———. "Zur Theologie der Sexualität und der Ehe." Pages 117–42 in *Theologie der Ehe.* Edited by Gerhard Krems and Reinhard Mumm. Regensburg-Göttingen: Pustet, 1969.

Werdermann, Hermann. *Luthers Wittenberger Gemeinde.* Gütersloh: Bertelsmann, 1929.

Westermann, Claus. *Genesis.* Biblischer Kommentar, Altes Testament, 1.1. Neukirchen: Neukirchener, 1974.

———. *Das Loben Gottes in den Psalmen.* 3d ed. Göttingen: Vandenhoeck & Ruprecht, 1963.

——. *Der Segen in der Bibel und im Handeln der Kirche*. Munich: Kaiser, 1968.

Wibbing, Siegfried. *Die Tugend- und Lasterkataloge im Neuen Testament und ihre Traditionsgeschichte unter besonderer Berücksichtigung der Qumrantexte*. Berlin: Töpelmann, 1959.

Wildberger, Hans. "Israel und sein Land." *Evangelische Theologie* 19 (1956): 404–22.

Wittram, Reinhard. "Möglichkeiten und Grenzen der Geschichtswissenschaft." *Zeitschrift für Theologie und Kirche* 62 (1965): 430–57.

Wolf, Ernst. "Politia Christi: Das Problem der Sozialethik im Luthertum (1948)." Pages 214–42 in vol. 1 of *Peregrinatio*. Munich: Kaiser, 1954.

——. "Zur Frage des Naturrechts bei Thomas von Aquin und bei Luther (1951)." Pages 183–213 in vol. 1 of *Peregrinatio*. Munich: Kaiser, 1954.

Wolff, Hans Walter. *Hosea*. Biblischer Kommentar, Altes Testament 14.1. Neukirchen: Neukirchener, 1961.

Wolff, Johannes. *Beichtbüchlein des Magisters Johannes Wolff* (1478). Edited by F. W. Battenberg. Gießen: Töpelmann, 1907.

Würthwein, Ernst. *Der Text des Alten Testaments*. Stuttgart: Privileg. Württ. Bibelanstalt, 1952.

Zahn, Theodor. *Geschichte des Sonntags, vornehmlich in der alten Kirche*. Hannover, 1878.

Zahrnt, Heinz. *Luther deutet Geschichte*. Munich: Müller, 1952.

Zarcke, Lilly. "Der Begriff der Liebe in Luthers Äußerungen über die Ehe." *Theologische Blätter* 10 (1931): 45–49.

——. "Der geistliche Sinn der Ehe bei Luther." *Theologische Studien und Kritiken* 106 (1934/35): 20–39.

Zezschwitz, C. A. Gerhard von. *System der christlich kirchlichen Katechetik*. 2d ed. Leipzig, 1872.

Zimmerli, Walther. *Ezechiel*. Biblischer Kommentar, Altes Testament 13. Neukirchen: Neukirchener, 1969.

——. "Ich bin Jahwe (1953)." Pages 11–40 in *Gottes Offenbarung: Gesammelte Aufsätze zum Alten Testament*. Munich: Kaiser, 1963.

——. "Das zweite Gebot (1950)." Pages 234–48 in *Gottes Offenbarung: Gesammelte Aufsätze zum Alten Testament*. Munich: Kaiser, 1963.

CPSIA information can be obtained
at www.ICGtesting.com
Printed in the USA
FFOW05n0951191217

9 780758 611970